THE
AUSTRALIAN
MOMENT

George Megalogenis is an author and journalist with three decades' experience in the media. *The Australian Moment* won the 2013 Prime Minister's Literary Award for Non-fiction and the 2012 Walkley Award for Non-fiction, and formed the basis for the ABC documentary series *Making Australia Great*. He is also the author of *Australia's Second Chance*, *Faultlines*, *The Longest Decade*, *Quarterly Essay 40: Trivial Pursuit – Leadership and the End of the Reform Era* and *Quarterly Essay 61: Balancing Act – Australia Between Recession and Renewal*.

For Amalia, Thomai, Anna and Gigi

George Megalogenis

THE AUSTRALIAN MOMENT

How we were made for these times

PENGUIN BOOKS

PENGUIN BOOKS

UK | USA | Canada | Ireland | Australia
India | New Zealand | South Africa | China

Penguin Books is part of the Penguin Random House group of companies
whose addresses can be found at global.penguinrandomhouse.com.

First published by Penguin Group (Australia), 2012
Revised edition published by Penguin Group (Australia), 2015
This edition published by Penguin Random House Australia Pty Ltd, 2016

1 3 5 7 9 10 8 6 4 2

Cover design by Alex Ross © Penguin Random House Australia Pty Ltd
Text design by John Canty © Penguin Random House Australia Pty Ltd
Cover photographs: Sydney skyline inigoarza/Getty Images, sky Shutterstock
Typeset in Adobe Caslon Pro by Post Pre-Press Group, Brisbane, Queensland
Colour separation by Splitting Image Colour Studio, Clayton, Victoria
Printed and bound in Australia by Griffin Press, an accredited
ISO AS/NZS 14001 Environmental Management Systems printer.

National Library of Australia
Cataloguing-in-Publication data:

Megalogenis, George
The Australian moment / George Megalogenis
9780143783503 (paperback)

Economics – Australia
Financial crises
Australia – Politics and government – History
Australia – Economic conditions
Australia – Economic policy

320.994

penguin.com.au

CONTENTS

THE SURGE

INTRODUCTION

In the four decades since the United States first put a man on the moon, the world's richest nation has suffered seven recessions. For three of those four decades, every American economic ailment was transmitted to Australia and amplified. We were struck down by one of the worst bouts of stagflation in the developed world in the 1970s and again in the early 1980s, and a frightening recession in the early 1990s that felt like it would never end.

Then history took an unusual turn. The US recessions that haunted the new millennium did not have Australia's name on them. We did share in the American humiliations in Afghanistan and Iraq, as we had done in Vietnam. But the cord of economic dependency was severed. We didn't just break from the US business cycle, but from the West more generally. Australia, uniquely, has avoided the first three super crashes of the digital age – the Asian financial meltdown, the tech wreck and the big one, the Great Recession, which we branded the 'global financial crisis'.

A single escape might be put down to luck, two to good management. But a third is the stuff of legend. Understandably, the rest of the world wants to know if Australia has cracked globalisation's secret code for prosperity.

The idea that a nation of almost 23 million people accounting for less than 2 per cent of world production might hold the key to the future does not fit with the humble story we have told ourselves since federation, that we are a spoilt people in charge of a minerals-rich continent, a quarry with a view. The laconic side of our character wants to downplay the achievement. The insecure side assumes that we will succumb soon enough – if the United States didn't break the Australian economy in the last decade, then China must in this one.

The truth is we prefer to think the Great Recession wasn't real. Or that it was confined to the North Atlantic. Or that the mining boom bailed us out. Or that it just wasn't our turn. That, like the Olympic skater Steven Bradbury, we stole the gold after everyone else in the race fell over. Sporting success like Bradbury's we can explain: we are persistent. The same goes for an Oscar: we are charming. Or even a Nobel Prize in science: we can be smart. Yet we're uncomfortable with the global spotlight upon us, being asked questions we're too scared to pose for ourselves.

But what if we are 'the last best hope on Earth', which was the phrase Abraham Lincoln used to describe the American project in the nineteenth century? The nation that reflects the best of the world back to it? There is a good case to be made on Australia's behalf.

Consider the flaws of the world's five richest nations. The United States has a market too free and a political discourse too toxically partisan for its own good. China, Japan and Germany, placed second to fourth on the global income ladder, are monocultures condemned to premature ageing because they don't have the national confidence for mass immigration. The UK, ranked fifth, is the nation closest to ours, but its economy relies on the futility of financial transactions, and its eternal hang-up about class makes it a poor host for new arrivals.

Our economy is open, but not out of control, because government still sticks its nose where it belongs to regulate the banks and to provide a decent social safety net. Our society, too, is as open as any, with an immigration program sourced in almost equal measure from the old world of Europe and the new world of Asia. In fact, the Asian-born now outnumber the British-born. We do hyphens better than the Americans – Greek-Australian, Italian-Australian, Chinese-Australian, Indian-Australian – and our banks are safer than the Bank of England.

We still have a self-sabotaging streak. Apathy and parochialism ensure that the national focus never strays beyond the bitumen tomb of suburbia. ('Did you see what they paid for that awful house up the street?') Our largest city, Sydney, has caught the global disease of intolerance. Our politicians are getting duller by the doorstop, and we have few genuine heroes to look up to.

In a group setting, we are wilfully inarticulate. The chant 'Aussie, Aussie, Aussie! Oi, Oi, Oi!' is a form of national Tourette's. This tone-deaf cry acts as a human shield to protect us, and the rest of the world, from taking Australia too seriously. Only a people that genuinely fear self-reflection would carry on like this. Perhaps that is why we continue to celebrate the military defeat at Gallipoli, as an extension of our aggressive adolescence, a young nation still not ready to find an independent voice. The Anzac tradition serves the dual purpose of making us feel like victims while giving vent, in some sections of the community, to a boorish, the-world-can-get-stuffed patriotism.

We are better than that. This book will argue on behalf of the Australian miracle through our response to external events. It starts with the oil shock of 1973 and ends with the Great Recession of 2008–09. Both episodes broke the American, European and Japanese enterprises. Only the first did the same to Australia's. What we learned in close to four decades is what makes us more versatile today than any other first-world nation.

The story is told from two complementary perspectives: through the reaction of the people, and through the institutions of government and the bureaucracy. Economics informs the narrative because it provides the best device for interpreting human behaviour. For example, why do Australians react better when they think they will lose something than when they receive a windfall? Some of the episodes may be familiar, while others will be new to readers. Much of what we remember, together, needs to be re-examined to decide whether Australia can, indeed, become a global role model.

I re-interviewed five of the six prime ministers who governed through Australia's transformation: Malcolm Fraser, Bob Hawke, Paul Keating, John Howard and Kevin Rudd. Graham Freudenberg kindly agreed to speak on behalf of Gough Whitlam, who wished this book well but declined an interview.

I asked Fraser, Hawke, Keating and Howard to think outside their own legacy egos to reflect on the positive contributions of one another. Through their combined praise we can identify the unique elements of the Australian project, and hopefully inspire our next generation of politicians to build on it.

There are, of course, tensions. The competing versions of Australia are apparent in the alliances between the former leaders. Hawke praises Howard so he can take a chip at Keating. Fraser gives credit to Keating, and Keating reciprocates so, together, they diminish Hawke and Howard by comparison. Howard applauds Hawke so he can reduce Keating. Hawke and Howard are Australian triumphalists, who think there is nothing wrong with the nation as it is. Keating and Fraser are Australian cosmopolitans, who see room for improvement. Rudd discusses his role in Australia's Great Escape of 2008–09. He also reflects on why he subsequently lost community support during the recovery from the recession we didn't have.

The rough rule of thumb for the Australian character is that we are greedy in good times and inspired in bad. Or as *The Economist* magazine once put it, 'Australia is one of the best managers of adversity the world has seen – and the worst manager of prosperity'.

The circumstances of our sidestepping the major global downturns may never be repeated, and our lessons may not translate for every first-world nation. But the days of us looking to the British and Americans for inspiration and comfort have passed. Now it's our turn to tell them how the world works – assuming we can break the lockjaw that strikes us when the conversation is serious, and avoid the reflex hubris that comes when others acknowledge our victories. Even if we manage to revert to mediocrity, the Australian Moment will be of interest for decades to come, as a reminder of what worked, and what might yet be.

1970 Golden Age ends with first US recession in 10 years. Hawke becomes ACTU president. **1971** McMahon topples Gorton to become PM. Gough visits China, Nixon follows. Nixon dismantles Bretton Woods Agreement. **1972** Watergate. Whitlam ends 23 years of conservative rule, and abolishes conscription, pulls Australia out of the Vietnam War and commissions a report on colour TV all on the first day. **1973** Gough's tariff shock. First OPEC oil shock. commences. **1974** term after early passed. resigns. collapses loses the Cyclone Colour TV Fraser

THE
SHOCKS

Another US recession Whitlam wins second election. Medibank Nixon Economy and Labor budget plot. Tracy. **1975** introduced. topples

Snedden. Saigon falls. Loans affair claims Cairns and Connor. Fraser obstructs budget. Indonesia invades East Timor. Whitlam government dismissed. Fraser's Coalition wins election in landslide. **1976** Recession ends, but inflation remains in double digits. Mao Zedong dies. Australian dollar under attack and devalued. Carter elected US president. **1977** 'Advance Australia Fair' wins national song referendum. Australian Democrats founded. Packer establishes rebel cricket competition. Fraser wins second landslide. Hayden replaces Whitlam. **1978** Hilton Hotel bombing. Vietnamese refugee crisis accelerates; cabinet lifts intake above 10,000.

I

THREE YEARS LATE
TO THE PARTY

Every rich nation reveals its character in its most selfish generation: the baby boomers.

In their prime, Australia's boomers had very old-fashioned
views about what constituted bad behaviour. In an opinion poll
taken in 1972, the year Gough Whitlam came to power, barely one
in ten Australians thought it was 'all right' to smoke pot (10 per
cent), avoid paying public transport fares (9 per cent) or throw cans
at the umpire or referee at a sporting match (2 per cent). At least
twice as many gave a moral pass to cheating on income tax (22 per
cent) or keeping the money if a department store handed back too
much change by mistake (19 per cent). By then, the Vietnam War
was a lost political cause, with a majority of voters wanting Australia to pull out, yet only 27 per cent of people thought it was 'all
right' to avoid registering for military service. Our baby boomers
were chips off the old block. Like their parents, they were rorters,
not radicals.

They had kept hitting the snooze button during the 1960s,
resisting the decade's urge for revolt. When they finally marched
against the Vietnam War in numbers too big to ignore, they

behaved more like Gandhi than Guevara. In Melbourne, the
fulcrum of the first mass moratorium in 1970, *The Age* newspaper
concluded its coverage by applauding protesters and police alike.
'The moratorium was, among other things, three days of genuinely peaceful demonstration. The Chief Commissioner of Police,
Mr Wilby, felt justified in congratulating the force on its restraint
and tolerance.' It read like the publicity blurb for the Woodstock
festival the previous year, which promised 'three days of peace and
music' in upstate New York. In Sydney there was also a 'minimum
of violence', although national newspaper *The Australian* noted the
unfortunate, but mildly amusing, case of a 'police constable [who]
was knocked unconscious by a tomato dropped from the top of a
department store'.

Our belated embrace of the '60s, with Whitlam's election in
1972, put our political system almost permanently out of synch
with the rest of the world, with the common view being that Australia followed overseas trends with a time delay. Whitlam became
prime minister twelve years after the Americans had elected John
F. Kennedy, and eight years after the British had their equivalent
turn leftward with Harold Wilson. Take any American presidential election or British general election that marked a national
mood shift since then and you can flip the result for Australia.
When economic rationalism was ascendant in the 1980s with
Ronald Reagan in the White House and Margaret Thatcher in
Number 10 Downing Street, we gave Labor another chance under
Bob Hawke. When the Americans and British switched to the
centre-left charisma of Bill Clinton and Tony Blair in the 1990s,
we opted for the nostalgic conservatism of John Howard.

But are we behind, or ahead of the pack? Our leaders prefer
to think the latter. Malcolm Fraser says he predated Reagan and
Thatcher as an advocate of small government, and Paul Keating claims, with some justification, that he wrote the Third Way
manual for Blair. The more likely explanation is that Australia's

size, location and mineral wealth changes the way our southern mind processes things. While we crouched behind the tariff wall, we were behind. But once we opened our economy we gave ourselves the opportunity to pick world trends ahead of our larger, less nimble friends. The common thread between the tardy and the prophetic Australia was our star-spotter's ability to identify the next big player in the international scene through our resources sector, which was the one part of our economy that was always exposed to competition.

Before Gough Whitlam, Australia seemed to draw its prime ministers from three plodding political archetypes: the working man who stood for the Labor Party, most notably Ben Chifley; the Labor defector who switched to the conservatives, most infamously Billy Hughes, and more benignly Joe Lyons; and the conservative lawyer, the most successful of whom was Robert Menzies, the founder of the modern Liberal Party.

Whitlam was the first Labor leader to jump the containment lines of class and ideology. He was born in the eastern Melbourne suburb of Kew in 1916, raised in Canberra, and studied at university in Sydney – the three cities that would come to define cosmopolitan Australia. Whitlam served in the Second World War as a navigator for the Royal Australian Air Force, and was a lawyer before he became a politician. His first twenty years in parliament had been in opposition, watching Menzies perfect the art of do-nothing government, while he fought the conservatives on his own side to modernise the Labor platform.

His predecessor, the seventy-year-old Arthur Calwell, was 'the last . . . the greatest and the most articulate of the red-blooded racists in the early tradition of the Australian Labor Party', according to the legendary speechwriter who worked for both men, Graham Freudenberg. Under Calwell, Labor had lost three elections in a row, in 1961, '63 and '66, each by a larger margin than the one before it. The leader before Calwell, Doc Evatt, had lost three elections of his own in the 1950s. As the defeats accumulated, so did the party's martyr complex. Labor people blamed Menzies for scaring people into believing Australia was at risk of communist invasion from the north. They blamed conservative Catholics for splitting from the Labor Party to form the Democratic Labor Party and direct their second preference votes to the class enemy, the Liberals.

By contrast with Labor's paranoid old guard, Whitlam was a ruthless pragmatist. He didn't govern that way, but in opposition he was the epitome of the professional politician. In his six years as opposition leader, he used the new medium of television to broaden Labor's appeal to the middle classes, redefining the working man's party into a party for all employees, male and female, blue collar and white collar. This involved the careful mixing of progressive with practical policies. His boldest visions were in foreign affairs. He wanted Australia to be truly independent by ending its involvement in the Vietnam War, making friends with the then isolated China and offering nationhood to our only colony, Papua New Guinea. But in domestic policy, he remained fixated on the Australian suburbs, promising more spending on education, a universal healthcare scheme, equal pay for women, and sewerage to every home. One of the puzzles of the so-called Golden Age in the 1950s and '60s, as Whitlam often noted, was that almost every home had a TV, but the Liberal and Country parties had been too stingy to provide sewerage to the same addresses.

Whitlam emerged in an era in which it was widely accepted that the national government ought to sit back and allow the states to provide public services (or not). One of Whitlam's most radical positions was to be a centralist. He issued the social reform challenge at his first press conference as opposition leader, in February 1967: 'There would be no other country with which we compare ourselves in which the national government takes so little responsibility, shows so little initiative in, say, education and health, as is the case in Australia, [or] where the natural resources, the things which we can develop with the greatest skill and speed and profit, are passing so rapidly into foreign hands.' A self-described 'democratic socialist', Whitlam explained his ideology in a follow-up article for *The Australian*, which Rupert Murdoch had founded three years earlier and would use to help get Labor elected. 'As units in the economy grow larger and become more international and as society becomes more technological and urban, so social-ism becomes more relevant and urgent. The forces which man is unleashing in the world must be the subject of public and not exclu-sively private decision and control,' Whitlam wrote. 'Democratic socialism is a philosophy about the value of man. It is an attitude towards one's fellow man. Today, it is not concerned merely with rationing scarcity and eliminating exploitation. It means planning for abundance and creating opportunities.'

He was lifting, consciously, from the welfare manual of US president Lyndon Baines Johnson. In a speech in May 1964, six months after the Kennedy assassination and almost three years before Whitlam took the Labor leadership, LBJ outlined his ambition to eliminate poverty and racial inequality. 'The challenge of the next half-century,' he said, 'is whether we have the wisdom to use [our] wealth to enrich and elevate our national life, and to advance the quality of our American civilization . . . [We] have the opportunity to move not only toward the rich society and the powerful society, but upward to the Great Society.' It was, essen-tially, a continuation of the Kennedy agenda, but with the addition of billions of dollars of new government spending. The LBJ agenda included the Civil Rights act, the Medicare health scheme for the elderly, urban renewal, protection for the environment and spend-ing on the arts, and was largely implemented before Whitlam had a chance to develop his own program. Original thinker though Whitlam might have seemed in an Australian context, what he was really trying to achieve was a form of policy catch-up to align conservative Australia with the progressive consensus in the US and the UK in the 1960s. He would have to learn for himself what LBJ had already discovered: the price of pursuing social reform on borrowed money was the unleashing of inflation, which posed an even greater threat to social cohesion than the problems he was trying to solve.

Robert Menzies had left the Liberal–Country Party government in strong electoral shape when he retired on Australia Day 1966, after sixteen consecutive years as prime minister. His successor, Harold Holt, led the Coalition to a landslide victory in November that year, but was soon unnerved by the new Labor leader, Gough Whitlam. Tragedy struck in December 1967 when Holt disappeared, presumed drowned after going for a swim at Cheviot Beach, on Victoria's Mornington Peninsula. His death seemed to unglue the government, and personality clashes, long suppressed under Menzies, became public property. The Country Party leader and deputy prime minister, Jack McEwen, didn't want the treasurer, Billy McMahon, to take Holt's place, and told the nation so. The Liberal Party turned to John Gorton, who it thought would be able to match Whitlam's television appeal. The straight-talking Gorton was popular for a while but his own side quickly grew to loathe his erratic decision-making style, and many didn't mind telling the electorate what they thought about him, either.

Whitlam assumed it would take him two terms to win office, and didn't expect to get so close at his first general election as leader on 25 October 1969. Gorton's Coalition government suffered a primary vote swing of 7 per cent against it. Labor picked up 17 seats; just four more and David Williamson need never have written his play *Don's Party*. Gorton was saved by his home state of Victoria, and where the DLP influence was the strongest.

But while he didn't expect to win, it turned out to be Whitlam's catastrophe that he lost. He had developed his program for social reform on the assumption that Australia's never-ending growth would pay for it, or at least pay off the debt it required. The 1969 election was held when the economy had achieved full employment and inflation was still at modest levels. Freudenberg says, with hindsight, that this would have been the ideal year to take office, before the Program (as Labor's ambitious reform plan was dubbed) 'became so overloaded with specifics': 'If we had been in government in the last three years of the post-war growth, the Program would have been more manageable and the times would have been more compatible with the Program.' But the economy was about to run into a global recession, in part caused by the cost of building the Great Society – not that anyone saw it at the time. The near-miss of 1969 nonetheless energised Labor: surely the next election would yield the remaining few seats of government. On the government side, there was a heavy sense of fatigue. Immediately after the election, Gorton faced a leadership challenge from McMahon, but survived. The next tilt came barely a year later, in March 1971, when McMahon took advantage of a very public falling out between Gorton and his young defence minister, Malcolm Fraser. The nation was transfixed as Fraser gave his reason for resigning from cabinet in a speech to parliament.

'Since his election to office, the prime minister has seriously damaged the Liberal Party and cast aside the stability and sense of direction of earlier times . . . [His] unreasoned drive to get his own way, his obstinacy, impetuous and emotional reactions, have imposed strains upon the Liberal Party, the government and the public service. I do not believe he is fit to hold the great office of prime minister, and I cannot serve in his government.'

Gorton lost his job to McMahon the next day, 10 March, but refused to go quietly and stood for the deputy leader's job, which he won. He awarded himself Fraser's portfolio, guaranteeing that instability would continue. Five months later, McMahon sacked Gorton from the ministry.

Such was the paralysis within government that in some respects Whitlam didn't need to have won the election: he was able to change national policy from opposition. One initiative deserves special consideration because it placed him ahead of world opinion, and earned Australia a stunning commercial advantage for the eventual challenges of the digital age. For some time, communist China had been annoyed by Australia's continued refusal to formally recognise its existence, and in early 1971, as Gorton's leadership was crumbling, threatened to cut its trade contract with the Australian Wheat Board. Whitlam, on the urging of the Labor Party's federal secretary, Mick Young, moved to exploit the opportunity for high diplomacy and domestic political mischief. The Australian opposition leader sent a cable to Chinese premier Zhou Enlai in April, suggesting that a delegation from the Labor Party visit Beijing. Freudenberg and others advised Whitlam to be cautious, 'because it was by any measure a great risk politically'. As Freudenberg recalls, China's rise in the early twenty-first century was by no means obvious in the third quarter of the twentieth. It was an international pariah, as a communist state, and unlike the USSR, very poor. 'To the extent that in the '70s we thought of China in terms of trade, it was really as a very big market for primary products,' he says. 'There was the old cliché: if we could persuade every Chinese person to have a spoonful of sugar a year that would take care of the Queensland sugar crop, and if every Chinese person wore one sock that would take care of the wool clip.' But wheat was the immediate motive for Whitlam: it was felt that Canada was moving towards recognising China and stood to gain a significant section of our trade with the sleeping Asian giant.

For a while, it seemed Whitlam had lost his gamble. Initially, China was slow to respond, giving McMahon – by now

Gorton's successor – a chance to taunt Whitlam. But McMahon was silenced when the Chinese finally accepted. Whitlam and his group arrived on 2 July 1971, and Whitlam met with Zhou three days later. They talked about the Vietnam War, trade, the McMahon government's reluctance to recognise China, and their mutual dislike of the US foreign policy in Asia in the 1950s and '60s.

Whitlam: 'The American people have broken President Lyndon Baines Johnson, and if Richard Milhous Nixon does not continue to withdraw his forces from Vietnam, they will destroy him similarly. The Australian people have had a bitter experience in going all the way with LBJ. They know the American people made him change his policy and they will never again allow an American president to send troops to another country in this way.'

Zhou: 'I have similar sentiments to you. Such a very good appraisal of the American people. I do believe the American people will rise up and restrict the policies of the American president and overthrow him.'

McMahon was outraged that the opposition leader was giving policy advice to Nixon from enemy territory. 'In no time at all, Mr Zhou had Mr Whitlam on a hook and he played him as a fisherman plays a trout,' the prime minister said. Whitlam had 'insulted just about most of our friends and allies in Asia and the Pacific'. But Whitlam had chanced on history. The US secretary of state, Dr Henry Kissinger, had a secret meeting with Zhou later that week. Whitlam left China on 13 July, with McMahon assuming Labor had learned nothing from the Cold War and had gifted the Coalition a fresh deck of communist cards to play at the coming election. On 15 July, Nixon announced his 'shock' – he was going to China, as the first step on what he called a 'journey for peace'. McMahon was suddenly yesterday's man, and the nation counted down to the inevitable change of government.

On the same day Richard Nixon sided with Gough Whitlam on China, McMahon's treasurer, Bill Snedden, put his name to a prescient cabinet submission. It warned that Australia was facing its gravest economic threat in a generation. 'Inflation of 6 per cent per annum, or thereabouts, is a most serious matter,' Snedden wrote. 'We have to go back nearly twenty years to find a period when consumer prices were rising faster than they are today. At this rate of inflation, the distortion of relative incomes and the incitement to speculative activities begins to seriously disrupt economic growth, and the antagonisms stirred up as the different economic groups contend to preserve their share of the national product becomes more difficult to deal with.' Snedden feared that this growing economic pressure could expose the fractures in Australian society, between bosses and workers, and between the baby boomers and their parents. But his grave tone was undermined by his cautious recommendation. 'In our attempts to deal with the economic problem to date, we have emphasised that our aim is to bring inflationary forces under control by gradual means without the disruption to production and employment which more drastic measures would entail. The restraint on Commonwealth spending which I am proposing would be fully consistent with that aim.' By restraint, he had in mind not harsh cutbacks, but a slowing of the rate of increase in public expenditure in the 1971–72 budget. This represented a far softer approach than the Menzies government, which had dealt with the inflation threat from the Korean War wool boom in an uncharacteristically aggressive but effective manner. Menzies increased a raft of taxes and withheld 20 per cent of farmers' income. The toughest measure Snedden announced in his 1971–72 budget doubled the charge for patients buying medicines under the pharmaceutical benefits scheme from 50 cents to a dollar.

In fact, what Snedden had felt were the first winds from the gathering storm that would sink Australia. The storm had a name: 'stagflation'. It's a term now greatly feared, but then little known.

It had been coined in 1965 by British conservative
Macleod. But it was now taking its most menacing f
where LBJ had tried to pursue his Great Society w
ning an increasingly costly war in Vietnam. When Johnson began
his first term in his own right in January 1965, inflation was 1.1
per cent and unemployment 4.9 per cent. Contemporary economic
theory told him that he could achieve full employment with just a
little more government spending, so he bet the budget on keeping
the first rate steady, and slashing the second. But the theory was
wrong. The deficit exploded from 0.2 per cent of domestic product
in 1965 to 2.9 per cent of GDP in 1968 – the highest level since the
end of the Second World War. And the money was spent to no
avail: consumer prices jumped but the dole queues didn't get any
shorter because the cost of employing people was rising as well.
When the Republican Richard Nixon was sworn in as president
in January 1969, inflation was at 4.7 per cent and unemployment
at 3.4 per cent, but instead of changing course, Nixon accelerated,
borrowing even more to fight the losing war in Asia. Inflation and
unemployment both crossed 6 per cent over the course of 1970 as
the economy slipped into its first recession in a decade, and 'stagflation' entered the pop cultural lexicon through Marvin Gaye's
protest song 'Inner City Blues (Make Me Wanna Holler)', which
made the connection between rising household costs and Vietnam.

One of the casualties of American stagflation was the so-called
Bretton Woods Agreement, which had governed post-war exchange
rate policies between nations. The US dollar was the system's
reserve currency, and it could be converted into gold, whose price
had been fixed at US$35 an ounce since 1934. As any trader knows,
if one price is fixed there is money to be made by speculating on
the price that changes. Once inflation started the rise, the Americans began funding their deficits by printing money, but this
ruse would rebound when creditor nations wanted to be paid in
gold, not greenbacks. The global market was telling the US to get

its house in order, but Nixon changed the rules of the game on 15 August 1971 when he suspended the convertibility of the dollar into gold. He also imposed a 10 per cent surcharge on imports and cut the US foreign aid budget by 10 per cent. This was the second Nixon 'shock' and it hurt Australia as much as relations with China would help us, by introducing a new level of unpredictability to our own economy.

Nixon forced other nations to choose. They could either join the US in leaving it to the market to set the price of their currency, or re-assert control in other ways. The market would sit in judgement whatever happened. Those nations that were slow in dealing with inflation would have their currencies attacked through the withdrawal of foreign investment.

The McMahon government took what seemed to be the soft but safe option, switching from the British pound to the American dollar as the guide for our currency. That is, the price was still fixed by the government, but it would be changed from time to time in response to what the US dollar did. But the greenback was more volatile, and suddenly our dollar was jumping all over the place after forty years of stability.

Hindsight says that 1971–72 marked a shallow recession in Australia, around two years after the US had theirs. The Coalition was caught out. It had responded to the inflation threat with a tight budget in 1971–72, but the unemployment rate, which had been below 2 per cent throughout the '60s, suddenly jumped towards an unthinkable 3 per cent. So McMahon panicked and began spending to restore jobs, and passed up whatever chance he might have had to place a lid on inflation. Whitlam mocked the government in his reply to the 1972–73 budget, which had tried to turn the growth tap back on. 'Not since the early 1950s has Australia been presented in two successive years with two such contradictory budgets as this year's and last year's,' Whitlam said. 'Last year, all brakes on, this year, in the words of the prime minister, all stops out.' McMahon's fiscal flip-flopping had destroyed what remaining claim the Coalition had to managing the nation's finances. There was no choice, really, but to give Whitlam his turn.

Our vulnerability came from a very simple misunderstanding of what had fuelled the Golden Age. We, like most rich nations, thought that government could still manipulate the economy through its own spending activities to secure full employment. Our version of intervention, constructed by supposedly pro-market conservatives, and endorsed by conservative and communist trade unions alike, placed politicians and bureaucrats at the heart of the big transactions. Government in those days controlled every price – tariffs, interest rates and the exchange rate – and the Arbitration Commission set wages. It was capitalism with a socialist hand. The income from the rural and mining sectors, which were exposed to the international market, was used to protect the domestic manufacturing sector from those same competitive forces. So we sold Japan our minerals but our tariffs ensured that we wouldn't buy their cars in return, while also protecting the high wages that made our cars expensive. The scheme worked so long as our export prices held up and inflation remained as low as it had through the '60s, when we were approaching full employment. Once nirvana had been achieved, however, workers kept asking for more without offering anything in return. The Coalition thought it had enough tools at its disposal to finetune the economy, but the world was rapidly changing. Inflation was damaging relationships within nations and between them. To think that a few politicians working from their offices in the bush capital of Canberra could defend Australian interests against this new uncertainty was fanciful. But they knew no other way. The Coalition, and then Labor, persisted with the old approach of price fixing until the world imposed the wake-up call of a deep recession. Even then, it would take many years for the right mix of policies to emerge.

The warning that the Australian economy had entered a new,

unstable phase could be seen in the unusual behaviour of the share market. In the spring of 1969, the price of nickel surged because of the demands of the Vietnam War and industrial action against a major supplier in Canada. The popular imagination was grabbed by Poseidon, which had been an unsuccessful mining operation until a prospector it had hired struck nickel in Windarra, Western Australia. Shares in the company had been trading at 80 cents at the start of September 1969. By Friday, 26 September, the price had doubled to $1.85. On the Monday, it was $5.60. And so it kept escalating until it peaked at $278 on 13 February 1970 (or $2730 in 2010 dollars). The media initially treated the Poseidon boom as a horse race. There is a revealing pair of front-page photos in the *Sydney Morning Herald* of 10 October 1969, juxtaposing the scene in the stock exchange's public gallery with the chaos on the trading floor, where dealers are yelling, moaning, sweating. Neatly dressed women clutching their purses, and men with binoculars, watch in orderly bemusement. They could be waiting for the curtain to rise at the theatre. The headline atop the photos reduced the scene to its mug-punting essence: 'Poseidon is way out in front as dealers go round the bend'. While shares in Poseidon itself quickly rose out of the reach of mum and dad investors, the lure of capital gain meant that contagion spread to other mining projects. Insider trading had not yet been outlawed, so those who understood the game would push rumours about a new stock, watch the price soar and sell their stake at a monster profit before the venture was exposed as unviable. The idea of buying at $1 and watching the price increase ten- or fifty-fold within days lured more and more middle-class people who had never played the market before. Then, just as suddenly, the price of nickel collapsed. In the rout that followed, mining stocks lost two-thirds of their value between January 1970 and November 1971 and many ordinary Australian households had their life savings wiped out. The nation that was turning leftward had just revealed its gullible side.

There is no magic formula to determine when a people lose their sense of perspective. The Poseidon boom came eight years after the most recent recession, in 1961, and twenty-four years after the end of the Second World War. The backdrop of full employment is one explanation for the madness; another is that Japan had replaced Britain as our number-one export market by 1967 and its demand for our minerals went to our heads. The quarry sits in an unusual part of the national psyche. The income that is drawn from mining is not connected to the everyday Australian experience in the same way that farming is. Even if most of us don't live in the bush, we know, intuitively, that its economy is subject to boom and bust cycles through the caprice of climate. If it rains at the wrong time, a crop is destroyed. But when an unknowable Asian nation asks us to dig on its behalf, we assume the boom will never end.

This global and local turmoil brought to prominence not just Gough Whitlam, but also a telegenic trade union chief. Bob Hawke managed to play both sides of the arguments between labour and capital, promoting big pay claims then stepping in to resolve the high-profile strikes that routinely shut down the economy. Hawke was born in Bordertown, South Australia, in 1929, grew up in Perth, and went to Oxford as a Rhodes Scholar, where he set beer-drinking records and wrote a thesis on the history of wage fixation in Australia. He served an eleven-year apprenticeship at the peak trade union body, the ACTU, before taking over as its president in 1970. Hawke's rise heralded a more militant approach from the trade unions. His first year in charge marked the first occasion since the Korean War wool boom that average earnings had increased by more than 10 per cent. The number of industrial disputes that year had increased by more than a third to 2738. In Hawke's second year in charge, 1971, another double-digit pay increase was achieved, and a then record 3 million working days were lost across the economy. Hawke was chasing a version of LBJ's Great Society, believing that workers could grab a larger slice of the national income pie without pricing themselves out of their jobs. The obedient Australia of the 1960s had entered the 1970s with a taste for self-destruction.

The greatest social problem facing Australia, Whitlam said in his campaign launch speech on 13 November 1972, was 'the good use of expanding leisure'. To this end, he promised community and sporting centres based around local schools, and cheaper domestic airfares so Australians could holiday interstate. This is not to make light of the smaller items in the Program, but to place it in the high-growth context in which it was developed. The speech, which called on a sheltered people to embrace the modern world, is better known for its goose-bump opening, 'Men and women of Australia . . .'.

'The decision we will make for our country on 2 December is a choice between the past and the future, between the habits and fears of the past, and the demands and opportunities of the future. There are moments in history when the whole fate and future of nations can be decided by a single decision. For Australia, this is such a time.'

The speech was optimistic, but the setting was one of apparent crisis. 'Will you again entrust the nation's economy to the men who deliberately, but needlessly, created Australia's worst unemployment for ten years?' Whitlam asked voters. 'Or to the same men who have presided over the worst inflation in twenty years?' The Program was now bulging with spending and other social policy commitments. In order of appearance in the campaign launch speech, they included the promise of an education for all children and the scrapping of tertiary education fees; an increase in the basic pension to 25 per cent of average weekly earnings; a universal health insurance scheme, to be known as Medibank; rebuilding infrastructure in the nation's cities and towns; the immediate abolition of conscription; and land rights for Aboriginal Australians.

The first priority was the restoration of 'genuine full employment'. Whitlam posed the rhetorical question: where would the money come from to pay for the Program? The answer was through the proceeds of economic growth. The economy, which the Coalition had mismanaged, was to be restored by government intervention.

Whitlam's victory was less decisive than it might have been. Labor achieved a primary vote of 49.6 per cent, which in past campaigns would have delivered a landslide in terms of seats on the floor of the House of Representatives. In 1929, a primary vote of 48.8 per cent secured 46 of the then 75 seats for James Scullin's doomed government. In 1943, John Curtin turned a primary vote of 49.9 per cent into 49 seats out of 74.

Whitlam won just 67 of the 125 seats, for a majority of eight after the appointment of a speaker. If he had enjoyed the strike rates of Scullin and Curtin, the final tally would have been closer to 80 seats. 'We have won them in the suburbs of Sydney and Melbourne, because that is where so many people live,' Whitlam explained at his first post-victory press conference, on 5 December. It was the first modern election to be won without an anchor in the bush. Labor gained six seats in New South Wales, another four in Victoria and one each in Queensland and Tasmania. Against this, it lost two seats in Western Australia and one each in Victoria and South Australia, leaving it with a net increase of just eight. It was a respectable win, but with the nation split across state lines. Labor had the majority of seats in New South Wales, South Australia and Tasmania, while the Coalition retained the majority of seats in Victoria, Queensland and Western Australia.

On that first day of power, 5 December, Whitlam had his eye firmly on the living room. He established an interim cabinet of two with his deputy, Lance Barnard, to commence governing while votes were still being counted in the closer seats. The reason for the urgency was that the final election result would not be known until Friday week, 15 December, he said. A full meeting of the Labor caucus to elect the ministry could not be held until the Monday following that. 'There are certain things I believe must be put in hand by the incoming government before then,' the prime minister-elect explained. And what was it that couldn't wait for a fortnight? The first item of business for the two-man government was the abolition of conscription. There was no reason why conscientious objectors should spend another two weeks in jail when the public had voted for their pardon. The second priority that day was to begin the process of introducing colour television to Australia through a formal request to the Tariff Board to review the matter. The third was to declare the new government's support for equal pay for women in a submission to the Arbitration Commission. From the opening brushstrokes, Whitlam was working on pictures big and small, and in his fever to complete every project he unsettled the city-folk who had given him a mandate to change the nation.

2

THE GOUGH SHOCK

The cultural divide in Australia in the early 1970s was between the smug and the smug – the locals who didn't care what the rest of the world thought of us, and the expats who wanted to tell their new friends in London that the typical Australian was a suburban slob. Both were expressions of inferiority, and Barry Humphries caught the contradiction best with his loud-mouthed creation Barry McKenzie, and his aunt, Edna Everage of Moonee Ponds. Gough Whitlam's victory enticed many of the exiles home, and generated what author Robert Drewe described as a 'rare feeling of national self-respect'.

'It's not as if we're suddenly a big-shot country,' he wrote in an article for *The Australian*, 'but the fact is that Labor restored some dignity to the conduct of our national affairs at a time when we had all come more or less to expect nothing but ill from political action. Without precedent in the history of British-style governments, it set out to make up for lost time by immediately implementing its campaign promises. Australians blinked as within weeks we recognised China, ended conscription, abolished race as a criterion of our immigration policy, began reform of the health service, supported equal pay for women, abolished British honours, increased arts subsidies, put contraceptives on the medical benefits list, took the tax off Australian wine, moved to stop the slaughter of kangaroos and crocodiles, and searched for a new national anthem.'

Drewe saw the first hundred days of the Whitlam government as a form of national awakening. Yet this new Australia asserted its newfound independence, from Britain and the United States, with all the grace of a seventeen-year-old on his final day at high school. There is a scene in the first Barry McKenzie movie that captures the double edge of the rebellion. Bazza is forcibly taken to a London psychiatrist's office, where he is asked when he started having delusions.

'If you really want to know, it all started when I paid through the nose for a ticket and landed up a shit creek called England,' he barked.

'So, you hate the mother country, do you?' the psychiatrist replied.

The mother country had abandoned us by formally joining the Common Market on New Year's Day 1973 after years of knocking on Europe's door. 'Our traditional markets are failing,' Margaret Thatcher, then the education minister in Edward Heath's Conservative government, had been telling her electorate. Australia, Canada and the new Commonwealth were forming close links with countries near them, she said, so 'Britain must look urgently elsewhere for trade'. Britain supplied more than half our imports at the end of the 1940s, but the figure declined rapidly through the '50s and '60s as our chequebooks pointed to the United States and then Japan. By the time Britain had joined the European Union, we were buying just 19 per cent of our imports from her, compared to 21 per cent from the US and 18 per cent from Japan. Britain's loss of influence, while inevitable, troubled older Australians. To this group – the Menzies generation, who would love the Queen till the day they died – Whitlam's modernity was viewed as decadent, and his desire for a non-aligned foreign policy was dangerous.

Another anxiety of national identity was based on gender. Australian women were more culturally assertive in the early 1970s than Australian men had been in the previous decade, and this made the male baby boomer even more nostalgic for the world of his parents. One of the more conservative Labor politicians of the time, the member for Blaxland in Sydney's west since 1969, was two years too old to be counted as a baby boomer. But former rock-band manager Paul Keating spoke for boomer men when he complained about the economic pressures that were undermining the single-income family.

'Husbands have been forced to send their wives to work in order to provide the necessaries of life. Young mothers have been forced out of their homes by economic pressure,' he had told parliament in his maiden speech, on 17 March 1970. 'We must not forget that this government has been in office for twenty years. It has had the duty and the opportunity to rectify the present situation. Family life is the very basis of our nationhood. In the last couple of years, the Government has boasted about the increasing number of women in the work force. Rather than something to be proud of I feel that this is something of which we should be ashamed . . . [Is the government] doing anything to put the working wife back in her home? It is not. It engages in a lot of claptrap.'

Feminism had two of its most recognisable spokeswomen in Melbourne-born expats. Germaine Greer's polemic *The Female Eunuch* was published in 1970 and Helen Reddy's pop anthem 'I Am Woman' reached number one on the American Billboard charts on 9 December 1972, the week after the election. Between these two signposts, Australia's best known bloke, ACTU president Bob Hawke, became the unintended pin-up for the bewildered male. During a television appearance in 1971 with feminist and communist Zelda D'Aprano, the trade union boss became the nation's groper-in-chief. As Blanche d'Alpuget wrote in her biography, Hawke touched D'Aprano's shoulder 'to find out, as he explained, if she was wearing a bra'. 'D'Aprano was a postal worker. Hawke asked her, "You mean M-A-I-L Exchange, don't you?" The feminist magazine *Mejane* named him Male Chauvinist of the Month and feminists never forgave him.'

Excessive displays of manliness are a telltale sign of an insecure nation – and an immature one. The top-rating local television program in the early 1970s was *Number 96*, a crass and sometimes funny soapie in the unAustralian setting of a block of flats. The male characters were either macho or uptight. The female cast took their clothes off, while those too old to join in the romp gossiped about what everyone else was doing.

Male aggression played out on the sports field too. Following their free-flowing Victorian Football League grand final in 1972, which delivered the highest combined score on record, the Richmond Tigers and the Carlton Blues played off again in 1973, but this time it resembled a pub brawl, with players taking cheap shots at one another. By the summer of 1974–75, when the Whitlam government was disintegrating, the nation got its kicks watching Lillee and Thommo hurl bouncers at the English cricket team in what was dubbed 'the Ashes of Terror'.

What was driving the grumpiness of the Australian bloke, apart from the uncomfortable rise of feminism, was the deterioration of the economy. Inflation had crossed 10 per cent by the September quarter 1973, when the more violent of the two Richmond–Carlton grand finals was played.

Plot any chart from the early '70s, and the two figures that take off together like a Concorde jet are wages and inflation. Labor inherited an inflation rate of around 6 per cent and a wages system that had been delivering average pay rises of about 10 per cent a year in the final term of the Coalition government. The first financial year of the Whitlam government, 1973–74, saw inflation

almost double from 8.2 per cent to 14.4 per cent, and average earnings jump by 17.6 per cent. The new government was both enabler
and victim. It used the public service as a trendsetter to promote
its campaign for equal pay and better conditions, and this added
to the wage–price spiral. The aggressive pursuit of the Program
created a scarcity of labour, such was the number of new public servants hired to expand the reach of the national government
in areas like education and health. Yet Labor was also hostage to
its brothers-in-arms in the trade union movement, who wanted a
larger slice of national income for wages at the expense of profits.
Workers in the private sector went on strike to secure the sorts of
pay rises that were being offered in the public sector. Who was to
blame?

Paul Keating's reading of events is not entirely uncharacteristic, nor entirely unfair. He says inflation triggered a 'shares battle'
between government, labour and capital. 'It's not well understood,
but Bob [Hawke] nearly destroyed the economy twice in the 1970s,
by the first wage explosion under the Whitlam government, which
Bob presided over, and, of course, the later one under Malcolm
Fraser and treasurer John Howard in 1979 to '82.'

Hawke, elected the Labor Party's federal president in 1973,
wanted to be prime minister – everyone knew that. And part of
the job audition, to Hawke's way of thinking, was to speak out
whenever Whitlam made a mistake. Each sought to shower the
economy with income when the last thing the nation needed
was more cash chasing prices ever higher. Like kids at a birthday party scrambling for the last slice of cake, they didn't mind if
they smashed every plate on the table to achieve their democratic
socialist objectives.

Hawke rejects this argument. He says Whitlam had no interest
in economics and resisted his offer to arrange some tutoring on the
subject. 'In the latter part of '72, when it looked like we were going
to win, I said to him, "You'll make great social changes, you'll do

good things internationally, but your government will live or die on what you do with the economy",' Hawke recalls. 'I said, "You don't know anything about economics, let me organise someone to talk to you a few hours a week", but he wouldn't do it.'

But let's not fall for political history's trap of blaming one man alone. Whitlam understood the importance of economics, especially in his first year, but underestimated, as did many others, how hard it would be to remove inflation from the system. He also led a government of eccentric rivals and was advised by a bureaucracy that did not appreciate the need for new thinking. Labor's frontline ministers had shared two decades in opposition, when the dominant policy concern was foreign affairs not economics. The treasurer, Frank Crean, knew his numbers. He had a commerce degree from the University of Melbourne, and worked in the tax department for eight years before entering the Victorian parliament in 1945 at the age of twenty-nine. He went federal in 1951. But his qualifications couldn't compensate for his inability to impose discipline as the government's bean counter. Crean was no match for the three big personalities of the cabinet – Jim Cairns, Clyde Cameron and Rex Connor.

Cairns, a former Victorian policeman, had an economics degree from the University of Melbourne, and received his PhD from Oxford for his thesis on the welfare state in Australia. He entered parliament in 1955, at the age of forty-one, challenged Whitlam for the Labor leadership in 1968 and had been the public face of Australia's peaceful dissent at the Vietnam moratorium marches. Cameron, the minister for labour, was a former shearer and trade union leader. He picked the worst possible time to become a federal Labor politician, winning the Adelaide seat of Hindmarsh in 1949, at the age of thirty-six, and hence did the whole 23-year stretch of opposition. When he came to power, he was determined to use it, and, as Keating says, 'started a public sector wage round all by himself as minister for labour'. Connor, the minister for minerals and energy was a late bloomer, entering federal parliament in 1963 at the age of fifty-six, after serving thirteen years in the New South Wales state parliament. He was the most senior Labor figure to have run his own business before politics, including a car yard in Wollongong during the Great Depression. When Labor took office, Crean, born in the same year as Whitlam, was fifty-six years old, Cairns fifty-eight, Cameron fifty-nine and Connor sixty-five. Their lack of governing experience created a perfect storm of policy errors.

Although accused of a lack of interest in economics, Gough Whitlam surprised the nation just seven months into his term by embracing the most aggressive pro-market reform on the policy menu. Without warning, he announced that on 18 July 1973 all tariffs would be reduced by 25 per cent. The Australian deregulation program began here, two years after the end of the Bretton Woods Agreement, and a decade before the next Labor government floated the dollar.

The campaign to reduce protection had never been a popular cause, but it brought some interesting people to the front line of the public argument. Most notable were two immigrant economists: Fred Gruen, who was one of the young Austrian- and German-born men deported from England to Australia on the *Dunera* in 1940, and Max Corden, who left Nazi Germany as a young boy with his parents to start a new life in Melbourne in 1939. They made the intellectual case for reform. Contrarian Liberal MP Bert Kelly (a farmer before he became the federal member for the rural South Australian seat of Wakefield) and the head of the Tariff Board, Alf Rattigan (a self-made man from the mining town of Kalgoorlie in Western Australia), took the argument to the political sphere. Each man had chipped away at the edifice of entitlement in the 1960s, arguing that protection made industry lazy and hurt Australian consumers, who were forced to pay higher prices for inferior goods.

Tariffs were originally designed as a revenue measure to fund the national government in the early years of federation. But their meaning quickly changed to defending jobs, wages and industry. The policy gained a xenophobic taint. Australian-made products were supposed to be better than the cheaper foreign version. This led, for instance, to arcane distinctions at the kitchen table between butter and margarine. By 1940, the Victorian minister for agriculture told his state parliament that foreign margarine was made 'so closely resembling butter in both appearance and flavour that this product has become a serious competitor of butter for table use, and now constitutes an increasingly grave menace for the dairying industry'. Not all margarine was bad, mind you – cooking margarine was made from 'beef and mutton fat produced in Australia'. The problem was table margarine, which 'consists mainly of vegetable oils grown by black labour and imported into Australia duty-free'. Coloured hands using new technology: it wasn't the Australian way.

The idea of buying something directly from overseas undermined our self-worth. What sort of country were we if we couldn't make things? Our closed economy had more in common with the old communist bloc, complete with black-and-white television and unreliable automobiles. The most absurd expression of our technical prowess was the Leyland P76. Judged car of the year in 1973 by *Wheels* magazine, it soon became the punch line to a national joke, as design flaws, strikes and soaring oil prices saw the model discontinued after just 18 000 vehicles had been produced. (The P76 did offer one glimpse of the big-is-better future: the capacious boot was supposed to fit a 44-gallon drum, which in the modern language of the working family would be a Bugaboo pram.)

Whitlam seemed an unlikely convert to the anti-protection cause. His reform program was concerned with increasing the size of the national government, not reducing its income by forgoing revenue from tariffs. And as a Labor prime minister, surely the last thing he would want to do was put a single job on the line. But Whitlam's agenda ran a little deeper than that: he wanted the opportunity to restructure the economy in order to free labour for other work, such as providing sewerage to more than a million homes, and creating new government departments for Aboriginal affairs and the environment. 'While these changes can be expected to require some workers to move from one employment to another, this must be seen against the existing high level of unfulfilled [job] vacancies and rising employment opportunity,' Whitlam explained in a joint statement with Jim Cairns, the trade minister. However, moving pieces of labour across the economy's chess table was not the reason for the dramatic announcement. It was a policy decision born with the haste of crisis rather than the long reflection of strategy: Whitlam's main motivation was to check rising inflation by reducing the cost of imported goods.

As the cabinet papers reflect, no submission on the across-the-board tariff cut was presented and the fight against inflation was the only reason given for it. 'All tariffs [will] be reduced by a quarter,' decision No. 968 stated. 'This is designed to reduce local prices of imported goods by slightly under 6 per cent.' The cabinet debate was fiery. Whitlam calculated that that best form of attack was to throw a convert into the front line, so he allowed Cairns, who had switched from protectionist to fervent reformist, to take up the fight. 'Whitlam only played a minor role in the cabinet discussions,' journalist Alan Reid wrote. 'He announced the recommendations. He left Cairns to carry the ball, which was shrewd. But for Cairns's advocacy, the recommendation would probably have never been endorsed.'

Cairns argued that the only way to relieve the pressure of shortages and inflation was through more imported goods. Among those in the no camp, Doug McLelland, the media minister, said lower tariffs would not reduce the cost of living for workers: 'All it would give them would be cheaper transistor radios, TV sets, cameras and electrical goods. Prices for foodstuffs were pushing up the cost of living, and the foodstuffs were produced in Australia and did not come from overseas.'

Still, the slight majority of the new cabinet were persuaded by the need to do something about inflation and Whitlam prevailed by a vote of sixteen to eleven. The media applauded this measure like no other in the entire Whitlam era. The *Australian Financial Review* praised it as 'undeniably one of the most forthright and courageous economic decisions taken by any Australian government'. One of the journalists who had campaigned for lower tariffs, Alan Wood, had been tipped off ahead of the cabinet meeting but chose not to break the story for fear of alerting vested interests.

Removing protection for industry fitted with the logic of a more open Australia. Yet Whitlam wanted to hold on to the remaining three prices set by government and the bureaucracy – wages, interest rates and the exchange rate. What he and his ministers, the ACTU and the conservative-minded bureaucracy didn't realise then was that inflation couldn't be dealt with until Australia had let go of those prices as well. But no other Western nation knew this at the time, so Whitlam can be excused.

It suits neither side to credit Whitlam for firing the starter's gun for deregulation because Labor people like to commemorate the social policies, while conservatives prefer to remind older voters about runaway inflation and unemployment. Yet Whitlam's tariff 'shock' (everything was reported as a shock in the 1970s, because the developed world was losing its bearings) stands alongside the relationship with China as his key contribution to the Australian Moment in the twenty-first century. Graham Freudenberg says there is little on the public record about the tariff cut because it wasn't part of the original Program. 'One of the reasons why I'm not up to par on the issue is that I never wrote any speeches on it.

You won't find any exposition of Whitlam's views on this as you can on almost any other issue of importance. It is characteristic Whitlam, in that it represented a bold stroke, and he loved the bold stroke, as in China and so on.'

In the short term, though, the policy was a case study of sound theory poorly implemented. There was no risk assessment made to determine which industries and communities required assistance to smooth the transition from one line of work to another. The tariff cuts coincided with a downturn in the economy, and were blamed for the lost jobs, which undermined the reform cause for a numbers of years. Also, the fire of inflation was burning on so many fronts that the arrival of cheaper imported goods could not douse it.

Whitlam's next attempt to wrestle with inflation was in the first week of October 1973, when he asked the minister for social security, Bill Hayden, to present cabinet with a hard-hitting paper on the topic. That Hayden, not Frank Crean, was given the call showed that prime minister was losing faith in his treasurer. Freudenberg recalls Whitlam's view: 'Frank couldn't argue the government's case with Treasury, and he didn't argue the Treasury's case in the cabinet.' Crean was overseas when the meeting was held.

Hayden was another Labor minister with an economics degree, from the University of Queensland. He had been a Queensland police officer before entering parliament in 1961, at the age of twenty-eight, and was in government a month before his fortieth birthday. The Whitlam government would have been an entirely different beast if Hayden had been appointed its first treasurer, not its last; Hayden would have fought the big-spending trio of Cairns, Cameron and Connor.

Hayden had been nagging his colleagues all year to slow the delivery of their cherished election promises until the economy could more easily afford them. His presentation to cabinet contained a blunt warning that inflation, if left unchecked, would kill the government. 'Price increases have accelerated since we came to office,' he wrote in a submission dated 5 October. 'We can fairly argue that this is not all our doing: but we must recognise that after ten months in office such arguments no longer cut much ice with the people and that increasingly they are looking to *us* to deal with the situation.'

The language of the document is fascinating, as it assumed ministers had no prior knowledge of the dangers of inflation, which was a comment on how the problem seemed to have snuck up on Australia after the stability of the Golden Age. Hayden explained the threat with, literally, a bricks'n'mortar anecdote, referring to advertisements in the Sydney press offering bricklayers up to $40 a day for a six-day week. 'Some may ask what is wrong with that. The labourer, it may be said, is worthy of his hire. And so, in a sensible world, he is . . . [But] the sharp increases in the wages of bricklayers and carpenters are going onto the price of houses.' And that was hitting the swinging voters in the suburban mortgage belt, the new Labor heartland. 'Some of these now much more expensive houses are being bought by well-to-do people of one kind or another. But the great majority, of course, are being bought by ordinary men and women of modest means and little or no capital other than what they have been able to put together by their own hard work – and that of their wives, or, in some cases, parents.'

Hayden gave his colleagues a quick history lesson. 'During this century, runaway inflations have occurred to several countries, resulting in complete collapse of their monetary systems, devastation of the economy and impoverishment of large social classes. The social and political implications of these events have been profound.' He was careful not to suggest we were heading down the Argentinian road, let alone facing the hyperinflation of Germany's

Weimar Republic. 'Australia is not at that stage, but the present stage is bad enough. As the national government, it is our responsibility to regulate the economy successfully. The longer we let the present situation drift, the worse it will get. The worse it gets, the more intractable it will become to control. We cannot allow ourselves to drift into a position where severe demand management methods, involving recessionary economic policies with attendant unemployment and a grind down in production, are all that are left to us.'

Cabinet agreed to a follow-up meeting between the government's economic committee of ministers and officials from the Treasury department. This ranks as one of the saddest discussions in Australian politics, and was held as the inflation rate crossed 10 per cent for the first time in a generation. A well-meaning but unsophisticated government and a confident but equally misguided bureaucracy understood that the economy was in some sort of danger, but beyond that, the common ground disappeared. Each side should have brought an interpreter with them, because they were speaking different languages. Treasury viewed the arrival of the Whitlam government with suspicion. Its default position under the previous Coalition regime had been to argue against any dramatic change in policy. Labor's big spending agenda was the antithesis of Treasury doctrine. Labor reciprocated the suspicion because it saw Treasury as a member of the ruling elite that had held Australia back for two decades.

The minutes of the 12 October discussion found ministers wanting to 'shield' low- and middle-income earners from the pain of tackling inflation, an approach Treasury thought naive. Jim Cairns explained: 'An increase in interest rates must be accompanied by offsetting benefits to selected groups. Equity must be considered if measures are to be politically acceptable.'

Interest rates, which were set by government on the persuasive advice of the Treasury, had been raised as an anti-inflation measure during the previous month, taking the home mortgage from 7 per cent to 8.4 per cent, and imposing a credit squeeze. A single increase of this magnitude was unprecedented, although an even larger one of 2 per cent to 10.4 per cent was to come the following July. Treasury secretary Sir Frederick Wheeler told Cairns there was no point giving some groups a discount on their loans: 'Once selectively is injected', he suggested, policy 'loses its effectiveness'. 'To the point of ineffectuality,' Whitlam added, revealing him to be more open to Treasury thinking than is commonly assumed. In 1973, at least, he was prepared to consider the need for restraint.

Sir Frederick believed that economic management and equity should not be confused, and he said so, coldly. If his intention had been to humble the government, he failed. Ministers engaged in a competition to belittle the Treasury officials. Rex Connor asked 'who was worst hit by inflation?' Sir Frederick said it was the 'little man'. Clyde Cameron asked if the higher interest rates would lead to a rise in unemployment. Treasury deputy secretary John Stone said 'it was not possible to give an easy answer'. Sir Frederick said it was a 'large question' and then ducked it: 'There is no indication that the change in the interest rates will cause general unemployment,' he said. Cameron was unimpressed. Although these cabinet minutes are toned down, the tension is still apparent. Cameron recorded a more colourful version of his argument with Sir Frederick on whether home buyers were suffering. He quoted Sir Frederick as having said: 'Well, you see, it's like this, minister: the amount of interest they pay is more than compensated for by the capital accretion that comes to the value of their home.' Cameron didn't see the funny-money logic in the answer – all credit crises are preceded by the delusion that interest rates don't matter because the capital gain will always triumph. Perhaps Sir Frederick was joking. Either way, Cameron had his comrades laughing when he quipped: 'I see, so when a man comes home from work and his wife tells him she has nothing for dinner because the increased mortgage repayments have exhausted her housekeeping budget, he can say, "Well, don't worry, darling, just give me a plate of capital accretion."' Whitlam took Sir Frederick's side and said, 'Well, if you are going to be insulting, I'll move on.'

Four days later, on 16 October 1973, the Organization of the Petroleum Exporting Countries delivered their shock that came to define the age. The price of crude was increased by 70 per cent, and production was to be cut by 5 per cent each month until Israel withdrew from the Arab territories it had occupied since 1967. The market price for oil soon quadrupled and the full effects were felt in Australia in early 1974. It was a classic price fix, a cartel screwing its customers because it could. The difference now was that the developing world was doing it to the first world, and the main target was the United States.

There are few genuinely crazy years outside of a world war when nations lose their mind together. 1973 is one such year. The oil shock created a sudden, inexplicable scarcity for rich societies. Recessions, which had seemed like mere blips in activity in the affluent 1960s, were an ever-present menace in the 1970s as a consequence of higher oil prices. In Australia, and elsewhere, prosperity for ordinary folk was measured by a car and a house in the suburbs. They were big purchases made easier on the wallet by cheap petrol and low interest rates.

OPEC didn't create stagflation, but it did accelerate the problem by increasing transport costs, which fed through to other prices in the economy. Although businesses cut back on staff, they still passed on the higher costs to others in the production chain. The month before the oil shock, the US was already afflicted with an inflation rate of 7.4 per cent and an unemployment rate of 4.8 per cent. Our second-largest trading partner, Britain, was also exposed with inflation at 9.2 per cent and unemployment at 3.5 per cent. Japan, meanwhile, had more inflation and less unemployment – 14.4 per cent of the former and only 1.2 per cent of the latter.

Australia, with an inflation rate of 10.1 per cent and an unemployment rate of 2.1 per cent, needed a friend that it could continue to trade with, to act as a buffer against any global recession. Japan, the largest customer for our minerals and other exports, and the world's second-largest economy behind the US, seemed the most obvious candidate. Japan boomed through the American recession of 1970, and this helped Australia avoid a serious downturn then – an early prophecy of the role China would play for us during the Great Recession in 2008–09. But when the US slipped into its second recession of the decade in December 1973, Japan, which was heavily dependent on Arab oil, followed in 1974, with its first contraction since the end of the Second World War.

The meaning of the oil shock has changed with the hindsight of the global financial crisis. OPEC had used the political pretext of the Yom Kippur War to blackmail the first-world economies, but there was also some economic logic to what they were doing. The price of oil had been fixed by long-term contracts, and in US dollars that were declining in real value after the collapse of the Bretton Woods Agreement. But the cost of pretty much every other product that the developing world bought from the first world, most notably food, was soaring. It never occurred to the Americans, in particular, that if they pushed inflation on to the international economy, through the deficits they had accumulated to build the Great Society and to fight the Vietnam War in the 1960s, that the developing world would one day push back.

History repeats, first as stagflation then as subprime. The global meltdown of 1974–75 is connected to the Great Recession by the common denominator of American hubris. Just swap Iraq for Vietnam, the credit bubble for the Great Society, and China for OPEC. Each crisis began with US excess and spread to Europe and the British Isles by guilt of association. In each case, the inter-national economy was paralysed by a mismatch between deficit and surplus nations. The deficit nations in the West indulged their citizens by telling them to keep spending. The surplus nations in the East punished their citizens by refusing to spread their new-found wealth. So customer and banker, West and East, continued to warp the global financial system until both sides lost. In 1974–75 it was too much inflation; in 2008–09 it was too much debt that crashed the global economy.

The oil shock was preceded by a breakdown in the American political system. The year 1973 had begun hopefully enough when the United States signed a truce with the North Vietnamese on 27 January, less than two months after Gough Whitlam had ended our involvement in that miserable war. Peace did wonders for the reputation of the re-elected Richard Nixon. The president's job approval rating jumped 16 per cent to 67 per cent immediately after the announcement of the war's end. But the trust implied in that level of support was shattered in a matter of months as the culpability for the bungled attempt to bug the Democratic National Committee the previous year crept closer to his office. As a result of the Watergate scandal, Nixon lost senior staff members H.R. Haldeman and John Ehrlichman, attorney-general Richard Kleindienst and White House counsel John Dean, on 30 April. The drama moved to the surreal in July with the revelation that Nixon had bugged his own office, which meant the argument over whether he knew about the break-in, or had been involved in the cover-up afterwards, could be resolved by pressing play on the secret tapes. Only, Nixon was reluctant to hand over the evidence, and when he finally did, a crucial seventeen-minute section had been mysteriously erased.

By September 1973, the US was showing its dark side again in foreign relations, by backing a military coup in Chile to topple the democratically elected socialist government of Salvador Allende. A separate scandal claimed vice-president Spiro Agnew, who resigned on 10 October after pleading no contest to a tax cheating charge. Ten days later, Nixon pushed Watergate into even more dangerous territory by firing the Justice Department's special prosecutor Archibald Cox, which prompted the protest resignations of attorney-general Elliot Richardson and deputy attorney-general William Ruckelshaus. The Arab–Israeli War straddled these head-spinning events, starting on the Jewish holy day Yom Kippur, 6 October, and ending in stalemate on 25 October. By November, Nixon's job approval rating was just 27 per cent. He was telling a startled nation that he welcomed the scrutiny of Watergate because 'people have got to know whether their president is a crook – well, I'm not a crook'.

The chaos that infected Western politics throughout the 1970s and spilled over to the once-tranquil continent of Australia had its origin in these two related transactions: Watergate and the oil shock. Watergate shifted the balance of power between government and the media. Before that story ignited, a US president, or even an Australian prime minister, was given the benefit of the office. After Watergate, reporters would treat their leaders as frauds until they could prove otherwise. The oil shock fed into the new cynicism by puncturing the myth that our governments could be masters of the economy. But Whitlam was a naive democrat at heart. He wanted to deliver to the letter of his Program, as it had been outlined to voters in 1972, and he didn't see the change in the international climate in 1973 as reason enough to stop spending.

3

A GATHERING CRISIS

First impressions can be telling. The Americans took Labor's election victory in 1972 as the end of a great friendship. The United States ambassador to Australia, Marshall Green, advised his boss, secretary of state Dr Henry Kissinger, that the relationship between the two countries was 'cooling'. In a briefing paper prepared ahead of Gough Whitlam's first official trip to the US as prime minister, Green betrayed the superpower's sensitivity by noting that Whitlam and others had been disrespectful to the Americans. 'Australia has undergone a fundamental reorientation of its internal and external policies since the visit to Washington by then Prime Minister McMahon in November 1971,' Green wrote in July 1973. 'The reorientation of its external policies in part has been a deliberate choice of Prime Minister Whitlam and in part has been accentuated in its impact by the critical and occasionally abusive tone used by Whitlam and some of his senior Ministers in expressing opposition to certain US policies.'

Green described the Australian Labor Party as 'an eclectic and often factionalized coalition of trade union members, traditional radicals, miscellaneous Marxists, and, most significantly, with a leadership and growing majority of middle-class origins'. He added: 'The ALP is often referred to as a "Labor" party but it would probably be more accurate to refer to it as a Democratic party to the left of center'.

The recently declassified US State Department cables offer a fresh way to tell the story of Australia's descent into political and economic chaos in 1974 and '75, through the loose lips of the main players in the Labor government, conservative opposition, the ACTU and the media. The documents are both painful and amusing, for they reveal the petty treachery of Australia's elite. Bob Hawke briefed against Whitlam, opposition leader Bill Snedden briefed against his Coalition partner Doug Anthony, and Rupert Murdoch briefed against everyone. Whitlam, interestingly, comes across as the least malicious. The harshest thing he had to say about a colleague was that Jim Cairns had been 'bloody silly' in publicly attacking US foreign policy.

The Americans viewed Whitlam's first year and a half in office, 1973 and early 1974, as a period of 'confidence and experimentation' in Australia. They noted, however, that the Coalition effectively controlled the Senate and was preparing to use its numbers to bring on an early election, which Labor was expected to lose.

The Whitlam era was only four months old when the Liberal leader in the Senate, Reg Withers, told the people they might be forced to reconsider the choice they had made in 1972: 'The Senate was deliberately set up by the founding fathers with its enormous powers to act as a check and a balance to protect the interests of the smaller states from the excesses of the larger. Because of the temporary electoral insanity of the two most populous Australian states, the Senate may well be called upon to protect the national interest by exercising its undoubted constitutional rights and powers.' This betrayed a born-to-rule mentality on the part of the Liberals, and helps explain their subsequent attempts to topple Labor by any means.

The declaration of war was formalised, coincidentally, on the day Whitlam and Cairns announced the 25 per cent cut in tariffs, 18 July 1973. Opposition leader Bill Snedden convened a meeting in Sydney with the leaders of the six state Liberal parties, and their six state party presidents, to demand Whitlam call a snap election. They said voters should be given the opportunity to rule on Labor's failure to deal with 'galloping inflation', its 'dictatorial attempts' to centralise power in Canberra, its 'tolerance' of strikes, and its 'betray[al] of our friends by insulting the US'.

It was no idle threat. The conservatives ruled in the three largest states, New South Wales, Victoria and Queensland, and in the federal Senate they shared the balance of power with the DLP. But the power the Coalition was threatening to exercise was not given to them by the people in 1972. The government that Whitlam formed was being scrutinised by a Senate that comprised members elected in 1967, when Harold Holt was prime minister, and in 1970, when John Gorton was running the country. There hadn't been a Senate election in 1972 – the so-called states' chamber had been out of synch with the lower house ever since Robert Menzies had called an early poll in 1963 for the House of Representatives only.

There was much in the Whitlam Program with which the old Senate quibbled, including Labor's plans for a national health scheme, Medibank, and the redrawing of the federal electoral boundaries to reduce the disparity in size between seats. To the conservatives, Medibank was akin to communism and they felt entitled to oppose it even though Whitlam had an explicit mandate for its introduction. But electoral reform was an even more pressing concern because it sought to remove the bias in the old rules towards the bush, and thus the electoral base of the junior Coalition partner, the Country Party.

Whitlam was not above a little scheming himself. He tried to shuffle the Senate numbers in his favour by offering a foreign

posting to the Queensland DLP senator Vince Gair. The appointment was secretly approved on 21 March 1974, the same day that
Whitlam called a half-Senate election only for 18 May. This meant
that 31, not 30, Senate spots would be contested, which made it
possible for Labor to gain the extra seat it needed to grasp Senate
control. When the story broke, Snedden called Whitlam's sleight
of hand 'the most shameful event by any government in Australia's
history'. The conservatives activated their plan to force an early
general election by threatening to block the so-called supply bills,
which allow the government to pay, among other things, the wages
of public servants. Menzies, now a private citizen estranged from
the party he had formed, was appalled by the breach of convention.
'The idiots who now run the Liberal Party will drive me around
the bend,' Menzies wrote to his daughter Heather on 8 April 1974.
'Their last move is to deny supply to the present government in
the Senate. Now, this is something that shocks me. The House of
Representatives is the House that is in charge of finances of the
country. The Senate can quite properly reject individual bills, but
for the Senate to deny supply to the government of the country is
a matter without precedent.'

Although Queensland premier Joh Bjelke-Petersen engineered a plan that successfully thwarted the Gair manoeuvre – by
speeding through the writs for his state's Senate vacancies before
Gair had time to resign – Whitlam took the Snedden bait, calling for the dissolution of both houses of parliament for 18 May.
He reasoned, correctly, that the economy was slowing and that
now was the best time to revive the mandate of 1972. As it happened, the biggest spending part of the Program, Medibank,
still lay ahead for the government. So did the introduction of
no-fault divorce. What had been delivered to date was the end
of conscription, the recognition of China and the establishment of
three new departments for Aboriginal affairs, the environment
and urban planning. What Whitlam might not have realised

was that his own side was speculating about his demise to the Americans.

Bob Hawke told the US consulate in Melbourne in April 1974 that Whitlam 'had made a massive blunder [and] had placed [the] ALP on [the] line' by calling an early election. Hawke dropped expletives into his assessment, but the embassy was too polite to record them. His rage was most evident when he talked about Whitlam's pro-Arab policies. 'Hawke says party lacks money and momentum. Predictably, he feels he will not be able to approach Jewish community for campaign funds, as in past, because of Whitlam's "unprintable" evenhanded "unprintable" Arab policy. Clyde Holding, ALP leader in Victoria . . . [said] the same thing separately.' The memo to Dr Kissinger concluded: 'Hawke was head of ACTU before 1972 ALP victory and he still will be if Whitlam loses. His reaction is probably index of trade union and party professional reaction. [The government's] 1972 campaign promises are largely unfulfilled and for reasons not wholly chargeable to senatorial obduracy. Prime Minister's habit of remaining above herd is not appreciated by herd.'

As the Americans got to know Hawke, and his ambition, they drew up a quick biography for internal use. They noted his love of drinking: 'His record of 12 seconds for downing 2 pints of bitter toppled from Guinness Book of Records only this year [1974]. Hawke in recent years has sacrificed speed for distance in this field.' And they noted his rivalry with Whitlam: 'Always political creature, Hawke obviously enjoys constant speculation about his future. Elected Federal President of ALP in 1973, Hawke has worn two hats with varying success. Usual conflict in objectives, between Labor political and Labor union groups, has arisen in Australia. Hawke is often in dispute with Prime Minister Whitlam, sometimes publicly. As big [a] continent [as Australia] is, it can't contain two super egocentrics like these, and their differences in foreign affairs frequently entertain public.' Hawke's fear that

Labor might lose seems reasonable given that the British conservative government of Edward Heath had just lost a snap election in February that year after one term in office.

In seeking a renewal of the 1972 mandate, Whitlam's campaign looked back, not to the future. Snedden also had his eyes fixed firmly on the past. He simply wanted to reverse the 1972 decision. 'The Labor experiment has been tried and it has failed,' the opposition leader said in his campaign launch speech, on 30 April. 'Through broken promises and sheer incompetence, the Labor Party has forfeited the chance you gave it to build Australia.'

The campaign lacked the buzz of '72. Snedden was a likeable person but wasn't taken seriously by the public. There was a sense of inconvenience in this election, coming just eighteen months after the last contest, and the result was not what the Coalition hoped for, because the electorate reaffirmed the '72 verdict.

Labor's primary vote of 49.3 per cent was down only 0.3 per cent on the benchmark of 'It's Time'. The government ceded three seats in New South Wales and another two in Queensland, but gained two in Victoria plus the newly created seats in Western Australia and the ACT, for a net loss of one seat. The main event was the fight for control of the Senate, and with all 60 spots on the line because of the double dissolution of parliament, the verdict was gridlock. Labor and the Coalition won an extra three places each and were tied at 29 seats each, with two independents, one of whom would soon rejoin the Liberal Party. The DLP, which had held five seats in the previous parliament, including Gair's, was wiped out. On the simple test of bums on the red leather of the Senate chamber, the Coalition was actually in a slightly worse strategic position than it had been during the Whitlam government's first term because the balance of power had switched from the DLP to two independents. If Whitlam had the numerical cunning of, say, a John Howard, he would have claimed victory on the night of the election. But there were a number of seats still in doubt and the Senate tally could have taken weeks to finalise. Whitlam waited until the middle of the next week to assert his renewed mandate. In the intervening period, the Coalition argued that Labor's claim to power was illegitimate because the vote had not been decisive either way.

Snedden refused to accept the final result, earning his place in the gaffe hall of fame by declaring: 'We were not defeated – we did not win enough seats to form a government.' The conservatives had been undone by their own impatience. They understood that Labor was losing control of the economy, but in their rush to the ballot box, they had picked the last decimal point in the cycle when Whitlam could pretend that stagflation might be avoided. The unemployment rate was still only 2.1 per cent when the poll was held, while inflation was at 13.7 per cent. In the US, the misery index was 10.7 per cent for inflation and 5.1 per cent for unemployment; in Britain it was 15.9 per cent and 3.6 per cent respectively. If Snedden had waited until later in the year, he would likely have become prime minister.

Snedden talked tough, but behind the scenes he assured the Americans that Labor hadn't lurched to the left. In an 'extended and frank' luncheon with Ambassador Green on 18 July 1974, two months after the election, 'he implied considerable parallels between his own views and those of members of the Labor Government on [a] number of issues, though not on defense policy.' Snedden, as the cabinet papers demonstrated in 1971 through his cautious approach to dealing with inflation, was every bit the interventionist that Whitlam was. The campaign talk by Snedden about Labor's threat to bring 'socialism' to Australia was just politics.

The sharpest observations Snedden had to offer were about his own team. 'Snedden touched at some length on personalities. He disparaged the performance of Country Party leader [Doug] Anthony in the elections, observing that Anthony's ill-considered statements and Snedden's repair work had consumed total of 6 of the 18 days of the campaign, and consequent loss of time had hurt. Snedden said it wasn't that Anthony's intentions were not all for the best. Anthony simply could not intellectually grasp the implications of some of the things he said.'

Ambassador Green could not quite get the drift of Snedden's view of foreign investment. It was Labor-like in its parochialism. 'He emphasised distinction between foreign ownership and foreign control, stating that he had no objection to continuing foreign ownership but would like to see provision over the long term for Australian control of major investments.' Surely he didn't mean nationalisation, which was the era's dirty word after Chile's socialist president, Salvador Allende, had grabbed control of the banks and the copper industry before the America-backed coup? What Snedden was talking about was the retention of fortress Australia. Foreigners were welcome as investors, but not as owners.

While Snedden raged against the dying of his political light, Hawke had recanted his pre-election view of Whitlam and was now talking up the prime minister to the Americans. The change in the relationship was recorded in a secret cable from Dr Kissinger back to Australia, based on a conversation Hawke had with an official in the US on 25 July 1974. Hawke, the document said, felt he had the support of Whitlam and Cairns 'for any move he might wish to make to succeed Whitlam if and when Whitlam decides to retire . . . Hawke opined that this would happen following next general election, which he speculated would be held before end of next year [1975].'

Hawke's ego was in overdrive: 'In response to a direct question about what he would do if the opportunity were to present itself, Hawke said he would have to make that decision on the basis of whether or not he had sufficient "guts" to fulfil what he called an "awesome responsibility". Hawke also said that he would be required to change his living habits, including drinking, for which he is renowned in Australian pub circles, if he became prime minister. On the question of drinking, Hawke made it clear that he likes "grog" and that it would be difficult indeed for him to turn the tap off completely. However, if the party had enough faith in him to honor him with the position, he would adopt a new public image.'

There was a discernible souring in the national mood during the winter of 1974. As the economy hurtled towards recession, the trade unions broke all previous records for strike action – 2809 industrial disputes, involving 2 million workers, and 6.3 million working days lost. This last figure was double the working days lost in 1971.

The unions flexed their muscle at the slightest provocation, and their campaign reached its apotheosis of absurdity when they got into a fight with Frank Sinatra on 9 July 1974. The American crooner had used the opening night of his tour in Melbourne to vent against Australia's journalists. The men were 'parasites, who had never done an honest day's work in their lives', while the women were 'broads and hookers'. The journalists' union demanded an apology, but Sinatra was unrepentant, so the argument escalated in the spirit of the times. The musicians' union declared the tour black, the hotel employees' union refused to deliver room service to Sinatra's suite at the Southern Cross Hotel, and the Transport Workers' Union refused to touch his plane. With only enough fuel to take him to Sydney, Sinatra was, in effect, a hostage of the ACTU. According to a page-one report in the *Sydney Morning Herald* on 11 July, Bob Hawke said: 'He'll never get out of Australia.' The two performers, Sinatra and Hawke, met that day, and after four hours of negotiation, peace was restored. Old Blue Eyes said sorry, the not-yet-Silver Bodgie called off the blockade, and the tour resumed.

A sample of the industrial disputes then underway ranged from a nationwide shutdown of the ports by ships' engineers and the threat of strike action by building workers in the ACT if poker machines were not introduced.

The civil disobedience extended to the government itself. On 24 July, the day before Bob Hawke talked himself up to the Americans, Gough Whitlam, Jim Cairns and Bill Hayden formed an unlikely alliance to urge Labor MPs to make a sacrifice. The trio wanted their colleagues to defer a proposed pay rise to show the community that politicians were willing to put their self-interest aside in the fight against inflation. What made this request unusual was that the prime minister and his colleagues were asking for a cabinet decision to be overturned. The Remuneration Tribunal had recommended the base salary for members of parliament be increased by $5500, or 37.9 per cent, to $20 000 per year. Cabinet had voted sixteen to eleven to accept the pay rise, against the protests of Whitlam, Cairns and Hayden. The three men hoped the back bench would be more reasonable, but the caucus rebelled. Hayden was booed when he addressed the group, Cairns was continually interrupted, and Whitlam provoked 'sarcastic and sometimes loud remarks', according to a report in *The Age* the following day. The vote for self-interest was fifty-one to forty. After the meeting, one annoyed government MP was quoted as saying: 'The party is not divided on ideological grounds. It is divided between the greedy, the cynical and the stupid on one hand, and the less greedy, less cynical and more intelligent on the other.' The following day the Senate did Whitlam a rare favour by rejecting the pay rise. The electorate was annoyed, and politicians never really recovered their dignity after this episode. Every subsequent pay rise would be seen by the media as an excuse to direct more outrage towards Canberra.

An urge for anarchy had overwhelmed the government after its narrow re-election win. Caucus declared its independence from its leader by electing Cairns to replace Whitlam's loyal lieutenant Lance Barnard as deputy prime minister. 'That had a negative psychological impact on Gough,' Graham Freudenberg says, 'because though Lance was not a strong figure in the government, he was immensely important to Whitlam personally as the one man he could trust, and the one who really knew the moods and the trends in caucus and, to an extent that Whitlam didn't have, with the public.' Cairns didn't watch Whitlam's back in the same way; if anything, he had a knife pointed at it. Cairns had presented himself to colleagues as keeper of the faith, who would defend Labor values as the government was facing its moment of truth on the economy, when unemployment began to climb along with inflation. Whitlam's instinct was to continue siding with the Treasury department, which wanted to fight inflation first. Cairns resented the cold-hearted calculation that unemployment would have to rise further to achieve the primary goal against inflation. In July, Treasury pushed for a range of tax increases to complement the higher interest rates it had already put in place, and provoked one of the defining internal battles of the Whitlam government.

Frank Crean, the treasurer who had been ignored by his colleagues in the first term, took up his department's argument and told cabinet that Australia 'had an inflationary crisis on its hands'. The spending bids that ministers had put in for that year's budget would push inflation past 20 per cent for 1974–75, he warned. 'The central problem now stems from the fact that wages have gone through the roof and show no sign of pausing on their upward trajectory.' The choice facing the government, he said, was to tighten its belt temporarily, or 'let inflation rip'. It is hard to imagine adults hearing this advice would choose the latter option, but Cairns spoke for the majority of the government when he argued that the Treasury approach would lead to higher-than-necessary unemployment. His view was that greater government spending would protect jobs.

Crean used even more strident language at the August cabinet meeting to finalise the budget. 'The coming budget represents what may be our last chance to check the economy's headlong rush towards hyper-inflation,' he said, before addressing Labor's article of faith that jobs should always come first. 'There is another viewpoint. That is that over-full employment must be maintained all of the time. I understand that viewpoint. But inflation of the order we are experiencing, let alone of the order in prospect, is so socially and economically destructive and divisive in its implication that we must ask ourselves whether for a time we should not have a different priority.'

Crean wanted new spending proposals pruned by $600 million and taxation increased by $400 million for 1974–75. These clawbacks would have reduced the planned increase in government expenditure from 32 to 27 per cent – 'a figure which, in our situation, would still take a lot of explaining,' Crean observed. Two days later, on 21 August, he wrote again to his colleagues to express his disappointment that they had rejected his advice for belt-tightening. He feared they had opted for 'the worst of all worlds'.

'So far from ensuring that unemployment does not rise unnecessarily our decisions are likely – especially in the longer term – to make it increasingly hard to sustain the level of employment opportunity that has for long been accepted as normal by the Australian workforce.'

Strong words, but Crean lost the debate because he wasn't forceful enough in pushing the anti-inflation cause. He presented the budget on 17 September 1974 in his own name, but it was really the work of Cairns. 'The world is beset by severe economic problems,' Crean said in his budget speech. 'Australia cannot insulate itself from them.' The extra spending he announced covered every conceivable portfolio. The largest item was a 78 per cent increase for education, on the back of a near-doubling in funding in the previous financial year. This was the heart of the Program and the looming recession was not seen as a reason to slow it down. All pensions and benefits had already been increased, because the budget's release had been delayed by the election. In the budget itself, the means test for the pension for those aged seventy to seventy-four was abolished. Aboriginal affairs and urban development also received increases of at least 60 per cent. Treasury staged its own form of industrial action, refusing to write the preamble for the budget because they didn't support its excessively Keynesian prescriptions.

Treasury made it harder for the government to make a sensible decision because it didn't pick the coming recession. As late as July 1974, the department was still insisting that unemployment would rise only marginally over the next twelve months 'from its present level of about 87 000 to around 100 000–110 000 by June 1975'. The forecast would be redundant within weeks. By December that year, unemployment had reached 267 000 and the economy had crashed. The deep recession Labor had wanted to avoid was now a reality.

'A pervasive sense of gloom' had taken hold, the United States embassy in Canberra said in a secret cable to the State Department in Washington, titled 'Australia's troubles and Whitlam's troubles – a gathering crisis'.

'There is in Australia an aura of selfishness and structural animosity, with the states against Canberra, the ALP caucus against Whitlam, the opposition after narrow political advantage, individual unions elbowing for material gain, corporations passing the cost of excessive wage settlements on to the consumer, rural interests claiming discrimination and none of these players motivated by concern for the national wellbeing.'

The pot was roaring at the kettle because the assessment was written on 29 August 1974, three weeks after Richard Nixon had finally ended the American agony by resigning the presidency. The document does, however, capture an interesting change of heart towards Whitlam. At the start of Whitlam's prime ministership, the Americans had viewed him with great suspicion. Now that they had seen the complexion of the rest of his cabinet, the last thing the US wanted was to have him replaced by Cairns.

'Whitlam's personal dominance of ALP and of Australian scene appears ended. He will surely recover from present uncharacteristic slump but is unlikely to regain his pre-eminent position. He has been challenged successfully by caucus – e.g. Cairns's election, parliamentary pay increases – and by his cabinet – economic policy, the budget. His inability to enlist union support is all too obvious. Whitlam's weakened position within ALP government has worrisome implications for US. We have relied upon his basic moderation and his support of US defense facilities and other US interests.'

Cairns, it was noted, had improved his image. 'He is more and more acceptable to business despite his frank socialist objective.' But the Americans weren't entirely sure. 'We still hesitate to regard him as a real alternative to Whitlam.'

Another confidant of the Americans at the time was the 'well-informed and extremely influential' Rupert Murdoch, who had just broken into the US newspaper market with two titles in San Antonio, Texas. His media stable at the time included the afternoon tabloid the *Daily Mirror* in Sydney, the national broadsheet *The Australian*, and the *News of the World* and *The Sun* in London. At a 'wide-ranging and apparently very candid' lunch on 15 November 1974 with Marshall Green and senior embassy officials, Murdoch looked into his crystal ball and saw Whitlam's demise. 'Australian elections are likely to take place in about one year, sparked by refusal of appropriations in the Senate. All signs point to a Liberal–Country victory, since the economy is in disturbingly bad condition and will probably not improve much of that time.'

Murdoch, whose name was misspelled as 'Murdock' in the cable, said that Bill Snedden would be the next prime minister. He didn't see Malcolm Fraser taking Snedden's place. Fraser was 'the most brilliant as well as the most courageous of the Liberals but is regarded as too inflexible and too arrogant by his colleagues'.

The Americans said Murdoch 'played a substantial role' in Labor's victory in 1972. 'He is satisfied that he took the correct position at that time, since it was essential to have a change after 23 years,' the ambassador wrote. 'Liberal–Country leadership had become increasingly weary intellectually. However, Murdock is disappointed by Labor's performance. He expects to support the opposition in the next election.'

Murdoch saw Whitlam as arrogant and lacking in basic people skills. He blamed Whitlam's policies for helping to cause the economic crisis. But the detail of his policy analysis was, frankly, poor. It echoed the muddle-headed thinking of the era that if only the government pulled the correct lever, the economy would return to its comfort zone of the 1960s.

'The government should be pursuing economic policies with a more selfish domestic focus. For example, the 25 per cent across-the-board tariff reductions, which appealed to Whitlam's orderly legal mind and liberal outlook, were a bad mistake and contributed needlessly to unemployment. A number of Australian industries require tariff protection and this problem should have been studied on a sector by sector basis. The government should have done more to contain interest rates and suppress food prices. Above all, it is inexcusable not to reduce government expenditures drastically at the present time to counter inflation.'

Murdoch wasn't a fan of the 'sharp, intellectual professionals of the Treasury department' whom he said had sold 'faulty proposals' to Whitlam and the then treasurer, Frank Crean. Murdoch said the 'weak, inadequate' Crean would be dumped for the 'puzzling and disturbing' Cairns. He thought Whitlam 'may find that

Cairns, a more facile politician than the prime minister, emerges unscathed while Whitlam himself continues to take the blame for inflation and the politically disastrous unemployment'. Ironically, Murdoch's desire for spending restraint echoed the positions of Whitlam and Crean. A last stand by Whitlam was possible, leading to his departure. 'Whitlam is quite capable even in the near future of becoming frustrated and laying down an "accept my policy or I quit" ultimatum to the caucus. Caucus might easily pick up this gauntlet and drop Whitlam in favour of Cairns.'

Murdoch favoured Hawke over Cairns. 'Bob Hawke is fiercely ambitious to become prime minister of Australia and could easily make it someday. He is intelligent and essentially moderate. He would be far preferable to Cairns but has little chance of defeating Cairns in the next few years. [He] sees the ALP going down to defeat and does not want to board the sinking ship.'

Economists struggle with human beings. Just when they think they have accumulated all the relationships in a society within the boundaries of a mathematical model, emotion will overwhelm all logic and create a bust no one sees coming. The three big crises of modern capitalism – the Great Depression in the 1930s, stagflation from the early 1970s to the early 1980s, and the Great Recession of the early twenty-first century – were preceded by an almost religious belief that one or other, the market or government, contained the secret code for perpetual growth.

The great insight of John Maynard Keynes was that societies trusting a free market to deliver full employment were bound to be disappointed because workers wouldn't accept the continued cuts in wages that competition would demand to deliver more products at lower prices. Keynes published *The General Theory of Employment, Interest and Money* in 1936, at the depth of the Great Depression. Those with a passing interest in economics would know his formula for gross domestic product – consumption plus investment plus government spending plus exports minus imports. No one had thought to give government a place in the GDP equation before. Keynes argued that when consumers closed their wallets, and businesses followed by laying off staff, leading to further falls in consumption, government had a role to play in propping up demand to prevent a depression.

Stagflation caused Keynes's views to fall out of favour because more government spending only added to the problem of the wage–price spiral. The monetarists, led internationally by Milton Friedman in the late '60s, and in Australia by John Stone in the '70s, turned Keynesianism on its head. To defeat stagflation, inflation must first be killed. Politicians were never entirely comfortable with this reasoning because it meant accepting a higher rate of unemployment than democracy said was tolerable. But the monetarists replied that full employment was no longer achievable; the trick was to find the rate of unemployment that did not provoke inflation.

Jim Cairns sounded like a convert of Friedman's in his first report to cabinet as treasurer, in January 1975. In fact, he seemed to be taking the side of the boss over the worker. He explained that 'there is a direct link between rising wage and salary costs and unemployment'. As wages were now rising faster than prices, company profits were being squeezed: 'In many companies there is concern that profits are vanishing altogether.' This was an extension of the problem that Keynes described. When companies saw their profits shrink in the '70s, they reacted as workers had when their wages were cut in the '30s: they stopped spending.

The 1974–75 budget was meant to increase expenditure by 32 per cent, and the deficit was supposed to be $570 million. Neither target was met. The final tally was a 46 per cent jump in spending, and a $2.5 billion deficit. But even all that intervention couldn't prevent recession because workers had pushed companies to breaking point with a 28.7 per cent increase in average wages in 1974–75.

Australia had caught up with the rest of the world by December 1974. It had an inflation rate of 16.3 per cent and an unemployment rate of 4.5 per cent. In the US, it was 12.1 per cent for inflation and 7.2 per cent for unemployment; in the UK 19.2 per cent and 3.8 per cent.

The Whitlam government offers a rolled-gold example of what not to do. It had spent in the boom of 1973, and spent even more in the bust of 1974 because it placed the delivery of its election promises above any consideration for the economic cycle. On both sides of the curve, it gave consumers and business the wrong message. In the boom, that message was 'Let's dance'; in the bust, it was 'The music stopped – what the hell, let's keep dancing.' Handing out cash when the economy is hot validates the greed that is the dominant emotion at the top of the cycle. Further stimulus in recession only reinforces the fear in the community that no one knows what to do. It is a perverse response, because the alternative to spending in recession is cutting entitlements and increasing taxes, which would make things worse. But the painful lesson was that government has to play a contrary hand to maintain the respect of the community. In a boom, it must resist the urge to spend, because only then can it spend with credibility in a bust. Stimulus only works from the moral and fiscal high ground of budget surplus.

Graham Freudenberg traces Whitlam's demise to the misreading of the 1974 election result. 'The tremendous impact of the oil shock was really ignored. The very fact that the '74 election was perceived by Whitlam and the government as a total endorsement of the Program really precluded some sensible rethinking of the Program. There was no question of starting afresh, so we were locked into our unfinished business.' He says the relationship with Treasury had 'deteriorated almost to the point of nullity' by the end of the year. The three arms of economic policy – the budget, interest rates and wages – were running at cross-purposes by the mid-1970s. The Whitlam government could barely control its own urge to spend and had little influence over the trade unions. This left the bureaucracy thinking it had to meet the stimulus with a fire hose. Treasury had effective control of interest rates, and it lifted them twice, in late '73 and again in mid '74, when the mortgage rate passed 10 per cent for the first time. Yet these increases were not enough to kill inflationary expectations. Treasury had echoed the government's policy error by damaging confidence without reducing the cost of living. The department didn't see that its failures of both imagination and routine forecasting had given Labor the licence to ignore it. 'Our economic advisers were not getting a hearing or perhaps giving their best advice,' says Freudenberg. 'For that I blame us more than them.' So Treasury had reason to be offended, and would soon have its revenge when it blew the whistle on the loans affair.

4

THE INGREDIENTS
FOR A CRACK-UP

A South Australian businessman knew someone who knew someone who had a spare $200 million to invest.

In September 1974, after a Greek community function in Adelaide, property developer Gerry Karidis invited his friend, labour minister Clyde Cameron, and others back to his house for drinks. The conversation turned to international finance at about 3 a.m. Karidis confided to Cameron that huge sums of money were waiting to be tapped on very favourable terms, and he knew who to call.

Karidis had already mentioned the opportunity to Don Dunstan, but the South Australian Labor premier wasn't interested. Cameron was, and immediately thought of his colleague Rex Connor, the minerals and energy minister, who had a really big idea to turn Australia into an energy superpower. Connor wanted to develop Australia's uranium, coal, gas and oil reserves to capitalise on the elevated commodity prices that flowed from the oil shock. The wish list of infrastructure projects included the completion of a gas pipeline from the Cooper Basin, in Queensland and South Australia, to Perth; three uranium mines in the

Northern Territory; and the electrification of heavy rail in New South Wales and Victoria. Australia was a resource-rich but capital-poor nation, so funds on this scale could only come from foreign investors. But both sides of politics worshipped at the altar of local ownership, as Bill Snedden had indicated privately to the Americans in 1974 and Gough Whitlam had argued publicly from his first press conference as opposition leader in 1967. That's why Connor sought loans, not joint venture partners. He thought these projects should be publicly owned.

Connor fancied himself as a working-man intellectual who understood business. He had little respect for either industry or media. The mining company executives he dealt with in his portfolio were 'hillbillies and mugs', the journalists of the parliamentary press gallery were 'apes'. Even so, he sourced most of his knowledge of the world from newspapers and journals – 'almost to the exclusion of all other reading', according to Laurie Oakes. 'And because he had read in *Time* magazine that 85 billion American dollars a year were flowing to oil-rich Arab countries which had nothing to spend such vast amounts on, he readily accepted the Karidis view,' Oakes reported.

'Bloody oath' he was interested in talking to Karidis, Connor told Cameron. Karidis promptly flew to Canberra, where he met with Connor, Cameron and Jim Cairns, who was acting prime minister while Whitlam was overseas.

By entertaining the idea that they could play the game of international finance on their own terms, without going through the Treasury, Cairns, Cameron and Connor – the three ministers who had ridiculed the economic bureaucracy at the showdown on inflation a year earlier – had just set the self-destruct button on the Whitlam government. On 11 November 1974, a year to the day before the government was dismissed, Karidis introduced a London-based Pakistani commodities trader, Tirath Khemlani, to Connor. Khemlani said he could secure a loan of us$4 billion

($3.056 billion in Australian dollars at the time) at an interest rate of 7.92 per cent, including fees. Local housing interest rates were at a then record 10.4 per cent. Comrade, this was a bargain.

Connor's motivation is easy to unpick. He knew that the money to fund his program could not come from the budget, because it was already in deficit, nor through regular loans, because the states would issue a veto. In those days, no level of government in Australia could raise funds overseas without the approval of the so-called Loans Council. He believed the states would agree after the money had been banked, because they wouldn't want to miss out on the projects.

He didn't need to guess the Treasury view, so Connor cut its minister, Frank Crean, out of the information loop. But the department got wind of the plan in early December 1974 and unleashed a blizzard of memos, warning the government against having any association with Khemlani. At a meeting on 9 December, the governor of the Reserve Bank, Sir John Phillips, and the head of Treasury, Sir Frederick Wheeler, tried to persuade Whitlam (now back in the country and in favour of the loans), Cairns, Connor and the attorney-general, Lionel Murphy, to drop the idea. They reminded the Labor men of the rush of foreign funds into Australia in 1972, which had pushed up inflation and necessitated a series of revaluations of the dollar against the greenback to cool demand. 'The proposal would result in a capital inflow a lot larger than in 1972 . . . [and] such a massive public outlay would affect private sector confidence. However, these arguments did not diminish the enthusiasm of ministers for the proposal,' according to a Treasury summary of the discussion. Connor explained the reason for his urgency in seeking the loan: 'Oil consumers were moving on a borrowing boycott on the Arabs to bring them to their knees. There was a need to get in quickly before this occurred.' That is, Australia should get its share before the West ganged up on the OPEC nations by imposing a tit-for-tat trade embargo.

Treasury's background checks on Khemlani showed he was at best unreliable, at worst a fraud. 'We have no evidence whatsoever that Mr Khemlani has any form of criminal record. The enquiries also indicated that he has no "track record" as an international financier either,' Sir Frederick wrote in a departmental minute. The Bank of England had told Treasury they considered the proposal to be in the 'funny money' category. 'The size of the loan is highly suspect. The Bank says that such large sums are simply not available from the Middle East, the Vatican, the Mafia or elsewhere,' a Treasury officer reported back to the department. 'The amount of the commission, 2–2.5 per cent, is consistent with a phoney offer. In the Bank's experience, offers with commissions of this magnitude are never genuine.'

But the government wasn't paying attention to the killjoys from Treasury. Whitlam had already shut out Crean from the initial meetings to consider the loans. When Whitlam appointed Cairns as treasurer on 11 December 1974, Sir Frederick saw an opportunity to step up his campaign. He told Cairns the government couldn't win either way: 'If the money is not there, the Government could find that its standing in international capital markets is badly damaged because of the attempt to obtain money through such dubious channels.' If the money did materialise, there would be 'continuing problems' because parliament and the Loans Council had been bypassed.

In a memo dated 13 December, a Treasury officer indulged his inner political correspondent by mentioning that the loans could trigger an early election: 'Finally – and at the risk of setting down a comment of a "political" kind – it should not be overlooked that, at the present time, the Opposition is clearly seeking an issue on which to go to the country. The mechanism for that purpose must clearly lie in either the Additional Appropriations process, or in the Supply process. At present, the position is only a generalised feeling of "popular unhappiness". A proposal of the present kind could provide a particular issue which the Opposition will no doubt be seeking.'

The Whitlam government approved the loan in the early hours of 14 December at a meeting of its executive council that comprised the prime minister, Cairns, Connor and Murphy. The governor-general, Sir John Kerr, rubber-stamped the document later. The authority to borrow was given directly to Connor, which made him the third most important member of the government after Whitlam and Cairns, the deputy prime minister. The authority reads, in part, like the Rudd Labor government's 2008–09 stimulus plan; a cash-splash to help Australia survive a world recession. 'The Australian Government needs immediate access to substantial sums of non-equity capital from abroad for temporary purposes, amongst other things to deal with exigencies arising out of the current world situation and the international energy crisis, to provide immediate protection for Australia's supply of minerals and energy and to deal with current and immediately foreseeable unemployment in Australia.'

The US$4 billion being sought was almost four times the total overseas borrowings of federal and state governments to that point. The $100 million commission Khemlani had been offered was almost double the Whitlam government's total spending on childcare in 1974–75. Fortunately for the nation, he couldn't deliver. The only sensible thing Labor did was to draft its agreement so tightly that Khemlani could only claim the commission after the money had been banked.

Treasury had an early win when it convinced Cairns to mount a counterattack against Connor. Cairns agreed with the assessment that Khemlani couldn't deliver the money. At a meeting on 21 December, a week after Connor had been given the authority to borrow, Cairns said 'there should be no more dealings with Khemlani'. Connor agreed to let it go. 'Mr Connor said there would be none by him. Ministers noted Mr Connor's statement that he did not propose to take any action pursuant to the executive council authority,' according to a record of the meeting by the Attorney-General's department. But it was not a statement Connor stuck to. Critically, he kept communication with Khemlani open. 'Why did Connor change his mind [after he said he would no longer deal with Khemlani]?' Graham Freudenberg wrote. 'The answer is he didn't, because in his heart he was still convinced that he would pull off the deal; he would show those little-minded men, clerks without vision, what bigness and courage and faith in Australia could do.'

'In the following weeks he lived for, almost literally lived with, his dream, waiting for the message that never came. His young friend and closest caucus colleague, Paul Keating, found him morning after morning, in March and April, asleep in his office, unshaven and dishevelled, waiting for the ring and rattle of the telex machine, which would herald Khemlani's message that he had at last delivered the goods. It never came . . . [and] Keating pleaded with him, "For God's sake, Rex, this is no way for a minister to behave".'

Someone in Treasury took out some institutional insurance by leaking the details of Connor's grand scheme to the Liberals. Opposition Treasury spokesman Phillip Lynch asked his first question on the matter on 13 February 1975.

Lynch: 'I address the question to the Minister for Minerals and Energy. Is the Government engaged in seeking massive overseas loan funds from the Middle East? If so, will he make a full explanation to the House?'

Connor: 'Matters relating to the currency, loans and the commercial credit of the nation should be handled with the utmost discretion. I am acting accordingly.'

The following month, Cairns inexplicably switched back from sceptic to participant. He decided that he too should get himself a loan for national development and picked the president of the Carlton Football Club, George Harris, as his intermediary.

Cairns was only after US$500 million, but his approach proved to be even more naive. Connor had been careful not to cover Khemlani's expenses – he would only be paid after the loan was secured. The letter that Cairns gave Harris was less precise and, thus, more problematic for the taxpayer.

The loans affair was a dummy run for the global financial crisis thirty-four years later. The two fiascos are connected by the same flawed assumption: that borrowing carries no risk if the purpose is nation-building. The oil shock delivered windfall surpluses to the Middle East that the West assumed would be better off back in the hands of the original consumer. 'There is an entirely new ball game in relation to international loan availability,' Connor told parliament on 22 May 1975. 'There is today a complete distortion of the world economy because of the availability of funds that have been generated in the purchase of Arab oil at increased prices. Today those funds are seeking to be recycled . . . [and] are looking for safe and reliable homes. There is no better place than Australia.' That is, Middle Eastern nations didn't know what to do with their sudden wealth, so it was only fair that the West take it back at a discount. It was both a scheme crazy enough to almost make sense, and an unusually arrogant way for a Whitlam government minister to view the developing world. A case of what's yours used to be mine and should be mine again.

America's hyper-capitalists looked at China's windfall surpluses of the new millennium in much the same way. The Chinese had built up their reserves by exporting cheap computers and TVs to the developed world, and by holding down the value of their own currency. It was a different form of appropriation to the oil shock because China's industrialisation drove down the price of technology, which suppressed headline inflation in the West. But it created the same dangerous imbalance between surplus and deficit nations. All this money had moved from West to East but the recipients weren't interested in spending it all on their own people. Why not borrow it back for a more worthy cause? How about a US housing bubble?

Labor people would object to the analogy because Connor's motivation was to secure Australian self-reliance, a laudable goal at a time when the old international order had broken down. But the subprime mortgage – the loan designed for people without money – was really no different in character to Connor's dream. The nation-building enterprise that triggered the GFC was a government-sanctioned push to permanently increase the home-ownership rate in the US by extending the bricks'n'mortar privileges of white America to blacks and Hispanics. US president George W. Bush declared his intention to civilise the market in a series of speeches in 2002. In October that year, he said: 'More and more people own their homes in America today. Two-thirds of all Americans own their homes, yet we have a problem here in America because fewer than half of the Hispanics and half the African-Americans own their home. That's a home-ownership gap. It's a gap that we've got to work together to close for the good of our country, for the sake of a more hopeful future. I set . . . a clear goal, that by the end of this decade we'll increase the number of minority homeowners by at least 5.5 million families.'

The GFC was preceded by the permissively low interest rates of the US Federal Reserve and a dangerous run-up in household debt across the developed world, Australia included. The 'recycling' of China's surpluses increased the supply of money at a time when the West was already over-geared. If only the Americans had studied their Australian history. They would have seen, in the loans affair, a lesson for the ages: to borrow to spend when you are already in debt can bring a nation down.

A trip to the main retail centres of the nation's capital cities or country towns in early 1975 would have revealed that a new kind of strike was underway. Shoppers were withdrawing their spending just as adamantly as workers had been withdrawing their labour. A record 19.7 per cent of household income was put aside as savings in the March quarter 1975. Hoarding had been a persistent feature of Australian life since the oil shock. Now it was reinforcing the recessionary spiral, as the closing of wallets in response to job losses saw businesses lay off even more staff. That summer, as Cyclone Tracy flattened Darwin, and Australia regained Test cricket's Ashes trophy from England, the economy reached its stagflation nadir, with unemployment rising again to 4.8 per cent, and the inflation rate peaking at 17.6 per cent.

In the counter-intuitive world of politics, the government that presides over the crash can sometimes appear the safer option. This was the perverse logic by which Gough Whitlam seemed to stage a personal recovery in early 1975. His opponent, Bill Snedden, had been weakened by a poorly executed leadership challenge from Malcolm Fraser the previous November, and this made him vulnerable when politicians returned to Canberra for a new parliamentary year in February. Whitlam remained master of his rhetorical domain on the floor of the House of Representatives, and he delivered a series of stunning performances. Whitlam's character assault against Snedden suited Fraser because it allowed him to pose the question to nervous Liberals: 'Could Gough beat us again?'

Fraser's move against Snedden signalled a new era in politics. It was the first time that a leader was wounded and then brought down with the help of a single, ambiguous public opinion poll. The Coalition's primary voting intention lead over Labor had narrowed from 17 points (55 per cent to 38 per cent) in December to just four points in February (48 per cent to 44), according to the Morgan Gallup poll. It might have been a blip. But Fraser's supporters invested devastating meaning to the numbers. They told colleagues that the electorate was having doubts about Snedden. Fraser's argument was not about ideology or even style of leadership. Snedden was well-liked in the party. What Fraser was offering was the certainty of victory, and his supporters kept pushing their case in the corridors of opposition until Snedden called a vote to resolve the matter. When the ballot was held on 21 March, Fraser prevailed by thirty-seven votes to twenty-seven. Snedden was the third Liberal leader that Whitlam had seen off, after John Gorton and Billy McMahon, and the first who did not get the chance to serve as prime minister.

Fraser was the prototype for the modern political animal – tertiary-educated, but without a substantial career before entering parliament. Born in Melbourne's wealthiest suburb of Toorak in 1930, his parents were graziers, and the young Fraser grew up on farms in New South Wales and then in Victoria's Western District. He also went to Oxford, where he graduated with an economics degree. Fraser was the youngest MP in his year, 1955, after winning the rural Victorian seat of Wannon at the age of twenty-five. His elevation to the Liberal leadership at the age of forty-four put him on course to become our youngest prime minister of the post-war period.

At his first press conference, the new opposition leader played down the idea of forcing an early election. But he left himself a rider: 'I generally believe that if a government is elected to power in the lower house and has the numbers and can maintain the numbers in the lower house, it is entitled to expect that it will govern for the three-year term, unless quite extraordinary events intervene.'

Fraser wasn't thinking much about the loans affair at the time. In a meeting with the American ambassador Marshall Green on 6 May 1975, he said the focus of his attack on the Whitlam government would be 'on basic foreign policy and security issues'. Green wrote: '[Fraser] was under no – repeat no – pressure from his own party ranks to have elections at this time. If elections were held today, Labor government would probably be out, but Liberal–Country parties would inherit a range of profound economic difficulties which were of the ALP's making. It was now best to let the government stew in its own juice and for the opposition to choose an appropriate time to make its bid for power, when it would hope to gain a strong working majority in both houses of parliament.'

While Fraser plotted, Whitlam purged his government of its economic policy troublemakers – Cairns, Cameron and Connor. He wanted a fresh start to tackle stagflation, and to regain his authority over the party, without the distractions of petrodollars or wages blowouts. He dealt with Connor first, revoking his authority to borrow on 20 May. The following month he used the pretext of the letter that Cairns wrote to George Harris to remove him from the treasurer's post. In his place, he appointed the tough-minded Bill Hayden. Cameron was pushed aside as labour minister for Jim McClelland, who was given a mandate to curb trade union power. These moves signalled a return to Treasury thinking for Whitlam. He had blown hot and cold on economics – tariff cuts in '73 and spending binges in '74. Now he was prepared to test the theory that inflation should be dealt with first, at the risk of higher unemployment. The choice had been made for Whitlam by the failure of the Cairns-inspired budget to prevent the deep recession now underway.

Cairns had a final appointment with controversy on 2 July 1975. He had signed three letters in total on behalf of Harris. Whitlam had been aware of the second and third when he demoted Cairns from Treasury to the environmental portfolio. Cairns professed no knowledge of the first in answer to a question in parliament. When that letter subsequently turned up, he was sacked from the ministry and stripped of his position as deputy prime minister. Whitlam called a special sitting of parliament a week later, on 9 July, in which he demanded the opposition 'put up or shut up'. The opposition had been enjoying the slow drip of revelation, using each new twist in the story to cry corruption and call on Whitlam to sack this or that minister. Every conceivable document was released to rule a line under the loans affair. Except Connor hadn't coughed up all his paperwork to Whitlam. When one of the unseen telexes did emerge, on 8 October, in an exclusive report written by the Melbourne *Herald*'s Peter Game, it was dated 23 May, three days after Connor had lost the authority to borrow.

Cairns and Connor were caught, Al Capone-style, for the dodge of misleading parliament, not the original sin of seeking petrodollars. But why all the fuss after the fact, when no money was raised and no commission paid? The crisis makes no sense without the backdrops of Watergate and the oil shock. There would have been no Arab surpluses to tempt Connor without the oil shock, and no sense of divine purpose for the opposition, bureaucracy and the media without Watergate. Labor had its legitimacy undermined by the accumulation of leaks to the media, and opposition. And still there was an element of bad timing that played its part in the drama. If Whitlam had his hands on all the relevant material in July, he might have sacked Connor in the same cycle as Cairns, and survived the year as prime minister. But the second execution was delayed until 14 October when Labor could least afford another scandal, because the Senate numbers had been switched by the intervention of two state premiers.

Recall that at the 1974 double dissolution election, voters gave Labor twenty-nine senators and the Coalition twenty-nine, leaving two independents. One month before Fraser ousted Snedden, New South Wales Liberal premier Tom Lewis decided he hated Whitlam enough to break the gentleman's agreement that in the event of the early retirement or death of a senator the casual vacancy should be filled by someone from the same party. When Lionel Murphy resigned from the Senate to join the High Court in February 1975, Lewis sent independent Cleaver Bunton to Canberra, to howls of protest from the government. Tough luck, Lewis thought – the Senate was the states' house. By his hand, the Senate numbers were now Labor twenty-eight, Coalition twenty-nine and three independents.

One of the existing independents then rejoined the Liberal Party, bringing the Coalition to thirty. But Fraser was still one vote short of a majority in the sixty-member Senate. That situation changed on 30 June, when respected Labor senator Bert Milliner passed away. Queensland National Party premier Joh Bjelke-Petersen rejected Labor's nominated replacement, Mal Colston, and sent little-known ALP member Albert Patrick Field instead. '[Field] was certainly no supporter of Whitlam or the ALP federal government,' journalist Alan Reid wrote. 'With other media people, I met Field on the day he arrived in Canberra. Field said he was an old-time ALP man. The Whitlam government was not an ALP government. It was more interested in looking after homosexuals than jobs and he would be helping to have Whitlam and his government thrown out of office.' Field didn't get the chance to cast his ballot for homophobia because the government launched a legal challenge against his appointment. Until that case was settled, the Coalition had a majority of thirty out of the remaining fifty-nine senators, against Labor's twenty-seven and the two independents. This was no standard political ploy, but the deliberate distortion of a federal election result, and over a dead man's body. Fraser didn't create this opportunity, but he felt no moral qualms about exploiting it. In his mind, Whitlam had already trashed democracy during the loans affair, so guerilla tactics were justified to restore conservative rule.

The Coalition used its ill-gotten gain of the Senate majority to obstruct Bill Hayden's 1975–76 budget. If there was any budget the Senate should have thwarted in the national interest, it was the previous year's. But the Coalition didn't have the balance of power then, and even if it did, Bill Snedden didn't want to risk a second election in the same year. Hayden's budget was designed to be Labor's correction for the previous two years of profligacy. On taking the treasurer's job in July, he provided his colleagues with a grim update on the economy, and their own culpability in adding to the burden of inflation.

'I am convinced that the symptoms of our economic malaise that have given rise to political opprobrium – high unemployment, stagnation of business activity, high interest rates, high marginal tax rates – all have their genesis in rapid inflation,' he wrote. 'There is no single cause of inflation, it is a complex process, but a significant contributing factor has been our attempt to push ahead a little too quickly with our social and economic goals. Barging up the centre of the field is not necessarily the most assured or quickest way to reach the goal.'

Ministers submitted proposals to increase spending by a further 33 per cent for 1975–76, which would have taken the budget deficit to $4.8 billion. Adding all those extra dollars to a high-inflation economy risked another round of price rises, which the trade unions would chase with another round of wage claims. Hayden resisted, and he did so with Whitlam's imprimatur: 'A deficit approaching $5000 million is a prescription for price increases of 25 per cent per annum and more; it is a prescription for the abject failure of economic management.' With the economy already in recession, Hayden thought that increased spending wouldn't deliver jobs, but would add to inflation. He asked for a deficit of half that amount – $2.5 billion – which would require cuts to existing spending programs. That figure would have been equal to the previous year's deficit. He almost got there, with a published deficit of $2.8 billion. In his budget night speech on 19 August, the new treasurer ended the pretence that jobs could be saved by more government intervention. 'Because of the structure of our mixed economy, where three out of four jobs are in the private sector, there are firm limits on how far the public sector should be stimulated in this recovery phase,' Hayden said. Labor was fighting inflation first, though not as righteously as Treasury wanted. The aim was to reduce inflation over two or three years, not defeat it in one burst of fiscal purity. 'Our present level of unemployment is too high. If we fail to control inflation, unemployment will get worse . . . we have therefore tried to find a middle way.'

The language of moderation and balance belied the revolution in Labor's thinking. The party of the working man, of public ownership and the fair go, was ready to take the side of business to restore growth. The tariff cut of 1973 had been the toe in the deregulation water for Labor. Hayden's emphasis on fighting inflation first was the baptism. This is the least understood part of the Whitlam experiment. Through naive trial and painful error, Labor was moving towards what is now recognised as the Hawke–Keating model: pro-market, but with a social safety net.

There was give and take in this budget: personal and company taxes were reduced in exchange for increases in beer, tobacco and fuel excise; spending for tertiary education, environment and urban development was cut in real terms, after counting for inflation, to make way for the $1.5 billion in funding required to introduce Medibank on 1 July 1975.

'The Hayden budget surprised the Liberals,' Laurie Oakes wrote. 'They had been confident that the Labor government would be unable to produce a budget which would be seen as responsible. Some commentators saw it as the most significant federal budget since the war.' The Liberal leader could read the press reaction as well as anyone, and seemed to put up the white flag. Two days after the budget's release, Fraser declared the Coalition's intention to pass it: 'We'll be following normal procedure in the Senate and with the knowledge we have at the moment, at this stage it would be our intention to allow it a passage through the Senate.' But he was hedging, in the expectation that Labor would soon revert to its habit of chaos and grant the opposition the extraordinary circumstances he said would justify using the Senate numbers to demand an early election. The excuse presented itself with the final act in the loans affair, when Rex Connor was sacked eight weeks after Hayden delivered his budget.

What Fraser couldn't do, though, was ask his colleagues in the Senate to block the budget outright. He was aware that some Liberals would not have supported this unprecedented step. In 1974, Bill Snedden had merely threatened to block supply, and Whitlam was eager to meet that challenge with an early election because the economy still favoured the incumbent. Blocking Labor's most responsible budget, with the economy in recession, was a risk Fraser wasn't prepared to take. He chose a more subtle path to secure an early election: he would delay the budget until Whitlam agreed to face the people. It was a lawyer's distinction, but the effect was the same – an unrepresentative Senate would be holding a democratically elected national government hostage until its political demands were met. Or to express it in the terms of the industrial conflicts of the times, the conservatives had gone on strike in pursuit of the pay rises that came with power.

Fraser announced the decision to delay the budget on 15 October, the morning after the axe fell on Connor. 'The Labor government of 1972–75 has been the most incompetent and disastrous government in the history of Australia,' he said. 'Although Australia has basically one of the strongest and healthiest economies in the world, in three years this has been brought to the brink of disaster by incompetence of the worst kind. Without reason or excuse the weakest sections of our community – those least able to defend themselves – have suffered needlessly. We now have the highest unemployment since the Great Depression and the worst prolonged inflation in our history.' And that was just Labor's failure to manage the economy. 'The disgraceful conduct of the government over the loans affair follows a long record of scandals,' he said. 'In just three years, nine of the government's senior minis-ter have either resigned, been dismissed or been demoted because of incompetence or impropriety.'

Whitlam met Fraser's hyperbole with his own, accusing the Liberal leader of 'constitutional revolution'. 'I make it clear that the government will not yield to pressure. We will not yield to blackmail. We will not be panicked. We will not turn over the government of this country to vested interests, pressure groups and newspaper pro-prietors whose tactics would destroy the standards and traditions of parliamentary government . . . Let there be no mistake about the gravity of Mr Fraser's intention. Parliamentary democracy is a com-plex and fragile thing. Around the world it is under challenge. And now it is being challenged in Australia by the very man who pro-fesses to be a man of principle.' Whitlam could have called another double-dissolution election. But the economy was in recession, so he stared down the Senate. Supply – the government's ability to pay the bills – was due to run out six weeks later, on 27 November. Whitlam reasoned that the Coalition couldn't hold out for that long.

At first, the polls surged for Labor because the community was repelled by Fraser's tactics. By the first week of November, the Americans were ready to write Fraser's political obituary. A cable from the embassy in Canberra to Washington reported that Fraser's gamble 'had back-fired badly'. 'The longer he refuses to budge the more likely it is that his personal popularity as well as the popularity of the opposition parties will continue to fall. Fraser is also having increasing difficulty holding opposition senators together.' The cable concludes: 'In our view, what Fraser has done is to rescue the Whitlam government from an almost impossible position . . . [Fraser] revealed poor judgement in withholding sup-ply and showed that he is unable to best Whitlam in parliamentary debate. Fraser has a number of potential rivals within the Liberal Party who might well be tempted to try and replace him as leader as a result of his performance to date.'

5

TESTING THE NATION'S CONSTITUTION

A sense of lawlessness had overwhelmed global politics in the 1970s. In chronological order, the abuses of power included the American bombing of Cambodia, which had not been a party to the Vietnam War; the American intervention in Chile; the Arab invasion of Israel and the follow-up oil shock; the Turkish invasion of Cyprus, a member of the Commonwealth; and much closer to home, Indonesia's takeover of East Timor. Then there was the dismissal of the Whitlam Labor government by the representative of the Queen of England in Australia, exercising powers on her behalf that Elizabeth II did not have at home.

Australia's constitutional coup was the exception because of the lack of accompanying public disorder. The event bore an uncanny resemblance to a fixed horse race. The Labor backers shook their fists, tore up their betting slips in disgust and went home to watch the replay of Gough Whitlam's fighting words on the steps of the old parliament house. Even the trade union militants who walked off the job almost by reflex couldn't bring themselves to call a national strike when the government that shared its politics was ousted on 11 November 1975. The obedience that had made the 1960s a non-event

for Australia kicked in just when we needed it, to stop the chaos of
'75 descending to civil strife. The proclamation dissolving both
houses of parliament, and appointing Malcolm Fraser as caretaker
prime minister until an election was held, was read by governor-
general Sir John Kerr's official secretary, David Smith (he'd
performed the same service a year earlier on behalf of the previous
governor-general, Sir Paul Hasluck, to announce Whitlam's
double-dissolution election). But the absence of Kerr made him
appear cowardly. He had sacked the prime minister, but didn't have
the decency to face the people to explain his actions. Whitlam tow-
ered over Smith, and the noise from the crowd beneath them both
made it almost impossible to hear what Kerr's emissary was saying.
Whitlam then strode to the cluster of microphones and delivered his
most famous line. 'Well may we say God save the Queen, because
nothing will save the governor-general.' History had a co-star that
day – comedian and actor Garry McDonald in his Norman Gunston
persona. Gunston stood with Whitlam on the steps for a few seconds
and the juxtaposition of mock interviewer and deposed prime
minister gave the drama a twist of the absurd. Advance the highlights reel two years to the 1977 Melbourne Cup presentation, and a
tipsy governor-general is being booed by racegoers. 'Any little noises
that you may happen to hear are only static, it's just something wrong
with the system,' Kerr said, meaning the sound, not the nation itself.
Whitlam the orator, versus Kerr the drunk – the contest for history's
sympathy was over before either man left public life.

The Coalition had never accepted the legitimacy of either Labor
victory in 1972 or 1974. Now Labor had the excuse to see voters in
the same way as Reg Withers had when he accused them of suffering 'temporary insanity'. Many on the Labor side worried that the
party would sulk to the left, and consign itself to another generation in opposition. The bipartisan petulance posed a chicken and
egg riddle: whether the politicians were creating or reflecting the
national divisions.

Paul Keating, who had replaced Rex Connor in the ministry in October, gave the Americans a furious briefing at the US consul office in Sydney two days after 'the Dismissal', on 13 November. 'Governor-General Kerr's action is proof of "establishment's determination to get rid of Labor government at any cost",' Keating was quoted as saying.

He provided the Americans with an insight into what had driven Whitlam's approach to government. 'Keating acknowledged crisis reveals deep schizoid tendency in Australian constitution, which incorporates incompatible chunks of British Westminster and American federal systems. Cannot be corrected by [referendum] amendments in foreseeable future because of opposition from states, L/CP and conservative populace in countryside. Knowing this, and convinced the "establishment" would force Labor government out ASAP by any available means, Whitlam decided at outset [of] his administration in December 1972 to ram through as much new social reform as possible, saying: "They'll get us out. Let's do what we can while we are here." As Keating sees it, PrimeMin's prophecy has come true and if ALP loses this election "can the Labor Party which has held the Reds at bay all these years, do so any longer?"'

Much as it would have pleased the conservatives to see Labor succumb to another split, and another generation out of office, one-sided democracies do not serve the national interest. Both government and opposition come to take their respective positions, and through them the people, for granted. The group with power assumes it can do no wrong; the group without it has no interest in arguing otherwise to the electorate, because its members are too busy fighting among themselves for the right to claim purity in exile.

With hindsight, the Dismissal was a tragedy with no heroes, or even victims, just villains who were willing to take the system to places it had never been before. Whitlam, Fraser and Kerr share primary responsibility. 'We were really dealing with three crack-pots here,' Whitlam government minister John Wheeldon said, in probably the most succinct verdict on the crisis. 'We were just lucky that between them they didn't sink the country.'

Whitlam and Fraser needed a grown-up to intervene, to tell them to pull their heads in. But Kerr worried that Whitlam might sack him first so he engaged in a bit of politics himself, ignoring his duty to advise and warn his prime minister. By exercising a reserve power few people were aware of, and by deceiving his prime minister, Kerr became the most radical of the three main players.

Kerr misled Whitlam not just by refusing to advise him that dismissal was an option, but by operating to a different timetable. Whitlam assumed that he had another week or two to go before supply ran out. Kerr, on the other hand, had set 11 November as the deadline because that was the last possible date for the calling of a general election before Christmas. An even-handed governor-general would have let Whitlam know what the real deadline was. An even-handed chief justice of the High Court would have stayed out of the drama. But Sir Garfield Barwick relished the opportunity to become involved in what was a political matter, and when Kerr asked for advice he was happy to provide it.

While Whitlam, Fraser and Kerr share primary responsibility for the mess, Sir Garfield, the conservative state premiers and the loans affair duo of Rex Connor and Jim Cairns also deserve history's rebuke. Each suffered delusions of grandeur to match those of the principal actors. Each damaged the institution they served. The only leadership figure at the time who resisted the temptation to add their fist to the melee was Ian Chappell, the captain of the Australian Test cricket team.

The surprise was that the system corrected in favour of the office of prime minister. Watergate tarnished the office of president and created a rival power centre in the media. The Dismissal had the perverse effect of enhancing both the power of the prime minister and that of the national government. This was an inevitable trend in one respect, because globalisation would compel Canberra to accumulate more power at the expense of the states. Nevertheless, the examples of Tom Lewis and Joh Bjelke-Petersen undermined whatever faith the electorate might have had in premiers as honest brokers in their dealings with the national government. No future prime minister would allow the states to treat them as they had treated Gough Whitlam, or John Gorton. By the turn of the century, voters would be demanding that Canberra take over traditional state responsibilities, such as health care.

All future governors-general would stick to ceremony, with the occasional lapse into political commentary. In time, even the ribbon-cutting function would disappear from the job description, as prime ministers, most notably John Howard, assumed the role of de facto head of state. The High Court remained a source of controversy whilst the former Liberal Barwick and former Labor senator Lionel Murphy remained on the bench. But Australia recoiled at the American option of a more politicised court. While the US Supreme Court became another marker of the partisan divide in that country, Australia managed to return the High Court to its respected place above politics. It helped that there was no former politician appointed to the bench over the next thirty-five years.

The 1975 election was an anticlimax, the least controversial part of that mad year. Tens of thousands of people attended noisy campaign rallies, and the television news carried nightly images of a nation apparently at breaking point. But there was no riot to match, for instance, the pitched battled between police and protestors at the 1968 Democratic convention in Chicago. There was, however, one very serious incident. Letter bombs were mailed to Fraser,

Kerr and Bjelke-Petersen. The one addressed to the Queensland premier exploded before it got to his office, injuring two clerks.

Labor's predicament was so dire that it permitted the Liberal Party to run an almost exclusively negative campaign. It was brilliant, but it was false advertising because it created the impression that Australia's problems could be fixed by returning to the party that ruled before the crash. In one famous ad, titled 'The three dark years of Labor', a catalogue of shock-horror headlines flashed across the screen, accompanied by clips, newspaper tear-outs and still photos. All of it was in black and white: 'ASIO row', 'Murphy', 'Gair scandal', 'Inflation up', 'No tax relief', 'Crean sacked', 'OUT OF WORK', 'Jobs for the boys', 'Cairns sacked', 'Cameron sacked', 'Cope sacked', '$200m loans', 'Khemlani tells', 'ACTU', 'Connor sacked', and finally, '315,000 unemployed'. 'What you have just seen, the three dark years of Labor government, have been all their own work,' a male voice concludes. 'Let's turn on the lights.'

Labor ceded 29 of its remaining 65 seats, across all points of the electoral map – eight in New South Wales, six in Victoria, five in Queensland, four in both Western Australia and Tasmania, and one apiece in South Australia and the ACT. It was reduced to just one seat in both Queensland and Western Australia, and none in Tasmania. To compound the humiliation, Labor lost the popular vote after preferences in every state and territory, including the ACT, which had never happened before, or since. The Coalition also won control of the Senate, with 35 spots in an expanded chamber of 64.

In the Australian context, no young government had been rejected this decisively since 1931, when James Scullin's Labor regime was thrown out after one term. Technically speaking, the government of the day on 13 December 1975 was Fraser's caretaker administration, but it was Whitlam's Labor that was on trial. Yet Whitlam's defeat was unremarkable when compared with overseas experience. As former Reserve Bank governor Ian Macfarlane observed in his 2006 Boyer lecture, no Anglo government in power when stagflation set in won their next election: 'Governments that were in power during the 1974 and 1975 period were soon replaced; for example, the Heath Conservative government in the United Kingdom in 1974, the Whitlam Labor government in Australia in 1975, and the Ford Republican administration in the United States in 1976. Their replacements did not fare much better, with the Callaghan Labour government losing office in the United Kingdom in 1979 and the Carter Democratic administration losing in 1980.'

Labor had been an unruly government, but the system would have been better served if its term had been allowed to run a little longer, to 1976 or '77. One more Hayden budget would have been preferable to the cautious start of the Fraser Coalition government. An election win in his own right, without the assistance of the governor-general, would have spared Fraser the sense of illegitimacy he carried into office and allowed him to take more risks in the name of reform.

All the former prime ministers interviewed for this book are complimentary towards Gough Whitlam, but Malcolm Fraser is by far the most generous.

Fraser and Whitlam became good friends after politics. Fraser notes: 'Gough never seemed to bear the resentment to me that he certainly did to John Kerr, that he would have to Barwick, that he would have to [Liberal shadow attorney-general Bob] Ellicott . . . I'm not quite sure why there was that differentiation. Maybe he thought if the positions were reversed he would have done what I had done. He didn't appear to bear a personal animus.'

'Gough had a sense of Australian identity,' Fraser says. 'He had a vision for the future of an independent Australia. His language was sometimes extravagant – he quite often frightened people, especially people from Eastern Europe. And that came out of the

economic policies as much as anything else, and also a succession
of ministers who seriously let him down, amongst whom has to be
included poor old Rex Connor. He had a grand idea of Australia
with which I really wouldn't disagree. I think one of the more
important things we have in common is the sense of Australia as
an independent country.'

Bob Hawke: 'Gough brought the party up to date in many
ways. He related it a bit more toward current issues. I was trying
to do a lot of what he was doing, culling a lot of those sacred cows.
He was a true internationalist and regionalist, leading recognition
of China and so on – that was outstandingly important.'

Paul Keating says Whitlam helped Australia earn the world's
respect: 'Australia came very near the marginalisation that South
Africa experienced over racial discrimination, and our salvation
from that occurred through and with Gough Whitlam. What also
occurred was a recognition that we had to come to terms with some
international realities. The recognition of the People's Republic of
China was one; exiting Vietnam was another. The other thing I
credit him with is, of course, universal health insurance, which we
still have.'

John Howard says Whitlam could have extended his government's term if he had levelled with the electorate about the change
in the international economy. 'The historic mistake that Whitlam
made was not to confront the public with the radically changed
circumstance he inherited,' Howard says. 'The quadrupling of
world oil prices came after he came to power. It always seemed
to me that he could have hung a lot on that. He didn't get it. If
he had gone to the public and said, "Look, the old paradigm has
disappeared" – to use the modern jargon – "it's all now very different, we are living in an era of greater exchange rate volatility,
the oil price has quadrupled, and sorry folks, but we just can't any
longer afford to do some of these things". And if he had done that,
he could well have prolonged his government. But he manifested

no interest at all, and when he did, he sort of conducted a bit of a smash-and-grab raid on economic rationalism – the tariff cut of 25 per cent, which in the stream of things you'd say was a good policy.'

Howard acknowledges the power of Whitlam's ideas. 'Obviously a lot of people would see his social changes as beneficial. Things like equal pay – of course I agree with that – and universal health care is accepted, it's embedded.'

Whitlam had seemingly left Labor where he found it at the 1966 election, when Harold Holt's Coalition had achieved a post-war record vote after preferences of 56.9 per cent. Fraser's return was just below that figure, at 55.7 per cent. But dig beneath the national result and the swing back to the Coalition was exaggerated in Queensland and Western Australia. In New South Wales, Victoria and South Australia, Labor's losing vote was noticeably higher than it had been in '66. While many of the mortgage-holders in Sydney and Melbourne who supported Labor in '72 and '74 had reverted to the conservatives in '75, enough had stuck with the party of the centre-left to redraw the nation's political map, and offer it a second chance to remake Australia in the '80s and '90s.

The dichotomy is easily recognisable today. It is the rift between new and old Australia: the progressive south-east versus the contrary north and west. But there is an economic twist to the story that only makes sense now, after the GFC. Whitlam's electoral fortunes mirrored the commodities cycle. The terms of trade – the price Australia receives for its exports relative to the price it pays for its imports – surged in each election year that Whitlam had increased, or maintained, Labor's national vote – 1969, '72 and '74. The terms of trade crashed in Whitlam's final eighteen months in office, and the political fallout was felt most keenly in the mining states of Queensland and Western Australia. This is one of the more telling statistics of national politics. It helps explain Whitlam's appeal in good times: voters trusted him to invest the proceeds of prosperity on their behalf. But when Australia's purchasing power was reduced by falling commodity prices, the electorate pined for the Golden Age of the '50s and '60s, which it associated with conservative rule.

Whitlam, and through him the nation, was a victim of lousy timing. His government confronted an external shock less than a year into its life which neither the system nor the public had the maturity to handle. Rather than comprehend the abrupt change in Australia's economic circumstances, Labor and its conservative opponents turned to one another and said: 'It's your fault.' Most of the books on the period either ignore, or mention only in passing, the international setting. In this, historians have fallen for the same trap as the protagonists in seeing the Whitlam experiment as a domestic morality tale about the man and his Program. But the economic torpor and community anxiety that defined the period from 1972 to 1975, was common to the rich world. Australia's peak inflation rate of 17.6 per cent was in the middle of the pack at the time, with the British going as high as 26.9 per cent and the Japanese 24.8, while the Americans reached 12.2 per cent. Our unemployment rate hit 5.4 per cent under Whitlam. It went to 9 per cent under a Republican administration in the US, and 5.1 under British Labour. Only the Japanese and Swedish were able to keep unemployment below 2 per cent and slip the noose of 'stagflation'.

Whitlam's Program delivered the 1960s to Australia into a single three-year term. His leadership style was daring for its policy content and for his approach to public debate. Whitlam, unusually for an Australian leader, had an intellect he wasn't afraid to show off. He promoted art over sport and tertiary education over blue-collar labour.

But the self-imposed pressure to bring the nation up to date meant the size of government increased too quickly, from 18.7 per cent of gross domestic product in 1972–73 to 24.1 per cent in

1975–76. Whitlam tried to pay for the expansion out of the proceeds of growth. But when the revenue dried up with the global recession of 1974–75 and the collapse in our terms of trade, Labor kept spending. Hayden couldn't reverse the process, he could only slow it. This meant the budget would remain in deep deficit, which is the clearest expression of a nation living beyond its means. The test for Australia's political class was whether it could reset community expectations to rebalance the budget, and reduce inflation without shattering the social cohesion we had taken for granted in the previous decade.

6

THE AGE OF THE RORTER

Malcolm Fraser's stunning election victory did not lift the national mood. Three years in opposition had not been long enough for the conservatives to re-evaluate their own policies. Their time in the wilderness had been divided into three distinct phases of self-obsession: Billy Snedden's plan A to force an early election in 1974, the Snedden-versus-Fraser leadership tussle through the second half of 1974 and the start of 1975, and Fraser's plan B to force another earlier election.

Without a reform program of its own to occupy it, the new government found its agenda was being set by the bureaucracy. In the first cabinet meeting on the economy, in January 1976, Treasury re-asserted its authority through its new minister Phillip Lynch. 'We will not succeed in bringing down unemployment in any lasting fashion unless we first succeed in reining in inflation and breaking inflationary expectations,' Lynch told his colleagues. By that he meant accepting 'a continuing high level of unemployment for some time to come'. It was the Hayden formula, with a slightly harder edge. 'We need to be clear eyed about this,' Lynch warned. 'Our success, or lack of it, in bringing down the budget deficit will not only be the key to our success in controlling inflation, it will also be key to the general credibility of the government.'

But there was an immediate contradiction. Coalition ministers were behaving no differently behind closed doors to the Labor people they said had brought the economy to its knees. Lynch's stocktake of election promises found that the Coalition had offered voters too much in return for their ballots. 'It is sobering to note that the savings we have made to date are at this point far outweighed by the immediate cost of our election promises,' he said. '[And the] additional spending proposals already coming forward will, if approved, worsen the situation further.' The new government didn't seem to trust the people enough to ask for their support to fix the economy without bribing them.

Lynch's first budget, on 17 August 1976, established the pattern of the Fraser years: it roared with an aggressive language of austerity that was not matched with deep cuts to expenditure. The Hayden deficit for 1975–76 had finished at $3.5 billion. Lynch aimed for a substantial reduction to $2.6 billion in 1976–77. 'Those who, in the name of reducing unemployment, call for higher government spending, or bigger deficits, or full wage indexation, or devaluation of the dollar, are calling for higher – not lower – unemployment,' Lynch told the nation. But the tough talk didn't shift the inflation rate, which remained at 14.2 per cent at the end of 1976 – just 0.2 per cent lower than where Labor left it a year earlier.

Fraser regrets that spending wasn't cut further in the first budget. He and Lynch had a meeting with the Treasury secretary, Sir Fredrick Wheeler, at the beginning of 1976 during which they were told the government didn't need to do more. 'Look, you've done a pretty good job, the budget is coming around, but the economy has had enough shocks,' Fraser quotes Sir Fredrick as saying.

But there were more external shocks coming. The international money market was taking pot shots at any rich nation that had been slow to tackle inflation. Britain was the most high-profile victim. In November 1976, its inflation rate was still 15 per cent, and James Callaghan's Labour government was humiliatingly forced to submit a spending cuts program to the International Monetary Fund in exchange for a US$3.9 billion emergency loan (a Connor-esque 4.5 billion in Australian dollars at the time) to cover its debts. Australia was the next logical target. The market decided our dollar was overvalued because it didn't reflect the fall in our terms of trade, and was pulling funds out of the Australian economy until the government devalued.

The issue was too sensitive for Lynch to commit on paper. He gave cabinet an oral presentation on 28 November to explain why, three months after promising in his budget speech to defend the dollar, he would have to devalue it and risk compromising the fight against inflation by increasing the price of imports. Fraser says that once the decision to devalue was taken, he wanted to make sure there would only be one move down. 'Everyone accepted there should be a big devaluation, even Treasury, and I was determined that we would only have one. We weren't going to have a second. I had seen too many European economies devalue the minimum amount, and then they'd have to come back because the markets never believed them. I got [Reserve Bank governor] Harry Knight in my office, and I said, "Harry, nobody is arguing whether we devalue or not, so the question is the amount. What's the minimum devaluation in which you can guarantee the next move will be an appreciation?" Phillip Lynch was in the room, nobody else. He said, "Fifteen per cent, prime minister." And I said, "Harry, do you mind if I add two-and-a-half per cent on for safety?", and he said, "I suppose I can wear it."'

Cabinet also changed the arrangement for setting the currency. To avoid further dramatic swings either way, the treasurer would issue daily updates on the dollar, based on a basket of foreign currencies. They called it a 'dirty float' – a halfway-house measure that still left control of the currency to the government, and placed

Australia out of step with our major trading partners. The Americans, Japanese and British had all floated their currencies in the five years since the collapse of the Bretton Woods system. But the Coalition couldn't let go of the dollar because it didn't trust the rest of the world to set a fairer price for Australia. It accepted the Treasury advice that the Australian economy was too small to deregulate because the dollar would be overwhelmed by speculators with deep pockets. What Fraser and the bureaucracy didn't realise was that the market would continue to speculate against the government anyway.

Fraser presented himself as a pro-market ideologue, but was a protectionist in practice. Among the most powerful voices in his cabinet were Country Party leader Doug Anthony and Anthony's deputy Ian Sinclair, respectively the minister for trade and resources and the minister for primary industries. Anthony and Sinclair were agrarian socialists, the bush's answer to Labor interventionists such as Jim Cairns and Rex Connor. One of the first symbolic acts of the Fraser government was the restoration of a subsidy to farmers for superphosphate, which had been abolished by the Whitlam government.

Fraser preached restraint and his most memorable line was 'Life wasn't meant to be easy'. But his government could never get its spending under control, which was the necessary precondition for breaking Australia's inflation habit.

A pall of national self-loathing had set in almost immediately after the 1975 election. Our sporting teams, so long a source of trivial but endearing vanity for the Australian people, had commenced a losing streak that would make us feel even more miserable about ourselves. There were no gold medals at the 1976 Olympic Games in Montreal. The Ashes were ceded to the English in '77. And at the B-list Commonwealth Games in Edmonton in '78, Australia had its poorest return of the post-war era, falling from first to third on the medals table behind Canada and England. Many a loyal Australian wasted untold hours in front of their new colour televisions waiting for those precious minutes of recognition when the rest of the world applauded our athletes. It was a morbid pursuit; we watched from the other side of the world, in our evenings, as tracksuited robots from the Soviet Union and East Germany marched to the victory dais, or the Poms skittled our batsmen again. The Americans felt the same shiver of inferiority that we did, but they could still console themselves with the reflective glory of individual sports such tennis, golf and boxing. Australia had no era-defining world champions to speak of in the second half of the 1970s to compare with the heroes of the '60s such as Rod Laver in tennis, Lionel Rose in boxing and Dawn Fraser in swimming.

An earnest cabinet submission prepared after Edmonton said the decline in our 'international sports performance' was a serious issue. '[It] has caused widespread community concern because large numbers of Australians support and identify with our national sportsmen and sportswomen,' Ray Groom, the minister for the environment, community development and housing, wrote. 'Failure in international competition damages our self-image and national pride.' He noted that countries such as Canada and even New Zealand were spending many times the amount on sport that Australia was, and recommended that we follow their example. The finance department, which Fraser had recently established to keep an eye on government spending, called out the hypocrisy of seeking more funding for sport while asking the rest of the community to tighten its belt. '[Finance] sees strong reasons of principle why Commonwealth assistance to international sport should not be significantly increased, particularly at a time when the government's policy of expenditure restraint has resulted in cutbacks in areas that could well be regarded as of higher social priority.' But the flag-wavers prevailed over the fiscal puritans, and the Fraser government began the long march to return Australia to the podium, with a program that would eventually see us spending more taxpayer dollars for every Olympic gold medal than almost any other nation.

Fraser was more comfortable in the locker room than in the art gallery. He shared many of Whitlam's instincts on social policy – he supported Labor's position on Aboriginal land rights, and was keen to expand the previous government's multicultural agenda – but he didn't have Gough's love of the arts. As with most Victorians, Fraser over-identified with football, and his giant frame was easy to pick out in the post-match celebrations when his team, Carlton, won premierships on his watch in 1979, '81 and '82. It's not drawing too long a bow to say that in the economic misery of the Fraser years, a new model of Australian leadership was being forged, where prime minister became barracker-in-chief.

Sport, in turn, became political in the Fraser era. In Sydney's rugby league competition, the coach of the struggling Western Suburbs team, Roy Masters, used class warfare as a motivational tool. He dubbed his side 'the Fibros', after the working-class cottages that hemmed the city's west. They needed an enemy from the right side of the tracks that wouldn't attract the sympathy of neutral supporters. So the North Shore's Manly, cashed up and successful, like the suburb it represented, became 'the Silvertails' in this David and Goliath contest, and the 1978 season was transformed into an extended bout of world championship wrestling.

Masters preached the hypocrisy of 'honest violence'. A whack given to an opponent when the referee wasn't watching earned no penalty, so it wasn't illegal. If the other side retaliated, it was their fault because they had taken their eye off the ball. 'Western Suburbs players generally believed that they were perceived by the Manly people as second-class citizens, in the sense that Manly had the richer contracts, they lived on the northern beaches, they had blond hair, they were silvertails, and generally came from a more privileged background than the West's guys,' Masters explained years later. 'The guys believed it and they hooked on to the idea.'

One-day cricket deserves a special slot in the highlights reel of the Fraser years for what it said about both the state of industrial relations and the power of media moguls. The instant-coffee version of the game had been an afterthought to the regular five-day Tests until the Nine Network's Kerry Packer got into a fight with the Australian Cricket Board over broadcast rights in 1976, and again in '77. The Board had refused Packer's more generous bid in favour of the public broadcaster, the ABC. Undaunted, Packer decided to create his own competition, secretly signing up the best players in Australia, the West Indies, England, South Africa and Pakistan. The money Packer offered was well in excess of what any of the players had previously been paid to represent their countries. The Australians, in particular, had felt exploited by the establishment and were keen to make a statement.

The rebel competition was dubbed 'Packer's Circus', and ran for two seasons alongside the Establishment's Test series, starting in 1977–78. Packer's 'Super Tests' were poorly attended, but the one-day games held under lights drew large crowds and ratings. When the truce was struck in 1979, Packer got the broadcast rights, and the commodification of cricket was underway. As any employer would know, if you pay your workers more, the business can only survive if productivity improves. It was the increased workload – the limited-overs tournament at the end of the Test series – that the national team captain, Greg Chappell, blamed for the underarm incident, which became a marker for Australia's loss of self-respect.

The stakes were absurdly low, a fifty-over-a-side match between Australia and New Zealand, on 1 February 1981. The five-match series was level at one all, and with one ball to deliver in the third, the Kiwis required six runs to tie the scores. Australia had nothing to lose but its reputation. Chappell instructed his younger brother

Trevor to bowl that last delivery underarm, so that batsman Brian McKechnie couldn't hoick it over the fence. He said it was a 'cry for help': 'I wasn't fit. I mean, I was mentally wrung out, I was physically wrung out, and I was fed up with the whole system. Things seemed to be just closing in on us, and I suppose in my own case I felt they were closing in on me.' New Zealand prime minister Robert Muldoon spoke for both sides of the Tasman when he described the underarm incident as 'an act of cowardice'.

The only thing more cringe-making than the Chappell grubber was the jingle the Nine Network used to promote its broadcasts, 'C'mon Aussie C'mon'. If one-day cricket was an early warning of a shrinking public attention span, the song that came with it prophesised the shrill, winner-takes-all nationalism of later prime ministers Bob Hawke and John Howard. In the late 1970s, sport was both a warning of a more aggressive Australia and a pressure valve that allowed people to blow off steam in the stands and in their living rooms, without the violence spilling onto the streets. The anger was drawn from the sense that rules no longer mattered, and off-field it was demonstrated in the way employer and worker alike were rorting the taxation and wages systems.

In *The Lucky Country: Australia in the Sixties*, Donald Horne wrote off that generation's leaders as 'second-rate'. But he hedged his bets on the people themselves. 'The very skepticism of Australians and their delight in improvisation have meant that so far Australia has scraped through,' he wrote. 'A nation more concerned with styles of life than with achievement has managed to achieve what may be the most evenly prosperous society in the world. It has done this in a social climate largely inimical to originality and ambition – except sport – and in which there is less and less acclamation of hard work. According to the rules, Australia has not deserved its good fortune. It will be interesting to find out if the rules are wrong.'

The rules weren't wrong. When the rug of prosperity was pulled from under Australia, the people behaved as badly as their leaders by bending the rules. They took the lazy path to restoring the income they had lost to inflation by cheating on their tax. The technical trigger for the abuse was the discovery of loopholes in the legislation, and the absurdly high rates of tax that people had to pay at the time. But the emotional trigger was the Dismissal. The top end of town saw the restoration of conservative rule as a licence to recover their losses from the Whitlam years.

Tax avoidance emerged as a national problem soon after the 1976–77 budget was released. Business had received a concession on its trading stock to offset inflation, but the legislation, including anti-avoidance provisions, would not reach parliament until the following year. The window between announcement and legislation was exploited by both business and individuals, which together claimed $106 million in 'artificial losses' ($502 million in 2010 dollars). By 'artificial losses' the tax office meant deductions that had been concocted. These taxpayers had no previous history of making such claims, so it was fair to assume they were chasing the loophole they thought was there. The figure was many times what the government had intended with its concession. As the Australian Taxation Office became aware of the schemes, it decided to backdate the closure of the loophole to the start of the financial year. Trevor Boucher, then a second commissioner with the ATO, recalls that the effect of the anti-avoidance provisions was like stepping on an ants' nest, because there was an immediate backlash from people who had a stake in the schemes. The lobbyists appealed to the Coalition's sense of propriety. Why should any businessman or private citizen suffer financial penalty from retrospective changes to the law? The government blinked, and it never recovered its authority on tax matters. On 24 May 1977, cabinet agreed to remove the so-called retrospective clause. The loss to revenue was said to be 'considerable . . . varying from not less than $70 million to more than $100 million'.

Lynch issued another warning to tax avoiders in the 1977–78 budget, but Boucher says the promoters of schemes took this as a challenge to go even harder. By this stage, the ATO was reporting to the Fraser government that higher-income earners were claiming deductions that would wipe out all their tax liability for years to come. But the government was stuck in a rut of indecision.

It was John Howard, who replaced Lynch as treasurer during the 1977 election, who temporarily staunched the flow. He introduced legislation in the following April, backdated to the previous budget, over the protests of his own side. 'Howard caught a hell of a lot of schemes,' Boucher says. 'There was a bit of a row in party ranks about that, but [this time] they held firm.' But still the tax avoiders kept pushing the limits of the law and the resolve of the government. The new treasurer sent a note to the tax commissioner asking for advice on what the next step should be. Bill O'Reilly replied on 11 April 1978 that the ATO had a new worry, 'whereby companies that have a tax liability are stripped of assets so that there is nothing left to meet [their] tax [obligations]'. O'Reilly said the existing law wasn't tough enough, and so began one of the most excruciating battles between bureaucrat and government in Australian political history over the so-called 'bottom of the harbour' schemes, in which companies were deliberately sunk into bankruptcy before their tax was due. The investor would strip the assets and on-sell the title of the worthless company to the scheme promoter, who would then claim the losses. The ATO wanted tax cheats to face criminal sanction but the Coalition kept finding reasons to delay. The Country Party in Queensland and the Liberal Party in Western Australia led the backlash because some of their supporters were involved in the schemes. O'Reilly issued eighteen explicit warnings over the next two-and-a-half years before legislation was finally passed on 2 December 1980.

The extent of the Coalition's weakness can be seen in the boom in tax avoidance schemes generally that occurred on its watch. The

value of dubious deductions escalated ten-fold from $191 million
in 1976–77 to $2.052 billion in 1977–78 (almost $9 billion in 2010
dollars). As many as 10 000 taxpayers a year were involved in 'identified' tax avoidance schemes. The true number would have been
far greater had the definition extended beyond the schemes to the
cash economy, the hunting ground of the worker. Still, it was a bit
rich for the trade unions to be lectured about wage restraint when
the Coalition couldn't stop its own supporters from ripping off the
budget.

Malcolm Fraser faced his first re-election on 10 December 1977
with Gough Whitlam still his opponent. He had called the contest a year ahead of schedule, making this the fourth trip to the
ballot box for voters in five years. The Liberals ran another devastating negative campaign, dubbed 'Memories', to remind the
people that they didn't want to return to the turmoil of the loans
affair. But Fraser wanted vindication in his own right, so he spiced
his re-election pitch with the offer of generous tax cuts, which
were presented as a 'fistful of dollars' in the government's positive
advertisements.

The 1977 election, like its 1974 mirror, delivered a repeat of the
previous contest. The Coalition government lost five seats – two
to Labor, and three to a reduction in the size of the parliament. It
still had 86 seats out of 124, to Labor's 38, and it retained control
of the Senate. Both sides saw their primary vote drop as a new
centre party, the Australian Democrats, created by former Liberal
Don Chipp, scored 9.4 per cent on debut with a promise to 'keep
the bastards honest'. The Coalition and Labor contributed about a
third each of the Democrat vote.

Whitlam took the second landslide defeat more personally than
the first. He felt that the public, and the party, would never give
him another chance to lead the country, so he retired from public

life with two election wins and three losses. He was succeeded as
Labor leader by Bill Hayden.

There had been a whiff of scandal around the government during the campaign. Phillip Lynch had stood down as treasurer over
allegations of impropriety involving a land deal. While he was subsequently cleared, he didn't get his old job back from the 38-year-old
John Howard, who had been in parliament for just three years.
Howard was a reverse Whitlam: he grew up in a lower-middle
income household that was normally associated with the Labor
side of politics. But his parents were proud Menzies-Liberals, and
fiercely anti-trade union. The young Howard had attended the
selective public school Canterbury Boys High, in western Sydney's
Labor heartland, and graduated with a law degree from the University of Sydney. His electorate of Bennelong was a mix of fibro
and silvertail, wedged between the city's working-class west and
its affluent north.

Howard concedes he was promoted early. He was the nation's
seventh treasurer in eight years, and after the election the Treasury
secretary greeted the new minister with a jocular reference to the
revolving door. Howard says: 'When I had my first meeting with
Fred Wheeler at the end of 1977, he said to me in his very formal
way, "Treasurer, I've been secretary of the treasury for six years and
you are the sixth treasurer I have served." I recall saying to him,
"I'm glad you're retiring next year."'

Howard had the worst possible initiation to the job. The budget
deficit for 1977–78 was supposed to be just $2.2 billion, but it blew
out by 50 per cent to $3.3 billion because of spending over-runs and
a leaky revenue base. Howard picked up the Treasury tune, and
repeated the warnings of Hayden and Lynch for ministers to cut
spending. 'The outlook for the 1978–79 budget is one of extreme
concern,' he advised on 14 July 1978. 'The full impact of the decision
to reduce personal income tax rates and to lighten the tax burden on
business, together with reduced receipts in other areas, means that

budget receipts are forecast to fall in real terms.' Howard said the deficit as it stood would reach $5.2 billion. 'It is clear that a subsequent jump in the budgeted deficit would represent, and would be seen by the community as, a fundamental reversal of policy and a squandering of the hard-won gains of the past few years.'

The duality in Fraser's leadership style, his righteousness and his ruthless pragmatism, came into sharp relief during the internal debates for this budget. The promised tax cuts could not be afforded without new offsets, but the prime minister was squeamish about another round of spending cuts. So he decided to drop the tax cuts instead. The cancellation of the 'fistful of dollars' was agreed to on 31 July 1978, and confirmed in a follow-up letter from Fraser to Howard that began: 'My dear Treasurer . . .' There was no comparable episode in the post-war period when a government had bounced its own cheque to voters. For all his faults on the economic front, Whitlam had insisted that Labor honour every promise it made to voters.

Howard's first budget, like Lynch's last, failed to meet its target. The deficit was meant to fall from $3.3 billion to $2.8 billion; it came in at $3.5 billion, a figure no different in headline terms to what Hayden had left behind three years earlier. The following year, finance minister Eric Robinson explained to his colleagues how they had managed to muck things up. 'We inherited a huge budget deficit (of $3.5 billion) – equivalent to five per cent of GDP – in 1975–76,' he said in a briefing dated 9 March 1979. 'Following a substantial reduction in 1976–77, the deficit has persisted around the $3 billion mark and, in the absence of corrective action, we are facing the prospect of a $4 billion deficit next year. How can this be so?'. It was all our own doing, Robinson replied to his rhetorical question. New spending had a 'strong ongoing momentum' and previous tax cuts had 'reduced substantially the buoyancy of the tax system . . . Taken together, these influences have tended to perpetuate the imbalance between receipts and outlays.'

Howard says public opinion would not have tolerated even more drastic cuts. 'Once you've had a big breakout of spending [as occurred under Whitlam], it is incredibly difficult to reduce it in real terms.' He also says the tax cuts were a mistake, and they tarnished his reputation as treasurer even though he had not been involved in their formulation. 'I thought the tax cuts in '77 were not necessary and I was surprised by them, and of course, they unravelled very quickly and I had the problem.'

By its failure to live up to its promise of financial responsibility, the Fraser government guaranteed the nation's decline in the 1970s. By the decade's end, the economy was comatose. The inflation rate was back at 10.1 per cent and the unemployment rate was 6.1 per cent. We were not as badly off as the Americans, who had inflation at 13.3 per cent and unemployment at 6 per cent, or the British – 17.2 per cent and 5.6 per cent. But there was no solace in our stagflation being a little less severe.

A circle of mutually reinforcing rorting had become the Australian experience. The top end of town cheated on its tax, the trade unions walked off the job, and the best the government could do to keep the peace was to offer vicarious sporting glory in the future, on the taxpayer's tab.

When Australia had been fully employed and inflation still in single digits in 1969, just over half the population (51 per cent) trusted government to do the right thing. By 1979 that figure had collapsed to a record low of just 29 per cent. The proportion of voters not satisfied with democracy had almost doubled, from 23 to 45 per cent, over the same period. Fraser had achieved power without moral authority.

TRANSITIONS I:

FROM OLIVE TO YELLOW

My favourite opinion poll is the one that would have stopped my mother migrating to Australia if the government of the day had obeyed its findings. Taken in March 1951, the Australian Gallup Poll asked voters 'whether or not Australia should get immigrants' from seven listed nations. Each candidate for our acceptance was European, a mix of Allies and enemies from the Second World War. The Netherlands (78.4 per cent), Sweden (74.7) and France (57.8) recorded strong Yes votes. Of this group, only the Dutch would come to Australia in large enough numbers to be welcomed with the putdown of 'clog wogs'. Less popular were people from Greece (only 41.5 per cent of Australians wanted them), Yugoslavia (32.6) and Italy (26.6). To explain the discrepancy between Northern and Southern Europe, consider the response to the seventh nation tested in the poll – Germany. Unlike the Greeks, who had been on our side in the war, the Germans had the advantage of fair skin. The German approval rating was 53.9 per cent.

My father had come to Australia by ship in 1950, at age sixteen. He returned to the Ionian island of Ithaca three years later, missed his new home and came straight back. My mother migrated from the northern Greek province of Kastoria in 1962, at age twenty, one of two girls from her village to catch the subsidised flight to Australia that day. They shared a room above a fish-and-chips shop in the inner Melbourne suburb of Richmond with up to six other girls. By day, they would work in the shop; at night, Mum would cry into her pillow, between writing letters to her parents in the village. On Saturdays, all the girls would search for work in factories and shops. The chances of my mum and dad meeting in Greece would have been next to zero. They crossed paths at the Ithaca Club in the city, where Mum was a waitress. They married in 1963; I was born a year later.

In *The Lucky Country*, Donald Horne observed that the Australian-born children of Southern Europeans seemed to take longer to fit in. 'The children of Northern Europeans – principally German, Dutch and Polish – seem to "become Australian" most quickly; the children of Mediterranean Europeans – mostly Italians, Greeks and Yugoslavs – less quickly. The Greeks have their own churches; the Italians, with some tensions, simply attach themselves to Catholic parish churches but their sense of family is strong. These generalisations may apply most to the cases where there has been chain migration, where a significant part of one small community transfers itself in groups to Australia and attempts to continue its group life.' He should have waited until the olive-skinned had a chance to grow up before making that last call.

What Horne was projecting onto the children was the qualifications of the parents. The Southern European immigrants came from rougher stock than the Dutch and the Germans. Neither of my parents had completed primary school, for instance. But the Australian-born children of Southern Europeans did better at school and in the workforce than those whose parents came from the more advanced parts of the continent, or from the mother country of Great Britain. It was no accident of geography, or culture, or skin-colour, because the Australian-born children of Asian immigrants excelled in the same way.

'Those whose parents arrived in Australia in the post-war years have achieved better educational outcomes than those with Australian-born parents,' a report commissioned by the Howard Coalition government revealed in 2002. 'The study also found the second generation of people from Southern and Eastern Europe and Asia had a higher proportion of people with university qualifications and in professional occupations than the second generation whose parents migrated from the United Kingdom or other Western European countries.'

Migrate from a first-world nation and you are less likely to feel estranged on arrival. Interestingly, the third generation, the Australian-born grandchildren of these immigrants, returned to the national average on education and income. As a general rule, the Greeks of my parents' intake divided into two groups: those who paid off their own home quickly, and those who remained in debt so they could buy up as much of their street as possible. Greeks and Italians had higher home-ownership rates than the Australian-born.

Primary school was much harder for me than it was for my fairer-skinned younger sister. Years Five and Six, 1974 and '75, were the most miserable. I felt like ridicule's first recruit. Much of it was my doing because I didn't have the social tools to deflect the barbs. The system did do something very amusing to me in the Whitlam years, when a special needs teacher came to our school to round up all the pupils with unfamiliar surnames. She wanted to help us with our English. I didn't protest my proficiency because the stirrer in me wanted to see how long it would take for her to realise her mistake. I can't recall what I said when she finally got around to addressing me, but she was embarrassed for both of us that my English was adequate.

In my little world, the second half of the '70s marked a turning

point from outcast to just another Aussie kid. I had a strong sense
that I was beginning to fit in, and that the nation had a new
intake to worry about – the Vietnamese (and later the Cambo-
dian) boatpeople. Luckily I couldn't read an opinion poll in those
days, because the Greeks were no more popular than they had
been when my father migrated two decades earlier. In 1977, an *Age*
poll asked people to choose between six regional sources for new
immigrants. The British topped the survey, with the favour of 44.1
per cent of voters. Next were people from Northern and Western
Europe (27.1 per cent). As for the rest, the message seemed to be
'Don't bother applying'. Southern Europe had the support of 6.5
per cent of Australians; Asia, 6.2; Southern Africa, 2.4; and the
Middle East, 1 per cent.

The authorities shared the public scepticism towards Southern
Europeans. The Fraser government worried that the dole or disability pension might be going to undeserving hands and instructed
the Department of Social Security to tighten its procedures. Sydney's Greek community came in for particular attention after one
of its members accused fellow new Australians of a massive fraud
in which doctors signed false claims for benefits. This is where
the ethnic sickie, or 'Mediterranean back', entered the fractured
lexicon of the '70s.

The tabloids, encouraged by the policeman pursuing the case,
dubbed it 'the Greek social security conspiracy' and it dominated
the news in 1978. 'Those 181 people, mostly Greek people living in
inner city Sydney, were the subject of possibly the most massive
assault on the civil liberties of Australian citizens in the history
of this country,' Hawke Labor government minister Brian Howe
would tell parliament eight years later.

They were rounded up in well-publicised raids at 8 a.m. on 31
March 1978 that covered more than a hundred homes and five doctors' surgeries. The Commonwealth Police sent the sledgehammer
of a hundred of its finest officers to smash this cashew. The most

curious part of the case was that the accused were asked to hold up a sign with the word 'Greece' written on it when they had their mug shots taken.

Sydney's *Sun-Herald* described it as 'the biggest criminal investigation in Australian history'. 'Before the party is over, 1200 people will have been charged with "conspiring to defraud the Commonwealth",' the *Sun-Herald* thundered on 9 April. 'The racket is said to have been extracting $6 million a year from the Social Security Department and $500 000 a year from Medibank. Police also believe they have thwarted a graft scheme that cost gullible Greeks about $2.4 million in bribes. All this money tops anything that has been investigated or unearthed by any Australian police force, state or federal.'

At worst, the amount of money that was supposed to have been ripped off was around 5 per cent of the sum the government had already privately written off after its back-down on the retrospective tax avoidance legislation.

The case eventually cost the taxpayer $10 million, and dragged on for years before most of the accused were exonerated. The handful of people that were convicted received fines or were placed on good behaviour bonds. Only one doctor was sent to jail. The Hawke Labor government appointed a commission of inquiry headed by Dame Roma Mitchell, and her report prompted a $10 million compensation payout to the victims, bringing the total loss to the taxpayer to $20 million, not counting lawyers' fees. 'One wonders whether other communities, perhaps smaller communities less used to defending themselves, would have come off as well,' Labor's community services minister, Senator Don Grimes, said in 1986.

At the top of the first migration wave in the 1960s, 77 000 new Australians were being added to the population on average each year, after allowing for emigration and death. But the program had a predominately Anglo base, with only a spice of Mediterranean. The UK provided almost half the intake, 33 000 out of the 77 000 per year, including John and Moira Gillard, and their two daughters, Alison, aged seven, and Julia, aged four, who migrated from Wales to Adelaide in 1966. Greece was the second-largest source, at 8000 per year, and the only other nation to contribute more than 10 per cent of the total. Italy was third, at 6000 a year.

The Greeks and Italians didn't change Australia because there weren't enough of them to make a material difference to the nation's character. There were twice as many British immigrants, but while their influence was felt in popular culture, they didn't change Australia either. In fact, it was the reverse: the Poms, like the wogs and dagoes, were expected to fit in. Australians wanted it both ways. They saw immigration as a jump-start to national maturity, while reserving the right to lash out at the people and the places they came from.

Australians prefer not to hear that we hurt each new immigrant group because we see ourselves as terrific hosts. We are, but not in the way we imagine. Whenever voters are asked if they want more people to come here, a majority will either say we should stick to the present intake, or reduce it. There has never been a poll with clear majority support for a higher intake. Yet each new immigrant group has the same story to tell: after a rough initiation, they are quickly accepted as members of the national family.

To appreciate why, imagine the cultural conversation between the local and the immigrant. The new arrival is told to adopt Australian values. 'Okay,' the new arrival says, 'I'm here for a better life – what is it, exactly, that I have to do?' 'Er, dunno.' Knowing Don Bradman's batting average doesn't make you an Australian. Reciting the national anthem doesn't work either, because all our song offers is a nation young and free, with lots of money if you work hard enough for it. Most Australians will pause when asked to define the values that they want immigrants to live up to. Mateship, a fair go – these aren't uniquely Australian traits. Don't bring your blood feuds here – the evidence over successive waves is that the fights back home never translate to Australia, beyond the odd flare lit at a soccer game.

It is the absence of a settled Australian culture that makes this country so much easier to migrate to than the United States or the UK. The locals may insist you do the right thing or else, but the immigrants quickly learn to see through the bluff. Despite an intolerant streak that sometimes explodes into racism, Australians themselves are xenophobia's weakest link. When they meet the strangers they had feared through the media, the clenched fist they imagined they would raise becomes a handshake. We're pleased to meet you, because Australians are a genuinely friendly and generally open people.

To the new arrival, Australians are something else as well: a touch lazy. The hushed conversation in the Greek community I grew up in was that immigrants were prepared to work harder than the locals. John Howard once told me something similar about his childhood. 'When I was a young person you avoided getting served by an Australian waiter,' he said. 'A lot of Australians, a generation ago, resented anything to do with serving.'

All an immigrant has to live up to in Australia is the ideal of home ownership and the best education they can get for their children. Banal, perhaps, but it builds a much more cohesive nation than an explicit cultural contract that insists on fealty to flag and national anthem. The first battle hymn my mother taught me was the theme song for the Richmond Football Club.

As an island continent, Australia never had to deal with uninvited immigrants in the same way that the US – the original melting pot – did, due to its porous border with Mexico. But the Americans are more willing to absorb all comers because their muscular version of capitalism has no qualms about accommodating the world's huddled masses at the very bottom of the income ladder. Egalitarian Australia wants its immigrants to maintain the social compact by joining everyone else on the middle rung.

The end of the Vietnam War was a regional shock to rival the global shock of stagflation, and Malcolm Fraser's decision to open the door to relatively large numbers of refugees was just as radical as Gough Whitlam's across-the-board tariff cut had been earlier in the decade. Both events tested the same part of the Australian character: our insularity. The White Australia policy had been the social conceit to match the economic indulgence of protection. Unlike the removal of tariffs, the act of allowing the yellow-skinned to migrate was less traumatic than the half a century of contemplation that preceded it. Most Australians today would be unaware of the things that were said against Asians by past leaders.

The most revered prime ministers on both sides of politics believed in White Australia. Labor's wartime leader John Curtin said: 'This country shall remain forever the home of the descendants of those people who came here in peace in order to establish in the South Seas an outpost of the British race.' Even if you accept the context in which he spoke, with Australia at war with Japan in the Pacific, he meant that all Asians, including those on our side, would never be welcome.

Arthur Calwell, the nation's first immigration minister, attempted humour in parliament in 1947 when explaining the case of a Chinese-Australian by the name of Mr Wong, who was wrongly threatened with deportation under Labor's policy to return 15 000 wartime refugees to their homelands. In fact, Mr Wong had been in Australia for twenty years. Addressing the Liberal member for Balaclava, Thomas White, Calwell conceded a mistake had been made, but seemed to suggest that the falsely accused man wasn't half the Australian his political opponent was: 'An error may have been made in his case. The gentleman's name is Mr Wong. There are many Wongs in the Chinese community, but I have to say – and I'm sure that the honourable member for Balaclava will not mind me doing so – that two Wongs do not make a White.'

Robert Menzies defended White Australia for the sixteen consecutive years he served as Liberal prime minister between 1949 and 1966. It left Fraser with a parochial minefield to negotiate, because while the Vietnamese refugees were fleeing communism, to Australians who had grown up under Menzies, all Asians were supposed to be the same.

Fraser was the only openly pro-immigration prime minister to date on the Liberal side. Like Whitlam before him, he explicitly rejected the dogma of White Australia. Unlike Whitlam, he was in power long enough to change the colour of the immigration program, even though the numbers were, in themselves, modest. Barely 40 000 Australians were added to the pool of overseas-born per year over the course of the 1970s – almost half the average annual total of the previous decade. The Netherlands, Italy and Greece each dried up as source nations, with more people leaving Australia or passing away. This made the 1970s intake different on all counts. Smaller in size and non-Europe in make-up, it was the first to look deliberately to our neighbourhood. New Zealand supplied 9000 of the 40 000 per year, Vietnam 4000 and Lebanon 2500.

The Vietnamese and the Lebanese weren't the first groups to flee civil war to make a new home in Australia. But their misfortune was to land in a fracturing nation with a crumbling economy. The labour market couldn't extend the red carpet of full employment that greeted people like my parents in the '50s and '60s. The advice to the Fraser cabinet was that not all the Vietnamese and the Lebanese being received were genuine refugees. Immigration minister Michael Mackellar told cabinet in November 1978: 'Although the people leaving are being recognised by the UNHCR as refugees, there must now be a strong suspicion that the government of

Vietnam is engaging in a form of social engineering leading to a restructuring of its population. People are leaving Vietnam without official and adequate documentation, thus being thrust onto the rest of the world whether that world is ready to take them or not.' This is an early sign of an official suspicion that has endured. The asylum seeker was seen as a less worthy new Australian to the immigrant we had invited through the front door.

The positions of Australia and the US were 'not altogether in harmony', Mackellar conceded. The Americans wanted every person who left Vietnam to be taken in; Australian officials wanted to maintain control of the numbers. 'United States officials are asserting that anybody who opts to leave Vietnam, whether by stealth or by paying their way past officials and on to large boats, must be seen to be a refugee and should be treated accordingly. If Australia unreservedly pursued the sympathetic United States line, we could be giving the green light for a well-organised and large-scale transfer of people to our shores, not against any program of intake we had worked out, but possibly to a timetable and scale devised by another government and businessman.' This is a key insight, because the public position at the time was that Australia and the US were united on the refugee question.

Fraser had taken the side of the South Vietnamese refugees before the boats started coming to Australia. In fact, this had been the first-issue line of attack he launched as opposition leader against the Whitlam government. In April 1975, as Saigon was about to fall to the North Vietnamese, Fraser urged Gough Whitlam to evacuate large numbers of refugees. The Americans quietly cheered Fraser on. While it would be a mistake to view this as evidence of the conspiracy that some Labor people believe played a part in the Dismissal, it does show that Fraser and the Americans shared strategic information with one another.

Ambassador Marshall Green advised Gerald Ford's administration to be wary ahead of Whitlam's visit to the United States on

7–8 May that year. Whitlam would do 'all he can' to use the trip to tell voters back in Australia that the US 'understands' his position on Indochina and 'that we consider Australia's record in dealing with refugee issues to have been better than that of any other friend of the US'.

'Under normal circumstances, there would be no particular disadvantage to us in his being in a position to make such claims, drawing on US statements. However, in the current phase such statements will be more than just resented by opposition parties in Australia. They will undercut opposition's efforts directed at Australia's taking a more constructive role in dealing with Vietnamese refugees, as well as devoting more attention to Australia's security in the face of the Vietnamese debacle.'

Whitlam told President Ford that Australia would take its fair share, which the prime minister defined as half the level that Canada was committed to. But on Whitlam's return home, the Americans sensed there had been some backsliding. Green sent a follow-up note on 8 May, while Whitlam was still in the US, quoting sources in the Department of Foreign Affairs who were 'ashamed of the way the government is behaving'.

On 17 May, Henry Kissinger complained that the 'Australians are wriggling off the hook and we should make maximum effort to get them back on'. Green replied four days later that Whitlam 'regrettably has a "hang-up" about Vietnam, and basically a negative attitude on refugees'. By July, he was advising a US official preparing to visit Australia not to mention the issue at all. 'It would not – repeat not – be useful to discuss Australia's willingness to accept Vietnamese refugees. The Whitlam Government's attitude toward receiving any substantial number is rather negative and any suggestion that . . . [we are] pressing Australia to receive more refugees will incur resentment in Government and press.'

Whitlam had already made his antipathy plain behind closed doors in a meeting with Clyde Cameron, now the immigration

minister, and Don Willesee, the foreign affairs minister, on 21
April – nine days before Saigon fell. '[Willesee] wanted to get a
ruling on the admissibility of certain categories of refugees,' Cameron wrote. 'Whitlam stuck out his jaw and, grinding his teeth,
turned to Willesee and thundered, "I'm not having hundreds of
fucking Vietnamese Balts coming into this country with their
political and religious hatreds against us." I could have hugged
him for putting my own view so well.'

Fraser says: 'I don't really know what drove him because the
decision not to take people from Vietnam seemed so contrary to
the rest of his personality and other things he believed in.'

Graham Freudenberg says that while Cameron was not always
a reliable witness, the quote – even if accurate – was not racially
based. 'I want to discount utterly the idea that Whitlam's attitude
to the refugee question at any time was race-based. It just wasn't.
Even if you put the worst construction on that comment, it's not a
racist statement. It's a political statement about the Balts.'

Migrants in the 1970s tended to divide at the ballot box according to the tyranny or economic hardship from which they had
fled. So while Greeks and Italians could be relied on to vote for
Labor because they had escaped various forms of fascism, the anti-
communists from Croatia and the Baltic states of Estonia, Latvia
and Lithuania were seen as Liberal by the same reasoning. That's
what Whitlam meant by 'Vietnamese Balts'.

Whitlam's obsession, Freudenberg says, was that Vietnam
should not be treated as a pariah in the way that China had been
after the communist revolution in 1949. 'If, as Whitlam was, you
are committed to the idea of restoring Vietnam to the comity in
our region, you are not going to start off by telling a new government in their hour of victory – and whether we liked it or not, it
was a victory – that we're going to save as many as we can from
your dreadful regime.'

There may have been some hyperbole in Fraser's call from

opposition for Whitlam to accept as many as 50 000 refugees. But he meant it.

Yet Freudenberg points out that it was Whitlam, not Fraser, who had brought more Vietnamese to Australia in the first phase. 'I'm not disputing what happened later on, when Fraser, to his great credit, did take a great number, and they are the Vietnamese refugees who make such a great contribution to this county now. The phrase "boatpeople" relates to later years. [But] I don't think it's fair to sort of counterbalance what Fraser was able to do some years later with the situation in 1975. In the two years after the fall of Saigon, our record was better than Malcolm's.'

To look at Australia in the '70s is to see the reverse of twenty-first century attitudes on economic and social policy. We were a closed economy with an open heart back then. After the 11 September 2001 terror attacks on the US, no main-party politician in Australia would risk supporting the arrival of 5000 Afghani or Iraqi refugees, let alone 50 000. Certainly not from opposition, as Fraser had done.

Imagine a prime minister today brushing off the warning that Michael Mackellar issued in May 1979: 'This new situation has all the ingredients for one of the most controversial and divisive issues in Australia's history. A hostile public reaction, stimulated by traditional fears of the "yellow peril" and by concern about present high levels of unemployment, could not only jeopardise Government attempts to resolve the refugee problem but could also cause a head-on collision between domestic public opinion and Australia's foreign policy interests.' If too many boats exposed the 'porousness' of Australia's coastline, voters would demand action. But Mackellar was also mindful of what the neighbours thought. 'As a large, underpopulated, "white" country Australia would be especially vulnerable to international criticism if we failed to respond in a humane manner to the arrival of boat refugees from Asia on Australian territory.'

Mackellar's submission contains a brutal estimate of the number of Vietnamese refugees heading for camps in South-East Asia, and beyond to Australia, after subtracting the number that would drown at sea in the attempt. 'The future numbers of refugees involved could be 750 000 at a conservative estimate – 1 million ethnic Chinese plus a 50 per cent component for ethnic Vietnamese, less a mortality rate of 50 per cent.'

Fraser recalls that the immigration department always wanted a harder policy, but it never got in his way. 'The barriers were miniscule because I had a minister who was cooperative,' he says. 'When there was a submission that said we've got to establish a razor-wire jail in the middle of the desert, that took about thirty seconds of cabinet time to get rid of. Nobody in cabinet opposed the decision.'

He says the Vietnamese community knows it would not have been allowed into Australia if contemporary political attitudes had applied in the 1970s. 'The post-war migration would not have occurred if people played politics with race and religion. We had people who had been through the war, they had experienced the Depression, they knew what a tough life was about, and today's generation of politicians doesn't.'

The Coalition supported the South Vietnamese because Australia had fought with them in that wretched war. 'People were concerned about what was going to happen to them if they stayed behind, what was happening to them as they drowned at sea, because the Malays were shipping them back out to sea. We had to persuade the Malays to have a holding centre. To do that, we had to say that we and others would take huge numbers out of those centres, and the Americans did, the Canadians did and we did. And I think the Australian people received Vietnamese refugees, largely, with enormous generosity. They accepted that there was a moral obligation and there were special circumstances because we'd been fighting with them, and given them some commitments and not been able to fulfil those commitments.'

Australia's Vietnamese-born numbered 41 000, or 0.3 per cent of the population, by 1981. They reached 167 000 (0.9 per cent) by 1996, passing the Greek-born to become our fourth-largest immigrant group behind the British, New Zealanders and Italians. They'd suffer the same unthinking initiation as the Italians, with the Vietnamese 'triads' replacing the Mafia in the media's imagination of the worst thing that ever happened to Australia, while the New Zealanders replaced the Greeks as the ethnic group the tabloid mind associated with 'bludgers'.

But the Vietnamese changed Australia in the way that their European predecessors couldn't because they gave us confidence in our own region. For the first seventy years of federation, Australia assumed that Asians were incompatible with our first-world bloodline. Before the Vietnamese came, we assumed our neighbours wanted to share our living standards but would cling to their culture, form ghettoes and create general mayhem. It was a sentiment politicians would give voice to in the 1980s and '90s, when they misread the protests of minority in the community as a sign that the immigration program had failed. Without bipartisan support, the bar was set that much higher for the Vietnamese than for the Greeks and Italians. They cleared it by the turn of the century as their children repeated the success of the Southern Europeans. By 2002, one of their early critics, John Howard, was ready to pay the Vietnamese, and the Chinese who followed them, the ultimate compliment. He said they had become 'the new Greeks and Italians'.

1979 Iranian revolution, second oil shock. Thatcher becomes British PM. Carter declares war on inflation. Soviet Union invades Afghanistan. **1980** Chinese economic reforms take off. Fraser wins third term, Hawke enters parliament. Third US recession of stagflation era. Reagan elected president. **1981** Underarm incident. US recession breaks inflation. Wages breakout in Australia. **1982** Fraser beats Peacock. Hayden beats Hawke. Dollar falls below parity against greenback for first time. Recession hits. **1983** Hayden surrenders to Hawke, Fraser loses election. Unemployment tops 10%. Drought breaks, recession ends and Australia wins America's Cup. Dollar floated. **1984** Financial deregulation. Medicare introduced. Keating named world's greatest treasurer. Hawke defeats Peacock. **1985** Negative gearing abolished. Tax reform secured, without consumption tax. Howard topples Peacock. **1986**

THE RECONSTRUCTION

World oil price halved. 'Banana republic' crisis. Labor slashes spending. **1987** Joh for Canberra. Budget back in black. Hawke re-elected for Labor-record third term. Negative gearing reintroduced. October stock-market crash. Joh resigns as premier. **1988** Tariff cuts resume. Howard attacks Asian migration. Kirribilli agreement. Housing boom. **1989** Peacock topples Howard. Mortgage rate hits 17%. Tiananmen Square massacre. Berlin Wall falls. **1990** Hawke wins fourth term. Hewson rises. Thatcher resigns. 'Recession we had to have' in synch with US recession. **1991** Final round of tariff cuts. Inflation killed. Hewson releases Fightback! Keating topples Hawke. **1992** Compulsory super. Major secures fourth term for British conservatives. Clinton elected president. **1993** Unemployment reaches 11%. Keating's sweetest victory of all. Enterprise bargaining. Mabo native title legislation. **1994** Downer topples Hewson. Competition policy reform. **1995** Howard topples Downer. Keating signs defence agreement with Suharto. Howard says GST will 'never ever' be Coalition policy.

7

THE SIREN SONG OF
THE QUARRY

Something in the American mind snapped when the second oil shock came with the Iranian revolution in 1979. US president Jimmy Carter slammed his desk, his voice rising to a shout, as he delivered a televised address to the nation designed to jolt his people out of their malaise. 'I want to speak to you first tonight about a subject even more serious than energy or inflation,' he said on 15 July that year.

'The threat is nearly invisible in ordinary ways. It is a crisis of confidence. It is a crisis that strikes at the very heart and soul and spirit of our national will. We can see this crisis in the growing doubt about the meaning of our own lives and in the loss of a unity of purpose for our nation. The erosion of our confidence in the future is threatening to destroy the social and the political fabric of America.'

He sounded like the late Australian actor Peter Finch, who had caught the zeitgeist earlier in the decade in the movie *Network*. Playing the role of TV news anchor Howard Beale, he advised his viewers to open their windows and scream at the street below: 'I'm mad as hell, and I'm not going to take this anymore!'

Americans don't give Carter the same attention in the story of their decline in the 1970s and recovery in the 1980s as Richard Nixon or Ronald Reagan, because his one-term presidency between 1977 and 1980 was the Democrat exception to a two-decade-long Republican lock on the White House. But he happens to be the Western leader who made the first decisive move against inflation, and that sent the domino of deregulation tumbling towards Australia.

On 6 August 1979, Carter appointed Paul Volcker as chairman of the US Federal Reserve with an aggressive brief to kill inflation. Volcker had enough independence in theory, and enough respect from the US political establishment in practice, to keep pushing up interest rates until inflation surrendered. Twice he forced the official rate past 20 per cent, once in 1980 and again in '81, causing a double-dip recession in the US. Volcker reversed the Great Society. He took inflation from a high of 14.6 per cent in early 1980 to 2.5 per cent by mid-1983. Two million jobs were sacrificed, but the US emerged from this painful episode ready to reassert itself as a superpower.

The British also tried to kick their inflation habit in 1979. Margaret Thatcher's Conservatives won the general election in May that year with a mandate to break union power. Thatcher was the first of the economic rationalists in command of a rich nation. Ronald Reagan's defeat of Carter in November 1980 was the second, and Australia, with Malcolm Fraser in office, could tell itself that the conservative planets had aligned. But Fraser was no Thatcher or Reagan. He read the turmoil at the end of the '70s as the dawn of Australia's second Golden Age, paid for by a second mining boom.

In international affairs, 1979 was the decade's darkest year after '73. The West's standover man in Iran, Mohammad Reza Shah Pahlavi, was toppled by a fundamentalist revolution in January, and Iranian students overran the US embassy in Teheran in November that year, taking fifty-two staff hostage. The following month the Soviet Union invaded Afghanistan to suppress its own Islamist insurrection, which created a dilemma for the Americans – would they side with Allah or Marx? The US went with the anti-communist Mujahedeen, who were led by a young Saudi Arabian named Osama bin Laden.

The second oil shock, triggered by the Iranian revolution cutting supply, zigzagged throughout the year and doubled prices by the end of it. But the West reacted differently when compared to the first oil shock, by conserving energy and sourcing more of what it did consume from non-OPEC suppliers. But Australians were oblivious to what this change of behaviour meant for our terms of trade.

Initially, the higher price of oil was seen here as a godsend that would boost the price of all commodities, especially the raw material we had a continent full of – coal. Higher oil prices would also deliver a windfall to the budget through price-based levies on crude oil and liquid petroleum gas. John Howard recorded these two related thoughts in a briefing to cabinet in July 1979, as the second oil shock was underway. 'We should note that not all of the upward influences on prices are without benefit,' he wrote, sounding like a sharp lawyer who had just found his client a favourable loophole. 'Obviously, higher prices for beef and other commodities have greatly assisted our producers and aided the restoration of the balance of payments, and higher oil prices are necessary on conservation grounds. From others – notably the effects on prices of adverse wage and monetary developments – we can take no comfort at all. We should also note that, whatever policies are now pursued, we are almost certain to see a further significant acceleration of prices in the second half of 1979.'

While he had given up on cabinet agreeing to large spending cuts, Howard told his colleagues not to worry because he had an ace up his sleeve – the 'oil revenue windfall'. 'We now have within our grasp the only opportunity we are likely to have for some years to reduce the budget deficit substantially in a relatively painless way.' The key word here is 'painless' – the soft option was the first resort of the Fraser government.

The following year was an election year, and the Coalition's thoughts turned to how to cash in at the ballot box. Treasury had advised that the oil shock would trigger a mining boom in Australia. Without a trace of embarrassment, Fraser revived Rex Connor's grand dream to transform Australia into an energy superpower. He encouraged the states to borrow as much as they liked to build new coal-fired electricity generators in order to capitalise on our new advantage.

The shame here wasn't the conservative double standard but the willingness to believe that a second global energy crisis would end differently to the first; that the anticipated boom here wouldn't be followed by a bust. This was our special brain snap, because we were planning to splurge when the Americans and British were tightening their belts. On 17 March 1980, cabinet met to discuss the outlook and everyone was counting the dollars before they had arrived. Even Howard had caught the fever. 'It is now clear that a major expansion of private-sector investment, particularly in mining and resource development, is in prospect in the 1980s,' he wrote in a joint submission with finance minister Eric Robinson. 'Hard, aggregative data are not readily available, but the Minister for Industry and Commerce [Phillip Lynch] has indicated that at least $16 billion in total is involved in private-sector projects – including non-mining projects presently at or beyond the final feasibility stage. Other sources suggest broadly comparable magnitudes. Even allowing for the spreading of expenditure over a number of years, investment of this order would, assuming it proceeds as planned, be well in excess not only of recent levels but also of that experienced during the mining boom of the late sixties and early seventies.'

The 1980 election caught the Australian delusion. The contest itself between Malcolm Fraser and Bill Hayden reflected the political difficulties of both men. Fraser was beginning to grate with the electorate, and the polls suggested a Labor victory was likely. Hayden was seen as smart, but not strong enough to defeat Fraser. Labor acknowledged the public's reticence by having New South Wales premier Neville Wran and Bob Hawke, who had stepped down from the ACTU presidency to run for federal parliament in the northern Melbourne electorate of Wills, stand alongside Hayden on the campaign trail.

Both leaders fixated on the resources sector in their 1980 campaign launches. Hayden promised to freeze petrol prices for twelve months. Fraser talked up the mining boom: 'In my policy speech of 1977 I said Australia could look forward to $6000 million of development. Some amazement was expressed in this – even disbelief. Because the Labor Party had stopped development dead in its tracks. Yet in the two years after that [policy speech] more than $6000 million was invested in mining and manufacturing. And now, prospective investment is $29 000 million. This development promises to be as important to Australia and individual Australians as anything in the last thirty-five years.'

Fraser's estimate of $29 billion, comprising public and private investment, was almost six times Rex Connor's ambit claim for Arab petrodollars and almost double the $16 billion figure mentioned in cabinet earlier that year. No leader should ever put their name to such sums, even if most Australian leaders to that point had only a passing interest in economics.

The Treasury secretary at the time, John Stone, defends the advice on the mining boom, but not its interpretation. 'There was an element of rationality to the view,' he says. 'After the second oil shock, we had by that time moved to import price parity for our own oil, but more importantly what it did was push up the price of competing energy fuels, in particular coal.' What went wrong, Stone says, was the interpretation: 'as usual, the politicians ran away from rationality', by using the prospect of a mining boom to encourage the community to indulge itself.

The election on 18 October 1980 de-legitimised both Fraser and Hayden. The primary vote swing to Labor of 5.5 per cent was the second highest of the post-war period to that date. After preferences, the Coalition won the popular vote by 50.4 per cent to 49.6 per cent, although this concealed majority votes for Labor in the two biggest states, New South Wales and Victoria. Labor required 25 seats to form government, but won only 13. Seven of those 13 came from Fraser's home state of Victoria, where Labor achieved its first majority of seats since 1929. Hayden was also ignored in his home state, of Queensland, where Labor could only pick up two seats, bringing its total to five out of 19. In the Senate, voters took away the Coalition's majority and handed the balance of power to the Australian Democrats, and Tasmanian independent Brian Harradine, formerly of the Labor Party. At a time when the nation required decisive leadership, the public hedged by weakening the Coalition's control of the parliament.

Every leader overcorrects for the perceived flaw of their predecessor. Malcolm Fraser thought Gough Whitlam gave too much leeway to his ministers. This reinforced Fraser's own predisposition to micro-manage. 'Fraser was a dour talker but a compulsive consulter,' Paul Kelly wrote. 'On the phone to ministers at home, at work, on Friday night, Saturday night, Sunday morning, from anywhere in Australia or the world. Cabinet sat until ministers got sick, got tired and refused to come. [Firstly], Ivor Greenwood died, then Eric Robinson died. Peter Durack had a heart attack, Phillip Lynch became terribly ill; everybody worried about their health, and their wives told most of them to quit politics to escape Fraser.'

Yet all that activity didn't lead to much reform, because Whitlam had got there first on social policy and because Fraser didn't believe in the free-market cause to the same extent as Thatcher and Reagan. Frustration with five busy, but indecisive, years led to the formation of a ginger group of Liberal MPs to promote deregulation. They called themselves 'the Dries', and they used the developments in the US and the UK to argue the case for the winding back of government controls of the economy in Australia. John Howard began flirting with their agenda, but he didn't have the clout to persuade Fraser.

Howard did get the prime minister's support for a review of the financial system. The inquiry chairman, Keith Campbell of the Hooker Corporation, reported back to Howard in 1981 with recommendations to lift controls on both interest rates and the exchange rate. Fraser accepted the first half of the advice only, by allowing the money market to set the interest rates on which the government borrowed to fund the budget deficit. Under the old rules, the government fixed its own interest rates, and every other rate was benchmarked against the government bond. So, with a politician's eye on the domestic lending market, the government often set the price lower than it should have been. It didn't want to hurt home borrowers, or small business, so it was caught in a Catch-22 where the money market wouldn't give it enough to cover the budget deficit. To make up the shortfall, both the Whitlam and Fraser governments literally printed more money, adding to the burden of inflation.

The move to deregulate the interest rates on government securities came in two stages, in 1979 and 1981. This is overlooked, unfairly, by both sides in our economic reform story because it suits Hawke, Keating and Howard to claim that Fraser did nothing at all. The more accurate critique is that he didn't do enough. The recommendation to float the currency was rejected, and Howard didn't push it because his department was also dead against it.

The community, however, was oblivious to the finer points of economic policy. What Australians wanted after the 1980 election was a share of the promised mining bounty. The trade unions pushed for their largest wage increases since the Whitlam years. To back up the claims, industrial disputes exploded in 1981 to the reach their second-highest level on record after 1974. Fraser had urged business to resist, but they wouldn't use the legislation he had provided. 'In the late '70s, industry was doing very well, they didn't adequately see what was coming,' Fraser says. 'And, as they had done historically, under a bit of pressure, they acceded to demands.'

With Bob Hawke now in the parliament, Fraser took on the role of industrial peacemaker. The prime minister never got on with the former ACTU secretary, but Hawke's successor, Cliff Dolan, was more willing to deal. The Transport Workers' Union had walked off the job in the winter of 1981 to press for a $20-a-week pay rise. In Victoria, a state of emergency was declared as the supply of milk ran out. On 22 July, the federal government retaliated on two fronts, standing down striking Telecom workers, and moving to deregister the TWU. Dolan called Fraser and asked for a meeting. They convened a mini summit of ministers, ACTU officials and the president of the Arbitration Commission, Sir John Moore. The employers weren't invited. Fraser and Dolan came to an arrangement that ensured the prime minister wouldn't miss the royal wedding of Prince Charles and Diana Spencer on 29 July. The deal annoyed Sir John, and the employers, and he subsequently ended the indexation system which had held wage rises roughly in line with inflation, because the government and the unions wouldn't play by his rules.

The trade unions were looking for their share of El Dorado. They took Fraser at his word that there was a mining boom under-way, and the prime minister couldn't control the expectations he had unleashed. The critical error Australia made in this period goes beyond the details of the wages blowouts and budget deficits, and the missed opportunities to embrace economic reform. The national mindset from the prime minister down assumed we retained control of our destiny even though the rest of the world was clearly in crisis. There was almost a wilful denial about what the Americans were up to. They were atoning for the stagflation decade in an admittedly selfish but pro-growth way, by forcing down the price of oil. But they had to break the global economy, of which they accounted for a quarter of all production, before they could get their own house in order.

As the experience of the early '70s should have taught us, if America's recessions didn't hurt us the first time, we could be completely sunk by a double-dip. But when we missed Paul Volcker's first recession, in 1980, we once again failed to anticipate the second wave. The government, the ACTU and the media were still counting the IOUs from the non-existent mining boom when the bust came.

Volcker's second recession ran from August 1981 through to November 1982. Australia couldn't resist it, and the hole we were digging for ourselves was far deeper than theirs because our allies hadn't partied as hard as us. Average wages jumped by 13 per cent a year in 1980–81, '81–82 and '82–83. We were the only Anglo nation to allow double-digit pay rises in each of the three critical years that covered Volcker's war on inflation. Thatcher's Britain had one in 1981, and Reagan's America had none.

No one here saw the crash coming. The 1982–83 recession removed the final emotional defence for the old economic model, because it quickly became apparent that no job was safe. The recessions of the early '50s, '60s and mid '70s hurt at the kitchen table through the squeeze of higher interest rates. But they didn't lead to mass retrenchments, so the middle class felt insulated to an extent. Even the Whitlam recession of 1974–75 involved no net job losses, because the 42 000 male jobs that did disappear were offset by an increase of 62 000 in total female employment. Industry protection, for all its faults, provided enough cover then for businesses to hold on to their existing staff. The cost of recession was formally measured in lost production and higher unemployment, which affected new job seekers, not those already employed.

But no amount of tariff or government support could spare the workers this time, because they had demanded, and received, pay rises that broke the viability of their employers. Between January 1982 and April 1983, 229 000 jobs disappeared – 173 000 male positions and 56 000 female positions. Around half the jobs lost were in manufacturing, which was the sector that had been subjected to the largest pay claims. Paul Keating would later tell a metalworkers union chief that they were carrying the guilt of '100 000 dead members' around their necks.

The unemployment rate had been treading water at 6 per cent in January 1982 – where it had been for most of the past six years. By the 1983 election, held fourteen months later on 5 March, it was 9.9 per cent. It peaked at 10.4 per cent in September 1983, the first time the figure had hit double digits since the Great Depression.

This was one half of the crisis. The inflation rate, which usually falls in recession, kept rising because of the wages blowout. In mid 1981 it had been 8.7 per cent; by the September quarter 1982 it peaked at 12.5 per cent and was still 11.1 per cent when unemployment crossed the 10 per cent mark in the June quarter 1983. In the US and the UK, double-digit unemployment in the early '80s was enough to knock inflation out of their respective systems. Australia's inflation problem would linger for the remainder of the decade. To put Fraser's stagflation in another context, he had twice the unemployment rate and only a slightly lower inflation rate than Gough Whitlam had left behind in '75.

Even this dry recitation of fractions conceals the true extent of the assault on the national psyche. Labor's opinion polling at the end of 1982 found the threat of widespread job losses had created a subtle shift in community attitudes: 'It is our judgement that unemployment will be a major vote-switching issue in Australia in 1983, but the issue is really better thought of as involving personal financial security. While the hardline, anti-dole-bludger response appears to be on the decline, there is little evidence to suggest that unemployment is an issue because of sympathy for the person out of work. Rather, unemployment is a growing issue because ordinary suburban middle-class swinging voters are becoming personally more concerned about their own security.'

The onset of recession had destroyed the Whitlam government in the second half of 1974. John Howard didn't want the government to repeat the mistake of throwing money at the economy when it would lead to more inflation. He wanted to maintain the budget line, allowing the deficit to increase in response to the recession, but not add to it by announcing new government spending. John Stone, the Treasury secretary, wanted policy tightened to take the opportunity of recession to kill inflation. Fraser thought both men had underestimated the depths of the recession and began pushing for a classical Keynesian approach, using the government sector to fill the gap left by the private sector.

Fraser had his way, but Stone thought Howard shouldn't present a budget that changed policy course so obviously. He advised Howard to resign, and the treasurer did indeed canvass the option within his inner circle. But even though Howard's relations with both Fraser and Stone were almost irreparably strained, he decided to soldier on. The budget he delivered on 17 August 1982 wasn't all handouts; there was a crackdown on tax avoidance and an increase in sales tax, and on beer and cigarettes. But the revenue measures didn't cover the tax cuts and extra spending he announced. Among the goodies were an increase in family payments and relief for first-homebuyers to shield them from the high interest rates they were paying. Jim Cairns would have been proud.

Howard said the deficit for 1982–83 would be $1.674 billion, or 1 per cent of GDP – a trebling of the previous year's deficit of $549 million. 'The Government is confident that this deficit can be financed in a non-inflationary manner,' he said. He blamed the world recession, but, in a line Kevin Rudd repeated two-and-a-half decades later, argued that Australia had been spared the worst by government action.

'Few predicted the extent of the present world recession,' he said. 'For a period we in Australia were fortunate not to feel its full effects. Our economic policies and relative energy endowments created a more favourable investment climate in Australia than in most other countries. This sustained our economic growth beyond that of others. However, the continued deterioration of economic activity around the world with all its implications for trade and commodity and energy prices ultimately affected our exports. It also dampened enthusiasm for a number of mineral and energy related projects. These adverse international influences were compounded by a significant worsening on the domestic wages front. The need for maximum wage restraint has therefore been much in the government's mind in framing this budget.'

There was a sharp rebuke against Fraser in the budget papers themselves. One of the reasons for the spike in wages, Treasury wrote, 'was an apparent development of exaggerated expectations about the increases in national income that would be generated by the resource investment "boom" and, perhaps even more importantly, the speed with which this additional income would accrue. As a result, wage claims were formulated in anticipation of benefits which had not, in fact, yet begun to flow.' Howard approved the wording of this section.

Fraser says that Bob Hawke should share responsibility for the recession, even though he had entered parliament before wages blew out again, because Hawke had lit the fuse in his final year as ACTU president, in 1979. 'Inflation was coming down to 5 per cent, then we got hit by the second oil shock and two domestic events we weren't able to control adequately. One was the wages push from the ACTU, which involved a very substantial reduction in hours and a very substantial increase in wages [which Hawke had authored]. The other factor beyond our control was the very serious drought in 1981 and 1982.' Hawke says Fraser wasn't interested in cooperation. 'I pleaded with Fraser – let's sit down and work out a rational way of handling these things – but he refused to do it,' he says. Fraser notes that Keating has taken his side in this dispute.

In fact, the quarry had fooled Fraser and Hawke. Mineral wealth and national development for smaller economies have, traditionally, been mutually exclusive concepts. The richer a nation is in dirt, the poorer its people, because the rulers tend to hoard the wealth for themselves. But these judgements are always a matter of degree. The resource curse doesn't apply in the same way in Australia as it does in the OPEC nations or Russia, because we have the benefit of stable democratic institutions. And Australia is not the only Anglo, or part-Anglo, nation that mines for a living. The US and Canada have been doing it for longer. Where the resource curse really hurts Australia is through the short partisan memory of the political cycle. Past experience is never heeded if it belonged to the other side. So Fraser's government didn't bother to consider what it might learn from Labor's mistakes, and he condemned the nation to their repetition.

Politically, Fraser was finished by the recession. He had damaged his credibility by promising a 'fistful of dollars' in 1977, only to renege after the votes had been counted. But the declaration of a mining boom in 1980, before it was assured, gave false comfort to the nation that the rest of the world didn't matter. By 1983, Australians were ready to return Labor to office. But did they want Bill Hayden to be their next prime minister?

8

THE DROVER'S DOG
HAS HIS DAY

Bill Hayden is the forgotten man of Australia's great deregulation adventure. His failure to convince the electorate in his own name distracts from his role in developing the policies that ultimately changed Australia. Without Hayden's badgering in the bleak years of opposition after the Dismissal, Labor would not have been ready to govern when history called it again in 1983.

Hayden had taken the opposition leadership after the 1977 election with a vow to bring Labor to the 'progressive centre'. He disassociated the working man's party from the excesses of the Whitlam years by insisting on policies that were prudent. His big idea was the Prices and Incomes Accord: a formal agreement between a future Labor government and the trade unions to deliver wage restraint in exchange for greater social benefits. The reform drew from the lessons of Britain's so-called 'winter of discontent' in 1978–79, as witnessed by Hayden's touring shadow treasurer Ralph Willis. Their trade unions refused to accept an Accord-style social contract from James Callaghan's Labour government and the breakdown in that relationship helped Margaret Thatcher rise to power.

Hayden was fortunate in one respect that he didn't win the 1980 election, because it is unlikely he could have prevented the deep recession that began two years later. But bad luck stalked him, nonetheless, in the form of the charismatic Bob Hawke, whose entry into parliament in 1980 created a perpetual challenge to his leadership.

Meanwhile, Malcolm Fraser clashed behind the scenes with John Howard and publicly with Andrew Peacock. Fraser goaded Peacock into calling a leadership spill in April 1982, and the prime minister prevailed by a vote of fifty-four to twenty-seven. Hayden's position was more vulnerable. Hawke challenged him in July, and only just lost, forty-two to thirty-seven. It was the only time in the post-war period that Labor and Liberal have conducted leadership ballots in the same year.

Peacock and Hawke appeared, unconsciously, to be the same man: smooth operators who could charm voters through the medium of television. They were channelling a national urge for healing, to close the book on the divisions of the Whitlam and Fraser years. They were also viewed by their respective colleagues as lightweights.

With power already in their hands, the Liberals could easily dismiss Peacock's aspirations because Fraser was, despite his personal unpopularity, a winner. Hawke's claim to the Labor leadership mirrored the argument that Fraser had used against Bill Snedden in 1975: 'Hayden can't beat Fraser, I can.' But Labor MPs were, by predisposition, more idealistic than their Liberal counterparts and took longer to make the switch. Many found Hawke's pragmatism grating. The old guard were worried that he was merely interested in the acquisition and retention of power, not its use to further the Labor agenda. What Labor's left feared was the very thing that made Hawke popular with swinging voters: that he had moved too close to the class enemy of business. Hawke had renounced his socialist self of the '70s, and was preaching cooperation between labour and capital in the new decade.

Fraser professed not to mind who he faced at the next election, which was due to be held by the second half of 1983. But his apprehension was easy to read. He preferred Hayden to Hawke because the opinion polls told him he had a better chance against the existing opposition leader, and he began preparations for a snap poll in the spring of 1982, after the release of the big-spending budget. He was forced to cancel his plans after one of the most spectacular own goals in Australian politics put the problem of tax avoidance back on the front page.

Fraser was stung by a royal commission that he had set up during the previous election to embarrass the Labor Party. The inquiry, headed by Frank Costigan, had been asked to investigate the alleged rorting by the painters and dockers union. But the criminality he uncovered extended well beyond the wharves to the 'bottom of the harbour' schemes of big business. In his first report in December 1981, Costigan warned that the profits being made by the tax avoidance industry were 'comparable only to the heady days of the Victorian gold rush'. The August 1982 report was the third in the series and the political controversy swirled for weeks. Labor's primary target was Howard, who was forced in September to publicly release a telephone book's worth of advice from the tax office that the government had either ignored or taken too long to respond to.

Hayden's personal stocks lifted during the debate, and Fraser, ever the opportunist, adjusted his campaign clock for an election at the end of the year, before Hawke's challenge could gain a second wind. But Fraser's luck had run out. At the end of October, he was rushed to hospital with a bad back. 'I'm fine, thanks,' he told the waiting media pack asking about his health, 'but I'd be much better if you were out of the way.'

The year ended with a by-election that neither Fraser nor Hayden wanted, in the Melbourne bayside seat of Flinders, which was vacated by the retirement due to illness of the former deputy

Liberal leader and treasurer, Phillip Lynch. By-elections are the trial separations of politics; they give voters the chance to tell the government they are leaving, without having to file for divorce. Earlier that year, in March, Labor had taken Billy McMahon's seat of Lowe in Sydney, with a primary vote swing of 7 per cent, and 9.4 per cent after the distribution of preferences. Flinders had a margin of 5.5 per cent, and the expectation was that Labor would win easily. But the locals were not impressed with the gruff Labor candidate, Rogan Ward, or the bickering between Hayden and the ACTU over the final details of the Accord. The Liberal candidate, Peter Reith, held on after limiting the swing against the government to just 2.3 per cent after preferences, less than half what had been required for Labor to take the seat. The result was a shock to both sides and ensured Hayden would face a miserable summer of leadership speculation. This made Fraser even more eager to get back to work and draw up option C for an early election in March 1983.

Hawke's pursuit of the Labor leadership was as ugly as anything he had done in his trade union days. His version of manly strength was not that different to Fraser's: he belittled his opponents when on the winning side of an argument and blamed his allies when he lost. But he had the natural politician's capacity for contrition and reinvention, and he accepted that another challenge would split the party, and damage him, even if he won. So he quietly gathered the extra numbers with a view to persuading Hayden to surrender without a ballot. But Hayden was as stubborn as any man in politics, and was prepared to dig in.

The Hawke camp had targeted Hayden's most trusted confidant, Victorian senator John Button, who had entered parliament at the same election as John Howard in 1974. Button had been on the same side as Hawke in helping Gough Whitlam reform the Victorian Labor Party in 1970, but that's as far as the connection went. Button didn't like Hawke, and he wanted Hayden to contest the election. But after the Flinders by-election, Button reluctantly agreed that Labor's prospects would improve with Hawke as leader and he advised Hayden to stand aside in the new year.

Hayden resisted, and sought to demonstrate his authority by reshuffling the shadow ministry on 14 January 1983. The most significant move was the dumping of Ralph Willis as shadow treasurer for Paul Keating. It was four days before Keating's thirty-ninth birthday.

Button was not convinced that the reshuffle would help. He wrote to Hayden on 28 January, urging him, as a friend, to recon-sider his position: 'You said to me that you could not stand down for a "bastard" like Bob Hawke. In my experience in the Labor Party the fact that someone is a bastard – of one kind or another – has never been a disqualification for leadership of the party. It is a disability from which we all suffer in various degrees. I am personally not one of those who believes that we can necessarily coast into office on the coat-tails of a media performer and winner of popularity polls. On the other hand, I believe Hawke's leader-ship would give us a better chance of success and if the ALP is to be defeated in the next election I would personally prefer it to be under his leadership than yours. That might provoke some really hard thinking about where we are going.'

By 2 February, Hayden had made up his mind to yield to Hawke, in exchange for guarantees that none of his supporters would be demoted and that he would become foreign affairs minister upon victory. The following morning, as speculation of an early election intensified, Hayden decided his resignation should be announced before Fraser went to see the governor-general. Fraser, with the help of a leak within the Labor Party, sensed a move was on and rushed to finalise the paperwork for the election. He assumed, wrongly, that Hayden would fight.

There was some karma in the air that day, 3 February, as Labor appeared to be one step ahead of the man who had outfoxed them

so many times before. Governor-general Sir Ninian Stephen
wasn't ready to approve the election when Fraser called on him
without warning. Fraser had wanted to confirm the election at a
1 p.m. press conference, but he had to wait for Sir Ninian to finish
his lunch with the Polish ambassador, which pushed the prime
minister's media booking to later in the afternoon. Meanwhile,
in Brisbane, where the ALP executive was meeting, Hayden
resigned, although he made it clear he was a reluctant martyr.
He and Hawke faced the press at 1.25 p.m. Hayden said, bluntly:
'I am not convinced that the Labor Party would not win under my
leadership. I believe that a drover's dog could lead the Labor Party
to victory the way the country is and the way opinion polls are
showing up for the Labor Party.'

Hayden was about two years too late to the most significant
jobs of his political career. He should have been Whitlam's treasurer in 1973, not 1975; and he should have replaced Whitlam as
Labor leader after the 1975 defeat, but he baulked at Gough's offer
of succession. While the Liberals might have felt more comfortable facing him than Hawke, they acknowledge that Hayden made
Labor electable again. 'Hayden deserves credit for restoring their
economic credibility,' John Howard says.

The most dramatic day in politics since the Dismissal had one
final twist. Bob Hawke lost his temper when asked that evening
by television interviewer Richard Carleton, 'Do you have blood on
your hands?' The medium that had made Hawke the most recognisable man in Australia caught the flash of raw aggression in his
eyes, and beamed it into the living rooms of swinging voters. At a
campaign meeting later that night, one of Hawke's allies, Victorian state Labor secretary Bob Hogg, told him: 'If you go on like
that, you can kiss your arse goodbye.'

But voters were willing to excuse the brief reversion to the old,
ACTU-style Hawke, because they wanted to be rid of Fraser. The
prime minister, combative to the last, warned that people would

have to hide their money if Hawke took over: 'Under Labor it'd be safer under your bed than it would be in the banks. They would be robbing the savings of the people to pay for their mad and extravagant promises.' Hawke, not the world's funniest man, had the nation in stitches when he replied: 'They can't put them there because that's where the Commies are.'

Hawke had no time to develop his own policies, and the same could be said of Keating, who had been shadow treasurer only two-and-a-half weeks longer than Hawke had been leader. It would be Hayden's agenda they would be selling. The reforming duo of Hawke and Keating were, in fact, the accidental creation of Hayden.

The campaign launch speech was remarkable for its Keynesian orthodoxy. Hawke offered new spending to create jobs, a re-commitment to centralised wage-fixing, tax cuts, pension and dole increases, and cheaper petrol. There were two notable promises *not* to do things – there would be no capital gains tax, which was the issue that had caused Labor trouble at the previous election, and no reduction of protection for industry until the economic crisis was overcome. The most significant policy commitment was the reintroduction of Hayden's universal healthcare plan from 1975 – renamed Medicare.

The emphasis of the launch speech was reconciliation, the third 'R' that Hawke had personally added to Hayden's intended slogans of reconstruction and recovery. 'What we have to do is break out of the vicious cycle of confrontation imposed by seven long years of the Fraser government,' Hawke said. 'That will involve significant new expenditure, significant new investment from both the public and private sectors.' The Prices and Income Accord between Labor and the trade unions would ensure the recovery 'does not simply disappear in a new round of inflation'. But he was also interested in taking business with him. Hawke would convene a national eco-nomic summit of employers, unions and state governments to be held 'immediately on assuming office'.

Hawke's ambition for reconciliation raised the nation's hopes in the 1980s, just as his ambition to win workers the fattest pay packet possible had caught its flaws in the 1970s. This is not to discount his success as a politician, but to remember that he changed his persona with the times.

The last Australian Gallup Poll taken with Hayden as leader, in December 1982, had Labor's primary vote at 49.2 per cent, the Coalition at 43.9 per cent and the Australian Democrats on 6.1 per cent. The election result was Labor, 49.5 per cent; the Coalition, 43.6 per cent; and the Australian Democrats, 5 per cent. So the drover's dog would have won. Hawke guaranteed a handsome victory for Labor, but he didn't increase the margin so much as secure it.

There would be no question of legitimacy as there had been for Gough Whitlam, when the Liberals quibbled with the size of the win. Labor's vote after preferences was 53.2 per cent, the party's greatest winning margin in any post-war election. Every state and territory apart from Tasmania delivered a majority of Labor members. Six seats were picked up in Victoria (including Flinders), five each in New South Wales, Queensland and Western Australia, and one apiece in South Australia and the Northern Territory, for a total gain of 23. Labor finished with 75 seats out of 125, its largest share of the parliament since 1943. It even had one more senator than the Coalition, something that had not happened since the losing election of 1949.

Hindsight tells Fraser that he would have lost the election to Hayden anyway. 'The circumstances of the recession in March of '83 would have given Labor a victory [whoever was leader],' he says. His great regret is that he didn't wait to test Hawke on the floor of the house. 'If you went through to the following November or December, which in many ways become traditional months for elections, the drought was broken, rural industries looking a lot better, and there wasn't as much gloom around. I made a lousy decision and I shouldn't run away from it. But I really don't believe that Bob Hawke was one of the great parliamentary performers – and six or eight months in parliament, who knows? It mightn't have made any difference, it might have made some difference.'

To return to power so quickly after the heavy defeats of 1975 and '77 was remarkable. Labor's history to that date had been of short, controversial periods in government followed by long, acrimonious spells in opposition. The timing of Hawke's victory jarred with the conservative cycles in the US and the UK, where Ronald Reagan and Margaret Thatcher were on course for landslide re-elections. Just as we had rejected the radical spirit of the '60s by sticking with conservative governments, it seemed we wanted to greet the decade of economic rationalism from the centre-left.

The shock of election night, 5 March 1983, was in the reaction, not the result. Malcolm Fraser's patrician facade cracked as tears welled in his eyes, and the most pitiless politician of his generation revealed himself to be a sensitive man. Later, in retirement, he came to fascinate his former enemies and appal his former colleagues by embracing left-wing causes. He railed against deregulation, criticised American foreign policy and campaigned for a republic. He became best friends with Gough Whitlam. Where was this bleeding heart in government? Fraser claims it was there all along. 'During the Cold War, I was still against apartheid . . . all those things that appeared contrary to their perception of me as the Cold War warrior,' he says. Fraser used his time in office to change the colour of the nation's immigration program by accepting tens of thousands of Vietnamese refugees ahead of public opinion. With this, he filled in the missing chapter in the Whitlam social reform program. But history marks Fraser harshly for failing to connect his rhetoric of self-reliance with economic reform.

In his defence, Fraser says he faced a Treasury department

that resisted deregulation. 'It would have been a very brave, and possibly a very foolish, government that floated the dollar when both Treasury and Reserve Bank were against . . . They [Treasury] would come after you, I've got no doubt of that. There were occasions when I could see reflected in [newspaper] editorials Treasury thinking [which we had earlier rebuffed in private].'

Bob Hawke offers no substantive praise for Fraser's seven-and-a-half years in office. 'All Fraser's good things have been said and done since he finished as prime minister,' he laughs. 'But seriously, it's very difficult, objectively speaking, to think of anything. The one thing I will say for Fraser, he has always been impeccable on the question of race.'

Paul Keating is more generous: 'The great pity of Malcolm Fraser was the Dismissal de-legitimised his government. But that said, he did not fall into these phoney distinctions between the civic and the human community. Malcolm Fraser had the clarity of mind to recognise the human community beyond Australia with his Vietnamese refugee program, and within Australia with his general embrace of the notion of multiculturalism.'

John Howard praises Fraser for the tone, but not the content, of his message of restraint. 'There was a sense of disorder and economic chaos and government chaos when he came to power, and I think he restored a degree of order,' Howard says. 'His attitudes on economics were helpful in getting the rate of growth in government spending under control.' But Fraser made the mistake of trying to recreate the Golden Age based on a model that had lost its viability. 'He basically believed that what had worked in the 1950s and '60s would continue to work in the '70s. That was an understandable mindset because he was a child of that period.'

The Fraser years were not entirely wasted on the nation, but they do represent a large chunk of one of the darkest periods of our post-war era. Australia engaged in a decade-long tantrum from the first oil shock in October 1973 through to the global recession of

1982–83. Fraser's was the dominant voice for almost eight of those
ten years. Whitlam's achievements, and disasters, may be the more
interesting, but Fraser's example is the cautionary tale for Australia in the twenty-first century. His divisiveness in opposition,
and his inability to inspire the community in government, can
be sourced to the way he played his politics. He mistook aggression for strength, and activity for progress. The bleeding heart he
exposed in retirement may just be the remorse of a man who knew
he had almost taken Australia to where it should never go – down
the American road of entrenched partisanship.

The final word belongs to the hard numbers of Australia's
economic decline. When Whitlam took office, the unemployment rate was less than 3 per cent and manufacturing accounted
for almost one in four of all jobs in the economy (23.5 per cent).
When Fraser left office at the other end of the stagflation decade,
unemployment was in double digits, and manufacturing's share of
the workforce had collapsed to less than 18 per cent, with more
than 200 000 jobs disappearing in that ten-year period. It was an
experience most Western nations could relate to. The US shed
1.1 million manufacturing jobs, Germany 1.5 million and the UK
2.3 million. Adjusting for the size of each workforce, Australia's
blue-collar workers lost one in six manufacturing jobs (16.6 per
cent). Only the Netherlands (16.9 per cent) and the UK (29 per
cent) fared worse.

Fortunately for us, the international economics profession was
more concerned with the British and Dutch diseases at the time.
If they had bothered looking below the equator, they would have
diagnosed the Australian disease as the most virulent of all, with
an element of both strains – the resource curse of the Dutch and
the trade union curse of the British.

This is the backdrop to Australia's most remarkable transformation in peacetime. The collective policy failure of the Whitlam and
Fraser era forged a consensus for deregulation. The big-spending,

high-protection, high-inflation 1970s had exhausted the old economic model. Labor was chastened by the legacy of Whitlam, but empowered by the failure of Fraser. The Liberals, urged on most notably by Howard in opposition, wanted to make amends for leaving the nation in worse shape than they had found it.

9

LEARNING TO LET GO

The Australia of the early 1980s resembled the typical Greek or Italian immigrant household of its day. The children were impatient to leave home, but the parents didn't trust them in the outside world. They worried the boys would get into fights and the girls would lose their innocence, bringing disgrace to the family name. So they tried to hang on to their darlings well beyond their teens, risking dependency's trap in which the children turn into soft and greedy adults.

The basic human instinct to shield a child is heightened in an unfamiliar country. The parent can never truly know the culture so they can't tell if their children are fitting in. As a predominantly white settlement in Asia, Australia has always felt out of place in the world, even though it is itself an immigrant nation. Our fear of other countries, but not their people, created a choke in our character. While we insisted that our new citizens adapt, we reserved the right to protect ourselves from the region, and from international markets, because we didn't trust either to look after our young nation. The edifice of state paternalism – exchange rate controls, tariffs, centralised wage fixation, government ownership of business, and subsidies to close the gap in living standards between city and bush – was the loving, but twisted logic of the clingy immigrant parent.

There have been only two Australian leaders who ran the nation against the grain of its sheltered history, as pro-immigration and pro-market. Bob Hawke was the first. Paul Keating was the second. They didn't start public life so open-minded. The old Hawke of the ACTU days was an avowed socialist who wanted to increase the share of national income that went to wages, at the expense of profits. He also opposed Malcolm Fraser's generosity to the Vietnamese refugees. 'Any sovereign country has the right to determine how it will exercise its compassion and how it will increase its population,' Hawke had said during the 1977 election, as he urged Fraser to turn back a Vietnamese refugee boat heading for Darwin. The young Keating who entered parliament at the 1969 election thought Australia would be able to reduce its immigration intake if it paid local families to have more children. 'We could have a system of subsidies paid to families on a sliding scale according to the number of children they have. For example, on the birth of a fourth child $1000 might be deducted from the mortgage on a home; $1500 on the birth of a fifth child. These figures may sound high but they are not when we compare them with the cost of bringing migrants to this country. After all, the best migrant is the infant Australian.'

Hawke and Keating became prime minister and treasurer when Australia could no longer pretend to have complete control over its destiny. They were given a sharp reminder on taking office that the old protection model was broken beyond repair. Foreign investors had been pulling their money out of the economy in the month before the election, relieving themselves of the Australian dollars they thought were too expensive. It was the market's way of testing the economic policies of Labor – the same thing had happened to newly elected centre-left governments in France and

Sweden. Under the exchange controls of the time, the currency was traded through the Reserve Bank, and if someone was selling out of the dollar, they would do so by swapping it for foreign currency held by the Reserve Bank. They were betting that the new Labor regime would have to devalue the dollar to bring the money back onshore. The market couldn't lose because in the event of devaluation it could buy back the cheaper dollar with the foreign currency it had only just taken from the Reserve Bank, and pocket the difference. On the first working day after the 1983 election, Monday 7 March, funds continued to flow out of Australia. This was, in effect, a form of standover behaviour – accept our price for the dollar and we won't ransack your shop. It was also an early taste of the gathering power of globalisation to bend nation states to the will of the market.

On Tuesday, Hawke announced a 10 per cent reduction in the value of the dollar, from US94.15 cents to US85.49 cents. The prime minister-elect said the alternative was to let interest rates soar to bring back the foreign investment dollars by a more disruptive route to the real economy. But he stressed that the dollar would not suffer further abrupt changes. 'I wish to make these points clear. The decision to vary by a single, discrete change of 10 per cent is a decision forced on the government by the unique circumstances of the past fortnight. It is not intended to signal any change in government policy in regard to the setting of the Australian exchange rate. The present exchange rate management regime which has operated since 1977 will continue . . . [and] all subsequent movements in the exchange rate will follow the gradualist approach previously in force.'

That first press conference, with a nervous treasurer-elect sitting at his side, was remarkable for another reason. On the Sunday after the election, Treasury secretary John Stone advised Hawke and Keating that John Howard had left them with a world-beating budget deficit: 'The magnitude of the fiscal imbalance is unprecedented in Australia during peacetime, as is the level of government spending. The budget balance is projected to deteriorate from near zero to more than 6 per cent of GDP in a two-year period. The speed and magnitude of that deterioration is almost without precedent among the major OECD countries in the postwar period.'

The Fraser government's pre-election budget had already created a deficit of $4.5 billion for 1982–83, almost three times higher than originally forecasted. The slippage was due to the recession being deeper than expected, and to over-runs in Coalition spending. Howard had told voters that the deficit for the coming financial year, 1983–84, would be in the order of $6 billion. Stone advised him late in the campaign that it would be more like $9.6 billion. This information should have been released to the public, but Howard chose to stick to his own earlier estimate. As amusing as this revelation was for Hawke, because it meant the Fraser government had been as irresponsible as the Whitlam government, it made Labor's own campaign commitments suddenly unaffordable. Treasury had costed the Hawke agenda at $1.8 billion – $300 million above his own estimate. This would inflate Howard's parting deficit of $9.6 billion 'to almost $12 billion' in 1983–84, Treasury said.

Hawke told the assembled journalists that when he made his commitments to the Australian people, he had assumed the deficit would start at $6 billion, to which his policies would add another $1.5 billion. 'We've been thinking in the order of figures which are consistent with $7.5 billion and perhaps a little bit upward,' he said. To deliver those promises now, when the deficit was higher than he had been told, would be irresponsible. With that, he placed promises on hold, pending a review. Only Medicare would survive the subsequent cull without a scratch because it was the quid pro quo for the Accord.

On entering the treasurer's office in the old parliament house for the first time, Paul Keating found the room empty but for one symbolic reminder of its former occupant, John Howard. Keating describes the scene: 'All that was left were decks of foolscap paper, pencil sharpeners, style manuals. Sitting on one shelf which, I remember, was made of chipboard, was a copy of the Campbell Report, and its cover had faded in the sunlight to the point you could hardly read it. And I said to [adviser] Barry [Hughes], "Isn't that prophetic?" It had disappeared; it was just a thing of neglect.'

Keating wanted to revive the Campbell Report on financial deregulation, and was privately urged on to do so by Howard. But Labor had rejected its recommendations in opposition, most notably to float the dollar and allow the entry of foreign banks into the local market. To get around this ideological roadblock, the new treasurer appointed Vic Martin of the Mutual Life and Citizens Assurance Company to look again at the financial system in May. Keating expected – in fact, wanted – Martin to reaffirm Campbell. His colleagues would have declared war on him if he had told them what he was thinking at the start of the process.

Keating believed the old system was finished and the dollar should be taken out of the government's hands and left to the market. He was being encouraged down the deregulation path by the Reserve Bank governor, Bob Johnston. But Keating also had an insistent voice in his other ear, saying 'Don't do it'. Treasury secretary John Stone was adamant that a float wasn't in the national interest because Australia was too small to handle the volatility of the foreign exchange markets. 'There were mad tides of money swamping across the world,' Stone says of the stagflation decade. Treasury wanted to insulate the economy from the worst of these effects, he explains, and this advice had been consistent in the twelve years since the end of the Bretton Woods Agreement. Stone thought Treasury could set a fairer price for the dollar than the panicky market; in essence, he thought Treasury knew more than the market, and the market would eventually yield to its judgement.

Around the same time that Keating set up the Martin committee, Bob Hawke was being encouraged by his economic adviser, Professor Ross Garnaut, to float the dollar. Stone, Hawke and Garnaut were, coincidentally, all old boys of the selective co-ed public high school Perth Modern School.

The Hawke–Keating strategy to promote economic recovery relied on the Accord to secure wage restraint and a lower dollar to help Australian industry become more competitive. That assumed the dollar, once devalued, would stay down. But the speculators were driving the price back up. By September, the dollar had crept back towards US90 cents.

The new Labor government was learning on the job about Australia's vulnerability to the mood swings of globalisation. The Coalition, in accepting only half of the Campbell Report, had left behind a leaky system which increased the volatility in the real economy because interest rates – the price people felt in their daily lives – were being tugged this way then that, in order to fix another price that they were exposed to only when they travelled overseas, namely the dollar. 'Much of the volatility in interest rates springs from the fact that while domestic financial markets are now virtually deregulated and very flexible, the exchange rate is relatively inflexible. Variability is therefore thrust onto the domestic money supply and interest rates,' the governor of the Reserve Bank, Bob Johnston, wrote to Keating on 20 September.

It was counterintuitive, but Garnaut and Johnston reasoned that a free float of the dollar would reduce the volatility. It would also take the government, and thus the taxpayer, out of the transaction. Stone advised Keating to maintain control. 'We would support the Reserve Bank to the extent of agreeing that some change in the system is warranted,' the Treasury boss wrote to Keating on 16 October. 'But we believe that change in this area should be undertaken in stages. A complete and wholesale leap to a full market system overnight would be an act of faith to which the Government has no need to commit itself at this time and the consequences of which cannot clearly be foreseen.'

Through Garnaut, Hawke had a clear intellectual path to the float. Keating, on the other hand, had to deal with Stone, and he says this important detail is overlooked by those in the Hawke camp who say the prime minister had to drag a reluctant treasurer to the reform finish line. Keating offers new evidence that he wasn't a late convert.

'The Treasury lived in fear – particularly after Hawke had presided over two wages explosions, notwithstanding the economic summit and his preparedness to see the wage share adjusted down – they were waiting for, let's call it, the reminiscences of the '72–75 Whitlam government,' Keating recalls. 'John Stone was the economic face of Australia to the developed world, for good or for bad, so therefore the idea that Stone could be managed in a cavalier way by economic amateurs in the prime minister's office, and my own I might say, was of course nonsense.'

Keating says Garnaut misrepresented their respective roles in an interview he gave for Blanche d'Alpuget's second Hawke biography. The argument goes to timing: Garnaut said that Keating had to be convinced by Hawke to support the float, while Keating replies that it was the other way around, that he convinced Hawke.

'It is completely true to say that from April–May 1983 I had decided that we had to move [to a float],' Keating says. ' [It] is worth recording for history's sake, the first time Bob Hawke ever heard about a floating exchange rate after the election, was me saying so to him about April–May of 1983, and telling him that I had discussed this at length with the Reserve Bank and its governor, Bob Johnston.'

Johnston had developed a 'war book' early in the year to prepare for the float, which supports Keating's view of events that he was at least reform co-captain along with Hawke. The question is whether Keating blinked along the way. He says this is simply not true. 'Ross Garnaut is a way better self-promoter than he is an economist. His distortion of events leading up to the float was all about the aggrandisement of his own role as much as it was even of Hawke's. They go mainly to the end moments of the year-long odyssey towards the float, picking the right moment for it to happen. But that pick had to be my pick because I was the one, in the end, charged with doing it, succeeding in it and selling it,' Keating says. 'In the event it failed, I would have been executed . . . I would have been out of public life; they would have massacred me. And I had essentially a secretary to the Treasury who was vehemently opposed, and his senior deputies, too, also opposed. Even though the younger members of the executive group were in favour of it, and on my side – I'm talking here about Ted Evans, David Morgan and the older Bob Whitelaw – they were not running the department. There was never a time in 1983 after about April that Bob Hawke and I were not floating the Australian dollar. The rest of it was simply picking the moment.'

Hawke says of Keating, simply: 'In terms of his treasuryship, he was a good treasurer. It took him some time, but he did pick up and he became a very good treasurer.' But he dismisses as laughable Keating's assertion that it was the treasurer who educated the prime minister about a floating exchange rate, and adds that Keating's comments against Garnaut are 'ridiculous' and that the float was a 'tender' topic for his former colleague. 'I have always been generous with him about the important part he played in the reform process. But it was just the fact that on this particular one he was behind the eight ball.'

Stone says he is inclined to believe Hawke and Garnaut over Keating. 'My own hunch is that Hawke, with Garnaut, was more responsible for the move.' Garnaut told d'Alpuget that Keating 'wasn't against [the float] per se, but he was still pretty dependent on Treasury thought that first year, so he let Stone carry most of the argument'.

It shouldn't really matter who was first – Keating or Hawke – because both were pulling in the same direction when it was time to act. Keating's hesitancy was understandable because Stone was firmly in the 'no' camp, and the new treasurer had seen what a department scorned had done to de-legitimise the Whitlam government over the loans affair, and the Fraser government over the budget deficit.

What isn't contested is that by late 1983, the government wanted to float the dollar, but Stone remained opposed. Keating, frustrated with Stone's position, began seeking out alternative advice from within the department. One such discussion can be revealed in detail for the first time.

On 23 October, a Sunday, Keating rang Ted Evans, a first assistant secretary at Treasury, who would later head the department under the Howard government. Keating told him that the option of floating the dollar had been discussed at a meeting of officials of Treasury and the Reserve Bank earlier in the week. He asked Evans for his opinion. Evans said it was not his business, but from an economic policy viewpoint, 'there now appeared to be clear advantages in a float'.

'There was, however, an important issue as to how one approached a float and there could be advantages in doing so in an evolutionary manner,' Evans cautioned.

Keating said he wanted to talk to Stone and his senior officers later that day. Keating then got in touch with Stone, who was unaware of the conversation with Evans. No slight was intended, because Evans told Stone about it later. But Stone felt that Keating had gone behind his back.

At the evening meeting on 23 October, Keating asked the officers, one by one, for their view. Evans recorded that Keating 'was inclined to float'. Evans wanted to know what role the government would play once the dollar was floated – would it direct the Reserve Bank to step in to support it when it was in trouble? Evans thought there would be 'little gain in a float' if the government maintained control through other means. Keating didn't answer, so Evans gave his support for an evolutionary float, adding his name to the list of other officers in favour.

On 28 October, Hawke announced the first baby step. The so-called forward rate would be floated, leaving the spot rate fixed. Historically, the Reserve Bank effectively fixed two prices for the dollar each trading day – the forward rate when the market opened and the spot rate when the market closed. Hawke and Keating were allowing the market to set the price throughout the day, but retaining the power of the Reserve Bank to reset the dollar at the close of the day's trading. Hawke made the announcement, and deliberately played down its implications so as not to spook the market. 'These changes, though largely technical, should assist in moderating the volatility of day-to-day flows of funds across the foreign exchanges,' he said.

Stone detected, correctly, that this baby step would quickly lead to the leap of faith of full deregulation, and he continued to urge caution. More money poured into Australia throughout November, in part because economic activity was picking up after the recession. The first week of December settled the debate. On the evening of 8 December, a call came to the Reserve Bank from its New York office that another large sum was coming Australia's way, bringing the total capital inflow for the month so far to around $1.5 billion. Melbourne businessman John Elliott was responsible for $900 million of this amount because he needed the overseas funds for his pursuit of the brewer Carlton United.

Later that evening, Hawke and Keating agreed to a full float, with back-up controls on the amount of currency that could be traded. Keating rang Johnston at 1.30 a.m. to advise him to close the foreign exchange market that morning, a Friday.

Johnston and two senior Reserve Bank officers flew to Canberra carrying the 'war book' in a black plastic folder. They joined the secretaries from the prime minister's department and Treasury for a meeting with Hawke and Keating in Hawke's office at 10 a.m. It was to be Stone's last stand. He told everyone in the room that the floating of the dollar reminded him of the Whitlam government's 25 per cent cut in tariffs ten years earlier, which had been done without Treasury's support and without any serious paperwork on the implications of the move. Floating the dollar and removing capital controls would have a greater political impact than the tariff cut, he added. Johnston replied that the old system was broken anyway. In his biography of Keating, John Edwards records that Johnston had let Stone handle that month's crisis because he no longer wanted the responsibility for a model that didn't work. 'For the last nine days we have made asses of ourselves,' Johnston said. Edwards wrote: '[Johnston argued] that under present arrangements the Reserve Bank could not effectively carry out monetary policy. He said interest rates had been pushed lower to deter capital inflow, but they were unsustainably low.'

Keating took his own notes at the meeting. He records Stone as saying: 'The problem for the government if we move to some kind of float is what it does for other things. A 5 per cent depreciation is looking like a 20 per cent tariff cut – a major shock injected into the system . . . If we are going to give the economy a shock I would rather give it to the financial sector than the productive sector. I'd be surprised if we didn't end up at 95 cents. Markets don't work very well in foreign exchange – they overshoot.'

Paul Keating, not Bob Hawke, delivered the historic announcement to float the dollar. John Stone did not appear at the press conference, but Bob Johnston did, marking a subtle shift in institutional power from the Canberra-based Treasury to the Sydney-based

Reserve Bank. Keating's words that afternoon, 9 December, were almost a little too routine, as if the gravity of what the government had decided had not quite sunk in. He said the changes made on 28 October to float the forward rate were designed 'to give the banks and other market participants' time to adjust. 'The government has now decided to take these changes significantly further by allowing the spot market, as well as the forward market, to float. The government has also decided to abolish a major part of the existing exchange controls.' He said the 'speculators would now be speculating against themselves, rather than against the Australian government' because the Reserve Bank would no longer be fixing the price of the dollar at the end of the day.

It was a technician's introduction to a brave new world, with none of the vivid imagery that Keating become famous for later in the decade. The Reserve Bank officials flew back to Sydney that night to prepare for the future. John Howard was on the same flight and complimented them on their day's work. 'I ran into Bob Johnston and Don Sanders. I congratulated them, I said it was terrific,' Howard says. 'My understanding is it was Johnston and Hawke who were responsible for the float. Keating was apprehensive.'

On the first day of the new order, Monday, 12 December, the dollar finished at US91.75 cents, and was below US90 cents by the end of the week. The float itself was an anticlimax because there was no run on the dollar, exactly as Labor had predicted, and hoped.

The public reaction to the float was initially muted because the dollar didn't seem to do anything unusual in the free market. The float gave an immediate boast to the confidence of the government, and in particular to Keating. He had held his own in a debate with the most formidable bureaucrat in the nation. The relationship between Hawke and Keating bloomed as a result. The prime minister realised that the treasurer could be trusted with big reforms. Most importantly for the government, the float had removed any residual doubts from the Whitlam years about Labor's ability to manage the economy.

Stone has come to view the decision as brilliant, despite his earlier opposition. He says the float was 'the most important economic decision in the post-war period and probably the best'. Malcolm Fraser wishes he had seen past Treasury intransigence and allowed it to happen on his watch.

The world had forced the government's hand in so much as the decision was taken at a time of crisis. But there is no denying that Hawke and Keating were on top of their briefs, and were leading, rather than being led. The ego detail of who converted first to the cause doesn't diminish either man's achievement. This reform required a gut call, and new governments have been better at making decisions on this scale than older governments, which are burdened by the inertia of incumbency and a fear of the electorate that increases with each escape at the ballot box.

The float marked the birth of a new type of Australia. The nation that had shielded itself from the world for eight decades was now prepared to make its own luck with a reform program more daring than most others. This is why so many people want to claim paternity for the float – because they know it began the transformation that led, eventually, to Australia being the last rich nation standing as the global financial crisis mushroomed into the Great Recession in the twenty-first century.

IO

A LICENCE TO REFORM

The choice moment in the economic cycle to take power is just before a V-shaped recovery, when the retrenched are about to be re-employed. Most recoveries don't fit the V-shape ideal, because businesses are reluctant to take on any new staff until they are certain the economy is out of danger. While they hesitate to rehire, the unemployment rate can continue to creep up for a year or more after the recession has ended. This is referred to, disparagingly, as a jobless recovery and can be a honeymoon killer for a new leader.

The Australian habit of changing governments, whether consciously or otherwise, on the eve of an external shock makes a V-shape recovery nigh-on impossible. Robert Menzies was hit with a wool boom within a year of taking office, Gough Whitlam had the oil shock, and Malcolm Fraser arrived in the middle of stagflation. For Bob Hawke, an early setback seemed part of the employment contract.

But Hawke had luck that no prime minister before or since has come close to replicating. His was the only government in Australian history to be greeted by a V-shaped recovery. One of the easiest-to-forget elements of the Hawke–Keating reform partnership is the benign international environment in the first phase of their project. Australia itself was in crisis, but the global economy was in rare good health. The crucial element of this good fortune was the United States. The American recession had ended in December 1982, with the loss of 2 million jobs in twenty months. In the first twelve months of the recovery, 4 million jobs were created. By the year to May 1984, annual jobs growth had reached an unheard of 5.5 million.

The US was surging without the handicap of inflation for the first time since the '50s, and Japan was also recovering strongly. Australia couldn't really lose in this favourable setting. Our gross domestic product recorded its fastest turnaround in history, from a contraction of 3.4 per cent in the first twelve months to the June quarter 1983 – Fraser's final year – to an eye-popping increase of 7.8 per cent in the twelve months to the June quarter 1984, the first year Hawke could claim as his own. Australian businesses had, in fact, resumed hiring in the June quarter 1983, before the recession had officially ended. It took just took fourteen months, to May 1984, to recover all the 230 000 jobs that had been lost in recession.

By 1984, Hawke was easily the most admired man in the nation, nominated by 31 per cent of voters, followed by marathon runner Robert de Castella (7 per cent) and Queensland premier Joh Bjelke-Petersen (4.8). The Australian Gallup Poll taken in February that year also found Hazel Hawke was the third most admired woman (6.4 per cent) behind journalist Ita Buttrose (11.6), and singer Olivia Newton-John (7.8). In March, Hawke's job approval rating had reached 80 per cent.

For Australians to hero-worship someone other than a sportsman contains a riddle. Was it Hawke that we really loved? Or was it relief that the drought had broken, the economy was recovering and we finally had a grown-up government in charge after the Whitlam–Fraser decade? The answer can be found in who our most admired overseas personalities were. Margaret Thatcher was first pick (19.8 per cent), followed by the Queen (12.3) and Ronald Reagan (7). Politicians were the new black in the 1980s: their popularity reflected a rise in national confidence across the developed world. The music charts were dominated by flag-waving songs. Men at Work's 'Down Under', a cheeky, catchy song which rhymed 'language' with 'vegemite sandwich', became a global anthem for Australia, reaching number one simultaneously in the US and the UK in 1983. By 1985, the rest of the world was cheering the stars and stripes, as Bruce Springsteen's 'Born in the USA', originally written as a protest song, was inverted into a celebratory chant by giddy audiences in Australia, Japan, the UK and Europe.

Hawke's numbers, while unusual by Australian standards, were not unique to the times. In the US, Reagan's approval rating had soared over the course of 1983, from a low of 35 per cent in January to 54 per cent by December. In Britain, Thatcher had a similar experience, although her sharp rise in popularity was aided by the Falklands War. Her satisfaction rating had bottomed at 25 per cent in December 1981. Six months later, after the Argentinian surrender, it had doubled to 59, and was still at 54 per cent a year on, in June '83.

Hawke's popularity, and the recovery that reinforced it, provided Labor with its economic reform alibi. It allowed the party of the working man to become the party of the market, and align Australia to the spirit of the 1980s. Hawke could adapt the Reagan and Thatcher agenda for local tastes because he had crossover appeal to Liberal voters. But this didn't mean Hawke switched rich people into Labor voters. The electoral majority Hawke relied on was the one Gough Whitlam had initially seized in the mortgage belts of Melbourne and Sydney – the Robert Menzies middle class. Deregulation didn't offend these voters, so long as they had well-paying jobs and access to decent public services. It was the promise of the reforms meshing with the good vibes of a V-shaped recovery that allowed Labor to go as far as it did down the road of deregulation, from the float to banking reform in the opening phase, to the removal of tariffs in the second phase and finally to the abolition of centralised wage-fixing in the third. The irony is that it was the old economic model that delivered the first flush of growth in 1983–84. But the limitations of that structure were soon apparent because the problem of inflation returned. By the middle of the decade the consumer price index was back above 8 per cent.

Paul Keating harboured a well-informed grudge against Australia's sheltered banking system dating back to his formative years in parliament in the '70s. In September 1977, as Labor's shadow minister for national resources and overseas trade, Keating complained that Australian mining companies were being starved of finance by the local banks, forcing them to 'sell off their equity to foreign corporations to get adequate capital to develop . . . this young nation's massive mineral endowment'. He suggested, radically for those times, that 'perhaps the answer to this problem is the opening up of the banking licences in Australia to world banking competition, so that some of the smug executives in Australian banks will have to get out and compete instead of having their business given to them on a plate by the provisions of the Banking Act'.

Douglas W. Stride, the managing director of the nation's fifth-largest bank, the Commercial Bank of Australia, took the speech personally and sent a letter to the staff at every branch to chide the upstart Mr Keating. 'This bank takes a stance of restraint in the area of politics,' Mr Stride wrote. 'However, we consider the threat to the employment opportunities of our staff warrants comment at this stage. The CBA is not afraid of competition and believes in free enterprise. However, a substantial change in our structure, which has been developed to benefit Australian requirements and is very labor intensive, would be inevitable if we are to survive in the face of Mr Keating's proposal.'

In Keating's telling of Labor's reform story, letters such as these, from Australia's protective but unproductive past, demonstrate that he had the deregulation instinct years before Bob Hawke. He sees Hawke's conversion to the cause through the prism of the ACTU-led wage explosions of the '70s. 'The reason that the Hawke government began its period with an economic summit is because Bob Hawke with his ACTU hat on had succeeded in really destroying the profit share in GDP,' Keating says. 'In other words, the ACTU, through industrial campaigns, were able to bring across to them a national income share gain to labour higher than was sustainable. This is why we began the 1983 government with unemployment in double digits and inflation the same. When Bob Hawke is looking for wage restraint post-1983 he's doing it very much as a reformed smoker – the smoking being the two enormous wage breakouts of '73–75 and '79–82.'

Hawke argues that *he* had the knowledge, and that Keating was the one who needed tutoring. 'I was in a fortunate position that by the time I came to parliament in the '80s, I really did have a better understanding of the Australian economy and the region than just about anyone else in Australian politics, I guess,' Hawke says. 'We had Gough, who not only knew nothing about economics, he was frightened of it. And then Fraser came in and he was frightened of economics in almost the same way as Whitlam was. At this period, when you needed leadership, it was virtually lacking in the '70s. The thing I've quoted many times, the thing that was very much burned into my mind, was Lee Kuan Yew's comment in 1980 – if Australia keeps going the way it is, it is going to finish up "the poor white trash of Asia".' Lee's argument was that Australia couldn't keep up with the growth of the Asian tiger economies. 'And he was right, so we had to have some fundamental changes,' Hawke says. 'Paul knew nothing at the start, but he was a quick learner.'

What neither ego can admit is the extent to which the economic reform program had to be improvised in government, in response to the threshold decision to float the dollar. Once Hawke and Keating accepted the judgement of the international market-place, they had to look at the economy from the perspective of Australian business. This is where Keating's old-fashioned bank bashing met with the new creed of deregulation. In 1984, the treasurer began urging his Labor colleagues to take the side of the overseas financial class. 'For too long there's been a view in the Labor Party that what we've got to do out there in the community is control everything,' he said in a newspaper interview in February that year. 'Government control of economic policy and the financial system has done what, particularly over the past decade? Only given us a miserable growth rate, one which is not creating enough jobs . . . What we have to say is that we have to get the private sector in with the government to have, as far as possible, parallel objectives. It requires a bit of bigness on our part, and I think Bob Hawke has that bigness in him.'

They were kin then: Hawke the proud father and Keating the loyal son. Hawke gave Keating free rein to pursue the entry of foreign banks to Australia, and the treasurer achieved endorse-ment at the July 1984 ALP national conference. The government issued sixteen licences the following year, and by 1986 the financial reform project was essentially completed with the removal of the last of the controls that had prevented banks from setting an inter-est rate higher than 13.5 per cent for a home loan.

The commercial banks had greeted the 1980s by building national networks, in preparation for the deregulation they thought would come from the Fraser government. The CBA merged with the Bank of New South Wales to form Westpac, and the National Bank of Australasia combined with the Commercial Banking Company of Sydney to form the National Australia Bank. The two new players joined the two existing national banks, the pub-licly owned Commonwealth Bank and the private ANZ, to create a top-heavy playing field of four major banks, with a cluster of state government-owned banks beneath them. This structure was in place before Labor took office, creating an unintended trap for Keating's reforms. The big four, and the state banks, saw the foreign competition as a test of how many people they could lend to. They didn't care as much about the quality of the people who were asking for money, because the economy was doing well. The finance sector had been the nation's fastest-growing employer since the mid '70s – one of the few, in fact, to thrive in the stagflation decade. The rapid influx of bright young things had reduced institutional memory about the risks of a credit boom.

Keating's command of the Treasury portfolio was consolidated in the second half of 1984 by the resignation of John Stone as Treasury secretary. In his place, Keating appointed Bernie Fraser, whom Keating's first biographer, Edna Carew, described as a 'self-made man, interested in horses, keen on football [and] a man of the people'. The changing of the guard at Treasury further realigned the institutional forces. The Sydney-based Reserve Bank had already created a place for itself in the new deregulation order with its advocacy for the float. The media was largely onside. Now, Treasury was part of the program because it no longer saw its role as protecting the government from its own ideas. The final piece in the confidence puzzle for the young Labor government was world recognition, and it came at the end of 1984 when Keating was named Finance Minister of the Year, by *Euromoney* magazine. In presenting the award in November, the magazine's Sir Patrick Sergeant said Keating was Australia's 'most impressive treasurer since the war'. He was referring to the reform program, not Keating's political communication skills. But it was Keating's ability to translate economics for Australian voters, as well as for the know-it-alls in the media and his own party, that set him apart from his predecessors. In crises past, the treasurer ceded the microphone to the prime minister: it was Gough Whitlam, not Frank Crean or Jim Cairns, and Malcolm Fraser, not Phillip Lynch or

John Howard, who told Australians what ailed them. The brief exception to the rule was Bill Hayden, whose 1975 budget held the nation's attention briefly before Whitlam and Fraser resumed their conflict. In finding his voice in 1984, Keating, with Hawke's encouragement, had become the second-most important member of the government, and turned the treasurer's job from mere bean counter into the national pulse-taker.

The third-most important member of the government was not even in parliament. ACTU secretary Bill Kelty gave Labor what even Hawke couldn't offer Whitlam in the '70s: wage restraint. The Prices and Incomes Accord didn't interest Keating at first, but he was quickly persuaded by Kelty. In his most revealing interview on the topic, Kelty told Paul Kelly that he thought the Accord would die a quick, Treasury-assisted death after Labor took office. 'We had developed the Accord with Ralph Willis. He was the person you trusted, the person I trusted. He was the person on whom we had developed our whole relationship with the incoming government. Then Bill Hayden dumped Ralph for Paul.'

At their first meeting, Keating told Kelty he 'didn't think much' of the Accord. 'He told us that incomes policies never worked. He wasn't going to be lumbered with an Accord-type strategy.' But Keating and Kelty became fast friends in government, each seeing that little bit of policy genius in the other. 'Paul, I think, realised that there were a lot of genuine people who wanted to transform the labour movement in terms of employment . . . [and] the social wage.'

Keating, initially more cautious than Hawke on both the float and the Accord, was able to marry the two initiatives into a powerful political narrative. He told voters that Labor was creating an internationally competitive Australian economy. They believed him while the economy was growing, even though the subtext of the deregulation partnership with the trade unions was that workers would see their real wages fall to allow businesses to improve their own profitability.

The consent of the ACTU allowed Labor to distinguish itself from the American and British models in the 1980s. Reagan and Thatcher played the class warfare card, taking on workers in government-run sectors to establish their authority. Reagan defeated America's air traffic controllers in 1981; Thatcher prevailed in the violent dispute with British coal miners in 1984–85. Rupert Murdoch ran a parallel operation against the British printing union in 1986. Australia, on the other hand, saw industrial disputes return to their pre-1970s levels. The number of working days lost per 1000 workers tumbled from nearly 700 at the start of the '80s to less than 200 by 1985. Hawke's reformation was complete. He was no longer settling strikes after the fact, but preventing them from starting in the first place, with the carrot of the Accord.

The first phase of the Hawke–Keating economic reform program found willing guinea pigs in middle Australia. The baby boomers were in the prime of their lives in the 1980s, aged in their twenties and thirties and moving from young adulthood to the three Ms of marriage, mortgage and maternity. Social researcher Hugh Mackay says the boomers were the product of two contradictory influences: 'They were promised a rosy future, courtesy of the post-war economic miracle, and the prospect of no future at all, courtesy of a cold war that threatened to turn hot.' Immaturity defined them, and their catchcry became 'We're not here for a long time, we're here for a good time'. 'They were impatient to change the world, to flaunt convention, to discard their parents' values, to do things their way, to get what they wanted. With some justification, they also became firm believers in the idea that they are the "youngest generation" in history, and they behaved accordingly.'

One measure of their impatience was their embrace of debt.

The household savings ratio had never fallen below 10 per cent of income before the '80s. In three heady years between the December quarter '84 and the December quarter '87, it halved from 15.2 per cent to 7.5 per cent. Paul Keating had inadvertently encouraged the binge: financial deregulation connected with a pre-existing shift in public values. In one of his early reports into the nation's mind and mood in 1984, Mackay noted that the recent recession had crystallised a feeling in the community that money was worthless if it were left in the bank. 'The difficulty of saving had been a major pressure encouraging people to adopt a more enthusiastic attitude toward the use of credit,' McKay wrote. 'This, in turn, has begun the long process of a deep change in community attitudes from support for saving – as a virtue in itself – to support for spending – using money, rather than merely accumulating it. But people do not seem to be particularly conscious of this change in their own attitudes. On the contrary, they report that although coping with the recession has produced a need for more careful management of financial resources, life has generally continued "pretty much the same".'

The free-spending instincts of the baby boomers meshed with a new generation of businesspeople who courted the media spotlight, and became household names. A rich man's sport, yachting, had united the nation on 26 September 1983, when Perth-based property developer Alan Bond lifted the America's Cup. It was a sporting fairytale. The Australian challenger had to come back from a deficit of three races to one in the seven-race final series to end the New York Yacht Club's 126-year winning streak in the tournament. There was even a technological twist to the underdog's victory: the Australian boat had a rule-bending winged keel. Hawke joined the celebrations on the morning of the last race, and caught the zeitgeist when he said: 'Any boss who sacks anyone today for not turning up [to work] is a bum.' Bond and his crew were afforded a prompt parliamentary tribute the following week.

Hawke cited the words of President Reagan, who said, 'Alan Bond represents the kind of tenacity with which Americans and Australians can identify'.

'Indeed, with this victory Australia has been projected into American minds in unprecedented fashion,' the prime minister crowed. 'Coming on top of the success of Australian films in the United States, we are now firmly registered with Americans as a country worthy of attention. The economic benefit to Australia – both directly and indirectly, through tourism and other investments – will be very substantial.'

Bond was described by author Trevor Sykes as 'Australia's greatest salesman of his time, and perhaps ever'. Sykes' advice to anyone who met Bond for the first time was: 'Carry your arm in a sling, so you can't sign anything.'

The idea of the entrepreneur as national saviour sat alongside Hawke's image of himself as a bridge between capital and labour. Larrikins such as Bond and John Elliott weren't bosses, but patriots, carrying the Australian flag into overseas markets. We were all capitalists in the early '80s, blissfully unaware of the pitfalls of debt.

Bob Hawke looked at his and Labor's polling numbers, and the strength of the economy after the float of the dollar, and imagined a second-term landslide. His opponent, Andrew Peacock, was viewed within the government, and by many on his own side, as a lightweight. Hawke called an early election for 1 December 1984. It was Australia's seventh trip to the polling booth in twelve years, and Hawke misjudged the loyalty of the voter by insisting on a two-month-long campaign. Rather than increase the government's majority, as Hawke hoped, the result saw Labor's vote fall by 1.5 per cent after the distribution of preferences. The size of the parliament was expanded by 23 seats to 148, and this concealed the losses somewhat. Labor's total number rose by just seven seats to 82, while the Coalition increased theirs by 16 to 76. Labor improved its seat count in New South Wales, but went backwards in Victoria and lost its majority in Queensland. One possible mitigating factor was a high informal vote that year due to a change to the ballot paper for the Senate that some voters assumed, incorrectly, also applied to the lower house.

The verdict confirmed the true value of preferred leader polls – next to nothing. One the eve of the election, Hawke's approval rating was 75 per cent. Labor's two-party preferred vote on polling day was 51.8 per cent to the Coalition's 48.2 per cent. The gap of 23 per cent accounts for almost half the Coalition vote. That is, they liked Hawke, but had no intention of ever voting Labor, which doesn't normally win with a large majority in the Australian system.

The experience in Britain and the US – where first-term conservative administrations were also seeking re-election – was the opposite of Australia's. Their leaders *did* translate personal support into hard votes. In 1983, Thatcher won a second-term landslide, increasing the conservative majority by 101 seats to 144 in a parliament of 650. In 1984, Reagan was returned with forty-nine of the fifty states and 58.8 per cent of the popular vote – a swing of 8.1 per cent to the incumbent. On the other hand, elections in Canada and New Zealand saw government change hands decisively in 1984.

Hawke wanted to set Labor up for a decade in office, but the setback of '84 made the party feel mortal, again. This raises an intriguing question about the nature of Australia's relationship with their prime minister in the '80s. They didn't love him to the extent that Hawke wanted, but they accepted him. In their respective jurisdictions, Hawke, Thatcher and Reagan were giants, the last leaders that people were willing to believe in, and who the media treated with deference, if not reverence. Each presided over reform programs that, a generation later, are still viewed as the gold standard for their respective societies.

Hawke had come to the leadership as an outsider, with serious doubts about his temperament. He surprised his internal critics by running a classic cabinet government, giving ministers freedom to pursue their own agendas, and to debate one another's, so long as they didn't blow up the economy. Hawke was blessed with a large number of competent ministers, by Australian standards, with just the right balance between passion and pragmatism. Where Whitlam had eccentric soloists, each throwing the government off its rhythm, Hawke had hard heads in Keating, Peter Walsh, John Dawkins and Ralph Willis to maintain fiscal discipline. The spending ministers were also of a higher calibre, able to see both sides of the budget: John Button in industry, Neal Blewett in health, Don Grimes and then Brian Howe in social security, John Kerin in agriculture, and Kim Beazley in defence. Add Bill Hayden, then Gareth Evans, in foreign affairs, and it is unlikely that any government, Labor or Coalition, will ever see so many talented individuals in the one cabinet again.

Hawke didn't need to insist on teamwork because they had seen the two sides of the bad government coin in the stagflation decade – the free jazz of Whitlam, where ministers did their own thing, and the suffocation of Fraser, where they were micromanaged into indecision. Hawke deliberately aimed for a position between the two leadership extremes. But even if he had delusions of greater control, it is unlikely that ministers would have allowed him to dominate.

The most revealing study was the tax summit after the 1984 election. At a political level, Keating was humiliated because he lost his bid to introduce a 12.5 per cent broad-based consumption tax. But his fallback package released in September 1985 still rates as the most substantial reform of the taxation system in the post-war era. It gave higher-income earners their own version of the

Accord: generous tax cuts and a new tax credit for the shares they owned, in exchange for new taxes on capital gains and fringe benefits. The top personal tax rate was slashed from 60 cents to 49 cents in the dollar. It was, in effect, a reward to the very people who had ripped off the system in the bottom-of-the-harbour days.

Keating told parliament there was no point leaving marginal tax rates at punitive levels when the only people they punished were 'honest taxpayers'. 'It would be stupid not to recognise the lesson of recent history: taxpayers just will not pay ridiculously high marginal tax rates,' he said. 'The system invites abuse if it attempts to impose such a burden.' Hawke and Keating were happy to give money to the enemy bosses in the national interest. One small problem: unleashing capital and restraining labour didn't restore balance to the economy in the 1980s, it merely flipped the source of the nation's troubles. Trade union overkill in the '70s could be measured in double-digit inflation and unemployment. The marker of business excess in the '80s was debt. The irony here was that capital sat in judgement on itself. Banks lent, businesses splurged, and they both blamed the government when things got out of hand.

I I

GETTING AHEAD
OF THE GAME

The fear of foreign takeover runs deep in the Australian psyche. From the earliest days of federation, our leaders worried about invasion. They even built the national capital, Canberra, inland to protect it from naval attack. Deregulation was supposed to be an end to cowering. Instead, it found a new way to provoke the old insecurity, the current account deficit. Only a handful of people in the wider community had even heard of the concept until Paul Keating started talking about it.

The current account deficit is the difference between our exports and investment income overseas, minus imports and the money we pay to our creditors. Australia has always been in deficit to some extent on the current account because our small population could never hope to generate enough savings to fund the development of our resources and expand our cities. The rest of the world never minded lending to us in the past because the quarry, and before it the farm sector, generated decent rates of return. What changed in the 1980s was the trade balance in the current account – exports minus imports – also went into deficit, and this posed the question of national survival. If we couldn't pay our way in the world, because we couldn't sell enough exports to cover the cost of the imports we were now bringing in, then the world would send us into receivership.

This was the unexploded bomb Malcolm Fraser left behind with his premature declaration of a resources boom. The projects didn't take off as he had hoped, but the foreign borrowings and the imports did. Imports exceeded exports in each of the final three years of the Coalition government, and the deficit on the current account deficit peaked at 5.5 per cent of gross domestic product in 1981–82 – the worst result in thirty years.

Each year's current account deficit has to be funded by overseas loans, and Australia's net external debt had more than trebled, 'from $7.3 billion, or 6.3 per cent of GDP in 1979–80 to $52 billion, or 25.1 per cent of GDP in 1984–85', according to the budget papers. Half the nation's net debt was publicly sourced. It belonged to the Commonwealth government – through the accumulation of past budget deficits – and to various state authorities that Fraser had encouraged to borrow. 'There had been, of course, earlier occasions when Australia tapped foreign savings to finance resource investment on a very substantial scale. However, the previous such occasions [a decade or so earlier] had been followed fairly quickly by a closing of the current account deficit.' Not this time, the budget papers explained, because we spent the boom before it arrived.

In the aftermath of recession, the trade deficit disappeared and the current account deficit narrowed to 3.8 per cent of GDP in 1983–84, but Bob Hawke's V-shaped recovery sent it back to 6 per cent of GDP by 1985–86, as Australian consumers preferred imports over local products, while the rest of the world's demand for our exports failed to keep up. The forces driving Australian consumers to buy overseas were the same ones that left our local manufacturers with nothing to offer to world markets – we knew our products weren't that good, even though we told ourselves we would 'buy

Australian'. But there was a second factor: the Americans were pushing down the world price of oil, and this was reducing the value of our quarry, and through it our terms of trade. In the mid '80s, Australia looked like the typical Western household of the twenty-first century, living the high life on debt.

The dollar, once floated, was supposed to fall to make our exports cheaper to sell and our imports more expensive to buy. But the market didn't seem in much of a hurry to make this adjustment on our behalf. On the first anniversary of the float, 12 December 1984, the dollar was worth US84.78 cents. On the second anniversary, it was 68.40, but it had returned above US70 cents early in 1986. 'We believed the exchange rate to be dramatically overvalued and we couldn't understand why it had not drifted down,' Keating recalls. 'We were saying "What is keeping it – question mark, question mark – what is keeping it up?", then all of a sudden something happened and away it slides. The thing to realise was that it was doing what it was supposed to do. I mean, markets overshoot and they do things late sometimes, or early in some cases, but it was trying to find the right price, its true competitive price, to help correct the current account imbalance.'

The Australian Bureau of Statistics reported the balance payments on a monthly basis in those days, and each current account deficit contained in that release gave the market an excuse to play with the currency. On 13 May 1986, the deficit for April was almost $1.5 billion – about $600 million worse than the market expected. But the dollar didn't move by much, losing half a cent to close at US74.07 cents. Keating initially had no comment, but decided he would offer a detailed response the following morning, Wednesday 14 May, in a radio interview with Sydney talk-show host John Laws.

'I get the very clear feeling that we must let Australians know truthfully, honestly, earnestly, just what sort of an international hole Australia is in. It's the prices of our commodities – they are as bad in real terms since the Depression,' the treasurer said, speaking from a borrowed phone in the kitchen of a hotel in Melbourne. 'That's a fact of Australian life now; it's got nothing to do with the government. It's the price of commodities on world markets but it means an internal economic adjustment. And if we don't make it this time, we will never make it. If this government cannot get the adjustment, get manufacturing going again and keep moderate wage outcomes and a sensible economic policy, then Australia is basically done for. We will just end up being a third-rate economy.'

Laws asked Keating to explain what would happen if Australia did not get out of this hole. 'The prognosis is, the only way you deal with the massive current account imbalance is to close the economy down. You cut all growth to zero, you stop all the imports growing and unemployment starts rising again and profits fall apart, and we go back to being the kind of economy we were in 1982, or worse.' Keating said that once economic growth falls below 3 per cent a year, unemployment rises again. Laws, confusing his slow-downs and recessions with a depression, said: 'And then you have really induced a depression?' Keating replied: 'Then you have gone. You are a banana republic.'

It was those two words – 'banana republic' – that spooked everyone. The dollar fell by almost US4 cents and closed at US71.24 cents. The next morning, the *Sydney Morning Herald* had it both ways, playing down Keating's 'unfortunate phrases' in its news report, and talking up his courage in the editorial. 'There was nothing in [the] comments that would have been new for the money market, which had already digested the news of the poor April current account figure, and much that was reassuring for it,' a report below the fold of the front page said, while the editorial declared: 'Notwithstanding the unfavourable reaction of the foreign exchange market, Mr Keating has probably hit on exactly the right response.' In *The Age*, business commentator Terry McCrann was outraged: 'Paul Keating lost his cool yesterday. In the process, he single-handedly wiped two or three cents off the value of the dollar and destroyed the emerging stability in the Australian financial markets.'

Keating made a mistake, and he confided so to colleagues at the time. Strictly speaking, a banana republic was a one-crop Latin American economy that had sold its soul to the United States. To use the term in the context of a current account crisis might have had a ring of truth to it. A nation's viability, in its simplest form, is its ability to attract finance. If the money market judges an economy to be unproductive, the zero-sum of deficit borrowing kicks in, whereby a nation has to offer a higher interest rate to maintain its supply of credit, but the repayment burden forces the government into austerity measures at home, which reduce the economy's capacity to service those overseas obligations. The danger in Keating's comment was that the foreign lenders he was trying to impress might just have taken him literally and pulled their money out of Australia altogether. While he did achieve the devaluation he was looking for, the risk now was that the currency would go into freefall, sparking a crisis of confidence in the economy, and requiring countermeasures to prop up the dollar – which would defeat the purpose of the float.

The interview also triggered a power struggle between Hawke and Keating over who ran economic policy, and with it the government. The relationship between the two had become increasingly tetchy since the last election. Keating had not forgiven Hawke for vetoing his 12.5 per cent consumption tax. Now their argument would break through the closed doors of government and into the harsh light of public scrutiny.

Hawke was flying to Tokyo when Keating gave the banana republic interview. Hawke's agitation turned to fury on 16 May when Keating announced a mini summit of government, employers and trade unions. Two days later, the Hawke caravan landed in Beijing. The reporters travelling with him were given an 'off-the-record briefing' that the summit had been scaled back, and would be run by the acting prime minister, Lionel Bowen, not Keating. It was Hawke's way of saying he had slapped down the presumptuous Keating. The following day's headlines in Australia declared Hawke was back in charge. He arranged for a conference call to ministers to tell them the same thing.

Paul Kelly records that Keating listened to Hawke with a newspaper on his lap, ticking off each point that the prime minister made against him. When Hawke was finished, Keating let rip. His colleagues cautioned him: 'Be careful, the Chinese will be listening.'

'Fuck the Chinese,' Keating barked back. 'Just what is the point of this bullshit, Bob?'

Hawke asked: 'Who's that?'

'Who the fuck do you think it is?' Keating replied. 'We've got problems here and we're trying to solve them. Just what the hell do you think you're playing at?'

Voters didn't get to hear that part, but they knew the two had been fighting. Hawke later admitted he had briefed journalists in Beijing, and Keating attacked Hawke's advisers, whom he dubbed 'the Manchu court'. Labor looked like it had reverted to the ego eruptions of the Whitlam era.

On Hawke's return to Australia, the prime minister and treasurer resolved their personal differences, and took a joint decision to press for a tougher budget and to ask the trade unions to give up a little more for the Accord. Hawke announced that he would be giving a televised address to the nation. The swing in the political and community mood, from the optimism of the float and financial deregulation to the doom of the banana republic, was partly due to Keating's startling warning and partly due to a slowing of the real economy. Hawke wanted to set the record straight for the people. Yes, this was indeed a crisis, but it wasn't entirely our fault.

Hawke's fireside chat on 11 June 1986 explained the fall in the terms of trade: 'Our exports of commodities such as wool, wheat, coal and iron ore have, for a long time, been a major source of our national income. While the prices we pay for our imports have continued to rise, the prices we get for these exports have for a considerable period been gradually and now dramatically declining.'

He said Australians had to accept a temporary reduction in living standards and permanently increase their standard of effort. The speech contained a cringe-making passage that unintentionally confirmed the shallowness of the national talent pool. Hawke name-checked four Australians who had achieved international fame: marathon runner Robert de Castella, opera singer Joan Sutherland, and the designer of the America's Cup-winning boat with its winged keel, Ben Lexcen, and the boat's skipper, John Bertrand. He wanted their example to drive a renaissance of Australian industry to beat the terms-of-trade trap.

'I want us to get the same sense of shared pride when an Australian manufacturing or services firm wins a contract against the best international competition – and let me assure you they can do it, they are doing it. It requires the same elements as have brought Deek, Joan, Ben and John to the top.'

He listed the elements of success, like a motivational speaker firing up the delegates at the end of a sales convention: 'Confidence in yourselves, your product and those around you. Readiness to work with great application and dedication. Eagerness to use the best available advice and technology. Preparedness to forgo present satisfaction for greater long-term reward. Total commitment.' The following day the dollar lost almost a cent, to US68.79 cents. The market had wanted an austerity campaign, but Hawke delivered a pep talk.

The substance of his speech was the deferral of promised tax cuts for three months, and a call to trade unions to accept further wage restraint. Cabinet then went to work to finalise the budget. The budget deficit for the present financial year was supposed to have been $4.9 billion, but it had blown out to $5.7 billion. Keating told the expenditure review committee (ECR) of cabinet he wanted the next deficit to have 'a four in front of it'.

The government greeted the new financial year on 1 July by re-imposing a 15 per cent tax on certain foreign investments. This withholding tax was another example of Labor getting used to the quirks of the market. It had been removed in 1983 to declare that Australia was open for investment, but the market exploited the generosity and drained $400 million from the budget in two years. Labor had created a loophole without meaning to, and closed it. But the market responded to the return of the tax by slashing another 5 cents from the dollar in a week. It was at US62.89 cents by 8 July. This was simply payback: there had been no material change in the outlook for the economy that week to explain a fall in the currency of that size. Now the government feared the dollar would overshoot, sparking a run on the nation.

Finance minister Peter Walsh wrote in his memoir that government spending had been be held to a real increase of 1.1 per cent in 1986–87 when the currency crisis forced ministers to go back to the chopping block. 'When the ERC met to wrap up the budget's final detail on Monday 28 July, there was widespread apprehension that the dollar would continue to fall, possibly to below 60 cents, which was perceived to be a psychological barrier below which it might go into freefall,' Walsh wrote. 'During the ERC meeting Keating had in front of him a small portable Reuters screen upon which he could dial, every minute or so, the latest foreign exchange quotes from Sydney. He was calling them out, "below 62, below 61, below 60, below 59". Finally it bottomed at US57.2 cents and only then because the Reserve Bank intervened heavily. I was closer to despair than I had been even in 1975. We had not been a bad government, certainly not by Australian standards, and we did not deserve the catastrophe inflicted on us.'

That day, Reserve Bank governor Bob Johnston confided to

Keating that he did not know what to do. What the ministers did next sealed the government's reputation. Keating appeased investors by again removing the tax on certain foreign invesments, and the ERC returned to find another round of cuts so that government spending would increase no further than the inflation rate. In reality, they did even better than that, achieving a small reduction in real spending. The stingy budget was released on 19 August with a forecast deficit of $3.5 billion for 1986–87. The dollar lost a further cent the following day, to us61.55 cents, and finished the month at us60.85 cents. Critically, it did not again fall below the us60 cent mark the government had told itself was the threshold between pain and outright panic. On 11 September 1986, the credit rating agency Moody's Investor Services downgraded the national government's AAA rating to AA1 because of the current account deficit.

The second phase of the deregulation program was dictated by the experience of the currency crisis. To date, Hawke and Keating had been playing catch-up, completing the unfinished business of the Fraser years on the float, financial deregulation and tax reform. Now they would try to get ahead of the game so the money market wouldn't catch the nation out again. The two most important additions to the economic program were the return of the federal budget to surplus for the first time in over thirty years, and the resumption of tariff cuts after a fifteen-year hiatus. The fiscal repair continued into 1987, an election year. Among the new measures were the abolition of the dole for sixteen- and seventeen-year-olds, and the means testing of family payments. The cuts brought the deficit to less than 1 per cent of GDP. 'This achievement compares starkly with the United States, where the federal deficit has hovered around 5 per cent of gross domestic product for five years,' Keating said. The tariff cuts would come after the election, assuming the government was first forgiven at the ballot box for the loss of national esteem that came with a lower dollar. Labor had set itself a unique test in Australian history: it would be seeking a fresh mandate for austerity.

The 1987 campaign was that last occasion that the consensus-based Labor model could be dismantled and replaced with the Reagan and Thatcher model, which took direct aim at trade union power. Opposition leader John Howard preached smaller government and greater individual freedom. He offered tax cuts, which Labor did not match, a rollback of the new taxes on capital gains and fringe benefits, the removal of the asset tests on the age pension, and the dismantling of Medicare. 'Only through a lift in the productivity of this nation can we close the gap permanently between our imports and our exports,' Howard said. 'And the only way that we will close that gap is to give to every individual man and woman in Australia the incentive and the encouragement to work harder.' Bob Hawke delivered a frugal campaign launch, with one notable promise, that 'by 1990 no Australian child would be living in poverty'. The written speech had said 'would *need* to be living in poverty' but the prime minister had dropped the qualification.

The times didn't suit Howard, because the conservatives were almost irreparably divided. There had already been one leadership change in the term, when Howard replaced Andrew Peacock almost by chance in September 1985. Peacock had wanted to remove Howard as deputy, but when that vote failed, Peacock quit the leadership, gifting Howard the top job. The accidental leader duly sacked Peacock from the shadow ministry in March 1987 after an expletive-soaked car phone conversation about Howard with Victorian Liberal leader Jeff Kennett. Their exchange was taped by a disability rights group using a scanner and released to the media. The fight between Peacock and Howard was the main bout within the Liberal Party, and the bickering helped to keep Labor in power for longer than it was used to historically.

Queensland premier Joh Bjelke-Petersen had brought a surreal dimension to the feud when he announced in February 1987 that he wanted to be prime minister. He courted Peacock as his deputy and wanted to lure John Stone out of retirement to begin a second public career as a politician. Peacock didn't sign up, but Stone did and stood successfully for the Senate for the National Party. Labor worried for a while that Bjelke-Petersen might snatch votes from one part of Labor's base – 'the unskilled male workers with low education and low income', according to Labor polling detailed in Paul Kelly's seminal work on the 1980s, *The End of Certainty*. But Bjelke-Petersen was a coalition wrecker, not a national vote magnet. His gatecreashing cameo exposed the weakness of Howard's first incarnation as leader, and laid bare the instability between the Coalition partners.

In April, the National Party, unable to decide between Bjelke-Petersen and their federal leader, Ian Sinclair, left the Coalition. Joh never made it to Canberra, but his grab for power was a harbinger of a cultural rift in Australia, between Queensland, the state that most resembles the American south in its embrace of god and guns, and the two big cosmopolitan states of New South Wales and Victoria. Queensland would never be truly comfortable or relaxed with deregulation, and it would continue to exert a subtropical veto over the national affairs, even after Joh had departed the scene.

For Hawke, the conservative division was the gift that kept giving. He thought about an early election for May, but decided against it. Then Keating helped talk him into a winter election on 11 July 1987, after the delivery of the economic statement on 13 May. The fiscal stars aligned for Labor late in the campaign when Howard admitted, after checking and double-checking his tax package, that it had a 'technical error' worth $540 million over three years. Keating said the black hole was more like $1.6 billion. 'Nothing contained in Keating's statement undermines the integrity, viability or the achievability of the package,' Howard insisted.

And still the electorate toyed with the idea of dumping the government for the side of politics that couldn't add up. Hindsight shows the economy was very weak, and had almost slipped into recession in 1986. Inflation was 9.3 per cent in the year to the June quarter 1987, and the unemployment rate was 8.1 per cent in July. Come the election, Labor's primary vote fell 1.7 per cent to 45.8 per cent. It recovered almost half that swing on preferences to deliver a popular vote of 50.8 per cent – down just 0.9 per cent on 1984. Despite that small final swing against it, Labor managed to increase its seat count by four to 86 out of 148. The four extra seats came from the traditionally anti-Labor Queensland – where Coalition infighting had damaged Howard the most. This restored Labor to a majority in each mainland state. Elsewhere the government lost a seat in both New South Wales and Victoria, and picked one up in both Tasmania and the Northern Territory. Without the Queensland premier's attack on Howard's leadership, the result would have been much closer. But that didn't diminish the achievement. No previous Labor government had won three elections in a row.

The post-election budget for 1987–88 went for even further cuts and aimed for balance, with spending forecast to be just $27 million more than revenue. It turned out to be a surplus of $2 billion as the economy was doing even better than expected – the first tangible sign that the reforms were paying off with a more efficient business sector that was taking advantage of the government getting out of it way. Based on the figuring used at the time, this was the first budget in the black since the early '50s.

But the progress was disrupted by the stock-market crash of October 1987. Even though it had virtually no spill-over to the real economy, governments around the world worried a global recession was at hand and instituted coordinated interest-rate cuts to support demand.

While the rest of the world sweated in the aftermath of the crash, Labor entered the bicentenary of white settlement in 1988 ready to declare mission accomplished. Another economic statement, on 25 May, finally revealed the detail of the tariff cuts. But they weren't to be slashed with the lightning-strike intensity of the Whitlam shock fifteen years earlier. The Keating method was gradual, a 20 per cent reduction in average protection levels over four years, on a so-called 'tops-down' basis. All those products with tariffs above 15 per cent would be reduced to 15 per cent; all those between 15 and 10 per cent moved to 10 per cent. However, the car industry would retain its own special regime. 'No Australian government has ever presented such a comprehensive program of change in a single package,' Keating said, with some justification. 'Spending cuts to deliver the largest budget surplus in our history, tax changes to put our companies at the cutting edge of world commerce, [and] changes to industry protection to promote competitiveness and efficiency.'

He should have stopped bragging at this point. The 1988–89 budget, handed down three months later, on 23 August, set the impossible goal of an economy where every irascible piece of data was moving in the same direction. 'This is the one that brings home the bacon,' Keating told the media. In his budget speech he ticked off the policy wins, starting with the halving of the current account deficit from its peak of three years ago. 'Our foreign debt burden has already stabilised and begun to fall. Inflation is down. Real wage increases are in prospect. Our rate of job growth is unmatched in the Western world. Business investment is rising rapidly. On the export front, new manufacturing activities and tourism have blossomed. On the import side, Australian factories are now supplying a wide range of goods that we used to buy from overseas. Unquestionably, a dramatically better state of affairs now exists than when I warned in 1986 of the threat of Australia degenerating to the status of a banana republic.' Every forecast he made that evening turned out to be wrong. It wasn't necessarily his fault – Treasury had misread the local and the international economy after the 1987 stock-market crash. The risk wasn't recession, but the reverse. A dangerous boom was building.

I 2

THE CULT OF PROPERTY

Paul Keating had noticed something was amiss while on holidays in Noosa, on Queensland's Sunshine Coast, an hour's drive north of Brisbane. The constant roar of construction work interrupted what he had hoped would be a quiet break with his family in January 1988. He telephoned Reserve Bank governor Bob Johnston to suggest that he look at raising interest rates, because the activity at the resort indicated the economy was stronger than they thought. Johnston didn't believe it was time to move just yet. Many of Australia's high-profile entrepreneurs had been burned in the stock-market crash three months earlier, and the Reserve Bank worried that higher interest rates would push them into bankruptcy, and with that bring down the commercial banks which had lent billions to them. 'We had big open positions,' Keating says of the over-leveraged corporate sector. 'We had [Robert] Holmes a Court on about $10 billion, we had [Rupert] Murdoch on about the same, we had Bond and [John] Spalvins, and these positions were rocky and they mattered to the balance sheets of a number of banks.' He says the Reserve Bank didn't pick that lower interest rates had created the conditions for a new boom as people moved their money out of shares and into commercial property.

The Australian fixation with bricks'n'mortar asserts itself at times of economic stress. Keating and his advisers weren't to know this because they had no experience of how quickly booms can get out of hand in a newly deregulated environment. The free-market manual told them that an overheating economy could be cooled by allowing a floating dollar to rise in value, by keeping the budget in surplus, by restraining wages, and by increasing interest rates. Keating ticked all these boxes, but the economy would not easily yield. While the entrepreneurs began buying up office towers, Australians punted on housing. Prices surged, Poseidon-like, by 20 per cent in 1987–88 and by almost 40 per cent in 1988–89.

Politics junkies and economists will never tire of debating what prompted the turmoil of the late '80s. The acknowledged errors on interest rates – the Reserve Bank's slowness to respond to the boom in 1988, and the overkill in 1989 – are the least-controversial part of the story today. What deserves greater attention is the stubborn refusal of households to take the hint of higher interest rates.

Pinpointing the catalyst for housing's part of the wider boom, and explaining its intensity, can only be done now, with the hindsight of more recent episodes. It wasn't the stock-market crash of October 1987, but one short paragraph in Keating's budget speech the month before. 'Since we have restored the integrity of the tax system by subjecting capital gains to tax, we are now in a position to permit the restoration of deductions against taxable income without exposing the revenue to the threat which existed before July 1985,' he said. 'The full interest costs of owning and maintaining rental property will now be deductible against income from any source.' By this he meant that negative gearing, the officially sanctioned tax perk that most Australians can recite off the top of their head, had been restored after a brief abolition.

Keating had removed the concession two years earlier as part of his opening round of tax reforms. He had described negative gearing back then as an 'outrageous rort', and he was correct. No other comparable country allows landlords to deduct the interest rate and other expenses they incur to run a rental property against any source of income, even wages. The norm elsewhere is for the deduction to be allowed against the rental income only. Any extra costs have to be carried forward to when the asset is sold, and deducted against the capital gain. Keating had explained in 1985 that negative gearing was 'one of the most blatantly abused tax shelters in the system'. He went further, by calling housing for what it really was: an unproductive investment that had the power to destroy an economy. 'In a capital-scarce country one must ration the capital carefully,' he said. 'Therefore, the capital must go to the most productive areas of the economy rather than into over-investment in real estate, or any other non-productive area of the economy.'

The back-down in September 1987 was forced on Keating by an incessant campaign from the housing lobby, which argued that there had been a landlord strike without the concession. The claim was dubious, but the treasurer had met his match. Australians felt too strongly about this particular tax break for Keating to be able to maintain the Treasury line. Peter Walsh said Keating told cabinet they 'had to do something to give our poor mug comrades in the New South Wales government some chance in the impending state election'. (They lost anyway.) The effect of the budget announcement was to invite existing home owners to buy second or third properties. The landlord rush squeezed out the new entrants to the market. There was a 30 per cent reduction in the number of first home-owner grant recipients between 1987–88 and '88–89 as prices jumped by 60 per cent over that two-year period.

As prices rose, so did interest rates, but that only intensified the cycle. The deregulation of home lending allowed people with the ability to borrow to keep doing so. In the past, the number of mortgages issued would be regulated as well as the interst rate charged. The public didn't want to miss out on the capital gain, or the tax deduction from negative gearing. The earliest available taxation records from that period show that landlords claimed $275 million more in deductions than they declared in rental income in 1989–90.

Australia's home-ownership rate is not remarkable in itself. It jumped from 53 per cent of households at the end of the Second World War to 70 per cent by 1961, and has remained at around that level ever since. Similar rates of home ownership have been achieved in the United States, Great Britain, Canada and New Zealand. Even the average size of our dwellings is unremarkable. Our typical home is around 50 per cent bigger than in Europe, but on par with New Zealand and Canada, and around 15 per cent smaller than the US.

What is different in Australia is the extent to which household wealth, and through that the sense of national wellbeing, is tied up in bricks'n'mortar. Housing had accounted for 52 per cent of all household wealth throughout the '60s, with the balance going to shares, other investments and consumer durables. It reached 60 per cent for the first time in 1973–74, during the boom of the Whitlam era. Keating's abolition of negative gearing returned the figure to 52 per cent by 1986–87. Then it jumped again to 59 two years later. It hasn't been below 58 since then, and the all-time peak was 70 per cent in 2004 – fulfilling Keating's original warning of property chewing up the nation's scarce capital. In the US, households have one third of their wealth in property, and two-thirds elsewhere.

'The home is gaining increasing stature as a symbol of power and privacy,' Hugh Mackay wrote in his July 1986 report into the attitudes of middle Australia. 'As people feel they are losing control over so many aspects of their lives, so the need grows for the sense of control and authority which home ownership brings.' This feeling started with the baby boomers, and it has repeated since as globalisation has made rich nations anxious about the rise of harder-working competitors from Asia.

Australians have always seen their houses as buffers against the external world. Originally, they were designed to shut out the continent's arid environment. Property serves as both fortress and open space for an anxious, but friendly people. When we invite friends over, we prefer to feed and water them in the backyard, not in the dining room, because it allows us to maintain the pretence of informality while protecting our inner sanctum. We talk to neighbours over the demilitarised zone of the back fence. And each generation endures the same deadly lesson that building a mansion on the edge of bushland doesn't protect the occupants from the firestorms that reach the city limits rarely, but inevitably.

In the same way, each generation needs reminding that house prices can fall. While Australia has so far avoided the busts that demoralised the Japanese in the '90s, and the Americans and British in the first decade of the twenty-first century, our property market is overvalued. Keating spread the fuel in the late '80s, then John Howard applied the flame-thrower in the next cycle.

The contemporary fixation with the tiniest movement in interest rates can be sourced to the economic tutorials Paul Keating conducted as he wrestled with the 1988–89 boom. He had the media and the public caught in a macabre game of data-watching, as we waited to see if the next number was a good one or a bad one, and if it were the latter, whether it would mean another tightening of the monetary screws.

Interest rates received more attention this time than in '86, when they were increased as part of the banana republic episode, because home mortgage rates were now deregulated for all new loans.

There were plenty of opportunities to speculate about interest rates. The treasurer would hold gruelling hour-long press conferences on the release of each monthly balance of payments. There was also a labour-force survey to comment on each month, although it was of less concern while unemployment was falling. Every three months there would be separate press conferences to decant the consumer price index and the national accounts, which tallied all the transactions in the economy to come up with an estimate of gross domestic product. Radio and television interviews would follow.

Keating's strength as a political communicator was the power of his imagery. He was able to simplify complex economic theory without talking down to the electorate. In one celebrated example in February 1989, after another bad current account deficit, he almost made higher interest rates sound like a welcome night at home after a run of too many parties.

'We have to live through this surge of wealth and employment and prosperity until it moderates and until we have a better balance between exports and imports. Basically the glass is now full and the effervescence is spilling over and that effervescence is the current account and inflation.'

Of all the numbers Keating addressed, inflation and unemployment were the most meaningful, while economic growth was the least informative because it was a snapshot of the immediate past and was subject to constant revision. The most dangerous series of the quartet was the balance of payments because it jumped around from month to month. But this was the one Keating was most concerned with because he had nominated the current account as the test of our international viability. Later, when he became prime minister, he pursued engagement with Asia with a similar thought in mind – to prove Australia's worth in the world.

Behind closed doors, however, Keating was having doubts about his harsh economic medicine. In a note he scribbled in the margins of a July 1989 report from the Treasury and Reserve Bank on the economic outlook, Keating said the forecasts 'made the twin deficit theory look like bullshit'. The twin deficit theory held that if the budget was in surplus then the current account deficit would narrow, because the government didn't have its hand in the savings jar, competing with productive business.

'By the end of the year under forecast [1989–90] the govt will have presided over an 8 percentage point shift in the PSBR [public sector borrowing requirement]. It must be a worldwide post-war record. Yet the current account will, according to these forecasts, be still 5 per cent of GDP. At least I can't be burdened with any more talk about re-weighting the instruments of policy. We now all know what utter crap that is.'

He had just given monetary policy one final tweak, taking the mortgage rate to 17 per cent, a number that is seared into our bricks'n'mortar consciousness. The setting of interest rates was, strictly speaking, the job of the Reserve Bank, but Keating was intimately involved in every decision. He owned the increases in a political sense because he announced them. The practice changed when Bernie Fraser replaced Bob Johnston as governor in September 1989. All future movements up or down would be declared by press release, in the governor's name on behalf of the Reserve Bank board. It was tentative first step to separating the Reserve from the treasurer, to demonstrate its independence in the formulation of monetary policy.

Keating and the Reserve Bank appeared to be at cross-purposes at the end of the '80s. The treasurer was still publicly asserting the current account was the prime target; the Reserve had its eye on inflation which, despite half a decade's worth of restraint showed by trade unions through the Accord, was still at 7.8 per cent at the end of 1989.

The conduct of monetary policy in this period was complicated by the behaviour of Australian businesses, which increased their risk-taking after the October 1987 stock-market crash. The banks, still chasing the false glory of market share, enabled the entrepreneurs to place double-or-nothing-style bets. This was our subprime moment, twenty years before the global economy succumbed to a much nastier version. Alan Bond, the best-known of the decade's businessmen, kept borrowing to add to his pile of assets. Before the crash, he was into mining and beer brewing, and had bought the Nine television network from Kerry Packer. After the crash, his big purchases included an American brewer, a Chilean telephone company, another Australian resource company, and the site for an office tower in Sydney. Fellow high-flyer Christopher Skase had created the Seven television network and a luxury tourist operation. Post-crash, he set his sight on Hollywood, making a bid for the MGM/United Artists film studio. Bond and Skase were chasing the Keating dream of an internationally competitive Australian economy. But they were over-leveraged. With each expensive addition to their empires, they left themselves exposed to any increase in interest rates. Between March 1988 and September 1989, the average interest rate charged to big business jumped from 13.25 per cent to 20.5 per cent as the Reserve tried to reclaim control of the economy, the strength of which it had underestimated. But they had moved into overkill territory. By the end of '89, both Bond and Skase were bankrupt.

Rupert Murdoch's business was also pushed to the brink of default. Keating had a hand in Murdoch's over-gearing. In 1986, reforms to media ownership policy, which forced proprietors to choose between newspapers and television stations in the nation's capital-city markets, created a bubble. Murdoch bought the nation's largest media company, Herald and Weekly Times, which his father Sir Keith had previously run. He kept the papers – Melbourne's *Sun* and the afternoon *Herald*, Brisbane's *Courier-Mail*, the Adelaide *Advertiser* and Hobart's *The Mercury* – and sold the HWT's interest in Melbourne's Seven Network, which ultimately ended up in the hands of Skase. Murdoch, like Bond and

Skase, was still buying and opening new businesses in 1989, when the national economy was slowing. Murdoch survived, and his recovery in the '90s was analogous to the nation's own path to international acclaim. The prudent one had been Packer, who sold his television network to Bond in 1987 for $1 billion – much more than it was worth – and bought it back at a discount at the end of 1989 when Bond's empire was teetering. Packer also thrived in the recovery, but unlike Murdoch, his ambition never reached much beyond Australia's shores.

Bond eventually went to jail, and the total losses of his various ventures were put at $5 billion. Skase lost $1.2 billion and then fled to Spain to avoid prosecution. Slumped in a wheelchair, and sucking desperately on an oxygen mask, he convinced the local courts to spare him extradition back to Australia on humanitarian grounds.

Bond and Skase had made their first big deals in the closed economy. But they never had the opportunity to bring down an economy until the entry of foreign banks fooled the local banks into engaging in a competition for market share, not quality customers.

The four largest banks wrote off a total of more than $17 billion in bad loans between 1989 and 1993. Two of the four, ANZ and Westpac, were responsible for $11 billion of that amount, and came close to insolvency. The commercial bank deficits effectively cancelled the good work of Keating and his colleagues in securing a federal budget surplus. The Victorian and South Australian state banks created another stress for the system. They had shed their traditional prudence to become involved in risky ventures on the well-meaning but dangerous premise that they were restoring full employment on behalf of their interventionist Labor governments. These two state banks went out of business with a further $6 billion in losses, which had to be underwritten by taxpayers. In Western Australia, the connections between a Labor state government and business became known as WA Inc., and the premier who forged the link, Brian Burke, went the same way as Bond – to prison.

Shady politics at the state level is as old as white settlement, but nothing the Labor premiers got up to in the '80s matched the corruption of Joh Bjelke-Petersen's government in Queensland. The premier accepted money in brown paper bags from business associates, demanded $1 million from Bond to settle a defamation action against the Nine Network, and only avoided a criminal conviction because a National Party supporter happened to be on the jury in his perjury trial.

Bjelke-Petersen had long lost the allure that had perhaps surprisingly made him the third-most admired Australian earlier in the decade. His forced resignation on 1 December 1987, after nineteen years as premier, and the defeat of the National Party government on 2 December 1989, ending thirty-two years of conservative rule in that state, was part of a sequence of old Australian political and business institutions that were declared morally or financially bankrupt in this period. Among the insolvent were the largest industrial group, Adelaide Steamship; the largest textile group, Linter; the second-largest newspaper group, Fairfax; and all three commercial television networks, Seven, Nine and Ten.

The authorities were not so much asleep, as unprepared for the social forces that were unleashed by deregulation. Author and business journalist Trevor Sykes put it best when he wrote: 'Never before in Australian history has so much money been channelled by so many people incompetent to lend it, into the hands of so many people incompetent to manage it.'

Deregulation taught the Reserve Bank and others in the official family that while the market should be encouraged, it could never be trusted. Australia wasn't the only nation with a home-grown financial crisis in the '80s, but we were one of the few to remember it when that experience would next be called on in the noughties.

There was an important lesson, too, for the community. Australians had invested too much faith in the entrepreneur in the

1980s. The collapse of Bond and Skase reminded us that there were some parts of the American dream that we couldn't abide.

The wild ride of deregulation revealed a nasty side of the Australian character. The grasping for capital gain was accompanied by an outbreak of xenophobia that the main parties found impossible to resist. The post-war bipartisanship on immigration was shattered on 1 August 1988 when John Howard, the unsuccessful opposition leader at the last election, called for a slowing in the Asian intake. Asked in a radio interview if the rate of Asian immigration was too fast, Howard replied by citing the views of the community: 'I think there are some people who believe it is.' When pressed for his own attitude, he said: 'I wouldn't like to see it greater. I am not in favour of going back to a White Australia policy. I do believe that if in the eyes of some in the community it's too great, it would be in our immediate-term interest and supportive of social cohesion if it were slowed down a little, so that the capacity of the community to absorb was greater.'

The Australian's Greg Sheridan said Howard's position was 'foolish and/or politically dishonest'. He mocked Howard, asking which Asians he wanted to deny entry to: 'Does he mean Polish Jews from Israel, Indian doctors, Hong Kong businessmen, Indo-Chinese refugees who fought alongside Australian troops in Vietnam?'

Howard's comments created a competition for outrage on the conservative side. National Party leader Ian Sinclair said there were too many Asians coming into Australia, while John Stone, now a Queensland National Party senator, said: 'Asian immigration has to be slowed. It is no use dancing around the bushes.' Australia had never had a debate quite like this before, but it had been part of the public landscape in Britain for a decade longer. As opposition leader, Margaret Thatcher had worried about the size of the intake from Pakistan. In a famous television interview on 27 January 1978, she said:

'I am the first to admit it is not easy to get clear figures from the Home Office about immigration, but there was a committee which looked at it and said that if we went on as we are then by the end of the century there would be four million people of the new Commonwealth or Pakistan here. Now, that is an awful lot and I think it means that people are really rather afraid that this country might be rather swamped by people with a different culture. And, you know, the British character has done so much for democracy, for law, and done so much throughout the world that if there is any fear that it might be swamped, people are going to react and be rather hostile to those coming in. So, if you want good race relations, you have got to allay peoples' fears on numbers.'

Thatcher, coincidentally, was in Australia at the time of the Asian immigration row and Howard's colleagues believe it affected his judgement because he didn't want the Iron Lady to see him back down.

On 25 August 1988, Bob Hawke moved a parliamentary motion to reaffirm that Australia supported a non-discriminatory immigration program. It said, in part 'that, whatever criteria are applied by Australian Governments in exercising their sovereign right to determine the composition of the immigration intake, race or ethnic origin shall never, explicitly or implicitly, be among them'.

Hawke turned the debate into one of character, to try to avoid making a martyr of Howard: 'Let me make it clear – and I want the leader of the opposition to know this – I do not accuse him of racism or of being a racist. In a sense, sadly, I make the more serious charge, I make the more damning indictment, of cynical opportunism, in a cynical grab for votes. His polling shows that there is this prejudice in the community and he has unleashed within his Coalition, and within the wider community, the most malevolent, the most hurtful, the most damaging and the most un-cohesive forces. Far from guaranteeing one Australia, he has guaranteed a divided Australia, a hurtfully divided Australia.'

Howard was unrepentant: 'The prime minister's moving of this motion today has been a totally political exercise. Our credentials on immigration cannot seriously be challenged. Nothing I have said over the past two or three weeks has been designed in any way to foster hostility towards any section of the Australian community, but I will never ever abandon the sovereign right of this country to decide who will be a permanent citizen of this nation.'

Four Liberals – Philip Ruddock, Ian Macphee, Steele Hall and Peter Baume – crossed the floor to vote with the government. Two others, including the former Fraser government immigration minister Michael Mackellar, abstained from voting. The seesaw of leadership instability on the Liberal side then tilted back in favour of the more moderate Andrew Peacock, who used the row to gather numbers for a challenge against his rival. Howard admits he lost his job to Peacock on 9 May 1989 because of his comments on the Asian intake.

The following month, Hawke was responsible for the next big step in the immigration program when he allowed tens of thousands of Chinese students to remain in Australia after the People's Liberation Army had crushed the protests in Beijing's Tiananmen Square on 4 June. Tears streamed down Hawke's face at a memorial service for the victims held at Parliament House five days later. But the scab of race, once scratched, can reinfect the body politic under the stress of recession.

13

RECESSION AS
NATION-BUILDER

Recessions are a normal part of economic life. Like taxes, they can be avoided for a time, but never truly beaten. The deep recessions are the ones nations remember and their retelling can darken the view of an era. The shallow ones barely warrant the title 'recession' because they don't come with the dislocation of widespread job losses and business failures. The stagflation decade contained two deep recessions, in the mid '70s and in 1982–83, which were obvious to people at the time, and two shallow ones, in 1971–72 and 1977, which economists debated after the fact. From the '80s onwards, there is just one worth exploring in detail: the deep recession Paul Keating said we had to have.

Establishing just what constituted a recession became part of the political sport ahead of the 1990 election. There was no independent panel of experts to rule on the matter, as in the United States, where the grandly named Business Cycle Dating Committee of the National Bureau of Economic Research issues press statements to confirm the start and end of recessions. The NBER considers a range of variables, including production and employment, and it usually takes about six to nine months after a recession has begun to have enough data to make an informed comment on the matter. Australians were too impatient, and narrowly focussed. The aesthete in Paul Keating had raised public expectations that statistics could be viewed as a window into the national soul, telling us if we were worthy or not. While he never said what would constitute a recession, the media and the opposition set the standard for him. If the economy contracted for six months – that is, if gross domestic product fell for two consecutive quarters – then that was a recession. No one can recall who decided this, but the benchmark was in common usage by the 1990 election. It was a silly standard because two small declines in GDP, without mass retrenchments, would be a recession, but a large collapse in one quarter, followed by a small rise in the next, would not. By this logic, the Whitlam government didn't preside over a 'technical' recession in 1974–75, even though it was seen as a deep recession in its day.

Keating promised a 'soft landing': he said the tough love of high interest rates, a succession of large budget surpluses and real wage cuts would simultaneously open the economy while also controlling the excesses of consumption, housing demand and business borrowing. That there had been no example of this happening before did not seem to concern him. Keating looks back at this period and imagines that in a more perfect world he might have tightened the screws earlier in 1988, before the boom got out hand, and eased them more rapidly in late 1989 and throughout 1990 to avoid a hard landing. 'The bank finally did lift interest rates too late and had to go to a much higher level,' Keating says. 'Then the new bank governor, Bernie Fraser, left them up too long. This was a very costly policy.' But the reforming and the managing were being done at the same time. Deregulation was still a relatively new experience for the nation, and this made a soft landing almost impossible.

Politically, the government knew that the community was

hurting, and behind the scenes, it had business chiefs and their bankers warning that recession was on its way. In mid '89, Bob Hawke embarked on an eighteen-day overseas trip with the advice of colleagues ringing in his ears that voters needed assistance. He gave serious consideration to introducing a mortgage relief scheme for homebuyers, and a new luxury tax to make imports more expensive. A third option was also discussed within his office, but never revealed to the media at the time: a 5 per cent consumption tax. Keating thought any policy change so close to the next election would be poison for the government. The voters would see the handout as confirmation the government had done the wrong thing, and that it had lost faith in its own policies. In 1974 and 1982, the Whitlam and Fraser governments had respectively surrendered to their worst Keynesian instincts as an attempt to buy their way back to political favour. But the very fact of their spending sprees had undermined public confidence. In 2007, when John Howard tried to secure another term by showering the electorate with cash, the same thing happened, but without a recession – his government too was thrown out of office. The Treasury department, conscious of the budget holes that Whitlam and Fraser left behind, urged Keating to defend the integrity of their project. With the help of Hawke's own staff, Keating was able to talk the prime minister back off the window ledge.

The problem wasn't one of courage, but of perspective and patience. Keating had lost sight of the fact that interest rates operate with a time delay. An extra half a per cent may not seem to matter from one month to the next, but the cumulative effect of half-a-dozen increases over the course of a year can be devastating if the changes are based on old data. Just like the previous two governments, Keating and his advisers failed to pick the turn in the economy. Interest rate policy was evolving from the Treasury- and government-influenced version of the '70s, to a less politicised but not quite independent model run by the Reserve Bank. Keating still wanted the right to announce the changes, so he owned them politically, even as he was ceding control. Bernie Fraser kept interest rates higher than they should have been because they didn't realise that the real job of monetary policy is to always be ahead of the curve – to increase before the economy overheats, and to cut before it crashes. But the political climate, strangely, wouldn't permit a defensive cut in interest rates. An amazing part of the public debate in late 1989 and early 1990, even as the electorate was screaming for help, was the incessant demands by economic commentators for more spending cuts or, failing that, a deferral or cancellation of the most recent tax cuts. No one could let go of the idea that what worked in the banana republic episode in 1986 must also work now, even though the budget was no longer in deficit.

Labor went into the 24 March 1990 election with two cuts in official interest rates and the promise there would be no recession. On the Wednesday before polling day, the national accounts for the December quarter were released and they showed the economy had gone backwards by 0.2 per cent, although growth for the calendar year was still 4.2 per cent. Keating said everything was going to plan: 'This is a beautiful set of numbers for us. Now that the rapid growth in demand has been reversed there is no need for interest rates to remain where they are. The government will be taking up this matter with the Reserve Bank in the first week or so after the election.' I had been travelling with Keating for most of that campaign, and my report the next day quoted three economists who agreed with him that there would be a soft landing, and one opposition politician who didn't. John Hewson, as shadow treasurer, said: 'We are in a recession, with worse to come.' They were all wrong: the recession was coming, but not just yet, because there would be one more rogue number to suggest the economy was still roaring.

The 1990 election was Labor's to lose. The change in the Liberal leadership from John Howard to Andrew Peacock the previous

May had not been popular with voters. Yet the seven-year-old government felt vulnerable and encouraged a protest vote as part of risky strategy to retain power through the back door of second preferences. Labor's private research found the mood of swinging voters was 'disillusioned, despondent and cynical'. Pollster Rod Cameron advised: 'The basic problem with Labor is that its economic policies have hurt middle-ground voters.' But Peacock did not inspire any confidence, which allowed Hawke to run as the devil you knew.

Hawke said he had 'no beef' with people who voted on single issues, especially on the environment, so long as they remembered to place the government's candidate ahead of the Coalition's. The public obliged, with Labor suffering its second-worst primary vote swing of the post-war era after 1975. Most of that came back as preferences, limiting the final swing to just 0.9 per cent. Even so, Labor lost the popular vote 49.9 per cent to 50.1 per cent, making Hawke's only the fourth government since 1949 to hold power with the support of less than half the nation. The previous three minority winners had been Robert Menzies in 1954 and '61, and John Gorton in '69.

It was an unusual campaign. In Victoria, the recession was fast approaching, and the old tensions between labour and capital were re-emerging. Melbourne's CBD resembled a shunting yard, as trams lay idle due to a public transport strike. But in New South Wales and Queensland, the nation felt a little less hassled. The election had caught a subtle power shift, from the old manufacturing heartland of Victoria to the services-based economies to the north.

Labor lost nine seats in Victoria, where the recession would claim the most jobs, and one each in South Australia and Western Australia. The common link between these three rust-belt states was financial mismanagement by their Labor governments. If no other seats had changed hands, federal Labor would have ceded its majority. But Labor picked up two seats in New South Wales and another two in Queensland, leaving it with 78 seats in total in a parliament of 148.

This victory did not carry the same sense of vindication as 1987. It was Hawke's fourth, and in some ways his most impressive, given the handicaps of a faltering economy and the age of the government. But the opinion polls immediately after the election recorded a steady decline in Labor's primary vote and a surge to the Coalition. A fifth term with Hawke at the helm appeared almost inconceivable and the chatter within the government, and the press gallery, was about when, not whether, Keating would take over. Defeat for the Coalition suggested the end of an era. Peacock was ready to stand down as leader, but first he had some unfinished business. John Howard wanted his old job back, but Peacock wasn't prepared to let this happen. So he held off conceding defeat to Hawke while he arranged the numbers for the cleanskin Hewson to become the new opposition leader.

Every recession should be necessary in the sense that it corrects an excess. Australia's experience in the stagflation decade had been miserable because two deep recessions in eight years did not cleanse the economy of its inflationary impulse. The Accord was supposed to deal with this by giving business a larger slice of national income as profits. It delivered on paper, with the wages share of national income falling from 61.9 per cent of GDP at the end of 1982 to 55.1 seven years later. The profit share rose from 18.9 per cent to 23.5, a transfer from labour to capital of more than $50 billion in 2010 dollars. It should have earned workers some gratitude, but businesses had borrowed against their windfall throughout the '80s and many didn't have the means or the wit to survive any landing, soft or hard.

Inflation remained sticky, despite seven years of uncharacteristic sacrifice by the trade unions. The consumer price index nudged back up to 8.6 per cent in the March quarter 1990, and the release of that news in April was exasperating for the government. At the end of May it was told by the statisticians that the economy had also rebounded by 1.8 per cent in the March quarter. This news was consigned to page fifteen of the nation's then highest-selling newspaper, Melbourne's *Sun News Pictorial*. Political correspondent Niki Savva and myself reported the story with all the false assumptions of the times, that our destiny could be divined in the last piece of data that landed on our desks:

'Australia is not in a recession – that was the good, if surprising, news yesterday which had the Hawke government cock-a-hoop. But the bad news for homebuyers is the government has no intention of dropping interest rates – the figures showed there was still too much buoyancy in the economy and the government will have to keep rates high to act as a check on demand. And the statistics raised questions about the effectiveness of the government's high interest rate strategy in controlling demand across the board.'

The numbers, when they turned unambiguously down, did so with a vengeance. Unemployment jumped from 6.3 per cent in April to 7.2 by August. The economy contracted by 0.4 per cent in the June quarter, and the nation placed itself on a form of data death-watch. On 29 November 1990, the statistics finally satisfied the definition we had latched on, with the news that GDP had crashed by 1.6 per cent in the September quarter. The press conference Paul Keating gave that day is drilled into the national memory. Before he entered the committee room in Parliament House to make his statement and take questions, the press gallery ran an impromptu sweep to see how long it would take him to say the R-word. The answer was six seconds. He saw no point in arguing the semantics. This was a policy-induced recession and Keating wanted his name on it, for good or ill.

'Well, I'll just give you a few comments on the national accounts.

And the first thing to say is the accounts do show that Australia is in recession. The most important thing about that is that this is a recession that Australia had to have. That the spending we had in the two years up to now was unsustainable, that we couldn't go on spending and consuming at the rate we were carrying the imports we were and the debt we were, and, of course, the erosion of our gains on inflation.' He said it was 'entirely possible' that the worst had already passed, and pointed out that 'policy generally has been conducted to encourage a sustainable recovery through 1991'.

As he spoke, the US economy, itself a victim of too much corporate bingeing in the 1980s, had slipped into recession. But history was playing with Keating that day. Subsequent revisions to the data pushed back the critical dates for Australia's 'technical' recession from the June and September quarters of 1990 to the March and June quarters of 1991. In other words, the recession-we-had-to-have press conference should not have been Keating's to conduct, because he was on the back bench, between his first and second leadership challenges.

A cheeky thought occurs with these revisions: Keating may have accidentally talked the nation into a deeper recession than what was coming to it. There is no way of knowing either way, but it is not an unreasonable proposition because economies turn on emotion. Booms and busts are the two extremes of the human condition, and the job of government is to moderate the mood swings. If recession is coming, it may not be wise for a treasurer to say 'Serves you right'. One thing is obvious now, as it was then: Australia went into recession at about the same time as the US, but we took a little longer to get out. The American recession ran from the September quarter 1990 to the March quarter 1991, according to the National Bureau of Economic Research. Ours, on the American definition, ran from the September quarter 1990 to the June quarter 1991, a recession that fits neatly into the 1990–91 financial year. But the two countries diverged on the most meaningful measure in these comparisons – jobs. American employers sacked 1.5 per cent of their workforce between March 1990 and May 1991; Australian employers retrenched twice as many – 3.9 per cent between July 1990 and February 1993. The US unemployment rate peaked at 7.8 per cent in June 1992. Australia's crossed 10 per cent in September 1991, and remained in double digits until July 1994. It reached a post-war high of 11.2 per cent in December 1992. The recession we had to have looked a lot like theirs from the early '80s because the individual pain of sacking or bankruptcy carried a national pay-off in the breaking of inflation. While the inflation-beating chairman of the US Federal Reserve, Paul Volcker, became an international hero, Keating's equivalent contribution in Australia in the early '90s receives no praise because it suits the conservative side of politics to treat him as an ogre, and because there was an undoubted element of policy error involved. Keating had been targeting the current account deficit, but landed the bigger prize of price stability by pushing the economy into a recession that no one who lived through would forget. Inflation fell to 3.4 per cent at the recession's end in the June quarter 1991, then it disappeared – it was at 1.2 per cent a year later, 1.9 a year after that, and 1.7 three years on, in the June quarter 1994.

But the price of low inflation was the removal of 253 000 men and 59 000 women from work. The recession was reinforced in the national memory because there was no V-shaped recovery. The total number of men employed in full-time work across the economy didn't return to its pre-recession peak of November 1989 until January 1998. The blokes who had fought for their chunk of Australia's inflation-diminished cake in the '70s, and had been on their best behaviour in the '80s through the Accord, were now told there was no place left for them in the mainstream. Yet many who weren't there still recall the recession because of the 17 per cent mortgage rate. That figure resonates louder than double-digit unemployment, because it became government's way of telling

Australians that, if pushed, another recession would be engineered to prevent inflation from dominating national life again.

Bernie Fraser regrets the mistakes on monetary policy, but points out that each easing in interest rates designed to cushion the economy had been controversial. 'There were fifteen reductions in interest rates between January 1990 and mid-1993, and almost every one of those reductions was criticised by the Coalition, and by media commentators. In retrospect, we should have taken interest rates down faster.'

Keating is unrepentant. 'Had I chosen to instruct the bank to lower the rates, had I pushed the treasurer's ultimate power under the Reserve Bank Act, the whole notion of the bank moving towards maturity as a stand-alone institution would have been destroyed. And I had in the governor the person I had the most faith in – Bernie Fraser – so I just wasn't prepared to do it. But I knew full well that the bank's intransigence in getting the rates up and the bank's intransigence in getting the rates down was going to kill me [politically].'

He doesn't regret saying this was the recession we had to have: 'I had my press secretary and staff say, "Oh, you should say you didn't mean to say that", and I might have said something generally to that effect. But, in fact, they always knew what I felt, and that was: Australia was about to go back to the dismal business of wage breakouts. And the seven years of the Accord and wage restraint would have been thrown out the door in the event that there wasn't a substantial slowdown. How you technically rate the slowdown – as a recession or a slowdown – is more or less beside the point. The fact is we had to have it. We went into the recession with the broadest measure of inflation at 4 per cent and we came out of it at 1. The thing that John Howard has to live down is that he went into his very, very deep recession with these 22 per cent interest rates and he still came out with 10 per cent inflation – there was no gain. We took another ten years [to kill inflation, compared to the Americans] because of Bob's wages explosions and Howard's incapacity to deal with wages policy.'

The recession's primary economic legacy was the defeat of inflation, which set Australia up for an unprecedented run of prosperity in the 1990s and beyond. The Reserve Bank was, ironically, the big institutional winner of the recession, although this would not become clear for another decade. Its delays in both raising and lowering interest rates taught it the value of the pre-emptive strike in the future. The political legacy was to make Keating the most unpopular person of the reform era.

Consider the contrariness of the Australian people at this time. When the economy was protected, recession was the rest of the world's fault; when it was deregulated, it was down to one man, Paul Keating.

'Australians recognise that their present economic difficulties are not of the government's making,' the Mackay Report had found in December 1982. Yet there was no reason to see us as an innocent victim back then. Double-digit unemployment and inflation was almost unique to Australia in the early '80s. In February 1991, a Saulwick Poll found 38.5 per cent believed federal government policies were responsible for our 'economic downturn'. Another 8.9 per cent said state government policies. World economic conditions were the explanation for 28.6 per cent, followed by trade unions (9.7) and big business (9.1). The only figures that jar are the last two. It would require a wilful misreading of the national accounts to believe that a generational-low wages share and a record high profit share meant that trade unions were relatively more culpable that business.

The early 1990s recession confirmed the selfish streak that had revealed itself in the boom, with middle Australia also taking aim at the victims of unemployment. 'Because the most obvious and frightening aspect of the recession is its effect on unemployment, many Australians have had their long-term anxieties about the "dole" and other aspects of the social security system reactivated,' the May 1991 Mackay Report found. 'Consistently, people claim that Australia's social security system is too generous, too "soft", too inclined to positively encourage "bludging", and to create too heavy a burden on "the workers".' Like the attitudes to the trade unions, the observations about welfare cheats are a flashback to the problems of the stagflation decade, rather than a sensible analysis of what was driving unemployment now.

Keating had the budget in surplus for three years in a row, and government spending back at pre-Whitlam levels – hardly proof of a generous handout system. But there was a persistent urge to punish. At the 1990 election, swinging voters stuck with Bob Hawke because they didn't think Andrew Peacock was up to the job. They wished there was a sharper choice, and the name John Howard was mentioned in Labor polling as someone that might have made a difference to the outcome. It is interesting that Howard would be seen as the future in the 1990s, when he was the treasurer who had lost control of the economy in the previous recession, and who had misled the people about the true size of the budget deficit. But a similar role reversal had made Hawke, the trade union boss in the '70s, appear the safest bet to reconcile the nation in the '80s, because he had learned from his mistakes. This is an unappreciated strength of the Australian system. The two-term limit for US presidents precludes someone who had governed poorly from returning a wiser leader the second time. Our three long-serving prime ministers – Robert Menzies, Bob Hawke and John Howard – had each split the nation in their previous incarnations as prime minister, treasurer or ACTU president. But the Liberals weren't ready to return to their past; they thought the future belonged to a trained economist – John Hewson.

14

THE DYNAMIC DUO
DISSOLVES

The decades-long legacy war between Bob Hawke and Paul Keating is, to their mind, primarily about authorship. But there is a personal dimension that goes beyond the normal rivalries of politics. Keating jokes that it would take a psychiatrist to write the definitive biography on their relationship. Hawke, the father, was fourteen years older, but a lair at heart. He wanted the son to be more laidback, and to love Australia unconditionally. Keating was born old. He judged the father, even as he looked up to him in the early years of the government, because he didn't approve of the womanising and the boozing. Each craved the other's respect, yet neither man had the humility to pay the other a genuine compliment because he thought that would acknowledge his own inadequacy. Hawke wished he had Keating's way with words; Keating wished he had Hawke's popularity.

The recession destroyed their partnership. On 7 December 1990, eight days after Keating declared it the recession we had to have, he gave an off-the-record address to the National Press Club that remains one of the most influential of the past generation. He meant for it to be read as a job application – he just didn't expect it to become public, nor for Hawke to use the reporting of it as the excuse to dishonour the private agreement they had struck at the prime minister's residence in Kirribilli two years earlier, for a handover of the leadership.

Keating was affected by the sudden death of Treasury secretary Chris Higgins the previous day. A keen runner with a serious heart condition, Higgins collapsed after completing a mini marathon in Canberra. One of the final pieces of advice he had written to Keating on 4 December was that a 'pick-up in spending and activity is in prospect through 1991 based on existing policy settings'. He said Treasury wouldn't oppose another interest rate cut, but it would be better 'to keep your powder dry until late January'.

Keating began by praising Higgins' service to the public, and then turned to the question of leadership. Australia, he said, never had a great leader: 'We've got to be led, and politics is about leading people. Now we've got to the stage where everyone thinks politicians are shits and that they're not worth two bob, and all the rest of it, and everyone kicks the shit out of us every time we get an increase in our salary. But politicians change the world, and politics and politicians are about leadership and our problem is – if you look at some of the great countries, of the great societies, like the United States – we've never had one great leader like they've had. The United States had three great leaders – Washington, Lincoln and Roosevelt – and at times in their history that leadership pushed them on to become the great country that they are. We've never had one such person, not one.'

'A decade ago, the national ethos of this country was the 35-hour week. You work thirty-five hours, you've got the house you wanted, the Commodore in the drive, the weekender. That was it.' He speculated that Australia's lack of ambition 'was probably because of the bounty of our resources and minerals . . . [It] might have been our convict past. God knows what it was, or whether it was the rip-off merchants that came with free settlement. But we missed out somewhere.' It was deregulation's version of Donald Horne's lucky country thesis.

There were enough barbs in there for Hawke to take it personally, although a leader more secure in his position might have laughed it off, or sacked Keating. Malcolm Fraser had called a leadership ballot when Andrew Peacock wasn't ready in 1982 and beat him handsomely. Hawke wanted to keep the peace and didn't think Keating would have the gall to challenge. In fact, Keating might have challenged immediately if Australia wasn't involved in the first Gulf War to push Saddam Hussein's armies out of Kuwait. While each man hesitated, they found time for one last reform to announce together, the 12 March 1991 industry statement that completed the tariff reduction program. A new general rate of 5 per cent would apply by 1996, replacing the two-tier system of 15 and 10 per cent tariffs. The motor vehicle industry would have its tariff reduced to 15 per cent, and for textiles, clothing and footwear it would be 25 per cent by 2000.

Keating told parliament: 'The package of measures announced today ends forever Australia's sorry association with the tariff as a device for industrial development. By turning its back on tariffs, Australia will be further propelled in its quest for international trade and efficiency, a search begun with the opening up of the economy in 1983 when we floated the dollar and abolished exchange controls.' It read like a farewell speech because it was. Keating didn't have another budget in him, and launched his first leadership challenge at the end of May 1991.

His public claim to Hawke's job was that the government needed a new-generation leader, otherwise it would ebb out of office. 'I made arrangements with Bob to try and avoid this kind of problem,' Keating told the Nine Network's Laurie Oakes in an interview on 2 June, a day before the first ballot. 'That is for a smooth, effective, sympathetic transition of both leadership and power within the party and to continue to regenerate ideas for the government . . . [I] don't resile from the fact that I have personal ambitions, but they're nothing like the ambitions I have for Australia.' He said Hawke couldn't win another election. Asked by Oakes if he thought he had a better chance, Keating said: 'I think that in terms of energy, leadership, a political strategy, injecting some esprit de corps into the government – giving it more cohesion and a sense of camaraderie, which I think it lacks at the moment – I think the answer is yes.'

Hawke was the nation's second-longest serving prime minister after Robert Menzies and the most popular on record. Undoubtedly John Curtin would have drawn a higher approval rating had similar opinion polls being conducted in his day, but Hawke had no peer in the post-war period. His argument against Keating was the one he had used against Bill Hayden: the people loved him. But at sixty-one years of age, and with the baggage of the recession and the revelation of the Kirribilli agreement, Hawke was losing his rock star quality.

Keating felt he was owed the leadership – he had a deal and he expected Hawke to honour it. Hawke felt that Keating wanted his turn even if it meant Labor would lose the next election. But Keating believed he had defended Hawke and given him courage when others were advising retreat, and when a more calculating politician might have allowed the leader to make his mistakes. Father and son could no longer stand the sight of one another. Hawke could never forgive Keating his ambition to better him; Keating could never forgive Hawke for refusing to acknowledge his loyalty. Hawke thought Keating was mad and the public would never warm to him. Keating thought Hawke was a narcissist who had used people all his life. The caucus didn't want to choose between them, preferring that Batman and Robin remain in place to contest one more election. But Keating didn't want to wear the boy wonder cape on behalf of the Hawke government anymore. He wanted Labor to fight in his own name, because it would fall to him anyway to rough up the John Hewson-led opposition.

Sitting prime ministers had been toppled before on the conservative side – most notably Menzies in 1941 and John Gorton thirty years later. But they had lost the confidence of their party rooms. Hawke was still the preferred prime minister within caucus, and Keating still had the second-most important job in the government. To challenge, and fail, meant giving up power and the right to steer the government's economic policies. It was a gamble made more extraordinary by the context: with the economy still in recession, Keating's decision to take on Hawke would inevitably distract the government from its day job – dealing with the recession he said he created. It was also an unusual claim for higher office. As the recession's author, Keating was assuming he would be more popular than the proven vote-magnet, Hawke.

The leadership ballot was supposed to be held on 1 June, but Hawke miscalculated by refusing to resign his position. He thought Keating should have the guts to demand a vote, but Keating reminded him that in 1982 Hayden had declared his position vacant. It was the first of a number of tactical errors that suggested Hawke was losing his nerve. Keating's supporters made a dash for Canberra airport after the first caucus meeting broke up to lock in Hawke's indecision, just in case he called them back for a second meeting that day. The challenger wanted the weekend to persuade a few more people to his side, to make his expected defeat respectable enough to warrant a second attempt later in the year. He didn't make up that much ground. When the leadership vote was taken the following Monday, 3 June, Hawke won easily, but not decisively – sixty-six to forty-four. Keating needed just twelve colleagues to defect to win next time.

Keating declared that he had only one shot in the locker and he had fired it. He told the media he would sit out the term on the back bench, but no one believed him. His farewell press conference as treasurer contained an amusing joust with the press gallery over his prediction for the next election. Would he please repeat his comment that Hawke couldn't win? No, Keating replied.

Michelle Grattan, *The Age*: 'Surely it wasn't just a line for the day?'

Keating: 'When I said it, I meant it, but the caucus doesn't believe me.'

Grattan: 'Do you still mean it?'

Keating: 'The caucus doesn't believe me. Now you want me to go and repeat it and I'm not going to.'

Grattan: 'No, just do you adhere to it still?'

Keating: 'No, Michelle, don't play silly word games with me please, darling.'

Second Journalist: 'Mr Keating, why don't you retract the statement now?'

Keating: 'Listen pal, I haven't seen you before so why don't you just be quiet.'

He explained the challenge was born out of frustration with Hawke's refusal to keep his side of their private pact. 'I was at the point where, if it had gone on too many more months, it would have been, I think, not worth my while to have sought to challenge. And I didn't want to be living with this question, would the promise be honoured, so I wanted it settled . . . [There] is something very healthy in public life about snatching it, there's a legitimacy about it, and I wanted to legitimise it.' He was pursuing power with the same righteous conviction that had driven Fraser throughout the '70s. Only, the '90s were nothing like the '70s because the nation was tiring of reform. Keating was seeking to revive a long-term government by promising even more change from the pit of recession.

John Kerin was given the biggest shoes to fill in public life. He had been minister for agriculture for eight years before he replaced Paul

Keating as treasurer. Bob Hawke hoped Kerin's plain-speaking manner would sever the cord between the government and Keating, and restore public confidence in Labor's stewardship of the economy. No fancy theories, no lectures, just the facts from one of the nicest guys in the cabinet.

By choosing to humanise the treasurer's position, Hawke had projected his own leadership values onto the job Keating had held for eight years. It was an experiment in a form of alternative political medicine for a government on life support, and it was doomed for a number of reasons. Kerin would always appear glib in comparison to Keating, and the press gallery would catch every hesitant statement and amplify it. Journalists missed Keating.

Kerin was a prisoner of Treasury advice. He took the job too late in the budget cycle to make that document his own – just as had happened to Keating when Hayden handed him the job – so he was stuck with the outline Keating had left him. He did change one aspect of the budget's presentation on 20 August 1991. There would be no six-hour lock-up of journalists to take them through the entrails of the budget papers. It was presented un-spun, so the media reports that evening and the next day began with one or other vested interest group offering their condemnation.

The Kerin budget is the one Treasury most regrets because it continued to misunderstand the depth and the nature of the recession. It delivered on Keating's earlier pledge to maintain fiscal discipline. New spending was to be offset by cuts, to guard against any early return to the boom conditions of the late '80s. The cut that defined the budget's economic and political miscalculation was in Labor's prized area of health policy. Kerin asked Australians to cough up $3.50 each time they visited the doctor. The co-payment was called a reform because it introduced a 'further price signal' to Medicare and would save the budget $1.65 billion over the next four years. But if it had a co-payment attached to it, Medicare lost its meaning as a universal health scheme funded directly out of the budget. Hawke had been assured that the left of the party would embrace the co-payment, but he was looking at the issue the wrong way around. Medicare was one of the few things that Labor stood for that people held dear to them. To say the program was unaffordable was code for accusing Australians of being hypochondriacs.

The budget itself was forecast to tumble into a deficit of $4.7 billion, after three consecutive surpluses, between 1987–88 and 1989–90, and a balanced outcome in 1990–91. Treasury explained at the start of the budget papers that the deficit was due to the slowdown in the economy, which had increased spending on unemployment benefits and reduced revenue collections. The structure of the budget was sound because new government policies weren't adding to the cyclical gap between revenue and spending. One hairy-chested boast jumps off the first page of the budget papers: 'As a percentage of GDP, outlays are still below the levels of the mid 1970s and most of the 1980s.' They were guarding the nation's coffers as if the economy was still booming.

'The forecasts that we were doing always showed that it was going to be a shallow downturn,' one senior Treasury officer recalls. 'There were data issues, and that wasn't entirely our fault. But where we were at fault, I think, is in the policy advice of the time, which was basically "sit on your hands". That wasn't only because our forecasts were [incorrectly] showing a fairly shallow dip. It was also because we didn't actually want to do anything.' Treasury should have been pressing for a temporary stimulus to avert the danger of unemployment remaining in double digits throughout 1992 and '93.

Unlike his predecessor, Kerin really did have only one salvo to fire, and the department aimed it for him at the government's foot. Treasury insisted on, and were granted, the right to test a theory that economic rationalists had held dear: fiscal policy should focus on the medium term, leaving the so-called automatic stabilisers in the budget – increased spending on unemployment and reduced revenue collections – to take care of the short-term with deficits. But the advice was killing the recovery for the same reason as the Reserve Bank's insistence that interest rates not be reduced too quickly. Tough love, especially after a recession that threatened the viability of the banking system, gives businesses no room to breathe. This defeats the point of fiscal policy as a stabilising force in the economy because it prolongs the social costs of the recession. The very thing Treasury was trying to avoid – the destruction of their hard-earned surplus – was made more likely by their refusal to protect jobs earlier in the process.

The political difficulty that Kerin posed for the government, and by direct association Hawke, was that he didn't have Keating's ability to poke holes in the Coalition's policies. And the government's second-most pressing task in 1991 after ending the recession was to burst the Hewson bubble.

John Hewson had offered himself as a fresh start for the Liberal Party and the nation. He was a professional – an economist by training. He was seventeen years younger than Bob Hawke and the only Liberal who didn't seem to flinch when Paul Keating attacked on the floor of the parliament. He was a Fraser-style moderate on social policy, but drier on economic policy than just about anyone in politics. By his very presence, the next election, due in 1993, would be about another wave of reform, not whether Australia should retreat or seek retribution against unseen forces.

Hewson sold himself as an anti-politician. He jaundiced view of government had been shaped by his brief experience as an adviser to Phillip Lynch and then John Howard. His self-belief came from the economic degrees he had obtained from the University of Sydney, the University of Saskatchewan, and another two, including his doctorate, from the John Hopkins University in Baltimore. He moved into merchant banking before the Coalition's 1983 defeat, and doubled as a business commentator. 'Keep an eye on him,' people would tell each other when Hewson entered parliament in 1987, at the same election as former Treasury secretary John Stone.

Hewson's colleagues, drained by the preceding decade's rivalry between Andrew Peacock and John Howard, accepted his argument that the Coalition should produce a detailed economic manifesto well ahead of the next election to erase the perception that the Coalition did not take reform seriously enough to make it all add up. The document was to be called Fightback! It was a Whitlamesque endeavour, a program so detailed it would require years to implement. Fightback! diagnosed the nation's malaise as too much government, and the cure involved taking the medicine that Bob Hawke and Paul Keating had refused to dispense – further massive cuts to public spending and deregulation of the labour market, sweetened by the largest personal tax cut in memory. He was, in effect, seeking a re-run of the 1987 election, combining the Hawke–Keating spending cuts with the Howard tax cuts. But all the attention would be on the tax reform at the centre of the package, the goods and services tax, which was to replace a raft of existing, less efficient indirect taxes.

As Hawke and Hewson prepared their respective arguments ahead of the imminent launch of Fightback, Keating was having an epiphany on the back bench. He decided the budget was getting in the way of the recovery and it was time to open the national wallet to encourage growth. This changed his argument against Hawke – he was renouncing what both of them had stood for in the middle of the year. Back then he was only pushing generational change. Now he had an interventionist program to pitch against both his own government and the Coalition. Strictly speaking, it didn't repudiate his former economic rationalist self because the circumstances of the recession justified a new course. But the political strategist in Keating appreciated that more government spending would assist his challenge for the leadership by shift-ing Labor members on the left away from Hawke. The former treasurer sweetened his pitch by promising to rescind John Kerin's Medicare co-payment.

Keating concedes that his reluctance to deploy the budget ear-lier in the recession was due, in part, to pride. 'It took from '85 to '90 to bring about the big consolidation of fiscal policy,' he says. 'The expenditure review committee had been meeting for seven and eight hours a day for three and four months a year for half a dozen years. We had all that grinding work to get outlays down and re-order Commonwealth spending, and you kind of protect those aggregates like you protect your own good name. So in that sense, in the ordinary course of things I would have kept the fiscal polish well and truly bright. But after I left the Treasury, following my first caucus ballot with Bob Hawke, I could just see that the economy was in far worse shape than the Treasury's belief that we were going to have some sort of soft landing. And so I got to the point of thinking, if I'm going to turn this around, fiscal policy has got to play a role.'

Three decades of public life had sharpened Bob Hawke's pres-entational skills, but they couldn't correct his tendency to circumnavigate the English language. The people didn't mind the prolixity because his optimism was infectious in the '80s. But the recession exposed the limits of his rhetoric. Under pressure, he was prone to hectoring, and voters didn't like this side of him. Hawke's, and Labor's, standing in the opinion polls remained poor throughout 1990 and '91. Hawke had at least 50 per cent of vot-ers dissatisfied with his performance as prime minister throughout this period, and Labor's primary vote never rose above 40 per cent.

John Hewson had a dream run against the cranky Hawke. The premise of his Fightback package – that more reform was needed to fix the economy – weakened Hawke because he couldn't reply with a stimulus package of his own without sacrificing Labor's claim to prudent budgeting. Hawke had just four weeks between Fightback's release on 21 November 1991 and the final sitting of parliament before the Christmas break to secure his position against Paul Keating. Then, he would have another year to bring Hewson back to earth before facing voters again in 1993. It was not out of the question, but he needed Labor's vote to improve after the public had seen Fightback to demonstrate that he could live without the former treasurer. But the forensic policy attack was Keating's forte, not Hawke's.

Fightback was accompanied by a marketing blitz. One glossy brochure mailed to voters took the exclamation marks beyond the absurd in its opening paragraph: 'Australia is in trouble and we can't go on the way we are! The Fightback Program to rebuild and reward Australia involves big change – and there's big gains for families, women, men and children. Taxes cut or abolished, so there'll be more jobs and greater benefits; paid for by a 15% GST, reduced government spending and by the tax cheats paying their fair share. It's total reform! It's fair reform! It's needed now!' Voters couldn't be expected to be across all the details. But the size of the document, and its scope, was impressive, and the Coalition was rewarded with an even larger lead in the opinion polls.

Hawke had nothing of substance to offer in reply. He said he would wait until all the government departments had looked at the numbers before making a more considered statement. The final question that Hawke took from Hewson in parliament captured the torture of a prime minister without a sharp script. Hewson taunted Hawke that his review of Fightback had yet to find any mistakes. Hawke replied with verbosity's last stand: 'In view of the fact that the opposition has left out from its inflation calculations the change to the healthcare arrangements, road user charges and the impact on interest rates, it is inevitable – I make this assertion here in this place – that its inflation forecast will be a substantial underestimate of the inflationary impact of its package. There is simply no question about that. Of course, that obviously also means, as the opposition's inflation estimate is an underestimate for the reason of the factors that have been excluded, that the compensation package will be manifestly inadequate. When the total analysis is complete we will be delighted to highlight, as we will, the complete inadequacy of the package in all its respects.'

Hawke was fighting the election before last, when John Howard's tax package was found to contain a double counting error. He was looking for a technical knock-out, to prove that Fightback was unreal. But to argue the detail was to accept Hewson's primary argument that the government had lost its policy nerve.

While Hawke relied on the experts to load his pistol, John Kerin was preparing for the release of the national accounts on 5 December 1991. He had been advised by Treasury they would confirm the recession had ended in the September quarter. No such luck. The statisticians reported that the economy had contracted for the sixth consecutive quarter. Kerin was at a loss to explain the minus sign, and when he sought help from journalists to remind him what GOS – the gross operating surplus, a measure of profits – stood for, his brief term as treasurer was over. Hawke sacked him the next day and appointed Ralph Willis, the man who had to stand aside for Keating almost nine years earlier when Bill Hayden was trying to save his own leadership.

The national accounts that cost Kerin his job marked the first anniversary of Keating's recession-we-had-to-have press conference, and they were as cruel to Kerin as they had been to his predecessor. The subsequent revisions to the data showed that GDP actually grew by 0.4 per cent in the September quarter, rather than fell by 0.3 per cent. The recovery was indeed underway, but Kerin wasn't to know this at the time.

A fortnight later, on 19 December, Hawke succumbed to the

Keating insurgency. The final days of his prime ministership made for painful public viewing as Hawke refused to accept the advice of his closest supporters to stand down. Keating's lieutenants held off from calling a second challenge, because they didn't quite have the numbers. When they were sure of a majority, they still hoped that Hawke would spare them the ordeal of another ballot. But Hawke wanted caucus to make the decision. The final result was closer than either man expected, with Keating winning fifty-six to fifty-one.

Asked how he wanted to be remembered, Hawke replied to the media that evening as he often did about himself, in the third person: 'I guess as a bloke who loved his country, still does, and loves Australians, and who was not essentially changed by high office. I hope they still will think of me as the Bob Hawke that they got to know: the larrikin trade union leader, who perhaps had sufficient common sense and intelligence to tone down his larrikinism to some extent, and to behave in the way a prime minister should if he's going to be a proper representative of his people, but who in the end is essentially a dinky-di Australian. I hope that that's the way they'll think of me.'

He was thinking of Keating as the lesser Australian when he spoke those words. Hawke felt Keating's interests weren't broad enough to connect with ordinary Australians. If this was ever true of Keating, it was doubly true of Hewson, but the Liberal leader had just seen off the prime minister who was once known by his published approval rating as 'Mr 75 per cent'.

Keating said that the government's poor response to Fightback had brought on the second challenge.

Journalist: 'How much responsibility do you bear, personally, for the turbulence that has virtually crippled the government over the last couple of weeks?'

Keating: 'Well, until a few minutes ago, I haven't made a public statement since 8 November. And I think I can say that if the government had been able to respond more fulsomely to the opposition's consumption tax package then the likelihood of this matter [the leadership] being debated before Christmas would have been remote.'

What he hinted at, but didn't spell out, was that he had already packed away his backbencher's office in room 101, on the first floor of the House of Representatives wing of parliament. Not in the expectation of victory, but in preparation for leaving politics. He admitted to confidants at the time that he had given up on a second challenge and would not be returning when parliament reconvened on 25 February 1992. But he had changed his mind when he saw that the release of Fightback had made the Coalition even more popular. The inability of Hawke and Kerin to rattle Hewson had gifted Keating a second act in public life. The next morning, 20 December, Keating was sworn in as prime minister by Governor-General Bill Hayden.

Bob Hawke's humbling exit, and his undignified lurch to celebrity and recrimination in retirement, did not diminish his achievement as prime minister. The 1980s reforms might have been more the work of Paul Keating and his advisers, but they were delivered in the name of Hawke's government. Labor had only been in power this long once before in its hundred-year history, in the Curtin–Chifley era between 1941 and 1949. But that regime began as a minority government, and won only two elections in its own right, in 1943 and 1946. Hawke's record of four successive election victories is unlikely to be matched by any future Labor leader.

The mistake Hawke made was to stay in power one year too long. In the very year Australians most needed their government, Labor was consumed by its own affairs. Even when they thought they were maintaining discipline by holding the line on fiscal policy, they were widening the gulf between government and the people it was supposed to serve. Hawke broke his word to Keating, and Keating was prepared to take the government to the brink to assert his claim to the leadership. Their argument was as indulgent as the one between Gough Whitlam and Malcolm Fraser in another recession year, 1975.

Nonetheless, Hawke remains the standout Australian leader of the post-war period. His strength was his ability to delegate. That is, he didn't play the role of know-it-all that Whitlam and Fraser had taken for granted in their respective governments. It would be wrong, though, to take this as a sign of humility. Hawke always assumed he was the smartest man in the building. Yet his ministers, and their departments, drove the policy agenda.

When Hawke pulled rank on Keating, it was on populist, not policy grounds. Ditching the consumption tax in '85 might have saved the government, but this is not easy to prove. Labor won re-election with massive spending cuts in '87 and with interest rates at 17 per cent in '90. The other reform where Hawke faltered was the introduction of competition in telecommunications. The company that most annoys Australians is the behemoth that Hawke built – Telstra. In 1990, Keating wanted to pit the old Telecom, which held the domestic telephone monopoly, in direct competition with a new private carrier created out of the old OTC, which handled overseas calls. Hawke sided with telecommunications minister Kim Beazley, who recommended a merger of Telecom with OTC to form Telstra. The new private sector rivals never stood a chance because Telstra maintained control of the network on which they would compete – a policy akin to allowing Qantas to own every airport terminal in the nation.

But these were exceptions that proved the rule. Hawke and Keating together gave Australia its most reformist government since the war. 'Even the most uncharitable person would have to acknowledge that in the Labor pantheon, both Hawke and Keating were economic reformers,' John Howard says. 'But I've got to say their job was made infinitely easier by the fact we didn't oppose them politically.'

The former prime ministers reveal a lot about themselves in what they say about each other's legacy. The views on Hawke are unanimous on the question of his leadership style.

Malcolm Fraser: 'I think he [Hawke] brought in the reforms that were necessary. He completed the steps that had been taken in relation to the capital market inquiry, he had his own inquiry, which was really just a rubber stamp about what Campbell was about, and that all went relatively smoothly. I also believe it was a period which ended the old and severe ideological differences which divided politicians in the late '40s, '50s and '60s, when Labor's left communism was still around, and that frightened a lot of people on the right side of politics. Labor people, from their point of view, would remember the '30s and be frightened about what the bosses were going to do to employees. I think the Hawke period demonstrated that in future the debate should be about competence, rather than severe ideological differences, and that was a very healthy change. You might argue that that in part occurred in Gough's time, but it didn't really. You had Jim Cairns, Clyde Cameron, Rex Connor – you had funny-money people, which was foolish. Gough's major fault was he thought the government would run itself if he thought he did his job. He didn't focus on economics.'

Keating offers a short pat on the back that inserts his own role into the picture, just as Hawke did when reflecting on Whitlam. 'Bob Hawke's perhaps important contribution,' Keating says, 'was to empower a collegiate cabinet to pursue strands of policy which were threaded to a common philosophy, and to give significant ministers generally their right to conduct the policy, that is, within the cabinet system.'

Howard is the most complimentary of Hawke. 'I thought Hawke was a good prime minister in his early years. I thought his reforms – the fact that he embedded a lot of the things I believed in, like financial deregulation, tariffs – were very good, and I thought that he was very effective as someone who ran a government.' Howard takes Hawke's side in the legacy dispute with Keating. 'I think that financial deregulation and tariffs . . . Hawke is more entitled to claim credit for those. I think the most courageous thing the Labor Party did in that whole period was tariff reform.'

Hawke changed Australia for the better by opening the economy. His was the first government in more than thirty years to handle external shocks successfully. The floating of the dollar in 1983 and the response to the banana republic crisis in 1986 were examples of leadership strength that taught Australia it could survive in the international marketplace.

When Hawke became prime minister in 1983, government was responsible for fixing the price of the currency, interest rates, tariffs and wages. Eight years on, the market determined the exchange rate, the Reserve Bank was about to assume full independence from the treasurer over monetary policy, and tariffs were being reduced to negligible levels. Of the old economic order, only the centralised wages system remained. He and Keating may never sort out who should get the first credit on any of these economic reforms. Like Lennon and McCartney, it is easier to say it alphabetically. The Hawke and Keating program could not have been developed in eight-and-a-half years in government without Hawke, the vote magnet, securing permission from the Australian people for Keating and other ministers to change the nation.

15

THE LAST SERIOUS ELECTION

Paul Keating didn't rate John Hewson. 'You all regard him as a fresh face, and good on him. In political terms he is – he has only been on the scene a couple of years. But he will never lift economics and politics to an art form. There's no Placido Domingo working in him . . . [I] walk on that stage and some performances will be better than others, but they are all up there trying to stream the economics and the politics together. Out there on the stage, doing the Placido Domingo. Hewson is doing the hall attendant number at the back of the theatre.' The sledge, delivered in his infamous press gallery dinner speech on 7 December 1990, betrayed Keating's concern that Australia was looking for a clean break, and that it would be Hewson who would catch the wave.

On the evening he became prime minister, 19 December 1991, Keating belittled the GST as a distraction: 'Dr Hewson has proposed what he believes is a plan for Australia,' he said. 'But it is the wrong plan. It's a plan which is about making a tenth-order issue about whether you tax income or expenditure into a first-order issue, when we know, all of us, that the first-order issues are employment, growth, investment, maintenance of low levels of inflation, further production, change in the workplace, enterprise bargaining, national economic efficiency.' That wouldn't stop Keating from launching a first-order scare campaign against the GST. It took some front to attack what he once supported. But Keating needed a populist hook to revive Labor's standing in the polls, and he was pragmatic enough to play the anti-GST card that was offered him.

The dilemma he grappled with in his first few weeks as prime minister was how to continue Labor's project to open the economy while also telling people that Hewson's manifesto was poison. That is, how hard could he push before he fell through the political trapdoor of hypocrisy? There was really not that much difference between the two leaders on the question of whether Australia was in need of more reform. Both saw the labour market as the final frontier, although Keating's sympathies would obviously remain with the trade unions. Both wanted to cut personal tax rates. Both were committed to removing industry protection and didn't believe the recession was a good enough reason to slow down that process. It wasn't in Keating's nature to oppose for its own sake; that brand of politics was for the smaller minds in the parliament. The fight against Hewson had to be on behalf of a greater cause, and Keating fixed on the idea that Fightback would destroy the Australian social safety net. Keating, the reforming treasurer, would use his prime ministership to define the no-go zones for deregulation. The lines he drew were in health care and the labour market, and they have held into the twenty-first century.

Fightback gave him two examples to work with. First, Hewson had been encouraged by John Kerin's Medicare co-payment policy and announced deeper cuts. The free hospital bed Australians had taken for granted since 1984 was limited to pensioners and welfare beneficiaries only. The rest of the population would be encouraged to take out private health insurance, and middle- and higher-income earners who didn't would be penalised with a 'surcharge approximately equal to the cost of basic private health insurance' on top of the existing Medicare levy. Fightback admitted that most people would have to pay every time they visited the GP. Second, Hewson wanted to abolish the dole for anyone who had been out of work for more than nine months.

But to turn Fightback into the wrong plan, Keating had to draw up one of his own to fast-track the recovery. As he mulled over the detail, his adviser, John Edwards, noticed something strange about the Fightback arithmetic. The GST didn't pay for the tax cuts. All the revenue it raised was used to abolish other indirect taxes, namely the wholesale sales tax, the excise on fuel and the state-based payroll tax. The income tax cuts, valued at $12.5 billion in a full year, were to be paid for through $9.5 billion in spending cuts and $3 billion in bracket creep – the process by which inflation drives workers into higher tax brackets.

Keating decided he could offer his own tax cuts via the same pot of money. They would form the surprise element of his competing manifesto, One Nation, which was designed to 'get Australia cracking again'. At a total cost of $8 billion, Keating's tax cuts were $4.5 billion cheaper than Hewson's, but they were calibrated to give more to middle-income families and less to upper-income earners. Keating wanted his tax cuts to start three months earlier than Hewson's, on 1 July 1994. The competition on tax cuts at a time of economic crisis showed that some political impulses of old Australia remained. Ten years earlier, Malcolm Fraser was prepared to sacrifice the budget bottom line to secure an early election win.

One Nation was launched on 26 February 1992 as a 'recession buster', and it translated Keating's back-bench epiphany on fiscal policy into hard cash. A one-off payment of $300 million was to be sent to families in April, worth between $125 and $250, depending on the number of children in the household. This payment became a template for future political escapes. John Howard used it in 2001 and 2004. Kevin Rudd used it in 2008 and 2009, to

中华人民共和国万岁

WARM SEND-OFF

Gough Whitlam is given a hero's send-off by Chinese premier Zhou Enlai in 1973 [top]. While Australia recognised China ahead of world opinion, we misread most of the other global trends of the '70s. The first oil shock of 1973 lured the Whitlam government into a farcical search for Arab petrodollars, with Tirath Khemlani [above left] as the middle man. The second oil shock of 1979 exposed the Fraser government. Malcolm Fraser didn't appreciate what US president Jimmy Carter was up to when he appointed Paul Volcker [left] as chairman of the US Federal Reserve that year.

Fairfax Syndication

Fairfax Syndication

Newspix / Peter Bull

Ton Linsen / Fairfax Syndication

A decade of strife: the bad-hair years of the '70s broke all known records for industrial disputation. BLF workers march up Macquarie Street, in Sydney, in 1973 [top left]. In politics, the street rally was all the rage as Whitlam faces a mob in Perth in 1974 [top right]. Social cohesion was further tested by the arrival of Vietnamese boatpeople in the second half of the decade. The era is symbolised by a notorious image from sport, when Trevor Chappell shamed us all with that underarm delivery in 1981.

Confidence returned in the '80s. Fraser was Australia's first barracker-in-chief. He played sports fan, complete with camera, as marathon runner Robert de Castella celebrated his gold at the 1982 Brisbane Commonwealth Games. Hawke was as comfortable in the role as he was with the entrepreneurial spirit, tickling America's Cup-winner Alan Bond. By the time we were toasting the bicentenary of white settlement in 1988, Australia felt like it was on top of the world. But there was a recession around the corner that we would never forget.

Russall McPhedran / Fairfax Syndication

Fairfax Syndication

Peter Morris / Fairfax Syndication

A gallery of rivals: the reform program has often been disrupted by tensions at the top. The American embassy observed that Australia wasn't big enough to contain the 'two super egocentrics', Whitlam and ACTU president Hawke. Fraser routinely humiliated his treasurer John Howard in cabinet, a relationship echoed by Howard's later treatment of Peter Costello. Howard's clashes with Andrew Peacock distracted the Liberals from effective opposition, and the party room continues to rumble with the rivalry of Malcolm Turnbull and Tony Abbott, forged in the republican debates of the '90s (pictured with journalist Paul Kelly). The exception was the productive way Hawke and Paul Keating managed to synchronise their ambitions, but that partnership eventually soured and the treasurer announced his challenge on 30 May 1991, the night before this image was taken of their last public appearance as a duo. Kevin Rudd and Julia Gillard reached boiling point before the government had even settled into its offices.

The '90s: another decade of anger. Howard, wearing bulletproof vest, explained gun-law reform to a sceptical audience in country Victoria in 1996. Pauline Hanson grabbed the voters that Howard had alienated and more than once almost brought down his Coalition government. With industrial disputes fallen to record lows, the boss went on strike in the 1998 waterfront dispute, when Patrick Corporation locked out its workers.

The two most significant speeches of the generation were for reconciliation: Paul Keating's Redfern address on 10 December 1992 and Kevin Rudd's parliamentary apology to the Stolen Generations on 13 February 2008. Hundreds of thousands of people marched across Sydney Harbour Bridge on 28 May 2000, but the prime minister between Keating and Rudd – Howard – was trapped on the issue. That left him the only former prime minister who didn't turn up to congratulate Rudd for the apology [above].

Australians measure their worth through their properties. Today's McMansions have more rooms housing fewer people in the typical family. Ours was the only property market in the rich world to record a capital gain during the Great Recession of 2008–09. Below, Rudd, flanked by his departmental secretary Terry Moran to his left and Treasury secretary Ken Henry to his right, discuss the stimulus package in October 2008.

Joe Armao / Fairfax Syndication

Glen McCurtayne / Fairfax Syndication

nurse households through the global financial crisis. One Nation also contained new spending on transport infrastructure and tax breaks for the car industry.

The funding for the One Nation tax cuts was to come from future budget surpluses. This was the most unbelievable part of the transaction because Keating wanted voters to trust that Treasury had regained its forecasting powers after the errors of the boom and the bust.

One Nation was presented as a more hopeful, more pragmatic document than Fightback. It made a virtue of government intervention, even though Keating now admits that some of the recovery claims were overblown. 'The public works components of it I took on not believing myself that they would have immediate employment consequences,' he says. 'But they were worth doing anyway, like the standardisation of the rail gauge from Melbourne to Adelaide, like building the Anzac Bridge in Sydney. But the notion that they were going to turn the economy around was wishful thinking. What I really wanted to do was a bigger spend directly [on infrastructure], but it was so verboten in the commentariat that no one believed it was the right thing to do.'

In April 1992, Hugh Mackay found voters warming to Keating in an unexpected way: 'When he was federal treasurer he was widely loathed in the community – although, as time wore on, he evoked a grudging respect for his persistence and commitment – and when he challenged Bob Hawke for the prime ministership, those negative feelings escalated into hostility and resentment. But now, to their own amazement, Australians are beginning to regard Paul Keating in a much more positive light; to feel that he is a stronger and more serious person than they previously thought; and certainly to feel that he now has an excellent chance of leading Labor to yet another election victory.'

We no longer blamed him for the recession and were now inclined to believe it would have happened to anyone. And we didn't miss Bob Hawke, whose undignified dash for cash included a TV interview, for a presumed fee, to announce his retirement from politics. At the by-election for Hawke's seat of Wills on 11 April 1992, Labor lost to an independent, local football hero Phil Cleary, who campaigned on old Australian values of protection. The Liberal candidate finished third, a warning that the nation was leaning left, not right.

The political power of Keating's program came from Hewson's response. As the opinion polls tightened, Hewson began showing an autocratic side. He said he would rather resign than change a single element of his blueprint. He picked fights with lobby groups and used increasingly personal language to attack political opponents – language that Keating was himself infamous for, but for which Hewson suffered more because the prime minister wasn't pretending to be the cleanskin. Keating joined the dots for voters by dubbing Hewson 'the feral abacus'.

Hewson was not as well-known as the press gallery assumed. Mackay wrote of how voters continually mispronounced Hewson's surname – 'Houston and Hewston being the most common errors'. 'Part of the sense of invisibility and unfamiliarity about John Hewson is a feeling that he came from nowhere. The electorate is surprisingly uninformed about Dr Hewson's academic background – often assuming that he is a medical practitioner – and there is no sense of his having served an apprenticeship in federal parliament.'

Hewson behaved like the prime minister-in-waiting, which echoed Gough Whitlam's approach. But Keating was no John Gorton or Billy McMahon. He used Hewson as a foil, to recast himself as the underdog.

If any journalist had second thoughts about their initial judgement that Labor was gone, the opinion polls would put them at ease again. The first round with Paul Keating as leader found Labor with a primary vote in the low 30s, and trailing the Coalition by as much 18 percentage points. The gap had been eliminated by the end of March, after the release of One Nation. But the electoral frost returned in winter, and the Coalition was back in front by 12 points at the end of August.

The gap in the polls was compounded by a blowout in the budget deficit that made Keating's promised tax cuts appear unaffordable less than six months after he had announced them. Keating had privately expressed his frustration at a meeting of the expenditure review committee on 20 May. He had shuffled the ministry after he toppled Bob Hawke, removing Ralph Willis from the treasury portfolio and replacing him with John Dawkins, whom he trusted would maintain Labor's reforming zeal. Willis was made finance minister and he clashed with Dawkins over the budget numbers. Dawkins began the discussion by telling his colleagues that the deficit was worse than feared. Willis was not amused that the budget had deteriorated since his brief period as treasurer. 'We should have known the revenue estimates were astray [when pre-paring One Nation],' health minister Neal Blewett recorded Willis as saying. 'Keating claimed that if he had been aware of the rev-enue shortfall at that time, he might well not have advocated tax cuts.'

The Dawkins budget confirmed that the previous year's deficit was almost double what had been forecast – $9.3 billion, instead of $4.7 billion. The present financial year, 1992–93, would see a deficit of $13.4 billion. The surplus that had been promised in One Nation by 1995–96 was now a deficit, which meant that about half the One Nation tax cuts – $4 billion – were in doubt. Keating is not one for public regret, but he should have announced the deferral of the second round of tax cuts at this point, before the election had been held. He would have won anyway, and would not have needed to repudiate his promise afterwards.

The surge in the deficit had two components. First, revenue

had collapsed to its lowest level as a share of the economy since 1973–74, while continued high unemployment meant there were fewer workers paying income tax. Company tax collections were still feeling the aftershocks of the recession. The One Nation tax cuts were predicated on bracket creep, but there was less of it now that inflation had been killed. Treasury did not yet understand the full implications of a low-inflation jobless recovery – a deficit that widens even when growth returns to the economy.

Yet Labor's poll numbers began to improve again. Perhaps the public didn't view this deficit with the same level of apprehension as the Whitlam–Fraser-era deficits because Keating had only recently delivered significant surpluses. The electorate's intuitive grasp of the economics was just about right. A passive budget, in the Kerin sense, or one as aggressive as Fightback, was of no use in a deep recession. But the window for government intervention was narrower than anyone realised. The problem with spending this late in the downturn was that the stimulus would arrive after the fact, when the economy was growing on its own again, thereby leaving the budget in deficit longer than would otherwise be the case. If the government had its time over again, it should have opened its wallet in Keating's final budget and Kerin's only budget, and begun to withdraw the stimulus in the Dawkins budget. That is how Kevin Rudd's Labor government played it successfully through the global financial crisis in 2008–09.

The politics of 1992 forced Keating to overcommit. He had to show the government was there for the people, and he had to claw back Hewson in the opinion polls. What was perplexing for the government and its advisers was that the recession itself had been brief, and not all that deep in terms of lost production. Australia was the second nation to recover after the United States, Bernie Fraser says.

The recession was in the labour market and in the national psyche. Blue-collar jobs were still being cut in recovery, and those who had been spared were being expected to work harder. Economists cheered because productivity – output per worker – was soaring. But there are no votes in a jobless recovery. Nor in one that allowed the banks to repair their books after the crazy lending of the late '80s. The banks were pocketing about one third of the value of each interest rate cut. The cash rate that the Reserve Bank of Australia used to signal the direction of interest rates was reduced by 13.25 percentage points between January 1990 and July 1993. The home mortgage rate was reduced by 8.25 points by September 1993 – a saving of 5 points for the banks. House prices were flat after the boom of the late '80s and this added to gloom in middle Australia. Our recovery in the early '90s was like the American experience after the Great Recession in 2008–09 – slow and sullen.

Given the miserable context in 1992, the debate between Keating and Hewson was strangely uplifting. I've never covered a more interesting contest. It was the last argument that the media didn't try to trivialise by asking each leader if they knew the price of a carton of milk – the quintessential 'gotcha', a seemingly simple question of detail designed to make the pollie stumble, for endless replay on the evening news.

Hewson used his parliamentary reply to the Dawkins budget to accept Keating's premise that the election was about the role of government. The speech, televised nationally, caught the anxiety that Australia was losing ground to the emerging economies in Asia.

Hewson reminded Keating that they were of the same vintage, and had grown up in a full-employment Australia: 'You would not have contemplated the possibility . . . that a so-called Labor government had created . . . one million unemployed. If you, prime minister, had suggested to me in those days that countries such as Hong Kong, Singapore, Taiwan and even Japan could have out-performed us significantly in the course of the period in which we grew up and, ultimately, matched our living standards, I would have genuinely thought you were out of your tree. Japan's standard of living was two-thirds that of ours in 1970. It passed us in 1980. Now we have less than two-thirds of its standard of living in the 1990s. Hong Kong, Singapore and Taiwan, places that do not have a lot of natural advantages in an economic sense, are about to match our standard of living in this decade.'

He said the 'principal difference' between Labor and the Coalition was that Labor had wanted an increasing role for government since the days of Whitlam, while the Coalition had always sided with the private sector. 'We believe in individual Australians and we believe in the forces of the market and the forces of competition. You believe in the big brother, the big, overbearing, suffocating government that is supposed to bring all the answers.'

He was meant to be addressing the nation, as the alternative prime minister, but he sounded like Keating's tutor, throwing back his student's economics exam paper with a big red F for 'fail' slashed across the front page. 'For far too long in this country we have kidded ourselves that you can load business with red tape, green tape, black tape and a host of cost disadvantages, without destroying national wealth. Perhaps most importantly to a lot of Australians, for far too long we have kidded ourselves that you can constantly knock your country and denigrate your flag without destroying national pride. Your concept of compassion –'

Keating broke the convention that the opposition leader's budget reply be heard in silence, and interjected: 'You are the one who has done that.'

Hewson replied: 'You should listen to this because it is very important. Your concept of compassion is to compensate people to whom you have denied choice, freedom and opportunity as a result of your policies. That is your idea of compassion. I remember you saying not long ago that when they fall off the pace you will reach back and pull them up. What you mean is that you will pull everyone else down to the lowest common denominator.'

Keating used this statement to sharpen his own critique of

Fightback, with devastating effect. 'The prime minister would never quote it back in the awkward form of the original,' Keating's speech writer, Don Watson, wrote. 'He would say "John Hewson says if you reach back for them, they will drag you down". Six months later he had developed such a way with the line you could sense a surge of shock and anger in the audience. Just as remarkably, you could sense it in yourself.'

Hewson misread his audience. Middle Australia didn't want to hear that the support they received from government in recession, and the services they expected of government in good times and bad, were indulgences that were holding back the country. They wanted a plan for the future, but not if it asked them to accept American- or Asian-style systems where work was relentless, health care and education were commodities to be bought, and the poor had only themselves to blame for their condition. Hewson never said the last bit, but that was the conclusion the electorate drew. Keating was for Medicare, Hewson was against it. Keating was for job creation, Hewson wanted to cancel the dole after nine months.

Paul Keating was still riding the reform horse himself. He had two complementary wages policies he wanted to pursue that had been left in the too-hard basket during his predecessor's terms. The first was to end centralised wage fixation. 'I could not do it when Bob Hawke was prime minister,' Keating says. 'He would not move from the award system.' Keating has received little credit for enterprise bargaining, under which workers negotiate directly with their bosses, because economists assumed he had pulled his punch – that further deregulation was possible but a Labor prime minister would never stand up his mates in the trade union movement. Keating says this view is nonsense because it doesn't take account of those workers who cannot look after themselves. 'In keeping with our partners the ACTU, and my partner in this, Bill Kelty, I was determined and always have been determined to maintain a reasonable system of minimum guarantees, and hence the safety net was part of the whole policy of enterprise bargaining. Those strong enough to get a bargain and take their share of the productivity saw wages growth really shoot up, but people like women in retail, kids in retail, people without any bargaining power, could only have their wages maintained or had any real growth attributed to them through a formal tribunal process.' The outline of the policy was released in the One Nation statement, and reinforced in the budget, but the detail would have to wait until after the election. Keating needed the trade unions to run a grassroots campaign against Fightback and didn't want to stretch that friendship by removing their monopoly rights in the workplace too soon.

The second reform was to superannuation. Under the Accord in the 1980s, the trade unions had agreed to modify their wage claims in exchange for a super benefit worth 3 per cent of their income. The scheme was limited to those covered by awards, but many employers ignored or were ignorant of, the arrangement. Keating wanted to lift super contributions to 9 per cent of income by 2000, and to bring all workers into the system, not just those covered by awards. The goal was to reduce the dependency on the age pension when the first of the baby boomers were due to retire in 2011. As the scheme reached maturity by the middle of the twenty-first century, an increasing number of people would be able to retire without requiring any government support.

This policy was in the same category as Medicare: the Coalition hated it, and opposed it with extravagant language. An example from John Howard, the industrial relations spokesman, in a radio interview on 10 July 1992: 'The obligation on the prime minister, the obligation on John Hewson, the obligation on me at the present time, is to try and put forward proposals that will help to ameliorate the desperate situation that Australia faces. Stopping a national wage increase would help, cutting immigration dramatically would help, adopting our youth wage proposal would help, putting off this stupid superannuation guarantee levy that costs tens of thousands . . . [of jobs] will help.'

With the Coalition voting against the legislation, Labor was forced to bargain with the Australian Democrats in the Senate. The negotiations between John Dawkins and Democrats superannuation spokesperson Cheryl Kernot were strained, but a compromise was eventually struck. The 9 per cent super target was maintained, but employers were given another two years (to 2002) to reach it. The reform received surprisingly mild coverage at the time, perhaps because the media was fixated on a Hewson victory. But it ranks as Keating's most publicly popular reform, and it served as an important backstop for the Australian economy during the global financial crisis in 2008–09. When the world's credit markets dried up, the $1 trillion held in local super funds were a handy source of finance for Australia's banks and industry. Keating wasn't thinking that far ahead, because no one imagined a GFC even in the darkest days of the early '90s recession. But one of the aims of compulsory super was to reduce Australia's reliance on foreign savings, and the GFC demonstrated the foresight of that reform.

The opposition began to lose its nerve towards the end of 1992. John Howard positioned himself for an unlikely draft to replace Hewson as Liberal leader. Howard never had the numbers, but he made his presence known with the launch of the Coalition's industrial relations policy, Jobsback!, on 20 October. In an interview with *The Australian* published that morning, Howard described industrial relations reform as more important than the GST. 'If I could do only one reform it would be industrial relations. Absolutely. But we can do a GST too.'

Industrial relations was, indeed, the final reform battleground, and Keating confirmed it for Howard on 5 November when he told parliament that if the Coalition won the election, Labor would allow the GST to pass through in the Senate, but would oppose Jobsback. 'I say to the opposition that, in the unlikely event of its becoming a government, the Labor Party would not obstruct the passage of the GST legislation in the Senate. I want it made totally clear that a vote for Hewson is a vote for the GST. No Democrats or any other group will save Australia from that.'

Publicly, Keating oozed confidence. When Hewson had asked in September why he wouldn't call an early election, Keating replied with the sledge of the decade: 'The answer is, mate, because I want to do you slowly. There has to be a bit of sport in this for all of us.' Privately, Keating was expecting an honourable loss. His most optimistic scenario was that Hewson would win narrowly, but that Senate obstruction of Jobsback would force the Coalition to call a double-dissolution election, which Keating hoped to win in his own right from opposition. Howard was looking at the future with a similar idea in mind – that Hewson wouldn't last long and that he might replace him in government. The conventional wisdom throughout '92 had been that no government could win re-election with unemployment in double digits. But the Liberals knew something that Labor didn't: the private polling showed the electorate were willing to give Keating a chance because they weren't yet ready to trust Hewson.

The 1993 election became winnable for Labor in November '92. The Newspolls either side of Keating's declaration that if Labor lost it wouldn't obstruct the GST, track a decisive shift in voting intentions. In late October, the Coalition led Labor by twelve points on the primary vote, 49 per cent to 37. The next survey, taken a fortnight later on the weekend of 6–8 November, found Labor had seized a four-point lead of 45 per cent to 41 – the first time in the term that it was in front. It wasn't a rogue poll, because this would be Labor's primary vote at the election the following March.

Swings this large between polls are rare without the jolt of a real world event. Keating's GST ploy and even the release of the Jobsback policy don't offer credible explanations on their own. The difference was the election of a Coalition government in Victoria on 3 October. The nation's second-largest state had suffered the worst of the recession because its manufacturing base bore the brunt of the job losses. Victorians were ready for change, but they didn't expect their new government to clobber them with a secret agenda for cut-throat deregulation.

The Liberal premier, Jeff Kennett, had taken the cautious road to office. His campaign invited voters to punish Labor, the 'guilty party'. The mandate Kennett claimed was to fix the state's finances. He said he couldn't specify just how he would do this until he had seen the true state of the budget. Barely three weeks after he was sworn in, Kennett pulled out the razor and the nation took notes.

On 28 October, Victorian's electricity, gas and water charges were increased by 10 per cent; motor vehicle registration fees were doubled; and a $100-per-household 'deficit reduction levy' was imposed. The following day, one in twenty of the state's public servants were sacked, and those who survived the cull had their 17.5 per cent holiday-pay loading taken away. Private sector workers were told they would lose their weekend penalty rates. On the third day of the revolution, 30 October, Kennett rushed through legislation awarding generous pay rises to senior government members, including a $160-a-week bonus for the industrial relations minister, Phil Gude. A new verb entered the political lexicon – 'Jeffed' – which meant to be sacked or shafted.

None of these changes had been mentioned in the state election campaign, and the public responded with the biggest street protests since the Vietnam War moratorium. What made Victorians fume, and the rest of the nation fearful, was that the Kennett program read like a full dress rehearsal for Fightback and Jobs-back. Rarely does a democratically elected government show such a different face after it wins. Individual promises may be broken as the new regime discovers the budget cupboard bare, or the numbers in the parliament force it to modify its agenda. But Kennett's intent was to bewilder. He wanted to confront every vested interest at once, so no individual group would have the right of an uninterrupted reply in the court of public opinion, or the time to unite with others around an agreed log of claims.

Keating secretly admired Kennett's method. He didn't have much time for Victorian Labor, which he blamed for denying him a soft landing for the economy in 1990–91, and was still blaming for the jobless recovery. But he couldn't abide Kennett's assault on the trade unions. In quick succession, Keating offered Victorian workers protection under the federal system, while Kennett backed down on the pay rises for himself and his ministers. So economists didn't get to test the proposition that cutting living standards for workers while increasing the remuneration of their boss – in this case, the government – leads to a more productive society.

Kennett's shock therapy came at the end of an agitated month, when Hewson had been attacking the tourism industry and accusing New South Wales Labor opposition leader Bob Carr of not being man enough to run the nation's largest state. 'You've got to be suspicious of a guy that doesn't drive, doesn't like kids and things like that. When he's up against a full-blooded Australian like John Fahey, he has not got a hope.' Hewson didn't stop at just ridiculing his political opponents, which was Keating's speciality. He was passing judgement on entire sections of the community. His most unusual critique was aimed at the one-third of the population that didn't own their own home. 'In any street, of course, it's always easy to tell the rented houses . . . they are the ones where the lawn isn't mowed, the plants aren't watered and the fences aren't fixed.' Hewson's approach anticipated by more than a decade the partisanship of the United States, where the voters of the other side are deemed to be unAustralian.

Keating had nothing to lose and Hewson wanted to win on his own terms. The match-up suggested that Keating would be the more political, but it was Hewson who blinked first and sacrificed his policy integrity. In December 1992, Hewson submitted to internal demands to modify Fightback. He removed food and childcare from the GST base, at a cost of $4.2 billion. The tax cuts were trimmed to take $2.2 billion away from higher-income earners, and the plan to deny the dole to the long-term unemployed was dropped. The package didn't add up, and the last-minute display of pragmatism reduced Hewson to just another politician, but made Labor people nervous because now Keating would be the issue again.

In the simple retelling of the 1993 election, Hewson threw it all away. The private polling of both sides detected a very late swing to the government, although Labor's still predicted a Coalition victory, while the Liberal's had Labor winning. The most common examples cited for the late swing were the street rallies Hewson held in the final week, which reinforced concerns about his temperament, and his earlier campaign stumble over how the GST would apply to a birthday cake.

But the polls showed a dead-heat in March '92, the Coalition well ahead between April and October, Labor in front in November and December, and the Coalition returning to the lead in January and February of the new year, and staying there until the final forty-eight hours of the campaign, when Labor caught them. The election had been a toss-up for twelve months. Yet politics still wants to record this as the unlosable election for Hewson.

It's time to rethink the 1993 election – its meaning at the time, and its contrary legacy for both sides. All the fractures in contemporary Australia between old and new, between city and country, between the coast and the inland regions and between states were there on election night, 13 March. Most of the press gallery, myself included, missed the significance of the state differences because we were gripped by Paul Keating's great escape.

Keating defied the dictum that Australians couldn't vote for a prime minister who didn't at least pretend to share their quasi-religious passion for sport. He was a classical music buff, preferring Mahler to Midnight Oil. He spoke up for the arts, knowing that when Gough Whitlam did so twenty years earlier, through the National Gallery of Australia's purchase of Jackson Pollock's *Blue Poles*, the media shrieked in horror and added it to the articles of impeachment against Labor.

Keating's support can best be understood through the Whitlam frame. The victory for 'the true believers', as Keating called it, had an echo of 1972. Labor won a majority of votes after preferences in New South Wales and Victoria, but the Coalition had the majorities in Queensland and Western Australia. This translated to four extra seats in Victoria and another three each in New South Wales and Tasmania. But Labor lost three seats in South Australia and two each in the mining states of Queensland and Western Australia, for a net gain of two seats nationally.

New South Wales and Victoria are the two most cosmopolitan states in the nation, and Keating's more compassionate pitch rang true with the tertiary degree holders and the non-English-speaking immigrants alike. In the mining states, which boasted fewer university-educated and fewer olive- and yellow-skinned immigrants than the national average, Keating's world view was never popular.

The rise of the suburban middle class in Sydney and Melbourne had ended the conservative hegemony in '72. It was Whitlam's agenda to improve services, from sewerage to higher education, that defined Labor's modern calling. Keating updated the message for recession by presenting Labor as the party of the social safety net. The GST worked as a political metaphor to place Labor on the side of the ordinary voter, but the GST wasn't the reason why the government was returned with an increased majority. The bread-and-butter issue that swung the most important votes Labor's way for conservative women was Medicare.

Keating's was the first sitting government since Harold Holt's in 1966 to record a swing to it. Labor's primary vote jumped by 5.5 points to 44.9 per cent, as the environmental protest vote which had gone to the Australian Democrats in 1990 came home. The Coalition's primary vote also rose by 0.8 to 44.3 per cent. After preferences, Labor had improved its popular vote by 1.5 to 51.4 per cent.

Keating's GST scare was Labor's revenge for the Red scares that Robert Menzies had used against it in the 1950s and '60s. An unpopular government was able to save itself by making the opposition the issue, and an unloved prime minister became a new form of national hero because he had seen off the threat of the Americanisation of Australian politics. Hewson had underestimated the extent to which Australians wanted government to look after them, and the next Coalition prime minister would have to offer the middle class a new form of protection to defeat Labor.

I 6

ROLLING BACK THE YEARS

Politicians had dishonoured tax cuts in the past and lived to win another election. Malcolm Fraser secured another term after his 1977 fistful of dollars was snatched back. Bob Hawke won three more times after he used John Howard's parting deficit to justify abandoning most of Labor's 1983 election program. But they were new to the job. After ten years in office as treasurer and prime minister, Paul Keating had no credits left in the political clemency bank.

John Dawkins told Keating the day after the 1993 election that the budget required some heavy pruning if it was to return to surplus. He wanted the tax cuts to be cancelled to make the job easier. Dawkins added a sting to the advice: if the tax cuts weren't dropped, he would resign as treasurer. Keating was in a bind because he had already legislated for the tax cuts. 'They are not a promise, they are law: L-A-W law,' he had said on one memorable occasion during the campaign.

They argued the detail for months before settling for the worst of both worlds. The first leg of the tax cuts was brought forward by seven months to November 1993, and offset by a $3.5 billion

increase in sales taxes and fuel excise. The second leg was deferred
by two years to 1998.

Labor's vote tumbled immediately after the release of the
1993–94 budget, and an open revolt from the caucus and the trade
unions followed. The Coalition, still smarting over the election
result, refused to pass the budget, leaving Labor to negotiate with
the Australian Democrats, two Western Australian Greens and
independent senator Brian Harradine, who shared the balance of
power. Keating says his government was marked for defeat from
that point on. But Keating's wasn't an isolated example. Across
the Atlantic, George Bush senior had just lost the presidency to
Bill Clinton for making a similar promise. 'Read my lips: no new
taxes,' he had told Americans. By that, Bush meant he wouldn't let
Congress force him to increase taxes in his first term. He had broken his vow in 1990, two years after making it, and his re-election
campaign in '92 was crowded out by questions of trust. They
were 'the six most destructive words in the history of presidential politics', according to Republican pollster Richard Wirthlin.
(Presumably, Nixon's 'I'm not a crook', uttered after the Watergate
scandal broke, were the four most destructive.)

The original dame of deregulation, Margaret Thatcher, was also
a recent victim of taxation policy. She had lost her job in November 1990 after her party room turned against her over a number
of issues, most notably her poll tax introduced in April that year.
The poll tax was called a 'community charge'; it replaced existing
council charges on property with a flat tax on individuals, whether
they owned property or not. Like the GST, it was a tax shuffle that
was supposed to deliver greater efficiency. But the losers rioted,
and the winners didn't thank Thatcher. Her successor, John Major,
promptly abandoned the poll tax for a softer option, and won a
fourth term for the conservatives in April 1992.

What Keating experienced with the 'L-A-W' tax cuts was
another form of the 'gotcha'. It was barely mentioned either in the

campaign or in the phoney war before it. On the sole occasion Keating used the phrase, no one had picked up on it – he couldn't get the press gallery interested in tax cuts until after the election. But then, as time went on, footage of him uttering the pledge came back to haunt him. And with each replay of the phrase 'L-A-W', people came to believe that they had expressly voted for tax cuts.

There are two reinforcing lessons from the Australian and British experiences in the early '90s. Long-term governments were able to squeeze an extra election victory, despite recession, because they had changed leaders (a lesson John Howard didn't heed a decade later). Keating and Major had both presented as the worker's friend, offering to ease the tax burden without the messy trade-offs involved in tax reform. But the re-elected were bound to disappoint people because of the Catch-22 of deregulation. Governments couldn't secure a return to previous certainties, they could only renew their authority by offering to stop someone else from adding to the reform burden.

Paul Keating wasn't interested in holding power for its own sake. He wanted to complete his economic reform agenda through enterprise bargaining, bringing Australia closer to Asia, and moving on to the big social reform that had eluded well-meaning governments on both sides since Harold Holt's: reconciliation with Indigenous Australians. Keating had given fair warning of his interest in reconciliation three months before the last election in his most well-known public speech, the Redfern Address, on 10 December 1992.

'We non-Aboriginal Australians should perhaps remind ourselves that Australia once reached out for us,' he said. 'Didn't Australia provide opportunity and care for the dispossessed Irish? The poor of Britain? The refugees from war and famine and persecution in the countries of Europe and Asia? Isn't it reasonable to say that if we can build a prosperous and remarkably harmonious multicultural society in Australia, surely we can find just solutions to the problems which beset the first Australians – the people to whom the most injustice has been done?

'And, as I say, the starting point might be to recognise that the problem starts with us non-Aboriginal Australians. It begins, I think, with the act of recognition. Recognition that it was we who did the dispossessing. We took the traditional lands and smashed the traditional way of life. We brought the diseases. The alcohol. We committed the murders. We took the children from their mothers. We practised discrimination and exclusion. It was our ignorance and our prejudice. And our failure to imagine that these things could be done to us. With some noble exceptions, we failed to make the most basic human response and enter into their hearts and minds. We failed to ask – how would I feel if this were done to me? As a consequence, we failed to see that what we were doing degraded all of us.'

In the normal meaning of the word 'mandate', Keating's increased majority at the 1993 election should have granted him the ability to pursue reconciliation without obstruction from the opposition. To add legal weight to his moral argument, Keating had a High Court judgement on his side. On 3 June 1992, the full court, by a majority of six to one, found that Indigenous people held a form of 'native title' to their traditional land if it had not been extinguished by the granting of another lease. The claim had been brought on by Eddie Mabo against the Queensland government and it related to the specific case of Mer, in the Murray Islands chain. The judgement debunked the notion of *terra nullius*, that no one occupied Australia before white settlement. Keating devoted much of 1993 to translating the judgement into legislation. His scheme allowed Indigenous people to access land that had not been converted to freehold title. Where rights co-existed – for instance, a lease over a rural property – the native title holder

could only access the land by agreement. Native title did not over-
take pre-existing rights. But the Coalition refused to negotiate,
and turned what could have been a bipartisan advance on a two-
century-old problem into a toxic argument.

The losers from deregulation had their first pyrrhic victory
through this debate. The private polling of both sides showed that
older white males who had been made redundant by the recession felt, incorrectly, that Indigenous Australians were receiving
privileges that were not available to them. The federal Coalition
was willing to feed their anxiety with ill-judged and inaccurate
warnings that native title could see people lose their backyards.
Mining companies and farmers joined the chorus calling for the
High Court decision to be wound back to deliver investment certainty. Even Victorian premier Jeff Kennett, who prided himself
on his open-mindedness, warned that private land could be under
threat, before retracting the comment.

John Hewson couldn't resist the urge to obstruct. The opposition leader assumed, incorrectly, that Keating couldn't satisfy the
kaleidoscope of grievance among the Senate minor parties.

Keating held his nerve and the legislation passed through the
Senate on 21 December 1993. Hewson lost his cool, describing it as
a 'day of shame'. The following morning he told parliament: 'The
Coalition is totally opposed to this piece of legislation. It is bad
legislation. It will prove to be a disaster for Australia. It goes way
beyond the High Court. It introduces inequities into the Australian system. It consciously sets out to divide the Australian nation
and there is only one thing you can do with bad legislation and
that is throw it out.'

Which way would public opinion settle? The level of rancour
suggested that Keating would suffer another dip, as occurred with
the budget when his dissatisfaction rating reached a record high of
75 per cent. But he had earned some respect, and his dissatisfaction rating fell by 11 points to 52 per cent in the month after the

legislation was secured. The system still rewarded politicians who got things done. By March 1994, Labor was back in front of the Coalition on the primary voting intention.

However, the public was less forgiving of Keating for pursuing closer relations with our nearest neighbour, Indonesia. We should know one another better, but the hang-ups of race and culture seem to get in the way. Misunderstanding is our common language. If one of our young tourists mucked up in Bali and ended the night in a police cell, the Australian media would whip itself into an indignant rage and demand the Indonesian legal system keep its hands off our citizen. But the innocent abroad would have been demonised at home if the same person had been pissed or stoned in the CBD of any Australian capital.

Keating thought Indonesia's President Suharto was worth befriending for the same pragmatic reason that Whitlam had sought out China's Zhou Enlai and Mao Zedong more than twenty years earlier. But Keating could never get the public to separate his interest in Jakarta from the plight of the East Timorese, and his diplomatic initiatives in the region were added to the stew of resentment that was brewing against Labor. All the opposition needed to do was find the right leader to give the public the confidence to dispose of the devil they knew too well.

John Hewson fell in May 1994 to the so-called 'dream team' of Alexander Downer and Peter Costello. John Howard had wanted to challenge, but was told not to apply. Downer was an example of where politics was heading. He was born into the profession – his father, Sir Alec, had been a cabinet minister in the Menzies government, and his grandfather, Sir John, a premier of South Australia and a senator in the first federal parliament. Alexander worked as an economist, diplomat and political staffer before entering parliament at the 1984 election, aged thirty-three. Both sides of politics would turn in desperation to candidates such as Downer as the economy settled into its longest boom. They'd come from seemingly nowhere, impress the public for a couple of opinion polls by feeding their latest complaint, then reveal their immaturity, and fade away. When their numbers dipped, the question of who should succeed them would be inserted into the next survey.

The opinion poll that had come closest to calling the previous election, Newspoll, began publishing a fortnightly survey in 1992. Two polls per month gave the political reporter a data crutch to match the statistics of the economics reporter. If the primary vote didn't show any change, you could look up the satisfaction rating of each leader, and if they yielded a yawn, check out who was the preferred prime minister. By the second half of 1994, Newspoll consistently showed Keating out-rating Downer as the preferred prime minister by a factor of two to one, which meant another round of speculation about leadership change.

Howard was circling and Downer was unable to deter him. Andrew Peacock, the man who had repeatedly thwarted Howard's previous attempts at resurrection, had finally removed the veto against his old rival. Howard didn't want to challenge, opting for a Hawke-style draft, but told Downer he would force a party-room ballot if necessary. The complication in this leadership tussle was the position of the Liberal deputy, Costello. Howard needed him to stay out of this fight, and offered a Kirribilli-style agreement to serve two terms before standing aside.

Downer resigned on Australia Day 1995, making history as the first main-party leader who was denied the opportunity to contest an election. (He redeemed himself by becoming the nation's longest-serving foreign affairs minister.) Howard greeted the media as leader four days later, on 30 January, as a new man. Earlier that month, Howard had disowned his former self on Asian immigration, in an interview with his former critic Greg Sheridan. 'I'm sorry . . . [if] my remarks were seen by Australians of Asian descent as suggesting that I regarded them in any way as lesser Australians than any other Australians,' he said, 'then I regret that very much.' Now, as leader, he would promise to keep Medicare, drop his industrial relations policy Jobsback, and even allow Australia to become a republic, if that's what the people wanted. So eager was he to minimise the policy difference between himself and Keating that Howard also agreed later to rule out a GST for all time, and to embrace the 1995 budget announcement to revive the repudiated 'L-A-W' tax cuts as a direct payment into workers' superannuation accounts.

Keating blames my employer, News Limited, for helping to resurrect Howard. 'Asking for sixteen years was the hard one to get over, of course it was – the equivalent of four successive presidential terms, pretty hard to do. But there was a great willingness on the part of the press to excuse Howard. *The Australian* had Greg Sheridan write the apologia interview, to say "He's okay, we've checked, he's not really a little suburban racist, he's okay", and that's what that interview really did – "We are clearing the decks for this guy to come back for a second time, but this time perhaps as prime minister."'

Howard was no more popular than Keating, but he had the advantage of nostalgia. Voters saw him as the man to take Australia back to what it had been, before deregulation and Asian immigration, even though Howard himself didn't want to return to the old ways with which they identified him.

The final political blow against Paul Keating coincided with John Howard's re-emergence. Inflation was stirring for the first time since the late 1980s. Even though unemployment had only just dropped below 10 per cent, the governor of the Reserve Bank, Bernie Fraser, wasn't willing to risk a repeat of the last boom, when his predecessor, Bob Johnston, moved to tighten monetary policy too late. Fraser struck three times between August and December

1994 for a combined increase of 2.75 percentage points to the official interest rate. The banks passed on the entire amount to home borrowers.

'As with the two previous increases, today's rise is intended to help sustain solid economic expansion with low inflation well into the future, that being the surest way to deliver on-going reductions in unemployment,' Fraser said on 14 December 1994. 'Timely increases in interest rates which succeed in heading off inflationary pressures before they take hold also mean that interest rate rises over the course of the cycle will be lower than would otherwise be necessary.' Fraser's actions carried the explicit threat of more to come if borrowing and spending didn't ease. It was a calculated official tantrum, and it worked as well as these things can. The inflation rate returned to the RBA's comfort zone within six months and stayed there for the remainder of the decade. But Keating was denied the vindication of a pre-election rate cut when the inflation threat had passed.

The opinion polls jumped in the Coalition's favour when Howard took over, and didn't budge after that.

The election verdict on 2 March 1996 was almost identical to the first Newspoll that tested Howard against Keating twelve months beforehand. Labor's primary vote collapsed by 6.2 per cent to 38.8, its lowest since the 1930s; the Coalition's primary vote was up 3 to 47.3 per cent. After the distribution of preferences, the Coalition's popular vote rose to 53.6, a swing of 5.1 per cent. The Coalition victory was as decisive as Bob Hawke's had been in '83, when Labor had polled 53.2 per cent in two-party terms. Keating paid, in the end, for his unpopularity. In his four-and-a-half years in office, his net personal rating remained below zero, with the proportion of voters who disapproved of his job performance always exceeding those who approved. After the heavy-duty policy debates of 1993, this election was about nothing, because Howard had accepted Keating's program.

The Coalition picked up 29 seats from Labor: 13 in New South Wales, 10 in Queensland, two in both Western Australia and South Australia and one in both Victoria and Tasmania. Labor lost a further two seats to anti-immigration independents in Queensland and Western Australia. Labor was reduced to just two seats out of 26 in Queensland, two out 12 in South Australia and three out of 14 in Western Australia. It was a rejection as decisive as Gough Whitlam's losses of '75 and '77, and Arthur Calwell's of '66. But the post-Keating Labor Party saw no need to reinvent itself. There would be no Gough Whitlam or Bill Hayden in the ranks to fashion a new agenda to restore Labor's trust with middle Australia. The leadership fell to Kim Beazley, a second-generation politician and one of the loveliest men in the parliament. He calculated that Labor needed some time to lick its wounds, and some distance from the reform program that had exhausted the electorate. It was a direct lift of Howard's risk-averse campaign strategy, and just as dishonest because it presumed that a return to government was simply a case of waiting for the incumbent to make mistakes. Howard's greatest political victory was in bringing Labor to his home court of poll-driven politics, leaving him free to recast the national identity debate that Keating had started.

Howard was only the second Liberal prime minister to come from Sydney, after Billy McMahon, and the first to win a general election. His home town put the Coalition on the right side of the nation's coming demographic wave, because population growth was moving northward, from the Australian Rules state of Victoria to the rugby league states of New South Wales and Queensland. Yet the voters who gave the Coalition its landslide saw themselves as the new forgotten people who had lost their nation to economic rationalism and multiculturalism.

The Coalition recorded its largest swings in seats with above-average Australian-born populations, in the Sydney and Brisbane mortgage belts and beyond. The biggest swing of the election was in Bill Hayden's old seat of Oxley, in Brisbane's south. No one expected Labor to lose there, but a perfect storm of local resentment and media notoriety combined to deliver an unlikely win for Pauline Hanson. She had stood as a Liberal, but was stripped of party endorsement mid-campaign after making a series of inflammatory statements against Aboriginal welfare. The people she spoke for came to adopt her surname – the Hansonites. Howard could make them feel better by attacking political correctness, but he couldn't restore their spot on the middle of the income ladder. His challenge, not apparent in the euphoria of election night celebrations, was to ride out the anti-incumbent wave, so he could catch the demographic wave. The Hansonites hadn't voted for him, but against Keating. The minute they realised that Howard shared Keating's faith in markets, they would point their pitchforks at him.

Paul Keating has few admirers among the former prime ministers. His strongest advocate, surprisingly, is Malcolm Fraser. 'Keating had a sense of identity and a sense of purpose for Australia,' Fraser says. 'He was let down by over-flamboyant language sometimes, but he did have part of what has been totally lacking lately – he had a vision of Australia for the future, possibly more so than Bob Hawke, but not more than Whitlam. But Keating understood economics, which Gough didn't, and I think it would have been interesting [if he had won in '96].'

Hawke offers praise on social policy. 'When I was there, I'm not saying he confected an interest in Aboriginal affairs, but it wasn't something that he actively pursued when he was treasurer. But when he became prime minister he did. He had the advantage of the Mabo decision, and the Redfern speech was a very important contribution to lifting the understanding and sense of responsibility for the Australian people.'

Howard is unexpectedly gracious towards Keating in one reform area that the Coalition had opposed him. 'I think his most significant thing was compulsory super, and I acknowledge he tried to bring in a broad-based indirect tax [as treasurer] and that he was undercut by Hawke and the unions. Having shown the courage and foresight on it in '85, he was completely political in '93 by running the campaign against Hewson.'

In winning the 1993 election, Keating had settled the future of Medicare as a universal health scheme.

'You should never underestimate the ongoing sensitivity of the electorate towards health policy,' Howard says. 'That's the reason why when I became leader in '95 I resolved that we had to reverse our de facto commitment to getting rid of Medicare, because I was convinced the Australian public wanted to keep it. And I think the health policy we produced in '93 made a bigger contribution to our defeat than many people . . . [realised].'

There is symmetry here between Labor's two most polarising prime ministers. Whitlam was more economically rational than the community remembers because he was the first to slash protection, in '73. Keating, likewise, was more of a bleeding heart than his image suggested because he saved Medicare twenty years later.

Keating was the first prime minister since Robert Menzies to leave the nation in better shape than he found it. Unemployment and inflation were falling together, and the economy was ready to stand on its own. In fact, the 1990s would be the only decade of the post-war era in which Australia's productivity grew by more than the rich world average.

It irks Keating to this day that the beneficiary of his and Hawke's reform work was Howard, a man whom he privately collaborated with in the early '80s but has loathed ever since. The last time they spoke was during the 2000 Sydney Olympics, when Keating teased Howard by saying that our gold medal winners wanted to hide the Union Jack in our flag when they climbed on the victory dais. The paradox of Keating's heavy electoral defeat is that he was the first prime minister to lose his job to an opponent who was too cautious to offer an alternate vision for the nation. Howard doesn't concede this point, because no new leader really believes that the vanquished can dictate the terms of a democratic handover. Yet Howard knew the nation was reform-weary. He capitalised on that mood by making Keating the election issue. But to do so, Howard had to agree with most of Keating's policies. The meeting of minds was inevitable on economic reform. But Keating bears responsibility for placing a clamp on Howard's ambition. He had unconsciously written the anti-reform scripts for the 1990s and beyond by his demolition of Fightback.

TRANSITIONS II:
FROM BLUE COLLAR
TO PINK COLLAR

The baby boomers assume they were the first to experience every modern social trend. From drugs to debt, they were on a generational search for ecstasy. Their adolescence marked the sexual revolution of the 1960s and feminism in the '70s. Their adulthood took in economic rationalism in the '80s. But their liberation terminated at the kitchen table. When the boomers started their families, the labour divided as it had for their parents. Dad went to work and mum stayed at home to raise the children.

The generational shift between old and new Australia is measured in the time a mother spends away from paid employment. The boomer mothers did not return to work until all their children had been packed off to primary school. As recently as 1986, the majority of mothers were still out of the labour force when their youngest was aged five.

The women who tried to have it all – career and kids – were from Generation X, born from 1964 to 1979. American pop culture dismissed the Xers as slackers. But Australia's were the hardest-working women in peacetime. By 2006, as the last of the Xers were having the first of their babies, the majority of mothers were back at work when their youngest was aged one. Most of those working mums were on part-time hours. The disparity between the single-income boomer household and the dual-income Xer household is explained by the quiet revolution that accompanied deregulation – the rise of the qualified woman. The final wave of boomers, born between 1959 and 1963, had only 20 per cent of men and 13 per cent of women going on to university. The final wave of Generation Xers, born between 1979 and 1983, boasted almost twice as many men (34 per cent) and almost three times as many women (35 per cent) in tertiary education.

The mainstream experience of migrant families predicted the experience of Generation X, but without the university degrees. A two-income household was the norm, and in the street I grew up in, in Melbourne's south-east, during the mid '60s and early '70s, the family with the newest arrival would often act as babysitter to the rest of us while our mothers were at work.

My father was born in 1934, my mother in 1942, so they were too old to be counted as baby boomers. Both worked for as long as I could remember. My father was a railway signalman. One of my earliest recollections is sitting with him in one of the signal boxes he manned, counting the trains that rattled through Torronga station. When he completed his night shift, he would crawl into bed just as we were rising from ours to get ready for school. He had the windows of the main bedroom blacked out, like Elvis in Graceland, to deny the morning sun. We'd try to make no noise as we ate breakfast, and tiptoe out via the back door. I had to wake him up once to tell him work was on the line. Could he work a second shift?

My mother had a knack for finding jobs with dream perks. She worked in a chocolate factory that would allow her to take home a handful of the week's output each Friday. She would cover them in plastic wrap and hand them to me before I went to play Saturday morning cricket for the under-12s. We hit the working-class jackpot when she became the head cleaner at the local Hoyts cinema, on the corner of Dandenong and Glenferrie roads, Malvern. The money was better than anything she had done before, but the work was backbreaking. The two-level theatre was beyond even her bulldozer strength, but rather than give up the position, she would sneak me in on weekends, a child labourer of eleven, to help out. I worked Sunday mornings.

The cinema had to be ready by midday, all 1200 seats, toilets upstairs and downstairs, the candy bar, and a Gone-With-the-Wind marble staircase that required a dousing to remove the sticky footprints of soft drink and choc tops from the night before. My work was in the stalls, pulling out the easy stuff from under the seats so Mum could sweep behind me with her broom with the sawn-off handle. I went on the payroll in my early teens, first as relief cleaner, and then full-time when I was studying at university. I squeezed in as many lectures and tutorials as I could in the two days I wasn't working. Social researchers might argue that necessity forced migrant women like my mother to juggle low-paid jobs with their duties at home. But as education levels rose in the Australian community, so did the number of working mothers.

Generations X and Y are terms of incomprehension. I prefer Generation W. The starting point is the same, covering people born from 1964 onwards, who were too young to remember The Beatles. Generation W, for 'women and wogs', is the first group in which women are better educated than men, and the Australian-born children of immigrants are better educated than their local peers. These people had no experience of working behind the tariff wall, so they should be counted as deregulation's recruits. The first wave of Generation W turned twenty years old in 1984, when the dollar had been floated and the banks were being opened up to competition. By delaying maternity, the Xers bought their first home after the boom of the '80s. The elevated entry cost would reinforce the pressure for the mother to return to work early, because two incomes were required to service the typical capital-city home loan. Property prices remained flat for most of the '90s and the absence of capital gain created the curious feeling among the winners of deregulation that they were being ripped off. Their frustrations meshed with the fury from the losers of deregulation – the baby-boomer men who would never again have jobs secure enough to keep mum at home – to create a new divide between the time-poor and the underclass.

The Whitlam and Fraser recessions, which preceded the entry of Generation W into the workforce, destroyed the jobs of 350 000 blue-collar men in the breadwinner sectors of manufacturing, construction and farming. On the eve of the first oil shock in 1973, almost half the men in work (48 per cent) were using their hands in these three areas. Manufacturing and construction accounted for 1.5 million jobs in total and farming another 350 000. By 1983, the number of manufacturing and construction jobs had fallen to 1.2 million, and farming had dropped to 300 000.

Bob Hawke was the last leader of his type. He was the bloke's prime minister, in charge of the country for the final decade when the male of old Australia felt the economy might still be on his side. Yet at the end of the Keating recession, another decade had been lost. Only 1.25 million were employed in manufacturing and construction in 1993, the same combined figure as ten years earlier. Farming was also treading water, with 300 000.

Those twenty years from the first oil shock to the 'recession we have to have' reduced the manufacturing sector from 27 per cent to 18 per cent of all male jobs, construction from 12 to 11 per cent and farming from 9 to 7 per cent. All the trouble was in manufacturing, but these men had nowhere else to go, because construction and farming didn't grow in net terms between the governments of Gough, Malcolm and Bob. The manufacturing jobs went offshore, first to the Asian tiger economies of South Korea, Taiwan and Singapore, and later, China.

Deregulation's first decade between 1983 and 1993 did create 1.4 million new jobs, even allowing for the recession. But two out of three of those jobs (900 000) went to women, and more than half of those (500 000) were part-time positions. The pink-collar jobs were divided almost equally between recreational services, community services, retail, and wholesale trade and financial services. In other words, the open economy called women to serve as shop assistants, nurses, teachers and lawyers. The men who prospered in the 1980s were tapped into the financial and property booms, namely builders, real estate agents, bank workers and financial advisers.

The recession of the early 1990s had been feminist without meaning to be. The Labor program to internationalise the economy was supposed to bring the best out of blue-collar men by creating new industries in high-end manufacturing. But the worker most suited to deregulation's demand for flexibility was female. She was prepared to work part-time, or accept a lower wage for doing the same job as the men in her workplace. The pattern would be repeated through the recovery, with women accounting for 1 million of the 1.8 million jobs created between 1993 and 2003. Once again, most of the new positions (600 000) were part-time. Manufacturing lost its status at the nation's top employer in 2002, replaced by the female employer of retail. It slipped to third on the ladder in 2006 behind the caring economy of health, aged and child care, another pink-collar employer. In 2011, it fell to fourth, swapping places with the blue collar sector of construction.

Going into the Keating recession, men in full-time work outnumbered women in full- and part-time work by almost 950 000. By 2009, those lines had crossed, with women in all work surpassing men in full-time work for the first time on record. Not even the mining boom could reverse this trend.

The movement from blue collar to pink collar predates deregulation, because female employment was rising even in the stagflation decade. It is the great myth of the Whitlam era that the pursuit of equal pay had bust the old economy. It had, in fact, encouraged women to work, and they took 400 000 of the 450 000 new jobs that were created between 1973 and 1983. But career opportunities were limited; the women who found work under Whitlam and Fraser were employed mainly in community services.

Tempting though it is to idealise Generation W for its skill set and feminine bias, it oozes cynicism. Growing up in the '70s meant no memory of life before television, when most Western societies believed their leaders were a little more honest, on average, than the people they served. Television taught Generation W to see the angle, the tricks of camera positioning and subliminal advertising. The decade of their childhood switched abruptly from the wonder of the moon landing to horror of the Vietnam War, from the promise of 'It's Time' to the conspiracy of the Dismissal. The media they consumed reinforced the cynicism. Watergate and Vietnam had made it impossible to see government in any other light.

Australia's Generation W was at the vanguard of popular culture's most cynical form, punk rock. The Saints were regarded as co-founders of the movement alongside The Ramones of New York and the Sex Pistols of London. The Saints hailed from Brisbane's south-west, and the band's guitarist, Ed Kuepper, said their music was reaction to the suffocatingly conservative state they grew up in: 'I think the band was able to develop a more obnoxious demeanour, thanks to our surroundings, than had everyone been nice.'

Generation W's later-born produced some of the funniest, most insightful local television of all, with *Frontline*, a spoof of current affairs television, catching the emptiness of the 1990s, and *Kath & Kim* allowing us to laugh at the whiny materialism of middle Australia in the noughties. All groups contain a paradox, and Generation W's was its failure to inspire either itself or the rest of the nation. It could interpret Australia with the sharp eye of the outsider, but it couldn't remake it in its own image because the boomers still set the tone of the national conversation.

The social divisions that existed behind the tariff wall – city versus country, and labour versus capital – had been resolved with an elaborate form of cross-subsidy. The bush was appeased through the rigging of electoral boundaries, which gave the Country Party a disproportionate return for its vote, while labour was bought off by centralised wage-fixing. Industry protection transferred national income from primary industries in the bush to manufacturing in the cities, and it allowed capital to pass on the higher cost of labour to consumers.

By liberalising the economy, the Hawke and Keating governments pulled apart the cat's-cradle relationships between city and country and between labour and capital in an unexpected way. City and country became more hostile towards one another. But the tension between labour and capital was released. Those with work wanted job security over wage rises, so they were less inclined to resort to industrial action. Competition, in turn, made business more reliant on quality workers. The old mateship models of militant trade unions and aloof employer associations had passed their use-by dates.

It was a woman's world, but she didn't feel like she was in command of her time. Politics had no interest in her views, beyond the question of which mother deserved the larger family payment – the working mum or the stay-at-home. The debate was misinformed by the notion that the choices made between part-time work and full-time care for children were somehow mutually exclusive. Mothers, in fact, moved between the two, often not because they wanted to, but out of necessity. And those who were at home needed help. In almost half the households where the father was working and the mother was at home, the family used some of form of childcare when the youngest was aged two. More than half of all sole parents who were not in the labour force used childcare when the youngest was aged one. But the men who ran the nation weren't ready for these real-world subtleties. They took sides in an imaginary mummy war. Labor was for the working mum, the Coalition for the traditional stay-at-home mother.

The baby-boomer men who lost their jobs to deregulation received more consistent bipartisan attention. They had voted Labor all their lives, but the Keating recession made their vote contestable and the woman who spoke for them, Pauline Hanson, threw a spanner in the political works by railing against the very people who were helping to build a new Australia – the immigrants.

Generation W is one of the keys to unlocking why we held our nerve when the Xers and Ys in the United States, Great Britain and Europe lost their collective heads in the twenty-first century. Better educated and more globally aware than any grouping before it in Australian history, Generation W is the flipside of the tetchy, entitled baby-boomer males of the stagflation decade. Where our old blokes issued the impossible demand that government look after them, our women and wogs assumed politics wasn't on their side, so they got on with their lives. But our new national calmness coincided with a sharp deterioration in our politics. The final phase in this story is the disconnection between leader and citizen as governments of both hues lost the confidence to pursue Australian greatness, just as we were revealing our true selves as one of the most cohesive and economically literate nations in the world.

1996 Howard returns Coalition to office after 13 years. Port Arthur massacre. Gun-law reform. Hanson's maiden speech attacks everyone. **1997** One Nation launched. Blair elected British PM. Asian financial crisis. Howard puts GST on table. Democrats leader Kernot defects to Labor. **1998** Suharto resigns. Waterfront dispute. Howard defeats Beazley with lowest 2PP vote on record. **1999** GST passes through Senate. Capital gains tax halved and housing booms. East Timor intervention. Monarchy 1 Republic 0. **2000** Y2K, GST and Sydney Olympics. Tech wreck. Bush elected president after 'hanging chads' case. **2001** Dollar falls below US50c for first time. First home-owner grant doubled. Another housing boom. US in recession. *Tampa*. September 11. Afghanistan. Howard defeats Beazley again.

THE SURGE

2002 Household savings fall below zero % of disposable income. *Kath & Kim*. Bali bombing. **2003** Iraq. Crean toppled, Latham beats Beazley. **2004** China boom drives up budget surplus. Baby bonus. Howard wins fourth term with control of Senate. **2005** Latham quits, becomes bestselling author. Beazley Mk II. WorkChoices and full sale of Telstra. **2006** Reserve Bank raises interest rates three times. Household savings recover. Costello clashes with Howard, but still doesn't challenge. Rudd topples Beazley. **2007** Terms of trade highest since Korean War wool boom. Rudd returns Labor to power for first time in almost 12 years. Australia signs Kyoto Protocol. **2008** New US recession, by far the deepest. Rudd makes Stolen Generation apology. Turnbull replaces Nelson. Lehman Brothers collapses, triggering GFC. Obama elected president. Australians patriotically go shopping. **2009** Australia officially avoids recession. Abbott defeats Turnbull. ETS deal collapses. **2010** Gillard topples Rudd. Australia's first hung parliament in 70 years. Dollar returns to parity for first time in 28 years.

17

PASSING THE TESTS

Our instincts were telling us not to follow the United States. To feel this in the 1990s, when the Americans had seen off their ideological and economic challengers in the Soviet Union and Japan, hinted at a new Australian view of the world. Hindsight says our timing was spot on. The last decade of the twentieth century was the time to break free of the US business and cultural cycles, before the back-to-back bubbles of the tech wreck and the global financial crisis blighted the first decade of the twenty-first century. Australia did so because it picked the American hubris.

The first example of a more independently minded Australia was as unexpected as it was tragic. On 28 April 1996, a 28-year-old loner, Martin Bryant, carried a military-style weapon and a lifetime of resentment to the Port Arthur tourist centre in Tasmania. He murdered thirty-five people and wounded eighteen others, and his face appeared on the front page of newspapers around the world. The nation was united in grief, but when John Howard announced he would seek uniform laws to ban all automatic and semi-automatic weapons, we promptly divided again along the city and country fault lines of the previous month's federal election.

Australia didn't share the gun fetish of the US, where the right to arms is part of the national foundation myth. But our politicians feared the farming and sporting shooters groups. Australia's gun lobby had marched on Labor governments in New South Wales and Victoria in the 1980s, overturning the proposed reforms that had followed a sequence of mass murders in Sydney and Melbourne. The new Howard government was aware of these precedents and that all the electoral risk was on the conservative side.

Howard conducted a ring-around of Coalition ministers for advice on how far he could afford to go. He asked the primary industries minister and future National Party leader John Anderson how many guns he kept on his farm. 'He said, "Your job is to explain to me and convince me as to what sort of firearms farmers need and legitimately must have access to,"' Anderson recalled. 'And I hesitated for a moment because I thought, oh, I don't quite know how to tell the prime minister that I have what he would regard as an arsenal.'

It took courage for Howard to act. But he did have Labor's support in the parliament, which assured the legislation's passage. I ask Howard if the assistance of opposition leader Kim Beazley was as important as his own endorsement of the Hawke–Keating deregulation program in the 1980s. 'But his urban female base would never have forgiven him if he opposed us,' is Howard's qualified reply. 'I thought his support was genuine.' It was just that Labor had less to lose by standing on principle than he did, he explains.

Gun-law reform acted as a cultural clarifier for Australia. Concern about crime, real and imagined, had been rising for some years. There had been twelve mass murders between 1981 and the start of 1996, claiming sixty-nine lives. In eight of those cases, the perpetrator was also killed. Port Arthur took the total number of deaths to 112.

The gun lobby assumed that Howard would back down, but it

underestimated his resolve and the role that public opinion played in reinforcing it. Howard drew comfort from the city-dwelling Labor supporters who wished him well, even though they said they would never vote for him. More than 700 000 guns were eventually given up under the buyback. The context is important. In the US, the bombing of a federal government building in Oklahoma, killing 168 people, had occurred only a year before Port Arthur, on 19 April 1995. But that event didn't prompt reform. US Democrat president Bill Clinton had tried to introduce gun-control legislation the previous year and the backlash had helped the Republicans seize control of both houses of Congress at the midterm elections – he wasn't game for another crackdown. That Howard was able to go further and not lose power demonstrated resilience in the Australian character, which would reappear just when we needed it in the second half of the '90s and into the twenty-first century.

The community spirit that John Howard touched upon after Port Arthur had a quicksilver quality to it. He couldn't harness it because the other part of the Australian character – the small-mindedness – also asserted itself in the '90s. This is the almost inexplicable part of our new global mind. As a people, we can make the big calls, from guns to the GFC, because we have a healthy suspicion of national fanaticism and international finance. But then we argue over the bill.

The debate over Peter Costello's first budget as treasurer, which ran either side of Port Arthur, brought out the whinger in us all.

Treasury had greeted Howard and Costello on the day after the election with the news that the budget had another hole in it. If cuts weren't made to spending, the deficit would reach $7.6 billion in 1996–97, the advice said. Howard had Paul Keating where he wanted him on history's page. It was Howard's parting deficit as treasurer in 1983 that had given Bob Hawke's incoming government the excuse to junk costly promises and to browbeat the conservatives. Now the legacy stain was on the other party.

Keating had said the budget would be balanced in underlying terms in 1996–97, and he was correct based on the numbers his government had been given in May 1995. But there'd been yet another slippage of revenue in the New Year. If Keating had had the sense to demand an update from Treasury for the election, he might have forced voters to reconsider their pick on the basis that a continued deficit meant Howard's promises could not be afforded. But Keating was in denial. He refused to countenance the possibility that Labor had lost its fire in its final term, so the campaign was conducted on the false assumption of a balanced budget.

Howard didn't come to this debate with clean hands. He had accepted Keating's word that the budget was balanced, even though private-sector forecaster Access Economic had already warned of an $8 billion deficit. No slicing and dicing of the language could alter the guarantee that Howard gave in his final appearance to the National Press Club before the election.

Question: '[What would happen if] you win the election and then you discover you are faced with a serious budget deficit blowout? [Under] what circumstances will you see it as necessary to cancel some of the many spending promises you have made to the electorate in the interests . . . [of] fiscal responsibility?'

Howard: 'Well, the commitments that we've made in relation to reduced taxation, and the other commitments we've made in our election policies, they will be delivered in full.'

When he was told of the actual deficit in March, Howard was caught somewhere between shock and amusement. His first instinct was to keep all his commitments, including the promise that there would be no new taxes or increases to existing ones. After thirteen years of Labor government, he thought there would surely be enough fat to trim. It was quickly agreed between Howard and Costello that the Coalition would cut spending by $8 billion, a target that was about $2 billion less than the equivalent savings in Fightback.

In May, Treasury added a further $2 billion to the savings task because the revenue estimates had deteriorated once again. It was the receipt of this second piece of advice – which couldn't be blamed on the former Labor regime – that forced Howard to agree to tax hikes, and to renege on other promises as well. Keating might have allowed himself a private chuckle because Howard now understood why the 'L-A-W' tax cuts could not be afforded in the short term: the fiscal problem was the revenue base, not the size of government. Low inflation and the stickiness of unemployment, which was still at 8 per cent when the Coalition took office, had conspired to leave the budget in deficit well into the recovery cycle. It was an unexpected price of restructuring the economy.

Howard found it hard to say sorry. He used a form of words that made his own side wince, and which he has long since regretted. He would keep the Coalition's 'core' promises, he said. The media quickly filled out the statement for him, reporting that he would be breaking his 'non-core' promises. When Hawke junked Labor's tax cuts and handouts after the 1983 election, he was applauded for his pragmatism. It had helped that he made his statement at the first available opportunity and in, for him, very plain language. Howard conducted a semantic argument about whether he had kept faith with the electorate. The media ridicule was out of proportion to the crime, but Howard brought it on himself because he wanted voters to believe he was different.

On 20 August 1996, Costello announced $7.2 billion in savings, $800 million short of the original two-year target of $8 billion. The spending cuts were valued at $5.2 billion, the revenue measures another $2 billion. The single largest cut was to tertiary education funding. The savings were expected to secure a small surplus of $1 billion in 1998–99. But this time Treasury was being too pessimistic. The budget was balanced a year ahead of schedule, and then it whirred back to surplus as Keating had said it would, jumping to $3.9 billion in 1998–99 – almost four times above Costello's original estimate – and then to $13 billion in 1999–2000.

Costello subsequently reversed many of the spending cuts, though not those to the universities or to the public broadcaster, the ABC. These choices were ideological. Howard and Costello agreed with the Hawke and Keating governments on the broad outline of the economic reform program – the float, financial deregulation, tariff cuts and surplus budgeting. But they rejected Labor's cultural agenda and used the budget to wind back Hawke's 'clever country' spending and Keating's funding for the arts. The savings from universities, for example, were not banked, but used to promote private sector schools.

Costello's first budget involved no lasting sacrifice. Labor had reduced the size of the national government from 27.3 per cent of GDP in 1984–85 to 22.7 per cent at the top of the previous boom, in 1989–90. Half those gains were lost in the recession and job-less recovery, and federal spending was at 25.5 per cent of GDP by 1995–96. The Coalition returned the benchmark to 23.1 per cent of GDP by 1999–2000.

The insistence on surplus budgeting is an enduring electoral trait that has served Australia well over the past generation. In the twenty-one years between 1987–88 and 2007–08, Labor and the Coalition delivered twelve surplus budgets between them, and another two were in balance. The Americans had just four sur-pluses in that period. The true value of our thrift would be apparent during the global financial crisis, when Australia avoided not just recession, but the large public debts that came with it.

Australians are, by disposition, an obedient people. We like to be led and want government to look after us. Yet we are wary of governments that borrow on our behalf. Howard felt the electoral double-standard from the outset; he needed a surplus to show that his administration was more prudent than the last, and to erase the bad memories of his time as treasurer. But he also knew the public wanted a return for their sacrifice. So he switched between purity and pragmatism, attacking the profligacy of his predecessor while building a middle-class welfare system that would become more generous than anything Gough Whitlam had advocated.

In the early years of his government, Howard was happy to appeal to those pining for old-world certainties, with a nod to the spirit of Menzies, but he wasn't prepared to turn back the clock to the economy that existed behind the tariff wall. Pauline Hanson's timing was immaculately destructive. She sensed that Howard was paying lip service to protection, and called his bluff. Less than one month after the first Costello budget the newly elected member for Ipswich poked at the tensions between city and county, and between new and old Australia, and created a grassroots movement against deregulation.

Her single independent vote on the floor of parliament was meaningless to a Coalition government with 94 seats out of 148. But Hanson's voice rattled the prime minister throughout his first term because she spoke to his people, and with an apparent clarity that he lacked. Her maiden speech to parliament on 10 September 1996 contained more deliberate provocations than a 2 a.m. pub brawl. The line that was most requoted was the one that echoed John Howard's previous position on immigration. 'I believe we are in danger of being swamped by Asians,' she said. 'They have their own culture and religion, form ghettoes and do not assimilate.'

Howard's office had prepared a statement in the expectation that Labor would ask the prime minister a question on the speech. It sought to correct her many inaccurate claims, without personally attacking her. Labor never asked the question, leaving Howard with a dilemma: did he initiate his own response, which would risk elevating her, or did he ignore her and hope she would fade away? He tried the latter, and to this day believes it was the correct decision. But he has very few people on his side who agree.

The deputy prime minister, Tim Fischer, the treasurer, Peter Costello, and the foreign affairs minister, Alexander Downer, were among the prominent members of the government who urged Howard to rebuke Hanson. Howard was annoyed each time they prodded him, and resented the implication that he was trafficking in xenophobia.

'I made a speech attacking Pauline Hanson pretty vehemently,' Downer told Fran Kelly in the ABC documentary *The Howard Years*, 'and I think I'm right in saying this: in nearly twelve years as the foreign minister I think it's pretty much the only time he [Howard] rang me to chastise me.' Howard wasn't impressed, Downer said. 'He said, "Well, you know, it's just going to leave me out there and the media are going to say: Well, Downer's doing the right thing, why doesn't Howard?"'

It was an unusually thin-skinned way for a prime minister with a large majority to behave. Howard couldn't bring himself to declare his outright opposition to Hanson because he felt he was being bullied by the media. Imagine how differently Australians would have seen him if he had told Hanson she was wrong in the way he had told the gun lobby that it was wrong. But Howard shared the concerns of her supporters about the pace of cultural change. He didn't see them as racists. Yet by refusing to put Hanson in her place, Howard created a monster.

Hanson formed her One Nation Party on 11 April 1997, and immediately pulled votes away from both the Coalition and Labor. One Nation's vote was higher the older the voter, with men aged over fifty offering the highest rate of support. By geography, the One Nation vote fell the closer one moved towards the CBD of each capital city, and the further one travelled south along the eastern seaboard. Country Queensland was One

Nation's stronghold; cosmopolitan Melbourne its softest point on the electoral map.

Howard had to choose between city and country, but the longer he hesitated, the more powerful One Nation became. Every mistake he had made in his response to Hanson was written onto the Queensland state electoral commission's tally board on the evening of 13 June 1998. It was the first election One Nation contested, and the new party stunned the nation by collecting the highest individual primary vote on the conservative side of politics – 22.7 per cent, to the Liberals' 16.1 per cent and the Nationals' 15.2 per cent.

Rob Borbidge's minority Coalition government had advised their supporters to place One Nation ahead of Labor when allocating their preference votes. Labor, by contrast, placed One Nation last. The Labor strategy had the advantage of mixing principle with raw politics. It was a pitch calculated to move city-based conservatives who didn't like One Nation into the Labor column.

The previous Queensland parliament had been hung, with the Coalition and Labor each on 44 seats. The balance of power belonged to the independent Liz Cunningham. She had sided with the Coalition, ending just over six years of Labor rule in February 1996. The Coalition thought 1998 would be another cliffhanger, so it held its nose and offered preferences to Hanson's party, even though she had vowed to destroy them.

The Coalition misunderstood the merry-go-round effect of One Nation. The Coalition primary vote collapsed by almost 18 per cent in total – around 14 per cent went to One Nation, and another 3 per cent went to Labor, based on post-election analysis by the parties. Labor calculated that it lost 7 per cent to One Nation, but the clawback of 3 per cent from the Coalition – namely, the anti-Hanson conservative voters in Brisbane – left Labor with a net swing against it of just 4 per cent.

Labor maintained its tally of 44 seats. The Coalition lost 12 seats to finish with 32. One Nation picked up 11 of those 12 seats and would have claimed the balance of power with just one more. But the twelfth seat went to another independent, Peter Wellington, who gave his support to Peter Beattie to form a minority Labor government.

Howard realised, too late, that Hanson was the real enemy. On the eve of the state election, he called Hanson's views 'deranged' in a vain attempt to dissuade Coalition voters from defecting. 'When he called me deranged, he was calling the majority of Queenslanders deranged,' Hanson replied. The volatility in Queensland was unusual, even by the state's own contrary standards. The people had dumped the Labor government of Wayne Goss in 1996, after two terms, left federal Labor with just two seats in the Howard landslide, then reverted to Labor at the state level after one term of Coalition rule. If Howard kept playing with the fire of Hansonism he would lose the next election.

The outbreak of xenophobia in Australia coincided with an economic catastrophe in the region. The Asian financial crisis began in July 1997, three months after the launch of One Nation, when Thailand's currency came under attack from speculators. The money market was betting that the baht, which was tied to the US dollar, would have to be devalued to deal with Thailand's large current account deficit. The Thai central bank resisted, but this only intensified the squeeze on the currency. Finally, it relented by agreeing to float the baht, whereupon it immediately lost 15 per cent of its value. Thailand slipped into a deep recession. The foreign investers, emboldened and frightened by the experience, began testing every other nation in the region. By the end of the year, the panic, and recession, had spread to Malaysia, Indonesia and even our second-largest export market, South Korea.

Australia's national interest was never in doubt. The Howard government would contribute to all three International Monetary Fund bailouts, for Thailand, South Korea and Indonesia. But the domestic cycle was pulling the Coalition towards a more isolationist stance.

Howard's main political concern was that the bailouts would be seen as self-defeating charity if the trouble in the region dragged Australia into recession. Was another recession really on the way so soon after the one we had to have? It felt that way to the government because the speculators didn't discriminate; they tested Australia as well. On 27 October 1997, the dollar dropped below us70 cents for the first time in almost four years. The next day, the Australian stock market lost 7.2 per cent after Wall Street recorded its biggest single-day points fall on record as part of its knee-jerk response to the Asian financial crisis.

It threatened to become a re-run of the banana republic episode a decade earlier. Back then, the money market had forced the Hawke government to slash spending to place a floor under the dollar. The budget was heading for surplus now, so it seemed a little unfair for Australia to be expected to do more on fiscal policy. Although it wasn't his call to make, as the Reserve Bank was now fully independent, Howard thought that interest rates might need to rise. This risked a recession, but his experience as treasurer had taught him that when there is pressure on the currency, the blunt weapon of monetary policy is eventually called on to make it attractive for foreign capital to remain. To Howard's relief, the new Reserve governor, Ian Macfarlane, decided to call everyone's bluff and leave monetary policy on hold. As Macfarlane explained to Howard, our currency was falling in an orderly fashion because that is what the theory of the float said would happen. The dollar was taking the shock to make our exports more competitive, allowing the domestic economy to continue functioning almost as if nothing had happened.

There was is no official date for when the Asian financial crisis passed us by. The first phase, which ended in 1997, didn't touch Australia at all. The dollar lost 8 cents in two months between mid October and Christmas and finished the year at 65.27 cents against the greenback. But critically there had been no banana republic-like collapse, and the real economy was still growing. This had a cathartic effect on Howard. No more would he, and Australia, be lectured about the superiority of the Asian model. The prime minister declared that we could deal now with the region on our own terms. 'We are no longer seen as some kind of anxious outsider clamouring to be a member of this spectacularly successful club,' Howard said. 'Rather we are seen as a strong, reliable, dependable, better-run, more successful, capable-of-punching-above-its-weight participant in the Asia-Pacific region.' The triumphalism was meant for domestic consumption. Paul Keating had said in the 1996 campaign that Asian leaders wouldn't deal with Howard. Well, they would now, with cap in hand, because they needed our money to save their economies. Tim Fischer said the 1996–97 budget cuts had come 'just in the nick of time'. 'If we had not done that, if we had built on the $10 billion deficit when we came into government, the IMF would have been in Australia by Melbourne Cup day 1997.' The comment was overdone because the IMF had no reason to come to Australia – almost whatever the deficit, the economy was run on sound principles. But the point about the surplus was undoubtedly correct because it allowed us, even then, to show we were the grown-up prepared to exercise restraint when all others were bingeing. To posterity's eye, which doesn't care which side was in government, it was a relief to see a tangible return from the economic reforms of the Hawke–Keating years.

But the government was nervous again in the middle of 1998 as our dollar began sliding for a second time. The crisis had now sent our nearest neighbour Indonesia into depression, and after weeks of violent street protests President Suharto resigned on 21 May. The following month, on 9 June 1998, our dollar fell below

US60 cents for the first time in twelve years. The next day it closed at US58.45 cents, the lowest level on record to that point, and didn't settle above US60 cents until October. Throughout this second phase, Howard worried, again, that a recession might strike.

Yet the rest of the world had already decided we were home free. In November 1998, the quotable American economist Paul Krugman called us the real 'miracle economy'. For policy-makers this was as good as sainthood. The term had been used to describe the Asian tiger economies earlier in the 1990s, before the market asked for its money back. Krugman said we had produced a 'textbook' response to the crisis. 'The puzzling thing is why Australia was able to do that when so many other countries haven't,' Professor Krugman said. 'There does seem to be a double standard out there in the market response. So far the rule is that white countries are allowed to have floating exchange rates and leave interest rates unchanged or even decrease them. The non-European countries, if they try the same thing, the currency slides 15 per cent, people say: "Oh my God, it's still a Third World country." The currency goes into freefall and they are obliged to raise interest rates to 75 per cent to defend it.'

Australia avoided the Asian financial crisis, primarily because ours was the only nation in the region whose central bank had not blinked. Macfarlane had been governor of the Reserve Bank for less than a year when Thailand came under attack. He admitted after his retirement that the bank had considered raising interest rates to defend the dollar, but decided against it because it would have created the perception that Australia had lost control. He didn't want to validate the market panic, or risk a domestic recession when inflation was in check. There was an official maturity to match the one in the community. 'The Reserve Bank has often been praised for lowering interest rates during this period, while other countries raised them,' Macfarlane said in his 2006 Boyer Lectures. 'In fact, we did not lower interest rates, but we did distinguish ourselves by not raising them. We were the only significant OECD country not to do so at any time in 1997 or 1998. We certainly thought about it, but in the end we judged that it would probably be unhelpful, and possibly seriously destabilising, as it turned out to be the case in New Zealand where rates were raised.'

New Zealand was the nation that Australian officials were subconsciously intimidated by. The little brother had replaced us as the star of economic rationalism in the '80s when Roger Douglas, the finance minister in David Lange's Labour government, had been named *Euromoney*'s 'world's greatest treasurer' in 1985, a year after our own Paul Keating. The Kiwis had done everything before us, including the GST. Their central bank was hardcore; only Germany's Bundesbank had a more fearsome reputation in the developed world for placing price stability above all else. So when the New Zealand Reserve Bank helped bring on a recession in 1997–98 by tightening monetary policy during the crisis, something just short of schadenfreude was felt here because their economic Haka didn't work as well as our more measured approach.

The Asian financial crisis tested the Australian model, and it was found to be more viable than Howard realised. He didn't have anything to do, really, but talk up the economy and resist the urgings of Hanson. In his days as treasurer, he would have been fiddling with the dollar and interest rates, and the markets would have eaten Australia alive. Howard says: 'I think the bank deserves credit. I think Macfarlane was a steady hand. I regard him as the standout economic official in my time as prime minister.'

Howard's experience in 1997–98 predicted the double edge of the global financial crisis ten years later. In both instances, a new government relied on the good policy work of its predecessor. The rest of the world would be amazed at how logical the whole operation seemed. But voters wouldn't thank the incumbent for the recession that didn't happen, and were annoyed whenever Howard talked about Australia's world-beating economy. Howard was struggling for the same reason as Keating had: the low-inflation recovery had yet to erase the memory of the recession. Unemployment was still stuck at around 8 per cent, while the total number of male full-time jobs remained below where they had been in 1989. As with gun-law reform, the community held together in a crisis before resuming the squabbles of the hip pocket.

Hugh Mackay's June 1998 'Mind & Mood' report found Australians had passed to the second stage of political disengagement – from anger to cynicism. The nation was lurching to the right, but not necessarily to Hanson. Attitudes were again hardening towards welfare recipients. But there was a hint of the long economic boom just around the corner. 'Curiously, a report which seems to contain such bad news actually offers some bright opportunities in the marketing and advertising context,' Mackay advised his business subscribers. 'Self-absorption often means self-indulgence, and, even though there is a kind of shutdown mentality in the community, many people will be prepared to spend money on products, services and experiences which help to insulate them from their insecurities.' Australians were preparing to party after a decade of painful adjustment. They would treat themselves by renovating the home, going on holidays or just eating out more. These were the indulgences of twenty-first century Western man. All Howard had to do was hold on long enough to ride the next boom.

18

HE OF THE NEVER EVER

The last successful reform of the deregulation era coincided, appropriately, with Australia's first escape from an American recession. The policy John Howard relied on to reconnect with middle Australia was the goods and services tax. But he had one small booby trap to disarm: he had ruled out a GST for all time at the previous federal election. Read his lips . . .

'So you've left open the door for a GST now, haven't you?' he was asked on 2 May 1995.

Howard: 'No, there's no way that a GST will ever be part of our policy.'

Journalist: 'Never ever?'

Howard: 'Never ever. It's dead. It was killed by the voters in the last election.'

That it was, but they didn't elect Howard to do nothing with power. The GST appealed to Howard because it allowed him to present to the nation as a man of conviction. That he needed to break another promise to prove to voters that he cared showed just how far he had fallen in their estimation in his first term.

There was no heroism in the initial stages of the GST debate.

Howard had single-handedly undermined the sales pitch for Peter Costello's second budget, in 1997, when he said he would not personally be claiming its centrepiece handout, a 15 per cent rebate on the tax people paid on their savings income, valued at $2 billion in total.

Costello was furious that Howard had got into an argument about the equity of the measure. On the Sunday after the budget, Howard decided to change the tax topic by agreeing that the GST should be on the table for future consideration. He began to redefine his 'never ever' promise to mean that he wouldn't be introducing a GST in his first term. He would seek an explicit mandate for tax reform in a second term. What could be more democratic? It was a brave move, but nonetheless disingenuous. The Coalition wouldn't have won by as many seats in '96 if voters thought the GST was an option for a second term.

'I couldn't see there being any alternative [to the GST],' Howard says. 'I had for years argued that governments had to keep undertaking reforms. I think one of the reasons we fell into a bit of a hole with the polls and everything in '97 was that people thought that we had run out of reform zeal. That was a view that was being fed into the electorate by [Jeff] Kennett and others. Whether it was fair or unfair, they were certainly doing it. And I always believed at some point we had to do something about indirect tax. And we did have a lot of electoral fat on our bone, and it's fair to say there's not much point having a huge majority and a lot of political capital in the bank unless you spend it on reform. Otherwise it would disappear.'

The GST had two things going for it as a reform. It replaced less efficient taxes, and the revenue it generated would increase more or less in line with economic growth, thus relieving future governments of the burden of inventing new levies to balance the budget each year. The old system taxed some goods at the federal level, while the states taxed some services, such as hotel beds. The

GST became official government policy in August 1997 after the High Court ruled that $5 billion in state indirect taxes on tobacco, alcohol and petrol had been collected in breach of the constitution. The judgement demonstrated that the existing indirect tax system was in need of repair, and it gave Howard the hook on which to hang his tax reform.

Howard had been in hospital with pneumonia, and was preparing to return to work when the judgement was handed down on 5 August. 'I spent a lot of time thinking in hospital,' he told me, for *The Longest Decade*. 'I had alluded to tax reform in an interview before I got crook. I had three weeks off. I was in hospital for a week and I had two weeks convalescence. I was off for virtually a month and when I came back I decided we had to do the GST.'

He was back at his desk on 11 August. Two days later, he announced that the GST would be Coalition policy for the next election. A ridiculous level of secrecy followed. The prime minister and treasurer worked on a single master copy of the tax package, which was never allowed to leave a secure room in the Treasury building in Canberra's parliamentary triangle. Only a handful of advisers were trusted to see it. The final policy, released a year later, on 13 August 1998, differed from John Hewson's Fightback in three important respects. The budget was in surplus, so there would be no need for further spending cuts to fund reductions in personal income tax. The GST would be set at 10 per cent, not 15 per cent, and the proceeds would be used to replace the wholesale sales tax only and nine smaller state taxes, but not payroll tax. Finally, the states would be handed the GST revenue, in exchange for an equivalent reduction in commonwealth funding. This was the canniest part of the politics, because the Coalition could argue that the rate could not increase in the future without the support of all the states.

The GST was no more popular in 1998 than it had been at the start of the decade, according to Newspoll. For Labor, this meant there was little political risk in opposing. The worst that could happen, Kim Beazley decided, was that Labor would fall a few seats short at the election, and surf to victory the next time. Timidity was Beazley's middle name. Once he committed Labor to opposing the GST, he settled on a literal approach. If Howard won the election, Labor would still say no in the Senate after the event. Paul Keating had taken the more provocative, but more credible position in 1993, when he said Labor would not stand in the GST's way if the Coalition secured a mandate for its introduction. The Australian Democrats saw an opportunity in Beazley's obstruction to offer themselves as honest brokers to deliver tax reform. They campaigned for their own GST, but with food excluded.

Labor repeated Keating's One Nation ploy by using the surplus to offer its own tax cuts without the GST. When the competing packages were lined up, voters suddenly had an insight into the values of the main political parties. Howard was giving more money to families where the father worked and the mother stayed at home, while Beazley favoured dual-income families. Howard promised the largest tax cuts to those on more than $50 000 a year; Beazley offered more to lower- and middle-income earners.

By reviving the GST as a life-or-death debate for Australia, Howard and Beazley unwittingly confirmed that politics was as exhausted as the electorate. The GST was a European idea from the '70s that should have implement here by the late '80s, after New Zealand had successfully bedded down its version, but which was now being presented as the most important reform to bring Australia into the twenty-first century. The start date for the GST would be 1 July 2000, six weeks before the opening ceremony of the Sydney Olympics, and six months after the world's computers were supposed to fall victim to the millennium bug.

The public didn't share Howard's GST obsession. There were surely more important things to argue about than tax reform – most notably, future-proofing the economy against further Asian-style financial crises, and using the proceeds of growth to settle Australia's longstanding environmental problems, from water supply to climate change, which was being treated as a serious issue at that time. Just after the polls closed at 6 p.m. on election night on 3 October 1998, Howard was shown an exit survey of voters from Liberal federal director Lynton Crosby. It reported Labor on 53 per cent and the Coalition 47 per cent after preferences. Howard broke the news to his family and prepared a concession speech.

The exit survey picked the winner of the popular vote, but was wrong on the margin. The Coalition lost by 51 per cent to 49, but still held on to government. Labor gained 19 seats – six in Queensland, four in Western Australia, three in Victoria, two in both New South Wales and Tasmania, and one apiece in South Australia and the Northern Territory. The swing after preferences of 4.6 per cent was Labor's highest since 1969, and it left the party requiring just eight more seats at the next election to form government. However, Labor's primary vote of 40.1 per cent was one of its lowest on record, only just above the 38.8 it received in the thrashing of 1966. Beazley, by his negativity, had failed to inspire the centre that had been the precondition for Labor's breakthrough victories of '72, '83 and even '93. The loser on the night was One Nation. It received a healthy primary vote of 8.4 per cent nationally, but couldn't translate it into influence. Pauline Hanson failed to win a second term in the House of Representatives, and the party's sole representative in the Senate didn't have the balance of power. Almost all of One Nation's support came from the Coalition, whose primary vote fell by 7.7 per cent to 39.5 per cent. To hold office against a swing that big required some luck.

After the election, I interviewed Crosby and he said he didn't know how they had won. The explanation is the Sydney mortgage belt, which had been the decisive factor for Gough Whitlam, Bob Hawke and Paul Keating in their big wins. In 1998, the home owners in the nation's most expensive property market warmed to

Howard over Beazley. The Coalition lost the popular vote in New South Wales by 51.5 per cent to 48.5, but retained 54 per cent of the seats – 27 out of 50. The GST appealed there because the tax cuts that came with it would help Sydneysiders meet their mortgage repayments.

Howard says he's unsure whether the government's near-demise in 1998 was due to the GST or One Nation. He mentions the seat of Macquarie, in Sydney's outer west. Older voters in the Blue Mountains turned against his government, while first-homebuyers in Sydney's outer suburbs stuck with the Liberal Party. The GST and One Nation are almost interchangeable in this analysis. Howard says self-funded retirees were the group most nervous about the GST. But the electoral map showed them to be the group most likely to embrace One Nation. 'Hanson hurt us in the election. The simple arithmetic of Hanson – she took 6 or 7 per cent off our primary vote but didn't hand it back to us through the preferences. I'll never know in the combination of the unease of the GST and Hanson which was the more dominant. They both played a role.'

John Howard was in a rush to legislate, and pushed his luck after the election by seeking to negotiate with the old Senate rather than waiting eight months for the Australian Democrats to assume the balance of power they had won at the election, on 1 July 1999. A technician might argue that the haste was justified because the proposed 1 July 2000 start date for the GST required a minimum of twelve months to prepare the economy for the new tax system. The new Senate would be eating into that time. But Howard could have done the honourable thing and started talking with the Democrats immediately after the election. He didn't, because while the old Senate was sitting, he had two independents he thought would pass the GST as it was proposed, with food taxed.

One was the wily Tasmanian Brian Harradine; the other was Mal Colston, the Labor man whom Joh Bjelke-Petersen had refused to send to Canberra to replace the late Bert Milliner in 1975. Colston had fallen out with Labor after the '96 election and quit the party. The Coalition gave him their support for the deputy presidency of the Senate, which provoked Labor into leaking details of his alleged rorting of parliamentary expenses in the past. When Colston faced fresh charges in '97, Howard bowed to public pressure and refused to accept the tainted vote. But the election victory in '98 gave Howard a political incentive to restore Colston's ballot. It was the first of many lapses of judgement that almost destroyed his ambition for tax reform. Colston was dying of cancer and his lawyers were able to keep him out of court. But the public had little sympathy for him, and while his vote was in play Howard appeared too clever by half.

In any case, Howard had misread Senator Harradine. He thought the Tasmanian independent would pass the GST in exchange for more cash compensation for vulnerable members of the community.

After agonising for six months, Harradine announced on 14 May 1999, a Friday, that he could not support the GST in any form. Howard was stunned. There was no fallback plan, because the Coalition had refused to even discuss the tax package with the Democrats. 'No, no, no, we are not going to exempt food,' the prime minister said in reply to Harradine's rebuff. He threatened a double-dissolution election, which would have pleased Labor. But Howard swallowed his pride over the weekend and agreed to approach the Democrats. After a few days of haggling, he accepted that food would have to come out of his GST, at a cost of $4 billion a year to the budget. To pay for the compromise, the tax cuts for higher-income earners were whittled back, and there was an arm wrestle about where the line would be drawn.

The Democrats party leader, Senator Meg Lees, became fast friends with Howard during the negotiation, but she didn't get

along with Peter Costello. The treasurer could see only complication ahead for himself. The tax office would have to set nitpicking
boundaries between fresh food, which was GST-free, and processed
food, which was taxed. He had said he didn't want to be sticking thermometers into chickens to decide if they were hot enough
to eat as a takeaway meal, which would mean they attracted the
GST. While Costello sniped at Lees across the cabinet table, the
deputy leader of the Democrats, Senator Natasha Stott Despoja,
was opposed to any deal. 'She didn't realise how close she came to
stopping it,' one source involved in the talks said. Mutual interest
prevailed, and Howard and Lees were able to silence their respective deputies long enough to strike an agreement. They announced
the package on 28 May 1999 in a joint press conference.

Both leaders had staked their careers on getting a deal done.
Lees wanted to show that the Democrats were a party of constructive reform.

The back-down saved Howard's leadership. 'It would have been
seen as a massive loss for Howard, after having won the election on
this thing by the skin of his teeth, that he couldn't get [it] through,'
the prime minister's then chief of staff, Arthur Sinodinos, says.
'I think it would have finished his leadership and would have
allowed Peter Costello to come up.' Howard says a GST of some
form was better than nothing at all, and concedes that the government would have been in trouble if he hadn't negotiated with the
Democrats. 'It would have been bad for the government and very
bad for me if we had walked away from the GST. And after all,
we won an election on it with food in, and the idea of giving up
was just unthinkable. I don't know that I sat down and thought
through what the implications for my leadership were. I just knew
it would be very bad for the government if we had walked away
from the GST, and something that is bad for the government is
always bad for the boss.'

The GST's birth was pain-free. The sky didn't fall in on the first shopping weekend, 1–2 July 2000. The consumer price index rate spiked in the September quarter, as it was meant to, then returned to earlier lows. Workers did as they were told and didn't ask for additional wage rises, because the tax cuts provided adequate compensation. The Reserve Bank had been increasing interest rates ahead of the GST's introduction, just to make sure no one got carried away. All seemed to be going to plan, except for one thing. The authorities had underestimated how the national obsession with property might encourage people to stoke another form of inflation.

The tax cuts Howard had given up to remove food from the GST troubled him. He felt he hadn't kept faith with his voters. The people affected by the deal with the Democrats were Liberal heartland, and were already annoyed by the 1996 budget measure to impose a levy of up to 15 per cent on their superannuation contributions. Couldn't the government do something else for them to make up for the tax cuts that they had to forgo to appease the Democrats? Howard found what he thought was the perfect measure – a pro-investment reduction in the capital gains tax. It was inserted into the business tax reform package Peter Costello released in September 1999. The capital gains tax had been one of Paul Keating's cherished reforms of the '80s. Howard never liked it, but it was collecting too much revenue to abolish. So he cut the effective rate in half by allowing investors to be taxed on only 50 per cent of their gain.

Trevor Boucher, the senior tax official who worked with Howard as treasurer to close the tax loopholes of the '70s, warned the tax break on capital gains would encourage avoiders 'like bees to a honey pot'. 'For my part, a dollar is a dollar is a dollar,' Boucher said. 'And people who earn their money get taxed in full on it. But a clever dollar that appears as a capital gain is now to be tax-preferred.'

In middle Australia, the baby boomers fancied it was time
to become landlords. Three reinforcing price signals encouraged
them to move into the housing market with a ferocity that echoed
the Poseidon boom thirty years earlier. The halving of the capital
gains tax burden combined with negative gearing and the imminent introduction of the GST, which was to increase the price of
building materials by 10 per cent, to make investment properties
seem like a sure bet. Repeat buyers bid against first-time buyers
and pushed up prices. In the frenzy, two years' worth of residential
building was squeezed into the first six months of 2000, leaving
a void after the GST's introduction on 1 July. The Reserve Bank
didn't see the danger, and was still increasing interest rates in
August when the economy was about to hit the wall.

On the eve of the 2000 Sydney Olympics, during which the opening and closing ceremonies paid mock tribute to two Australian
inventions for the backyard that were of no practical use to the
rest of the world – the Victa lawnmower and the Hills hoist –
American economist David Hale said it was not enough for
Australia to use technology after other people had invented it. We
needed our own products if we wanted to guarantee our future
prosperity, yet Australia doesn't have any large, globally dominant
information technology companies. 'You haven't had the good luck
of Finland and Sweden in producing companies such as Nokia
or Ericsson. Until you do, your stock market will not be a magnet
for capital flows into the IT and media entertainment sectors.'

It was advice best left ignored. The global economic order was
shifting. The United States had entered the new millennium confident that its model had ended history itself. The recovery from
its last recession in 1990–91 was the longest on record, beating by
a year the previous benchmark set in the '60s when prosperity ran
for nine years without pause. The American triumph was built on

technology; the internet had become the virtual railway of the twenty-first century, connecting far-flung people and businesses through their computers. Global investors chased American technology stocks, believing that this time the boom was the one that would last a lifetime.

Normal investment rules that weighed the price of a stock against the earnings were suspended because there was an almost religious belief that millions of customers would flock to these new companies. But the internet didn't guarantee profits, it destroyed them, because it allowed the Western consumer to believe they could have something for nothing.

The NASDAQ share index, which mainly covers tech stocks, peaked at 5048 points on 10 March 2000. Two-thirds of its value was wiped out over the next thirteen months, a figure comparable with our own mining-shares experience at the end of the '60s. On the tenth anniversary of the internet crash, the index was at 2368 – still less than half its value at the top of the boom. There was no defining event that burst the tech bubble, and most stock-market corrections don't normally lead to recession. But a US recession followed a year later.

Two million Americans, or 1.5 per cent of all those in work, were laid off between January 2001 and January 2002. By rights, Australia should have been sucked into this recession as well. The economy was slowing sharply because the GST had changed spending patterns – a boom before 1 July 2000 followed by a bust in the second half of the year. The nation's largest general insurer, HIH, collapsed in March 2001 with losses of up to $4 billion. One.Tel, the groovy new-economy telco that was bankrolled by the sons of Murdoch and Packer, went into administration at the end of May 2001, with debts of more than $600 million. The nation's second airline, Ansett, went under in September that year. But bad management was the common factor, not the wider economic cycle.

We kept growing because we weren't burdened by a tech wreck, and because John Howard had turned Keynesian to save his government. Howard first sensed the economy was in danger in early 2001 when the backlash against higher petrol prices meshed with small business frustration at the paperwork associated with the GST.

Petrol prices were approaching $1 per litre for the first time. The GST wasn't supposed to have anything to do with this – and it didn't – but the public didn't believe the government. 'We are getting killed on this,' the new National Party leader, John Anderson, told Howard. 'He was right,' Howard says. 'He was a bit more alive to it than either Peter or I was at the beginning. It transformed the political scene in a very short period of time because we had ended 2000 in pretty good shape, and suddenly we were in a lot of trouble.' The tax package had lowered fuel excise by an equivalent amount to cover the imposition of the GST. It wasn't a full refund because Treasury had said there were other benefits involved in the switch through the removal of other imposts. If the government didn't collect those savings on behalf of taxpayers, the oil companies would pocket them, and the price of petrol would be no different. The amount in dispute that the government insisted the oil companies cough up was just 1.5 cents per litre. When I ask Howard why all the fuss over such a small amount, joking that we treated it as the third oil shock, he chides me that motorists take the cost of petrol seriously.

'Petrol was the real killer because the mob thought that we'd chiselled them,' Howard says. 'Australians are incredibly sensitive about the cost of petrol. They love their motor cars and if they think that the government is adding to an externally induced burden on petrol prices they will really get cranky, and by 2001 the public was very unhappy and they felt they'd been chiselled on the switch. It wasn't a neat explanation – we'd cut excise supposedly to fully compensate for the price impact of the GST, but when we actually unravelled the onion we found that a tiny element of that was, according to the Treasury, embedded cost benefits [for the oil industry]. And try to explain that to the public, they'd say: "Did the reduction in excise exactly equal the impost of the GST?" "Well, mostly." And once you say "mostly", you are gone.'

Howard didn't need to consult an opinion poll to realise his government was being marched to the guillotine. The weakness in the economy and the ongoing problems with the GST had been the dominant factors in two state elections. On 10 February 2001, Labor won back government in Western Australia; on 17 February, Peter Beattie achieved an historic second-term landslide in Queensland with 66 of the state parliament's 89 seats. The Coalition there was reduced to 15 seats after, again, flirting with One Nation preferences.

Howard's political courage, like his recourse to contrition, was selective. He never said sorry to the Stolen Generations, and he was the last on his side to stand up to Pauline Hanson. But when the time came to apologise to motorists, he did it to excess. On 1 March, he agreed to the 1.5 cent cut in excise, after saying for months it was 'irresponsible'. He also abolished automatic indexation, so fuel excise would no longer be increased in line with inflation. His advisers were aghast because no one had asked for this. The hole in the budget would run to the billions over the long term. But he told them, calmly, that his government was finished if it had to answer for every small rise in petrol prices.

After the national accounts were released on 7 March, he was forced back to the handout well. They showed the economy had contracted in the final three months of 2000, the first minus since the bottom of the last recession, in mid 1991. The retreat in production was explained almost entirely by the slump in building activity after the pre-GST frenzy. To complete the miserable run of data for the government, for the first time in history the dollar had fallen below us50 cents.

Now it was the turn of the first-homebuyer to experience the prime ministerial remorse. Young families were being squeezed out of the property market by the baby boomers. Again, Howard's adviser's warned against an excessive handout. But he told them the government had to fix the problem.

Howard should have allowed the cycle to take its course. The first-time buyers who had been locked out in the 1999–2000 period would have returned in 2001 and 2002 as prices settled. But he was impatient and doubled the first home-owner grant from $7000 to $14 000 against the advice of Treasury. The grant sparked a new boom. In the year to October 2001, house prices soared by 21 per cent in Sydney and 26 per cent in Melbourne. This activity helped Australia avoid the US recession then underway, but it stored up trouble for the future.

First-homebuyers wanted to buy before prices escalated beyond their capacity to pay, but their eagerness kept pushing those prices higher. A key statistic of this period is the average loan taken out by a first-time buyer, which increased by more than 20 per cent for the first time on record. The $7000 increase in the grant that Howard had given them didn't close the deposit gap, it just fed into prices.

Howard's vote buying paid off when he finally turned the polling corner in the middle of 2001, after the budget delivered more relief for self-funded retirees at the price of a small deficit, which wasn't confirmed until after the election. Had Howard lost office that year, one can imagine the incoming Beazley government using that deficit to claim that Howard had left behind a black hole. The argument would have been easy to mount: the year before the GST's introduction, 1999–2000, the surplus stood at $13 billion, or 2 per cent of GDP. In 2001–02, the deficit was $1 billion, or 0.1 per cent of GDP. That two-year reduction of $14 billion was, in effect, the price of securing the GST and avoiding recession.

The great economic reform era that began tentatively with the tariff cut in 1973 before taking off with the float of the dollar in 1983, ended in the avalanche of post-GST bribes in 2001. Australians revealed their greedy side through the process. In his scramble to recover their support, Howard allowed the pendulum between leader and voter to swing too far to the latter.

Every voter that cried 'cost of living' was given a wad of cash to quieten them down. But then the next voter wanted the same. The competition for handouts infected the government itself. Howard and Costello argued, repeatedly, over the quantity and the content of the largesse. But it was Howard's government, not the Howard–Costello government: the prime minister always prevailed because the treasurer didn't want to take the fight to the public, even though, as Paul Keating demonstrated throughout the '80s, the deputy with the calculator can often pull rank on the leader with the chequebook. While Howard searched for the next payment to make to his target audience, Costello tried to reinforce a sense of purity by cutting income taxes as well. The upshot was taxes were no longer being collected to provide public services, or to build buffers in good times to deploy in bad times, but to churn back to the electorate. The budget became a frequent-voter program, with rewards based on loyalty, not need.

A carefully targeted tax and handout system should reduce welfare dependency as affluence spreads. The Coalition sacrificed this principle by increasing the number of households that received more in benefits than they paid back to the government in income tax. The ranks of the income tax-free club had been steady for most of the '90s. The Keating government had left the figure at 38 per cent of all households in 1996, when the unemployment rate was around 8 per cent. This included pensioners and the poor, but not those with full-time jobs. The Howard government lifted this benchmark by 4 percentage points to 42 per cent by 2004, when unemployment had fallen below 6 per cent. That is, the bottom four rungs of the income ladder, plus a fraction of those in the middle, the fifth rung, were income-tax free. The most interesting part of this transaction is in pinpointing the voters who moved from paying some tax in 1996 to getting more than they put in by 2004. Most were families with at least one parent in work.

The reform decades of the 1980s and 1990s had promised a more productive nation that could compete with the rest of the world. But the GST blotted the script by facilitating the rise of middle-class welfare in the twenty-first century. Subsidies that the Hawke and Keating governments had taught us to live without were being revived by Howard in an act of electoral appeasement. The defining symbols were the first home-owner grant and the baby bonus. The latter handout was promised at the 2001 election and supersized three years later. Political historians are inclined to score the baby bonus as a vote winner. But it was bad policy, because it reverted to the mentality of the 1970s, when every family was told it deserved to gorge on the magic pudding of government protection.

19

TUNING IN TO
GLOBALISATION

If Australians were to draw a reform map up to the twenty-first century, complete with missed turns, only one other people in the world would recognise the dates as matching with their own journey: the Chinese. They embraced the market in the 1980s but a heavy-handed government crackdown at the end of the decade almost destroyed the project. A period of introspection followed in the early '90s before confidence returned. The Asian financial crisis hurt, but in contrast to the experience of smaller neighbours, it didn't stop the national momentum.

China's great leap to capitalism was fated to coincide with Australia's economic miracle because the two nations had commenced their respective reforms at around the same time. It is not a stretch to say that both adapted to globalisation better than, say, the UK, because communist China and protected Australia looked at deregulation with a similar egalitarian eye. The point was to get rich without increasing the gap between the top and bottom.

The industrialisation of China and the decline of the United States need not have occurred in tandem. In fact, the lifting of hundreds of millions of Chinese out of poverty should have generated a virtuous circle of growth for the world's richest nation and its newest rival. But the Americans were losing their perspective before China had fully emerged. The US political system telegraphed its dysfunction when the November 2000 presidential election between the Democrat Al Gore and the Republican George W. Bush had to be settled by the Supreme Court. The tech wreck followed a few months later and then, out of a clear blue sky on 11 September 2001, Islamist terrorists flew hijacked airplanes into the symbols of US financial and military might, the twin towers in New York and the Pentagon in Washington. President Bush had the US embroiled in two unwinnable wars in Afghanistan and Iraq when China was still competing with Italy for sixth place on the world's income tables.

China and the US delivered conflicting signals to Australia. China showered the nation with cash, as its voracious appetite for our minerals elevated our terms of trade to their highest level since the gold rush of the 1850s. The Americans damaged our psyche. Their troubles sent a negative emotional shock our way that was almost equal to the positive income shock from the resources boom. The test of national temperament in the twenty-first century was to keep both our greed and fear at bay by investing the China windfall wisely, while resisting America's descent into paranoia.

John Howard was still trapped at the kitchen table in August 2001, arguing the detail of the GST, just before the world changed. The final pre-election Newspoll, taken in late August, found the prime minister with a job satisfaction rating of 40 per cent, and Labor and the Coalition tied on a primary vote of 40 per cent each. The best the Coalition could hope for was a narrow win, but precedent seemed to be on Labor's side because no government seeking a third term had achieved a swing to it before.

The question of whether Labor might have won became moot

after the infamous maritime incident north-west of Australia at the end of August. A boat carrying 460 mainly-Afghani asylum seekers got into difficulty in the Indian Ocean and was rescued at Australia's request by the Norwegian vessel MV *Tampa*. The people were meant to be taken back to Indonesia, but they insisted that the *Tampa* continue to their intended destination, Australia. Howard told them to stop, and SAS troops boarded the vessel to make sure the message was understood. After a frantic ring-around to find a neighbouring country that would take them for processing, Nauru agreed to become our detention centre. Athough the people seeking our protection were fleeing regimes with which we would soon go to war – the Taliban in Afghanistan and Saddam Hussein's in Iraq – public opinion was against the victims because we hadn't invited them to our shores. Howard had cornered Kim Beazley, forcing him to accept the government's response, then accusing him of flip-flopping when the Labor leader refused to support draconian and retrospective legislation to make the storming of the *Tampa* lawful.

Within a fortnight, the 11 September terror attacks on New York and Washington had settled the election in Howard's favour. By the end of the month, his rating was 61 per cent and the Coalition had eclipsed Labor by 50 per cent to 35 on the primary vote. The election was held on 10 November as Australian forces were being deployed to Afghanistan.

Whether the *Tampa* affair changed the way middle Australia thought about asylum seekers is difficult to say. Malcolm Fraser had accepted the Vietnamese boatpeople in the late '70s and the public didn't punish him for it. But the *Tampa* boatpeople were met with a diametrically opposed set of values. The truth here is that leadership dictated the national response, not the other way around. Howard set the tone and the electorate followed him.

The Coalition victory was less dramatic than the opinion polls had promised. It picked up two seats in New South Wales and one in Queensland, and lost one in Victoria, for a net result of plus two. After preferences, the Coalition won the popular vote 50.9 per cent to 49.1; a swing to it of 1.9 per cent. Labor's primary vote went backwards, but not necessarily to the Coalition. This was a more complicated election than its status quo finish suggested because the nation was actually shifting slightly leftward, from hard right to right, and from centre-left to left. The pattern can be seen by following the primary vote swings: One Nation's fell by 4.1 per cent; the Coalition's jumped by 3.5; Labor's fell 2.3; the Greens picked up 2.8 per cent. Howard had brought home some of his base from Pauline Hanson, while Kim Beazley had given up some of Labor's base to the Greens. The previous elections of 1996 and '98 suddenly made more sense: the party of the centre-left was still paying for the recession, which had splintered its heartland by sending older male voters first to Howard, then to Hanson and back to Howard again. While Labor sought to appease this voter by following Howard to the right, it opened another wound in its base as the cosmopolitan voter that Whitlam, Hawke and Keating had cultivated now looked to the Greens.

The passion of the 2001 campaign came from the subject of border protection. Howard's most memorable phrase – 'We will decide who comes to this country and the circumstances in which they come' – recalled Bob Hawke's attack on the Vietnamese in the 1977 election campaign. But Howard's political revival can be explained, simply, by bricks'n'mortar. The state that had been the most hostile to incumbents in the '90s was Queensland. Brisbane house prices had lagged behind those in Sydney and Melbourne during the landlord phase of the boom in 1999–2000, so existing home owners didn't have the false comfort of the capital gain to make them feel richer. But Brisbane caught up in 2001, with annual prices rising by 16 per cent in the year to October.

No one was really watching Australia at the time. The dollar spent much of 2001 below us50 cents, yet we had picked the next trend in capitalism: the debt-fuelled spending boom. People who had previously owned their homes outright re-borrowed. Every comparable Western nation – the US, Britain and Canada – would do the same. Part of this trend can be explained by the breaking of inflation. In the 1970s and '80s, household spending was constrained by high interest rates. After inflation had been tamed, families found that lower interest rates allowed them to borrow twice as much without increasing their repayment burden. It was only natural that some of this saving be translated into higher house prices, and household debt. The question no Western nation could answer before the global financial crisis was, when did they go too far?

House prices rose in Australia before anywhere else, so the household savings ratio fell further. Fittingly, the first episode of *Kath & Kim* screened on the ABC on 16 May 2002, in the very quarter the ratio went 'negative'; that is, the community as a whole was spending more than it was earning. As Kath and Kim divided their time between their suburban McMansion and the local shopping mall, the viewer was never told where their money came from. Their insipid menfolk, Kel and Brett, surely didn't make enough to support their perpetual consumption. But that was the point. Every level of society was enjoying themselves on the credit card. We all felt part of the bogan middle in the noughties.

The urge to retreat to the home and the shopping mall was reinforced by the turmoil in our immediate neighbourhood. Australia's relationship with Indonesia, the world's largest Muslim nation, had been less predictable after Suharto had been toppled in 1998. John Howard had taken the opportunity of the leadership change to suggest to new president B.J. Habibie that Jakarta give the East Timorese a vote on their future. Habibie surprised the world by responding with a pledge to grant East Timor independence by the end of 1999, if that was what the people wanted. They did, but the Indonesia-backed militias on the island retaliated with violence that compelled Australia to lead a military intervention force to secure the peace in September 1999.

The success of that operation restored Howard's standing in the polls, not quite to where he had been after Port Arthur, but it was instructive that Australians gravitated to Howard in a moment of crisis. Without realising it, his heroics in East Timor created a ripple that led ultimately to the *Tampa*. While Suharto was in power, the Indonesians were willing to prevent asylum seekers from making the dangerous trip across the Indian Ocean to Australia. That neighbourly favour was harder to call on after East Timor was granted independence, because the Indonesians had things other than Australia's interests on their mind. Relations between Jakarta and Canberra cooled noticeably between 1999 and 2001. Habibie wouldn't take Howard's call during the final days of the East Timor bloodbath, and neither would Megawati Sukarnoputri, who was president during the *Tampa* stand-off.

It is in this context that September 11 was felt with almost the same intensity in Australia as in the US. When terrorists struck Bali a year later, on 12 October 2002, killing 202 people, including eighty-eight young Australians and thirty-eight Indonesians, our subliminal fears about the Muslim nation to our north seemed to be validated. But Howard revived our previous cordial relations with Jakarta because our interests and theirs had realigned in the war against al Qaeda and its offshoots.

Howard gave the finest speech of his career in tribute to the dead.

'Our nation has been changed by this event,' he told a memorial service at the Australian consulate in Bali on 17 October.

'Perhaps we may not be so carefree as we have been in the past but we will never lose our openness, our sense of adventure. The young of Australia will always travel, they will always seek fun in different parts, they will always reach out to the young of other nations, they will always be open, fun-loving and decent men and women.

'So as we grapple inadequately and in despair to try and comprehend what has happened, let us gather ourselves together, let us wrap our arms not only around our fellow Australians, but our arms around the people of Indonesia, of Bali. Let us wrap our arms around the people of other nations and the friends and relatives of the nationals of other countries who died in this horrible event.

'Australia has been affected very deeply but the Australian spirit has not been broken; the spirit remains strong and free and open and tolerant. I know that is what all of those who lost their lives would have wanted and I know that is what those who grieve for them want.'

US president George W. Bush issued a similar call after the attacks of 11 September: 'When they [al Qaeda] struck, they wanted to create an atmosphere of fear. And one of the great goals of this nation's war is to restore public confidence in the airline industry. It's to tell the travelling public: "Get on board. Do your business around the country. Fly and enjoy America's great destination spots. Get down to Disney World in Florida. Take your families and enjoy life, the way we want it to be enjoyed."'

It wasn't quite a presidential order to go shopping, but the American – and Australian – people did so anyway. Bush and Howard became kindred spirits in stimulus and war; their response to the challenge of terrorism echoed LBJ's. They wanted to have it both ways, cloaking themselves in the war leader's battle fatigues while donning a Santa hat and beard to hand out goodies to the electorate. Bush and Howard judged their communities to be too precious to make a direct sacrifice for the war effort in Afghanistan, and then Iraq. The wars would be funded by borrowing, while households would be encouraged to borrow for themselves to enjoy the creature comforts of technology and property.

Howard indulged the electorate by breaking a longstanding convention of Australian politics that a handout to voters had to be matched by an offset elsewhere in the budget. The surplus, which began building again in 2002, was returned to voters as tax cuts and cash payments that created their own bubble logic: to impress the public, every subsequent handout had to be more generous than the last.

The Americans went even further, because they pushed their budget into deficit. Bill Clinton had completed his eight years as president with the largest surplus in US history – $236.2 billion, or 2.4 per cent of GDP in 2000. Bush rammed unfunded tax cuts through Congress, and few of his Republican colleagues seemed to mind the deficit that came with them. Unlike Howard, who was prepared to spread the benefits across the income ladder, Bush aimed his tax cuts almost exclusively at the top. When Bush stood successfully for re-election in 2004, the deficit was $412.7 billion, or 3.5 per cent of GDP.

LBJ's pursuit of the Vietnam War and the Great Society helped inject the poison of stagflation into the global economy in the second half of the '60s. The Bush wars in Afghanistan and Iraq, combined with a borrowing binge at home, spread the cancer of large, unsustainable government debts across the Western world in the noughties.

It is easy to write off John Howard's third term, between 2001 and 2004, as reform-lite. He does so himself, while emphasising that his hand was forced by overseas events. 'That period was very heavily dominated by national security issues – Afghanistan, the Bali bombing and Iraq,' he says. But his colleagues concede that he had run out of fresh ideas.

The election campaign in 2004 finished as a cakewalk, but it didn't seem likely earlier that year when Labor had taken the lead in the opinion polls under its new leader, Mark Latham, who had replaced Simon Crean.

Voters were unhappy because the Reserve Bank had remembered

enough about the early '90s recession to push back against the property boom. Interest rates were raised twice in 2002 and twice again in 2003. Sydney house prices had jumped by another 22 per cent in the twelve months after the 2001 election. Monetary policy worked on this occasion, a little late, but just in time to stop Sydney joining the subprime bubble that was about to inflate in the US. Sydney prices fell by 5 per cent over the course of 2004, but the timing was inconvenient for the government because Howard had a number of seats at risk.

At each election he had fought, Howard had tried to frame the choice around a single theme: Paul Keating in 1996, tax reform in 1998 and border protection in 2001. In 2004, he pledged to keep interest rates low and received more votes than he had with the GST or the *Tampa*. He had found the heart of middle Australia – the castle.

The Coalition picked up eight seats from Labor in electorates where there was an above-average concentration of home borrowers. Labor took four seats from the Coalition in electorates below the mortgage line. The Coalition increased its two-party vote by 1.8 per cent to 52.7, and it won control of the Senate for the first time since 1977.

Howard said he wouldn't waste the opportunity of his renewed mandate. But what was there left to be done? Political journalists didn't need to ask: all Howard had left was an old idea, something that he'd never been able to convince the people about in the previous two decades. The government would look again at reform of the workplace to provide greater freedom for employers to hire and fire, and to match pay with the conditions of the business, either up or down. The community was bewildered. Deregulation of the labour market did not fit with their twenty-first century image of Howard as father figure. He had encouraged Australians to enjoy themselves in the third term, in keeping with the ambition he had first set eight years earlier for Australia to be 'comfortable and relaxed'. Why was he letting their employer cut their entitlements in his fourth term?

Every rule in the reform book was broken with WorkChoices. It was sprung on the public with no warning and no debate. Howard had, in fact, explicitly ruled out another wave of reform. But he saw a twofold argument for further deregulation. First, Australia was running out of qualified workers by 2004, and the immigration program was being used to plug the gaps. A new mechanism for wage restraint was needed to prevent the China-led boom from overheating the economy. Second, there were still half a million unemployed Australians. To get them into work, the price of their labour had to fall. Howard never said this explicitly at the time, but he said so after his defeat. 'The people who didn't get penalty rates and overtime loadings for the period [WorkChoices] was in operation were the very people who needed that reform, the kids who couldn't break into the labour market – they got a job,' he says.

The WorkChoices policy relied on the same guiding philosophy as the Jobsback policy of 1992. Employer and employee would be trusted to bargain in good faith, without the bureaucracy dictating what was on and off the table. WorkChoices removed the 'no disadvantage test' from the government's previous legislation, which prohibited any deal that involved a reduction in pay or conditions. It also allowed firms with up to a hundred employees to sack whomever they wanted, without having to follow the process for a so-called 'fair dismissal'.

The GST had been argued for a year before the 1998 election, and the legislation had been debated line by line in Senate committee hearings for six months after the election. WorkChoices was rushed through the parliament with an almost obscene haste. The Coalition had taken control of the upper house on 1 July 2005, and the legislation was introduced into the lower house on 2 November that year. It passed through the Senate a month later, on 2 December.

The ACTU spent $8 million of its members' money on its radio and TV campaign. It was on the screens before the legislation was even released. This canny use of air time set a bad precedent for future reforms. The mining companies, with far deeper pockets, would use the same medium to bring down the next Labor prime minister. The Coalition government's taxpayer-funded campaign to defend WorkChoices was worth $121 million, while business groups kicked in with their own campaign. The stench of American big-money lobbying wafted through this argument.

The unstated but dominant reason for WorkChoices was political: to break what remained of trade union power. But Howard was seeking something that the open economy had already achieved through reduced trade union coverage and increased job insecurity for all employees. To push beyond that point was the impulse of the partisan, not that of a leader making a considered assessment of the data. The public sensed that Howard was taking the side of the boss for ideological reasons only.

Trade unions had represented 58 per cent of the workforce in 1975: 63 per cent of all male workers and 48 per cent of all female workers. The figures did not move much in the Fraser years, and 55 per cent of all workers still had a union ticket by the end of 1983, despite the recession. It was Bob Hawke, a former ACTU president, and Paul Keating, a child of Labor's New South Wales right faction, who broke the monopoly. After thirteen years of Labor government, trade union coverage had been reduced from just over half the workforce to less than one in three – 31 per cent of all workers (34 per cent male and 28 per cent female). As WorkChoices was being passed in 2005, the national figure was 22 per cent, with little difference between men (24 per cent) and women (21 per cent).

Howard the deregulationist thought WorkChoices could secure the profitability of businesses in the non-mining sector by allowing them to hire the unemployed at a lower wage. Howard the populist saw the China-sourced revenue windfalls to the budget from

2004 onwards as a re-election fund for his government. So when voters complained about WorkChoices, or higher interest rates, he always had another tax cut, or handout, up his sleeve. The budget would still be in surplus almost no matter how much he gave away because each year Treasury would revise up the revenue forecasts. But this only added to the threat of another rise in interest rates. The personal obsession with workplace reform took Howard's eye off the main game, which was to use the proceeds of the boom for nation-building, not wallet-lining.

'The big political error in WorkChoices, which I've acknowledged, was getting rid of the no-disadvantage test,' Howard says. 'If we had not done that, and if we had just done something on unfair dismissals – we had to do something on unfair dismissals, we clearly had a mandate for it – things might have been different.' Note the phrase 'political error'. Howard thinks the policy was sound and wants the Coalition to revisit it in the future.

'The most potent point of the union–Labor campaign on WorkChoices was that you'd lose your penalty rates and your overtime loadings. Now, in reality, because of the strength in the economy there was very little likelihood of that happening to many people.'

In fact, the biggest problem was that WorkChoices sought to solve a weakness in the Australian economy that no longer existed. The last wages breakout had occurred in the early '80s. Howard should have been thinking beyond his ideological comfort zone of Reagan and Thatcher to consider the new reform challenges that flowed from China.

It was too simplistic to see China as a sugar daddy. China was changing the nature of globalisation. It was pushing down the price of manufactured goods while increasing the price of energy. The Western household was being tempted with cheap TVs and computers, but their jobs wouldn't deliver the higher wages to pay the increased electricity bill that accompanied all those gadgets.

WorkChoices was, to put it bluntly, off the topic.

From the rest of the world's perspective, Australia could do no wrong in Howard's fourth term. The OECD report into our economy in 2006 said we had been making our own luck 'through the series of structural reforms and the introduction of robust macro-economic framework which have bolstered resilience'. It noted that our living standards had surpassed those of all the G7 nations except the United States. That is, the per-capita income of the typical Australian was superior to that of the Japanese, the Germans, the British, the Italians, the French and the Canadians. The IMF's managing director, Rodrigo de Rato, said: 'Other economies have much to learn from Australia, which is reaping the benefits of broad-ranging structural reforms that have generated high productivity growth and falling unemployment.'

Yet the personal economy felt like it was about to burst. Households were putting more money aside for the first time in a generation. By the end of 2006, the savings ratio had recovered to 4 per cent of disposable income, after being below zero between mid 2002 and mid 2005. The Australian public had worked out something most of the Western world didn't realise yet: the time for borrowing for the sake of spending had ended. Our households were tightening their belts before their government did.

The Reserve Bank became increasingly wary in 2006 and into 2007 about the government's willingness to throw another billion at the electorate. It wanted some of the windfall of the mining boom held back, to take the pressure off inflation. But the government either didn't understand the warnings or deliberately ignored them. Every time Howard spent, the Reserve Bank slammed the monetary policy brake. What WorkChoices took with one aspect of government policy, Howard tried to give back with tax cuts, which in turn the Reserve Bank took away again with higher interest rates.

Treasury secretary Ken Henry worried too, and told his staff so in a speech in April 2007 that damaged his relations with the government. In an election year 'there is a greater than usual risk of the development of policy proposals that are, frankly, bad', he said.

Henry thought the law of diminishing returns would apply to the 2007 contest. 'Expansionary fiscal policy tends to crowd out private activity,' he said. 'It puts upward pressure on prices, which, all things being equal, puts upwards pressure on interest rates.'

Henry was one of the most important bureaucrats of the deregulation generation. He was an adviser to Paul Keating as treasurer between 1985 and '91 before returning to the department. Henry gave advice on the case for a GST in '85 and against the GST in '93 (both times on behalf of Keating), and again for it in '98 when he was chairman of the Coalition government's tax taskforce operating out of Treasury. He was, in effect, the ghost-writer for the Howard–Costello GST and tax cuts package. By the time Ted Evans retired as Treasury secretary in April 2001, Henry was the logical successor. The leaking of his private speech echoed the Treasury wars with the Whitlam government in the '70s. Henry was annoyed that someone in Treasury made the speech public. The prime minister was angrier still and drew on the spirit of the WorkChoices to reduce Henry's pay by cancelling his performance bonus.

The opinion polls were shouting at John Howard. Australians were complaining about cost-of-living pressures. Yet the same voters wanted to do something about climate change and were prepared to pay. Which impulse to believe?

The environment was traditionally viewed as a second-tier political concern in Australia, behind economic management. So the Liberals put timber workers before forests while Labor would protect coal miners ahead of the atmosphere. The popular support for action on climate change broke these stereotypes for two mutually reinforcing reasons.

First, a long drought had been underway in southern and eastern Australia since 2001, and was being felt especially keenly in
the bush. The Murray-Darling River system, which runs from
Queensland through New South Wales and Victoria to South
Australia, providing water for the nation's food bowl, was suffering
its equal-driest period on record. At the same time, urban water
restrictions became a normal part of life. People weren't allowed to
hose their driveways clean or soak their lawns. The state governments that applied the restrictions worried that households would
revolt, but the opposite occurred. As one Labor premier at the
time told me, he couldn't ease the restrictions when dam storage
levels later improved in his state because the people enjoyed making the sacrifice.

Second, the political debates in the US and Britain were adding to Australian anxieties about climate change. The man that
George W. Bush had beaten at the 2000 election, Al Gore, was
enjoying a renaissance as an unlikely movie star. His documentary
An Inconvenient Truth opened to packed movie houses across Australia in September 2006. Howard didn't see the picture, but he
rushed to judgement anyway to say he wouldn't be 'taking policy
advice from films'.

British prime minister Tony Blair was in the Gore camp. On 30
October, the Labour government released a report commissioned
from economist Nicholas Stern. The Stern Review said climate
change was primarily an economic problem. 'Climate change is
the greatest market failure the world has ever seen,' was Stern's
blunt assessment. 'The costs of stabilising the climate are significant, but manageable; delay would be dangerous and much more
costly.'

Howard couldn't ignore Stern's finding. And the polls were
adamant: the prime minister's stubbornness on the Kyoto Protocol
was beginning to grate.

Howard thought Australia had struck a terrific deal at the

international meeting in Kyoto in December 1997. The agreement set variable targets for reducing greenhouse gas emissions across nations, with special consideration for those rich economies dependent on high-emitting energy sources. We were one of only three – along with Norway and Iceland – who were allowed to increase our emissions (ours was by 8 per cent) above 1990s levels by 2012. The rest of the developed world was to reduce theirs by at least 5 per cent. But Howard lost interest in ratifying the pro-Australian protocol after President Bush declared soon after taking office in 2001 that the agreement was 'fundamentally flawed'. Howard took the opportunity to pull Australia out. We would only move when the Americans did, he said.

Older and younger voters were the most adamant that they wanted to do something about climate change. The families in the middle were more concerned about the cost of childcare, another second-tier issue that had become as important in Howard's final term as interest rates.

Howard was not the man for these times, and it showed with the increasingly exaggerated gestures he made throughout the election year of 2007. In January, he offered $10 billion for a federal takeover of the Murray-Darling without consulting Treasury for advice on the numbers. In June, he became a convert to a market-based mechanism to deal with climate change after receiving his own report, written by Peter Shergold, the head of the prime minister's department.

Howard promised a 'domestic emissions trading system – that's a cap and trade system – beginning no later than 2012'. For years he had argued against Australia moving before anyone else in the region. Now he wanted to go first, as Australia had done with tariffs.

'Australia will continue to lead internationally on climate change,' he said, 'globally and in the Asia-Pacific region. Not in a way that lectures and moralises, but in a way that builds support for global action to tackle this enormous global challenge.'

With this, the climate change chameleon had covered all parts of the spectrum. Howard had been for the Kyoto Protocol before he was against it, and against emissions trading before he was for it.

Placing a price on greenhouse gasses was the first economic reform forced on Australia's politicians by the community. However, prior consent did not guarantee action because leaders on both sides did not trust the electorate to keep its end of the bargain.

Nevertheless, when voters said they wanted to make a contribution, they challenged the very premise of the Howard era: that a leader had to be seen to be giving more than he took from the taxpayer. Community attitudes had, in fact, been changing on Howard's watch. At the 1996 election, voters said they preferred less tax over an increase in social spending by a ratio of three to one – 57 per cent wanted a tax cut, and only 17 per cent wanted better services. The lines crossed for the first time at the 2004 election, and by 2007 the sentiment was running strongly the other way: only 34 per cent wanted less tax and 47 per cent wanted an increase in social spending.

The fashionable view is that Australians became less greedy the more money Howard threw at them. The likelier explanation is that bribing reaffirmed his political weakness, not the electorate's strength of character. Paul Keating had grasped this point at the top of the previous boom in 1989: if the government gave in to the public complaint about higher interest rates, it would be validating that critique. Although he didn't see the connection between the two, Howard was adding to the interest rate burden without a coherent plan for dealing with the mining boom.

As the people lost confidence in their prime minister, the Labor Party struggled with basic questions of political identity. In order to distance itself from Keating, Labor had stopped defending its own economic reform program after the 1996 landslide, and each subsequent election loss made it feel less certain about what it should stand for. John Howard was responsible only for the tail end of the reform project, but he managed to claim full credit for the electoral benefits that flowed from the long recovery. Labor seemed unable to point this out, and nor could it convincingly articulate that Howard was squandering the opportunity that the boom presented for another round of reforms.

To beat Howard, after ceding so much policy ground to him, Labor felt it had to rely on either a recession to discredit the Coalition's economic management, or an own goal like WorkChoices, which made people feel vulnerable at a time of plenty. Seeking power by default jarred with Labor's self-image as the party of reform. Bob Hawke didn't want to continue Malcolm Fraser's project, Gough Whitlam hadn't sold himself as a younger version of Billy McMahon, and John Curtin certainly didn't seek office so he could continue to rule as the young Robert Menzies. But the strategy Labor mapped for the 2007 election aimed to minimise the difference with Howard across tax and spending policies in order to isolate the difference on WorkChoices and climate change.

There is no simple explanation for why Labor had lost its reform zeal during the Howard era. Personnel played a part. The prosperity generation of politicians who entered parliament after the last recession had no memory of economic hardship, so they sweated the small stuff of the media and polling cycles. They were too young to have witnessed the glory days of Hawke and Keating, so they didn't know that reforms are polished through years of public debate and division. Howard was the only winner they had seen up close. His methods became theirs.

I lost count of the number of Labor people who complained privately that Howard played the politics of division and envy, only to hear them repeat his focus-group-tested lines in public about being tough on boatpeople or welfare bludgers, while rewarding this or that gainfully employed voter with more cash. Howard taught Labor to fear the electorate. So there was no policy reappraisal because the party's factional chiefs didn't want to risk the bad look of disunity. Yet Labor had made itself electable in the past only after it had developed a reform program through trial and argument. The risk of a split was balanced by the reward of a new idea.

Labor had just four leaders in almost thirty years between February 1967 and March 1996 – Whitlam, Hayden, Hawke and Keating. Each was a giant of the movement because they were prepared to update the party platform. Whitlam, Hawke and Keating had each been in public life for at least twenty years before becoming prime minister.

In the eleven years between 1996 and 2007, Howard witnessed five changes in the Labor leadership – from Kim Beazley to Simon Crean to Mark Latham, back to Beazley and finally on to Kevin Rudd. None could be said to have developed a single policy to rival the reforms of the past. Beazley and Crean were sons of Whitlam ministers. Latham and Rudd were loners who were able to create a constituency through the media, which they used to convince caucus to elect them. They played Hawke's game, without the experience. Latham had been in parliament just ten years before contesting the 2004 election. Rudd had just eight years' federal service before taking the Labor leadership at the end of 2006.

Kevin Rudd had built a formidable profile through the quality press as Labor's foreign affairs spokesperson, and through the morning television program *Sunrise*, where he had a weekly spot. His career before parliament had been out of the public eye. He had been a diplomat and a political staffer, and had run Queensland Labor premier Wayne Goss's office between 1989 and 1995. It was a CV not dissimilar to Alexander Downer's.

Rudd was marketed as a younger version of Howard. He was a brand in his own right, 'Kevino7', who existed above his own party.

He would get up earlier than Howard, talk for longer, and venture to places on the media dial where no leader had gone before – FM radio and TV comedy shows.

He infuriated Howard because the prime minister was aware of how Labor people viewed the private man. Rudd was an opportunist with a foul temper. He bullied staff and badmouthed his own colleagues. Press gallery journalists swapped examples of Rudd's self-regard. Howard couldn't see how the electorate would warm to such an egotist. But Howard had made Rudd – it was Howard's cynicism that created the vacuum for an earnest, evidence-based policy nerd rising from nowhere to lead the nation. Rudd didn't carry the baggage of Iraq or children overboard, or climate change or WorkChoices. And to top it off, he spoke the language of our new best friend in commerce, Mandarin. He appeared the right man for the new age and would offer Australians hope for a more honourable future. From his first week as Labor leader in December 2006, Rudd never looked like being rattled. The opinion polls moved decisively in his and Labor's favour, forcing Howard to shed almost everything he had believed in to try to snap the nation out of its reverie. He even watered down WorkChoices in May 2007, a month before announcing his support for emissions trading.

On the first working day of the election campaign, 15 October 2007, John Howard stood alongside the treasurer who wanted his job and together they promised the largest election tax cut in history, valued at $52 billion over four years from 2008–09 to 2011–12. No strings attached. The money would come out of the projected surplus, and would complement the tax cut in May that voters had not warmed to.

An hour or so after the government made its final tax cut offer, one of the senior people in the opposition rang me to ask what I thought. This conversation is commonplace in the press gallery.

The politician is not seeking advice, but fishing for how the media might cover the other side's announcement. I was prepared to play the game, because I wanted to know whether Labor would call Howard's bluff and say it wouldn't match the tax cuts.

What happens, I asked, if next week's inflation figure is a bad one and the Reserve Bank decides to increase interest rates? 'We'll just have to fucking wear it,' the contact told me, answering the question I didn't need to ask. Labor would agree with nine-tenths of the Coalition's tax cuts and keep their fingers crossed in office that they could afford to deliver them without blowing up the economy.

Glenn Stevens, who had replaced Ian Macfarlane as Reserve Bank governor the previous year, was in a difficult position. The September quarter consumer price index released on 24 October was worse than expected. The underlying inflation rate was pushing towards 3 per cent, and this necessitated another increase in interest rates. The next meeting of the Reserve Bank board was set for Melbourne Cup day, 6 November. The decision, announced the following day, raised the official cash rate by 25 basis points to 6.75 per cent – its highest level since 1996, and the tenth increase in the cycle since 2002. The press statement explaining the reasons referred to the financial troubles in the US. But Stevens still didn't see danger for Australia.

'The world economy is still expected to grow at an above-average pace, however, led by strong growth in China and other parts of Asia. High global commodity prices remain an important source of stimulus to Australian spending and activity.'

The key word here is 'stimulus'. Stevens did not believe the budget should be stimulating the economy at the top of the boom when China was already doing this.'

Howard is critical of Stevens: 'My political/economic argument was that the mid-campaign interest rate increase, the last one of our term in office, was an unnecessary, unwise decision. They had made their point about independence, nobody doubted it. There was an increase in August, for heaven's sake – that was only three months before the election. It might have been possible to avoid the sensitivity about a rate rise during the campaign if that adjustment had been made in December, and it wouldn't have been seen as a judgement on the incoming government.

'Peter [Costello] and I were surprised. We thought the [inflation] numbers would be more favourable to us – we were a bit taken aback. I think the problem with it was that people were writing about it until the numbers came out, and once the numbers came out, everyone knew, the bank had really talked itself into adjusting rates.'

Asked if he thought the campaign tax cuts might have influenced the Reserve's decision, Howard says: 'No, I don't think so. I think he felt he just had to do it to demonstrate his independence, which was unnecessary. Would that have made a difference in the [election] result? Probably not . . . it might have had an impact on the margin.' Howard never really lost the price-fixing impulse. He wanted political credit for the cuts in interest rates, and to shift blame to others for the increases. But he had left Stevens no choice. Inflation was stirring, and those tax cuts were, from the perspective of an overheating economy, too risky.

The spendathon of the 2007 campaign was surreal for many reasons. Australians had never seen election promises on this scale before. Howard even pulled out the chequebook after the interest rate rise, with a $2 billion a year handout to parents who sent their children to private schools the final offer of his 12 November campaign launch speech.

The focus groups that Howard had read so well in his previous eleven years recoiled at his profligacy. Two days later, Rudd addressed Labor's launch with a perfectly scripted counterattack. 'Today I am saying loud and clear that this sort of reckless spending must stop. I am determined that any commitments I make are first and foremost economically responsible. That's why the commitments I announced today will cost less than one quarter of those Mr Howard announced on Monday.'

Rudd wasn't as pure as he made out. Over the course of the campaign, Howard had out-spent Rudd by just $2 billion a year – $15 billion versus $13 billion, with each man's tax cuts accounting for the lion's share of the total. Neither package would be afford-able once the global financial crisis punched a hole in the federal budget.

John Howard was dismissed by the electorate for the same reason Paul Keating had been eleven years earlier: voters had grown tired, even sick, of him. The Coalition's defeat on 24 November 2007 was as comprehensive as the previous changes of government in '96 and '83. Labor won 25 seats – nine in Rudd's home state of Queensland, seven in New South Wales, three in South Australia, two in each of Victoria and Tasmania and one in each of Western Australia and the Northern Territory. The Liberals picked up two seats from Labor in the mining state of Western Australia, and one from an independent in New South Wales for a net loss of 22.

Labor's two-party vote of 52.7 per cent was identical to its 1972 victory, but it came with a larger seat count. The swing of 5.4 per cent was the third highest against a sitting government after '69 and '75. The catch was that Labor's primary vote of 43.4 per cent was around 6 points lower than its previous two entries into government in '72 and '83. It was even 1.5 points below Keating's winning effort in '93. The gap had gone to the new party to the left of Labor, the Greens.

Howard lost his own seat as well as his government. Defeat in Bennelong to Labor's Maxine McKew was driven, in part, by gender and race. The electorate was in a demographic hotspot, between Sydney's affluent, and safe Liberal north, and its ethnic west, which was Labor heartland. Howard's skilled immigration program had turned Bennelong into a marginal seat, and he would always run the risk that his rhetorical past would catch up with him. The Chinese-born constituted 10 per cent of the seat by 2007, the Korean-born 3 per cent and the Indian-born 2 per cent. The myth of Bennelong is that the Asian-born were always against Howard. They had, in fact, supported him, especially in 2001. The catch in 2007 was that the more recent arrivals were from mainland China, and they preferred the Mandarin-speaking Rudd.

Of all the former prime ministers, Howard is the one who generates the sharpest reactions. Malcolm Fraser offers no comment on his legacy, but simply: 'I can say he was a good treasurer.'

Keating insists on the right to attack, even though I asked for positive reflections only: 'In a nation of immigrants, John Howard let the racism genie out of the bottle. This is an act of high political irresponsibility and we are still suffering from it. I'd even go so far as to say that manifestations of this period in such things as the Cronulla riot [in 2005] has in its antecedents the notion that somewhere in officialdom at the top of the country it's all right to think poorly of people who come from a different background to yourself. This is, I think, a dreadful letdown for the country after it had succeeded so greatly in settling so many people from abroad, in perhaps the most successful multicultural experiment in the Western world.'

Bob Hawke has the most to say about Howard, both in his favour and against him.

On race, Hawke agrees with Keating: 'It was not just Howard directly, but part of the problem was that he gave so much oxygen to One Nation and Hanson, and I think he bears some responsibility for that. But I don't want to be too tough on Howard because the tendency amongst the labour movement is just to knock, knock, knock, knock – and there are many things on which I would knock him – but he was supportive of the reforms I made. He would have liked to have had a prime minister himself, when he was treasurer, who was supportive. But he did have a blind spot, a weak spot there [on race], and I think it's unfortunate. I don't think he sufficiently understood the way the world was changing, how the centre of economic gravity was moving across from the mid-Atlantic to the mid-Pacific and further, and from Australia's point of view – quite apart from the morality of it, which is fundamental – there was our economic interest.'

But Hawke admires Howard's grit: 'The one thing you have got to say about John, I suppose, more than anything else, is the absolute tenacity of the man, which I respect enormously. He handled the GST with integrity. Howard would never have become prime minister if Hewson had done what was the obvious thing to do and go to that '93 election and say, "I think it is worth looking at a GST, but I undertake not to introduce it in a first term." And if he had done that he would have got the result in '93 that Howard got in '96. It was just crazy, crazy politics. But Howard went about it with tenacity, and it took a degree of courage to take it to an election and win – and you've got to respect him for that.

'The other thing I respect about John is he started off very, very badly with respect to China, but he changed and continued the strong relationship going through Gough, Fraser and myself.'

Howard inherited an economy and an immigration program that were both open, but he played with the latter through the closed rhetoric of border protection and old Australian values. He ruled Australia for its most prosperous period on record, when, for the first time, we were able to avoid a financial meltdown in the region in 1997–98 and a mild global recession in 2001. But he never quite caught the opportunity of his period in office. He was too conscious of the past because his over-fifties voter base wanted reassurance that Australia wasn't being changed beyond comprehension by globalisation. That approach made sense during the testing period of the jobless recovery, in the late '90s. In the new millennium, it held the nation back. The increasingly erratic behaviour of the United States and the emergence of China were challenges that required a new thinking. But Howard looked at these issues through the wrong end of the telescope. America was a friend, right or wrong, so we went to Iraq to topple a regime that posed no threat to us, and to go looking for weapons of mass destruction it didn't possess. China was a friend, too, so we took her money without asking the logical question of where to invest it, let alone what the shift in global economic power from West to East meant for our society.

Howard wasn't too old for the job but he had run out of ideas after the introduction of the GST. His party, and the nation, would have been better served if he'd had the humility to retire after the 2004 election, at the latest. He didn't want to stand aside for Peter Costello, a man with whom he had little in common, and even less respect for the longer the treasurer asked for the job without forcing a challenge. In his desperation to buy one more election win in 2007, Howard put budgetary and interest rate policies at odds, as his spending provoked a tighter monetary response from the Reserve Bank just when the global economy was about to crash. The echoes of history were from '74 and '82, when Treasury was pushing up interest rates to counter the loose budgets inspired by Jim Cairns and Malcolm Fraser. Those two busts ended badly for Australia. This one, thankfully, would be different.

20

THE LAST RICH
NATION STANDING

Kevin Rudd governed on about four hours sleep a night. He had
set a manic pace for his staff, his colleagues, the media and the
wider community in his period as opposition leader. John Howard
couldn't believe that Rudd would make announcements on a Saturday, the unofficial day of rest for politicians when the television
news received its lowest rating of the week. The public loved this
side of him at first. 'Kevin07' was devoted enough to work 24/7.
Yet he had a strange sense of detachment once an announcement
had been made. He didn't like to return to old debates because his
restless mind had already darted off to another subject.

Winning government increased the number of people he could
conscript to his Sisyphean quest to be on top of every issue. Rudd
was a bureaucrat by training, and was always demanding a briefing
paper to be written for him. In the early months of his government, the nation's capital buzzed with the excitement of policy
renewal. Rudd signed the Kyoto Protocol in December 2007, and
in February 2008 delivered the apology to the Stolen Generations,
which Howard had refused to do. In April, he hosted an ideas
summit to plot a course for the future.

The community was impressed, and the opinion polls showed the new prime minister enjoying Bob Hawke-like ratings. But within the government, Rudd was accumulating enemies. The documents he demanded of the public service sat unread in his in-tray; the policies he floated in the media were never followed through to delivery. It was activity for its own sake. Nonetheless, the redeeming feature of this workaholic prime minister was he thrived in a genuine crisis.

On the morning of Tuesday, 30 September 2008, Rudd was awake at 5.45 a.m. His deputy chief of staff, Alister Jordan, had been up for more than an hour, pulling together a briefing on the vote just held in the United States Congress. The trigger for the global financial crisis – the biggest international shock since the oil crisis of the 1970s – is dated fifteen days earlier, when the US investment bank Lehman Brothers collapsed after the US Federal Reserve and Treasury couldn't find a finance house big enough to buy it. Lehman Brothers was a Wall Street institution. Older than the Australian federation, it was established in 1850. The debts it reported on the day of its bankruptcy totalled US$613 billion – around half the size of Australia's annual GDP. The panic spread across the globe in a nanosecond, as bank after bank that was owed money by Lehman Brothers realised they were entangled in a web of bad loans that could bring them all down together. But it was the vote to block the Bush administration's US$700 billion rescue package for the world's largest economy that brought the panic home to Australia. We were about to face globalisation's most dramatic test of temperament to date.

Rudd decided that he and treasurer Wayne Swan would blitz the early-morning media to assure Australians that our banks remained strong, better capitalised and less exposed to the sub-prime housing loans that were threatening the viability of banks overseas. The Australian Prudential Regulation Authority, which oversees the nation's financial system, was asked to update its

advice about the stability of the banks. That advice was delivered by 8.30 a.m. and the first of a series of meetings commenced
between Rudd, Swan, their respective heads of the Department of
Prime Minister and Cabinet and Treasury, Terry Moran and Ken
Henry, and senior government staff. Rudd had already managed to
make two important overseas calls, to British prime minister Gordon Brown and Australia's ambassador to Washington, Dennis
Richardson, to get their perspectives on the crisis. Rudd and Swan
held a press conference in Canberra at 9.45 a.m. – fifteen minutes
before the Australian share market opened – to reassure people
that the banks, and by extension the Australian economy, were
well-placed to weather the storm. Swan dropped a hint that the
government wouldn't insist the banks pass on the full amount of
the interest rate cut that the Reserve Bank was expected to deliver
after its regular monthly board meeting on the following Tuesday,
7 October.

Swan had been waiting to send this signal since Lehman
Brothers. In mid-September, Treasury detected an alarming spike
in the rates the banks were charging one another for the funds that
passed between them overnight. Rudd was unsure. He had to be
convinced that this was the right thing to do because the politician
in him felt that working families were struggling and would not
take too kindly to banks pocketing part of an interest rate cut.

The next day, 1 October, Rudd caught a flight to Perth to meet
with the state premiers. The prime minister's VIP jet is a tight
squeeze at the best of times. Rudd had a small work table in the
main cabin with two sets of passenger seats on either side of it.
A narrow aisle led to two other passenger seats within hearing
distance of the table. There were just seven seats in total, including
the prime minister's. But on this trip, nine people were gathered
for a midair meeting – Rudd, Swan, Moran, Dr Henry and five
key advisers. To accommodate the extra bodies, a couple of fold-
out canvas chairs without backs were pulled out and set down in

the aisle. The main item of business was whether to make Swan's hint explicit.

Labor had revelled in bank bashing; it had suited its election campaign against the Howard government because it reminded working families that he could not keep interest rates low. There was no room for nuance in this sort of populism. Banks were bad; the people who borrowed from them were victims. But the first rule of managing a financial crisis is to convince people to leave their money in the bank.

According to one official on the plane, Rudd made a point of saying that he was prepared to wear a bad day or two in the press. 'Forget about what is going to win us the news [cycle] or lose us the news [cycle], what is the most responsible thing to do?' The comment was revealing for its lack of self-awareness. To make an exception in these abnormal circumstances confirmed that the government took a short-sighted view of every other issue. Rudd had run the government the way he had run for office, on the principle of continuous campaigning. Each day was devoted to winning more favourable mentions in the media than his opponent.

There was no question that politics would have to take second place. The world's financial markets were in danger of freezing up, leaving banks without the cash to conduct their daily business. Rudd accepted the advice to cut the Australian banks some slack and give Australia the chance to escape the catastrophe.

The ever-present nightmare of capitalism is the run – when everyone heads for the exit at the same time. The mob banging on the locked door of a faltering bank, to retrieve deposits that weren't there, is one of the images of the Great Depression that is seared into the consciousness of people born many generations after the event.

The GFC began as a run between the bankers themselves. The panic of the moneyed elites is only understood by recalling what preceded it. The biggest banks in America, Europe and Japan had thought they had unlocked the secret to perpetual profit. They were to economic rationalism what the politicians of the 1970s had been to Keynesianism – the zealots who took the theory too far. The US Federal Reserve under its previous chairman, Alan Greenspan, believed in the infallibility of markets, and the inevitability of American success if markets were allowed to set their prices without a nosey regulator looking over their shoulder. Australia once held a similar view, but the experience of the late 1980s boom had identified the one market that deserved, in the national interest, to be kept on a shortish leash: the finance sector. The subprime loans were a global manifestation of the crazy lending Australia experienced in the '80s, when banks saw market share as the most important metric and forgot to ask the basic question of whether the person they were lending to could repay them.

Both sides of American politics had encouraged lower-income households to take out so-called subprime loans. These started with a low interest rate that later increased to more normal levels. The new insurance products the banks sold to one another that backed these loans assumed that house prices would keep rising – that is, there was no risk that these loans would turn bad, because even if the home borrower couldn't keep up with their repayments, the properties could be sold at a profit to the bank. But rather than reducing the risk to each lender, such insurance spread the risk across the entire system like a computer virus. All it took was for one big bank to fail and every bank that was connected to it would come under stress.

What fed this problem back into the real economy and ensured the global financial crisis became the Great Recession was the cascade of defaults that came when the subprime loans switched to their higher interest rates. Each distressed property put on the market drove the market lower. US house prices fell by about 20 per cent between 2006 and 2008, bringing all the tenpins in the economy down. The borrowers who lost their properties stopped spending, the banks who were left with the overvalued asset couldn't recover their money, and on it went, until every Western economy was staring into the abyss of the first synchronised global recession since the Great Depression.

Australia had been here once before. The 1929 election was held just a fortnight before the Wall Street crash that began the Great Depression. History's victim then was the Labor regime of James Scullin. The parallels with Kevin Rudd's government were eerie. Scullin had won power at the top of a boom, and the man he defeated, Stanley Melbourne Bruce, had lost not just office but his own seat of Flinders as well.

Bruce had been the most dominant figure in national politics in the 'Roaring Twenties', but was humbled for the same reason as John Howard – he wanted to deregulate the labour market. As Judith Brett wrote, Bruce had long believed that 'high wages were a major cause of Australia's economic difficulties'.

Bruce sought a fourth term on 12 October 1929 on a platform of industrial relations reform. He wanted to return Canberra's arbitration powers to the states, but his idea didn't catch the public's imagination and Labor won its largest majority to that date. *The Age* gave its readers a twelve-paragraph summary of the election result in the top right-hand corner of its front page. 'The Federal elections resulted in an overwhelming vote for the retention of a Federal arbitration system,' the report began. 'Figures show that the Bruce–Page government was routed . . . [and] the personal defeat of Mr. Bruce in Flinders is indicated. Other Ministers defeated are Messers. Marr and Abbott.'

There were large anti-government swings in wealthy seats such as Kooyong and Warringah. The final paragraph reminded Australians of their place in the world: 'The result stunned the conservative press in England – the Sunday "Times" observed that the development of the situation would be "awaited with deep anxiety, but that there was no cause for a panic".'

Scullin's government was sworn in on 22 October, only two days before Wall Street suffered the first of its crashes. Labor quickly split under the pressure, forcing Scullin to call an early election on 19 December 1931, which was lost in a landslide. The story was retold with gallows humour by Rudd government ministers in 2008.

Australia's response to the GFC was shaped by choices made during the final term of the Howard government. The critical period between 2004 and 2006, when the US housing market overheated, was an arm wrestle between the Coalition and the economic bureaucracy. John Howard was talking up property while the Reserve Bank was trying to cool it. The prime minister told voters to keep the faith because the property market would never falter: 'I haven't met anybody yet who's stopped me in the street and shaken their fist and said: "Howard, I'm angry with you; my house has got more valuable".' A quote like that can destroy a politician's reputation if what follows is a bust. The precondition for a bust was indeed there. House prices increased by at least 30 per cent in every city except Sydney between 2004 and 2007. The national's mining capital, Perth, recorded a 77 per cent increase; Melbourne 38 per cent, Brisbane 36 per cent, Adelaide 35 per cent and Hobart 30 per cent. In Sydney, voters continued to scream in Howard's final term because prices went up by just 5 per cent over that three-year period – a cut in real terms after inflation.

Sydney was Australia's finance capital and thus the city most prone to funny-money bubbles in the new millennium. But the timing of those Reserve Bank interest rate rises in 2002 and 2003 meant that Sydney was in a near recessionary state when the US property market was preparing to inflate. Sydney's western suburbs, the epicentre of the backlash against asylum seekers in 2001, would have been the most vulnerable to subprime-style lending.

Howard was annoyed with both the Reserve Bank and Treasury in his final term for hurting his battlers in Sydney's west, and for spreading the pain to Queensland, where the interest rate rises of 2006 and 2007 stung the most. The two institutions didn't always see eye to eye, but they reacted with the same instinctive suspicion of the boom. During a meeting of senior Treasury officials in 2004, the topic of recession had come up. 'Look around this room,' Martin Parkinson, the Treasury's deputy, whispered to the head of the department, Ken Henry. 'You and I are the only people who were here during the recession of the early 1990s.' From that observation came two top-secret workshops of senior officers to come up with a model to better handle the next recession, which seemed light years away at the time.

The review looked at the forecasting and policy-advice mistakes of 'the recession we had to have' only. But the cabinet records studied for this book show similar mistakes were made in the mid '70s and early '80s recessions. Treasury always missed the turn in the economy. And even after it acknowledged that recession was underway, it compounded its error by forecasting a soft landing. 'The view we came to out of those workshops was that, in periods of serious economic weakness, we in the department should be the first to say to government "do something". We shouldn't be the last,' Dr Henry told authors Lenore Taylor and David Uren.

The corporate memory in the Reserve Bank about the danger of an over-eager finance sector had almost vanished as well. The Howard government had taken away the Reserve's responsibilities for supervising the banks in 1998. That role had passed to the Australian Prudential Regulation Authority. Under the new arrangements, APRA was responsible for all financial services, including superannuation and insurance. But it had failed its first challenge in the most spectacular way by missing the warning signs in 2001 that HIH was about to collapse under the weight of criminal neglect. APRA accepted the rebuke given to it by the HIH Royal Commission in 2004 to become 'more sceptical, questioning and, where necessary, aggressive'. Peter Costello had already appointed John Laker as the new chairman in 2003. Dr Laker came from the Reserve Bank, and with him the corporate memory chain between the monetary authority and the regulator was reconnected.

To be fair to the banks, they hadn't forgotten the lessons of the early 1990s either. But the banks didn't get the chance to test whether they would resist the temptation of all those exotic loan products being pushed overseas because they were too busy issuing mortgages for the local property boom. Unlike the US and the UK, where borrowers can mail back the key to their bank if they can't keep up with their home loan repayments – leaving the bank to carry the loss until it can sell the house to someone else – Australian borrowers can't walk away without being sued. So when interest rates were being raised between 2002 and 2007, our mortgage belt took the hint and increased their repayments by more than the increase in their costs so they could reduce the principal owing. Household savings began to recover from 2006 despite higher interest rates, ironically, because families put their tax cuts straight into the bank, or onto their mortgage. That's how they expressed their dissatisfaction with Howard's bribes – by refusing to take his advice to keep enjoying themselves.

The battle readiness of Treasury and the Reserve Bank, and the strength of the local banks, gave the Rudd government a head start on the rest of the world. The other advantage was the state of the budget. Wayne Swan was able to deliver all of Labor's election promises, and book a surplus of $21.7 billion for 2008–09, 1.8 per cent of GDP. In the US, the deficit before the GFC had been 1.2 per cent of GDP.

Working in the other direction for the Australian balance sheet was the threat of inflation. The Reserve Bank had increased interest rates two more times after the election, in February and March 2008. The official cash rate had peaked at 7.25 per cent – the highest level since 1994. That last increase felt like overkill, and the Reserve Bank reversed the March tightening on 3 September, cutting the official interest rate by 0.25 percentage points.

The rear-view of economic statistics shows the US recession was entering its tenth month when Congress passed its bailout at the second attempt, on Saturday, 4 October 2008, Australian time. The stimulus would take another eight months to work its way through the economy, and in the meantime the recession deepened. 'The US started weakening from the March quarter 2008,' a senior Treasury official says. 'Their fiscal stimulus package didn't get out the door until the June quarter 2009 [when their economy bottomed]. It was too late.'

Technically speaking, the Americans tried to revive their economy before we defended ours. The Reserve Bank board met three days after Congress approved George W. Bush's stimulus. The Australian financial market was betting on back-to-back interest rate cuts of 0.5 percentage points in October and November. But the bank board decided that if interest rates had to be 1 percentage point lower, why should it wait a month? An immediate cut of 1 point to 6 per cent was announced and the rest of the world took note. It was a dramatic gesture. The US Federal Reserve also cut rates the next day, but by a smaller amount – 0.5 points to 1.5 per cent, because it was operating from a position of weakness. In his only media interview, Glenn Stevens told the Seven Network that his heart was in his mouth when he watched our dollar fall immediately after his announcement on 7 October. Then it stabilised and recovered after a few minutes, and everyone breathed easier. The float of the dollar, although almost twenty-five years old at this point, never fully erased the institutional fear that the market might one day overshoot. But on balance, the system had delivered the stability it promised.

But one large interest rate cut would not be enough to calm the nation. The news from overseas was diabolical and Treasury prepared a quick forecast for the government, to warn that the collapse of activity in the United States, Europe and Japan would almost certainly drag Australia into recession. The estimates that sent the sharpest jolt through Rudd and his senior ministers were that unemployment would double from around 4 per cent to between 8 and 9 per cent, and that the budget would tumble into deficit.

On the weekend of 11–12 October, Rudd convened a meeting with deputy prime minister Julia Gillard, finance minister Lindsay Tanner and their advisers. Treasurer Wayne Swan participated via a secure phone hook-up in Washington, where he had been attending the annual meetings of the IMF and the World Bank. The first order of business was to guarantee all bank deposits in Australia and the lending between banks. That decision was announced on the Sunday. 'Had we not acted we would have risked a run on the Australian banks on Monday for no good reason,' Kevin Rudd says. The other thing to be discussed was how much money the government would need to pump into the economy to cover for the retreat in private sector activity.

Ken Henry told the government to 'go early, go hard and go households', and he recommended around $5 billion. It was Rudd who doubled it, according to official sources, figuring that for the stimulus to make any difference it had to be worth about 1 per cent of GDP – more like $10 billion. Rudd won't comment on this detail, but he does confirm that he was looking for a gesture dramatic enough to assure employers they should hold on to their staff into the new year. It was too late to prevent the economy going backwards in the December quarter 2008, Rudd explains. 'What I was really concerned about is what happened in the first quarter of 2009. If you have a technical recession over two quarters, the combined impact that will have on confidence will be immeasurably greater than the impact in the real economy which would otherwise occur.' Paul Keating's definition of the 'recession we had to have' was a heavy presence in the room.

On 14 October, the first of the Rudd government's stimulus packages was unveiled. The great cash dump sent $9 billion to families and the elderly in early December to encourage them to do some Christmas shopping. Families received $1000 per child, a single pensioner received $1400 and a couple $2100. The first home-owner grant was doubled to $14000 for the purchase of existing homes, and trebled to $21000 for new dwellings, at a cost to the budget of $1.5 billion. Treasury didn't like this. It had argued for a doubling of the grant only. Again, it was Rudd who insisted on more.

The prime minister received his first inkling that the stimulus might work when he was doing some last-minute Christmas shopping in Sydney on 22 December. He called his wife, who was in New York, to ask what she wanted him to buy for her. 'The place I was at was chock-a-block,' Rudd recalls. 'Therese said, "I'm on the second floor of Macy's and it's empty."' Tom Albanese, the American-born chief executive of Rio Tinto, Australia's second-largest mining company, recalled his surprise at the antipodean response to the GFC: 'I'd been travelling all over the world last year [2009], in the depth of the recession, and the only place anywhere in the world where people were actually in restaurants was in Australia, as they were the only ones in the world that had any money.'

At a focus group I attended in the first week of the 2010 election campaign, I was struck by Generation W's attitude to the stimulus. My snapshot of middle Australia comprised eight women in their mid to late twenties, living in Melbourne's southern suburbs. All were first-homebuyers, married, partnered or single.

Asked what they did with their government payments, each reply was punctuated by a giggle:

'Shopping.'

'Shopping.'

'Paid off the credit card and then shopped again.'

'Went to Sydney.'

They felt guilty, but that's exactly what the money was meant for.

A second package was announced on 3 February 2009, comprising another $12 billion in cash payments to be delivered in mid-March, and $28 billion in infrastructure spending. The Senate trimmed the cash payments by $50 to $900 per family.

The Reserve Bank eased monetary policy a further four times, in November, December, February and April, bringing the official interest rate to just 3 per cent. The US Federal Reserve had stopped cutting four months before our central bank, in December 2008, because its official interest rate had already reached zero.

Dr Henry saw stimulus as a two-part play: cash to keep people spending in the first six months of the GFC, followed by government investment to fill the void left by a capital retreat. He kept reminding ministers that in 1990–91, private and government spending were falling together because of the mistaken view at the time that the budget surplus should be defended.

The Christmas stimulus came too late to prevent the economy contracting by 0.9 per cent in the December quarter. But it did something that was unappreciated at the time. Around the world, household consumption had collapsed. In Australia it fell by just 0.2 per cent, after declines of 0.4 per cent in the September quarter and 0.3 in the June quarter. There is no other period since records were first kept in 1959 when household consumption fell for three quarters in a row in Australia. But there wouldn't be a fourth quarter, and this is what spared us another contraction in GDP. Household consumption rebounded by 0.5 per cent in the March quarter and 0.8 per cent in the June quarter. The GDP figures for those two quarters were plus 10 per cent and plus 0.2 per cent respectively. Phase one had achieved its goal of avoiding an immediate recession.

The most controversial part of the stimulus was government investment in school buildings and the home insulation program. From an economic point of view, this public spending sealed the Great Escape from the GFC. Private investment would fall for five out of six quarters between the December quarter 2008 and the March quarter 2010 – other things being equal, this would have delivered a recession in the second half of 2009 based on past experience. But government investment did as Henry's blueprint predicted. It offset the fall in private investment so that total investment in the economy grew in the second half of 2009. It also helped that another housing boom was underway. The cheapest part of the stimulus had been the trebling of the first home-owner grant. But it had the same stunning effect in the real economy as Howard's original first home-owner ploy in 2001, by bringing forward the decision to buy for tens of thousands of young families. The grant fed straight into prices which when combined with historically low interest rates made existing home owners feel rich enough to keep spending. The short attention span of politics – and some frankly mischievous claims from the opposition and in the media that the stimulus was 'wasted' – is inclined to dismiss the government assistance as unnecessary. Nothing could be further from the truth, and the proof is in the response to Australian politicians and officials when they travel to economic and other forums overseas. The question everyone asks us is: 'How did you guys do it?'

But Treasury did get one thing wrong. It was still forecasting recession in 2009–10 because it didn't appreciate that a successful stimulus would make people happy enough to spend as if there was no crisis. So mild was the Australian downturn that the unemployment rate didn't even cross 6 per cent. It peaked at 5.9 in June 2009, when the American rate was already at 9.5 per cent, with still further to go past 10. By the end of 2010, our unemployment rate was back at 4.9 per cent – in the US it was still 9.4. One of the myths that has developed since, and which is reinforced by public opinion polls, is that China saved us. But China had a bigger slow-down than the United States in the first half of 2009. Australia's terms of trade fell for four quarters in a row from the December quarter 2008 to the September quarter 2009. The quarry wasn't as important as people thought. In fact, the state that went closest to recession in '08–09 was Queensland. The states which did most to spare Australia from the Great Recession were New South Wales and Victoria. New South Wales had been the weakest economy during the boom and this, interestingly, made it the most enthu-siastic recipient of the stimulus. Victoria had been the Goldilocks economy during the boom, neither too hot nor too cold, and it continued growing at about the national average.

The Rudd government deserves credit, primarily because it took the advice given to it to deploy the fiscal buffer it had inherited from the Howard government. A re-elected Coalition government might not have been so willing to listen. Howard, in particular, would have been carrying potential grudges against Ken Henry and Glenn Stevens – the former had criticised the Coalition in 2007, the latter had increased interest rates in the election cam-paign. The GFC might also have given Howard the excuse to further delay his promised leadership transition to Costello.

The institutional heroes of the GFC were undoubtedly the Reserve Bank and the Treasury. Monetary and fiscal policy moved in tandem for the first time. In recessions past, forecasting errors, institutional rivalries or the cack hand of government had con-spired to make things worse. The good work of the so-called official family reassured the public that serious people were man-aging the economy.

But recessions aren't avoided merely by managing the numbers. The public decides these things, and Australians demonstrated a new maturity in 2008–09. The old fight between labour and capital, which Howard had revived with WorkChoices, had melted away with the change of government. During the GFC itself, business cut hours to protect jobs, and workers, wearing their consumer hat, returned the favour by spending as an act of patriotic duty to defend business. Another personal factor was the immigration intake. One million new Australians were added to the population between 2001 and 2008, with almost 300 000 of those coming from China and India. Australia was still enjoying strong population growth throughout the crisis, and this helped to further prop up the demand for housing.

Australia was another country compared to the frightened, fractured place it had been during the bad-hair decade of the '70s. Although the petty complaints of prosperity returned after the first phase of the crisis had passed, this too was in keeping with the new Australian maturity. What mattered was that we had got the big call right. The return to the more regular programming of whingeing was the responsibility of the leaders who facilitated it: because once the crisis was over, they resumed the confected rivalry of politics.

The Australian Moment was thirty-five years in the making, starting with the Whitlam government's tariff cut and the formal recognition of China in the early '70s; the Fraser government's termination of the White Australia policy with the entry of the Vietnamese refugees in the second half of the '70s; the Hawke–Keating government economic reforms between 1983 and 1996; and the Howard government's consolidation of those reforms, and the super-charging of the immigration program after 2001. We tested and perfected our pragmatic version of deregulation a generation before the rest of the world awoke to the dangers of placing too much faith in the zeroes that globalisation can temporarily add to national income. For the first time in our history, we didn't want to be anyone or anywhere else.

Labor's election victory in November 2007 anticipated Barack Obama's US presidential triumph in November 2008. The popular votes were almost identical: 52.7 per cent for Labor and 52.9 per cent for Obama. The same groups of voters – young people, immigrants, lower-income earners, Indigenous Australians for Labor and African-Americans for Obama – helped decide the two elections. The economic cycle alone does not explain the similarities because Australians dismissed a conservative government at the top of a boom, while Obama emerged during recession. The psychic link between the two systems was the role the Iraq War played in undermining the credibility of the conservative side. The style of politics that flourished when the so-called war on terror was a vote-winner in the mid-noughties had rebounded on its practitioners after the peace in Iraq proved more bloody than the shock and awe of the invasion, and the subprime bubble burst. Australia, in dismissing Howard, had got ahead of the international political curve.

For voters aged under thirty-five, who had grown up with a cynical TV eye, Rudd and Obama were essentially the same person. They satisfied Generation W's craving for intelligence and authenticity. The two leaders were marketed as brands. Rudd was Kevin07; Obama was a poster, a bumper sticker and a cause. The expectations they fostered were almost impossible to fulfil in government. Generation W was demoralised when their dream candidates shed their genius in office to reveal themselves as easily intimidated politicians.

Australia had a happy downturn, but a nasty recovery. Voters were unwilling to give Rudd lasting credit for a recession averted. John Howard would have allowed himself a grin: the same thing happened to him after the Asian financial crisis in 1997–98. The people weren't interested that the economic model worked, they wanted something politics can never really guarantee – an end to the media and electoral cycles of negativity.

Rudd didn't take the opportunity presented by the GFC to reassess his agenda. He had on his plate his promise to deliver an emissions trading scheme, a review of the taxation system chaired by Ken Henry, and a possible federal takeover of public hospitals. Just one of these ventures would have taken up a normal three-year term to prepare the community, release and pass the necessary legislation and then deal with any hiccups of implementation. But this Labor government, despite its popularity in 2008–09, and its undoubted success during the GFC, was still trying to figure out what it wanted to do with power. Rudd's in-tray betrayed those eleven soulless years in opposition. He and the party were trying to find their reform voice in office.

This is a different problem to the one that confronted Gough Whitlam after the oil shock. Whitlam was emotionally and intellectually attached to his Program, and his determination to legislate, regardless of the change in economic circumstance, contained a certain innocent charm to it. Rudd had a Whitlam-like pride, but the policies he was persisting with had not been adequately explained to the electorate beforehand. There was no unifying theme. So the spectacle of Rudd juggling news ideas after the GFC created the impression of a government that didn't know what it wanted.

Compounding Labor's loss of direction was the nasty business of returning the budget to surplus, and the Reserve Bank's necessary task of returning interest rates to more normal levels. The recession we didn't have to have revealed a hole in the underlying structure of the budget. All those handouts of the Howard era came back to bite Labor because the GFC reset our income clock, by slashing company tax and capital gains tax collections. Wayne Swan's first budget, framed before the GFC, had predicted surpluses totalling $79.2 billion between 2008–09 and 2011–12. The stimulus over those four years was worth $66.7 billion, so, other things being equal, the budget should have remained in balance once the crisis had passed. But the total deficits for that four-year period came to $166.7 billion. As a share of gross domestic product, these deficits were larger than the Keating holes in the early to mid '90s. Although unemployment had dropped to half the level it was then, the deficits spoke to the broader economic truth that the Howard government had spent the proceeds of the first boom before the money had arrived. Nonetheless, the deficits were trifling when compared with our rich, but bankrupt, peers in the US, Japan, the UK and Europe. Total net government debt was forecast to peak at $132.6 billion, or 8.9 per cent of GDP, by 2011–12. Compared to the rest of the developed world, where government debts of up to 100 per cent of GDP were commonplace, Australia should have been pleased. But at home, the opposition was able to blame Labor – even though these were Howard's structural deficits – because Rudd and Swan had a curious inability to sell the government's achievements. Their polling told them the public didn't like deficits of any type, so they tried to avoid the issue, leaving a grateful opposition to fill the void by switching blame for the deficit to Labor.

Climate change was an issue Labor assumed the public already understood. The public, after all, had forced the debate onto the politicians in 2006. In the second half of 2009, it was time for action and the two-party system seemed ready to oblige, despite some misgivings. On the Labor side, ministers divided into two roughly equal camps: those who wanted to press ahead with an emissions trading scheme, and those who wanted to let the economy settle down after the GFC before taking on the reform. The goal of an ETS is to change the economy's energy mix, away from coal-fired electricity generation to lower-emitting sources such as wind or solar. But this can't be done without making existing energy sources more expensive. To impose this shock on the economy, even if the polls said the community was willing, required more than usual care.

Rudd wanted the legislation for his ETS passed before he flew to Copenhagen in December 2009 for the international meeting he thought would deliver a new climate-change agreement to replace the Kyoto Protocol. He also wanted to destroy the opposition at home – a self-defeating strategy given that he was also negotiating with a fellow believer. Malcolm Turnbull had replaced Brendan Nelson as opposition leader, ostensibly because Nelson had abandoned the Coalition's policy to act ahead of the world. The Liberal Party was riven between those who still wanted an ETS and those who did not believe that humankind was contributing to climate change. The National Party was always opposed to action, but its members had bitten their lip under Howard. Rudd did neither Turnbull nor himself any favours by trying to provoke a conservative split.

Turnbull lost his leadership to Tony Abbott on 1 December. Abbott was another climate chameleon – he was for an ETS before he was against it, and had even offered support for the alternative of a carbon tax. Rudd's legislation failed once Abbott repudiated the Coalition's own 2007 election platform, a denial of mandate that would have far-reaching consequences for Australian politics. In a way this was more brazen than the Senate obstruction in the 1970s. Back then there was an element of principle involved – the Coalition didn't agree with the Whitlam Program. Abbott was opposing for the sake of it. No previous opposition had overturned a policy that both sides had agreed to at the previous election.

Later that month, Rudd returned from Copenhagen a shattered man. He had sincerely believed that a global deal was possible, and that he would help seal it. But the world's two largest economies, the US and China, were at loggerheads and the meeting ended in recrimination, with no binding targets for further emissions reductions. With this, Abbott had an anti-reform card to play against

Labor that would borrow from Paul Keating's negative campaign against the GST a decade earlier. Abbott called the ETS 'a great big new tax on everything' and warned that Australia shouldn't go it alone. Rudd, the most consistently popular Labor leader since Bob Hawke, lost his bearings. He didn't want to talk about climate change anymore.

Climate change became the mechanism by which the community anger in a deeply recessed United States was transmitted to the last rich nation standing. The precondition for electoral revolt in Australia was the heavy GFC losses that the baby boomers nearing retirement had taken on their share portfolios and super-annuation nest eggs. These older voters were looking for someone or something to blame, and the ETS became the catalyst for their grievance. Abbott saw how the Tea Party movement in the US had successfully torn down Obama's approval rating, and applied the theory of continuous carping to Rudd. The prime minister obliged by losing his nerve.

In January 2010, Rudd ignored the urgings of his colleagues to call a double-dissolution election. In April, he walked away from the ETS, having once described climate change as 'the great moral challenge of our time'.

Abbott shrugged off the contradictions in his own position and revelled in playing the role of spoiler. He attacked Labor from right and left, accusing it of wasteful spending and unnecessary taxation. Suddenly, the nation's rhetoric took a turn for the '70s and 2010 became our maddest political year since 1975, even though we had what the rest of the world craved – a viable economy and a cohesive society. For decades, we had told ourselves we were lucky, but lazy. Now that we had earned the right to brag, politics found a way to undermine our national self-respect. The inconvenient truth for both sides is that voters like to be led; they want to know that their leaders are confident in their own policies. When Rudd walked away from his conviction on climate change, he unnerved the nation and placed a time bomb under his own leadership. The ghost of James Scullin was calling Rudd from the graveyard of one-term prime ministers.

The Rudd method also failed the policy test of the mining boom. In May 2010, he announced a new federal tax on mining profits to replace the state-based royalties which were levied on production. The policy was soundly based, because it offered a mechanism to catch a greater share of the revenue windfall for the budget, without hurting the viability of miners. The tax couldn't be passed on to consumers here because the Chinese were doing the buying. The money collected could be either set aside or spent on behalf of industries that were being squeezed by the boom. It was an intrinsically popular idea. Labor tested it first with its beloved focus groups, and they replied that the mining companies should pay their fair share for exploiting our resources. But Rudd did not bother with the finer points of consensus building. The public had no time to digest the theory – practically no one had heard of a super profits tax before it was announced – and the mining companies were given no time to negotiate the detail. The revenue estimates were included in Wayne Swan's third budget as a fait accompli before the promised consultations with industry were to begin.

The mining companies replied with an advertising campaign as powerful as the ACTU's attack on WorkChoices and the motor lobby's assault on the fuel excise. By June, Rudd's colleagues were fed up with his management style, and fearful of the opinion polls, which showed Rudd's personal rating in freefall after the ETS backflip and Labor and the Coalition tied at 50–50. Such was the loathing for him within the caucus that Rudd's leadership crumbled within hours of Julia Gillard's decision to challenge him on 23 June 2010. The nation had never seen a leadership coup quite like it before. Gillard had given no public warning. In fact, she had said nothing on the night. The television cameras caught a glimpse of her marching into Rudd's office for the showdown, but that was it. Around the parliament and the nearby restaurants and bars, Labor MPs swapped phone calls and text messages trying to second-guess the outcome. Rudd, meanwhile, had no one canvassing for him. He tried to talk Gillard out of challenging, but she was not for turning. He called a late-night press conference to say he would fight, but soon after returning to his office he realised he wouldn't be able to muster the numbers for even an honourable loss. The next morning, the nation awoke to the news that Gillard would be elected unopposed as our first female prime minister. Generation W had another icon, and she would disappoint even quicker than Rudd.

To those who practised or covered politics, the leadership change seemed a perfectly logical outcome. Rudd had lost his confidence and had stopped making decisions. The polite explanation was he had suffered burnout. Those close to the talks between them say Gillard concluded that Rudd wasn't ready to face an election. But to the public his demise was a shock – even though it was their opinion of Rudd, relayed through focus groups, that had convinced Labor to change prime ministers. Labor had conducted secret research in May and June to test voter attitudes to Rudd and Gillard. She was seen as 'real'; Rudd, they didn't know what he stood for.

Rudd served as prime minister for two years, six months and twenty-two days – only four months longer than Scullin. There should have been no parallel between the men, really. Rudd had successfully steered Australia through the Great Recession.

When we spoke for this book, Kevin Rudd had had more than a year to reflect on his demise. He believes the success of the stimulus created a communications trap for the government. 'If people haven't experienced a recession then they don't know what they have avoided,' he says. 'I think that's human nature.' He believes Tony Abbott had the simpler argument to mount in late 2009 and early 2010. 'The message "We are sinking in debt" was easier for an opportunistic opposition to sell, because . . . [the GFC] did represent a change in the debt numbers and it is easy to play with those numbers. Thirdly, inevitably with large-scale immediate capital projects, you are going to run into implementation difficulties.'

Rudd says voters would have understood the issues better with a little more exposure to what was going on in the rest of the world, through their contact with it as travellers and from the stories told to them by young people migrating here. If he had been allowed to keep his job he would have been able to make the case, he suggests. 'My view as prime minister was that by the time we got to an election I think people would have . . . [seen] a lot more of the economic carnage elsewhere in the world.'

He doesn't agree with me that he took on too much in his first term. On the contrary, he insists he had no choice but to keep his promises. 'The public would be less comprehending of me shelving pre-election commitments at that stage because they had no concept of what was happening globally.' But he concedes the decision to defer the ETS was 'wrong'. The one promise he didn't keep, because the Liberals withdrew their support, and because his own cabinet was divided on what to do next, became the catalyst for his removal.

Rudd had earned the right to tell the story of our escape to the rest of the world. But he couldn't convince his own side, let alone the Australian people, that they had achieved something special together.

TRANSITIONS III:

FROM ANALOG TO DIGITAL

He was a willing servant of the media. No question was too small for the prime minister to answer. He obliged with his opinions on loud-mouthed chefs, TV comedy sketches and attention-seeking visual artists. When he dropped the faux Aussie phrase 'fair shake of the sauce bottle' into an interview, I thought two could play this game. I tapped out a quick column in Rudd-speak – that is, in a voice that wasn't the prime minister's, or mine:

KEVIN, mate, hate to break this to you but this bloke bender you are on at the moment is not a good look.

The more you try to sound like a regular fella, the more you invite the punters to laugh at you.

They don't know who that bloke is anyway. I mean, who demands a 'fair shake of the sauce bottle, mate'? Real men switched to soy way back in the 1970s, when Bon Scott could still blow into a bagpipe.

You don't shake soy, you drizzle it, like those chefs on TV tell you to. And while I've got your attention, mate, stop trying to have an opinion on everything. You can't be a know-it-all and a bloke at the same time.

A bloke knows when to say: 'Dunno, don't care.' Equally, a man in your position should be able to say: 'Sorry, I don't have time to watch Gordon Ramsay – can't you see I'm running the bloody country?'

Rudd took it on the chin, and mentioned the article at his first public appearance that day: 'Well, I was having a Dad and Dave this morning – that's a shave – and I picked up my copy of the *Oz* and I saw – was it George Megalogenis? – having a go at me. And I thought, fair crack of the whip, don't come the raw prawn with me, George. Or, coming from Queensland, I'd say you'd get the rough end of the pineapple.'

It was June 2009. The global financial crisis had officially passed us by, with the previous week's national accounts showing the economy had grown in the March quarter. Peter Costello, perhaps not coincidentally, had just announced his retirement from politics and Labor people thought the next election was in the bag. They had worried the former treasurer might have given them a fright if he had taken the Liberal leadership. Rudd was in good spirits. To get a rise from a prime minister at the peak of his power might have been an unexpected and undeserved compliment, but it was more a comment on how easily Rudd could be distracted. My poor attempt at humour, and Rudd's much funnier response, sanctioned a national debate about whether he was being authentic. I wasn't living the Watergate dream here of holding power accountable, just feeding my profession's incessant demand for trivia.

The word 'media' is an unhelpful generalisation, like 'Asia' once was to the untrained Australian eye. Each decade finds the media reflecting, and refracting, a slightly different national voice. Each leader finds a new medium to cope with and exploit. Rudd was our first digital prime minister: outrageously popular, prone to hyperbole, gone before you got to know him, and the object of nostalgic longing after voters found his replacement didn't impress them either.

Rudd had brought the game-show scrutiny on himself because he routinely campaigned in places where politicians were rarely heard from, most notably FM radio. On the Sunday before polling day in 2007, Rudd deliberately avoided the ABC's political *Insiders* program for an appearance on the Ten Network's *Rove*, commercial television's most popular variety show at the time. The host, Rove McManus, had had an accidental role in Rudd's elevation as Labor leader the previous year. The incumbent, Kim Beazley, had opened a media conference by offering his condolences to McManus, whose 32-year-old wife, Belinda Emmett, had died of cancer. Beazley meant to say 'Rove McManus' but the name that tumbled from his lips by mistake was 'Karl Rove', the strategist for US president George W. Bush. The AAP wire report that day called it 'a major blunder'. Those within the Labor Party pushing for Rudd to replace Beazley used this slip of the tongue to bring on the challenge.

In the past, our leaders snuck into popular culture when it suited, but were never enslaved by it. Gough Whitlam made a cameo appearance in the second Barry McKenzie movie; Paul Keating had his picture on the cover of *Rolling Stone* magazine, wearing Ray Charles-style Ray-Bans. But these had been controlled exposures to soften the prime ministerial image. By going on *Rove*, Kevin07 permitted the medium to belittle him.

McManus offered a safe, policy-free interview, with a politically incorrect twist. The final question he would put to each guest was designed to sort out the cool from the uptight: 'Who would you turn gay for?' Harmless enough, but surely beneath the dignity of the office Rudd aspired to . . . The Labor leader didn't think so, because Rove offered him the thing every leader craved: unfiltered access to more than a million politically disengaged living rooms. Rudd allowed the question, and let the audience have a chuckle at the effrontery, before answering: 'There is only one person for me – my wife Therese.' Not to be denied the final word, Rove quipped: 'Is she a man?'

The Rove–Rudd show was seen by 1.386 million households – a city's worth more than the 214 000 who tuned in to *Insiders*, where the guest that morning had been deputy Labor leader Julia Gillard. It is hard to say if the appearance shifted one vote, but it empowered a level of discourse between media and prime minister that Australians had not seen before. In government, Rudd could never say 'No comment' when asked about anything, because he had already declared his eager availability as Kevin07.

Rudd told his colleagues that if they didn't feed the media, the media would eat the government. But it consumed him anyway, despite his perfect attendance record as a student of the digital age, because he let the media dictate his agenda. His surrender wasn't conscious. He thought that appearing each day, on every conceivable wavelength, would assure voters that he was there for them. But he was reacting, not leading, and the practised imprecision he used to deflect questions began to irritate. When he abandoned his emissions trading scheme in April 2010, he didn't call a full press conference to explain himself, as past leaders felt obliged to when dealing with bad news. Rudd had already booked a media appointment at a hospital that day.

The Rudd dismissal was a comment on the instant rush to judgement of twenty-first century politics. In eight years between 2002 and 2010, Australia had three prime ministers and seven opposition leaders. Rudd wasn't the first leader of the digital age to talk himself out of his own job. Howard had fallen into the same trap in his final year, 2007. He sensed the public was no longer listening to him, so he kept jumping from topic to topic, looking for that magic phrase, or handout, to reconnect with middle Australia. All it did was make him appear needy and easier to vote out of office.

Media technology is the third big change that defines Australia today, after the role of the region – through the people we import from it, and the rocks we sell back to it – and the feminisation of the workforce. The media – television, radio, print and the internet – screams at every rich nation. Leaders complain with some justification that the demands of the digital age are over-whelming the serious business of governing.

Tony Blair noted just after leaving office in 2007 that a large part of his time as British prime minister was spent 'coping with the media, its sheer scale, weight and constant hyperactivity'. Blair measured the compression of the news cycle by the number of top-ics he ran a day: 'When I fought the 1997 election we took an issue a day. In 2005, we had to have one for the morning, another for the afternoon and by the evening that agenda had already moved on.'

The reason Blair and Bill Clinton have such dismal legacies in the deeper ponds of British and US politics is that they wasted too much time thinking of the next line instead of honing policy. The Republican George W. Bush followed the Democrat Clinton by devoting more time to crafting the headline for invading Iraq – 'weapons of mass destruction' – than worrying about securing the peace afterwards.

The hypocrisy of the media is easy to confess: we reward leaders who appear fresh, only to punish them when they try to engage in the complexity of policy. The problem here isn't any single organi-sation or group of journalists displaying bias, or mistaking their own voice for that of the people they report to. Every era has its opinionated media. The digital age, however, has delivered a new type of power to the media that it never sought: the veto of white noise. Blair was right, there is too much of it.

But the media has also identified the inherent weakness of the twenty-first century Western leader. There is nothing more dis-turbing for a journalist to cover than a politician who behaves no better than they do, cutting corners to meet that day's deadline with a half-formed story or idea. Kevin Rudd was the first leader I've experienced that ceded the respect for his office by his willingness to serve the media. Julia Gillard and Tony Abbott compounded his errors by refusing to complete a sentence between them during the 2010 election campaign. The public isn't blameless here. It demands instant answers and encourages the media to embark on a hysterical search for the next messiah. Someone has to step back to restore the voice of leaders and the power of ideas.

First we have to end the weekly or fortnightly genuflecting to opinion polls. They are largely meaningless outside of election years. But the media has somehow allowed them to dictate their news judgement. It is lazy journalism, which perpetuates short-term thinking within the political parties.

Perhaps the public never really had that much awareness of the finer detail of policy debate, and the media through its 'sheer scale, weight and hyperactivity' has created the impression of mass engagement that isn't really there. How else to explain the gyrations in Australian attitudes on climate change, from support to hesitation to outright hostility? The issue destroyed two prime ministers and two opposition leaders between 2007 and 2010: John Howard in '07, for not embracing action quickly enough; Liberal leader Brendan Nelson in '08, for trying to overturn the Coalition policy; Malcolm Turnbull in '09, for wanting an ETS when half his party didn't believe the science; and Rudd in 2010, for trying to mollify nervous voters by delaying the ETS. Public opinion is less settled than the science of climate change, because no leader is prepared to argue a consistent position for long enough to secure even the most basic level of community understanding.

Gillard rushed to the election of 21 August 2010 with a non-policy. She ruled out a carbon tax, while saying her preference remained for a market-based mechanism. But she wouldn't proceed until community consensus had been re-established. That is, she tried to buy time in the digital age. Her personal rating dipped immediately after that announcement, and the rest of the campaign turned nasty as Rudd's supporters began leaking against her.

At the ballot box, Labor's primary vote fell by 5.3 per cent to 38, but most of it went to the Greens, who jumped by 4 points to 11.8 per cent. The Coalition's primary vote increased by 1.5 per cent to 43.6; a swing comparable to its 1984 result, but the pay-off was greater. Labor went into the campaign with 83 seats out 150 plus another five notional seats after the redistribution of electoral boundaries. It lost 16 seats on the pendulum – 14 to the Coalition, one to the Greens in Melbourne and another to an independent in Tasmania. But it picked up two seats from the Liberals in Victoria. Nine of the 12 seats Labor ceded to the Coalition in net terms were in Rudd's home state of Queensland, where the global financial crisis had hurt most. Labor was reduced to 72 seats, one fewer than the Coalition, but survived because the inconsistent Gillard was able to persuade three of the four independents and the sole Greens MP that she could offer more stable government than the inconsistent Abbott. The Coalition didn't accept the verdict of the parliament and demanded a fresh election. Abbott channelled Malcolm Fraser by creating a virtual hostage situation. He opposed everything Labor did, even its modest levy to help pay for the clean-up of Queensland after the devastating floods in the summer of 2010–11.

Gillard believed that the absence of a climate change policy had cost her government its majority. Yet when she changed her mind after the election and announced a carbon tax to start on 1 July 2012 followed by an ETS three years later, she was accused of deceit by her opponents. Amazingly, as the legislation was passing through the parliament, the man who had abandoned his principles – Rudd – was now preferred as prime minister over both Gillard and Abbott. Those pesky polls, if they were to be taken literally, were saying, 'Let's pretend that it's 2009 again'.

The digital age recalls the insecurity of the stagflation decade, when leaders lost their authority. Every institution in the 1970s failed: government, bureaucracy, the judiciary and the financial sector. Arguably only the media played a constructive role in debating the problems of the rich world. Today, the media is an intrinsic part of the problem. The personal irony for me, as an employee of News Limited, the Australian arm of Rupert Murdoch's global media company, is that his British operation has been embroiled in one of the defining scandals of the era, and closed the circle of Western cynicism that began with Watergate almost forty years earlier. The *News of the World* was like the so-called 'plumbers unit' of the Nixon White House. The populist tabloid hacked the mobile phones of people in the public eye often for the smallest of reasons – to gain column inches in the gossip pages.

Murdoch, more than any other international businessman, has been able to identify the character weakness of the Anglo world. In the US, his television network and newspapers reflect the American urge for politics as a form of civil war. In the UK, he has indulged a snobby populace with scandal and sport. In Australia, his tabloids place sport on the front and back pages, and downplay anything else apart from crime. Politics is the obsession of the national broadsheet, *The Australian*, a paper that is happiest when delivering an argument.

And yet, Australians are surely at ease with the world in a way we could not have imagined in the '70s. But we do have conflicting interpretations of our success. A new sense of separation exists between the well-travelled cosmopolitan and the well-travelled suburban triumphalist. One faction thinks the nation is on the verge of something special, so long as it drops the baggage of xenophobia. The other faction hears the elite's call for self-improvement as personal rebuke, which it is. The cosmopolitan is still craving the world's respect while the triumphalist insists on the right to offend.

362 THE AUSTRALIAN MOMENT

The triumphalists dominated the national conversation before the global financial crisis. You could hear their voice in the all-conquering Test cricket teams of Mark Taylor, Steve Waugh and Rick Ponting as they bullied their opponents with childish taunts. The sledging was unnecessary because these teams had some of the best players of any era. Yet they carried a form of Australian inferiority complex onto the field. They wanted to be feared. Respect was for losers. When they ceded the Ashes for the first time in a generation in 2005, it was almost a relief for us all because defeat turned them back into gentlemen. The hero to both nations from that series was Shane Warne, the scoundrel redeemed.

That year ended with world attention of the type that no nation seeks. The Cronulla riots pitted coward against coward. On 11 December 2005, a mob tried to purge the southern Sydney beach of Australians of Middle Eastern background. They swarmed at anyone with brown skin. The following night, Lebanese-Australian youth returned to the suburb in convoys, firing guns into the air, and smashing cars. *The Economist* – the magazine we like to quote back to ourselves now that it describes Australia as the next Golden State – dubbed Cronulla 'the race riots in paradise'.

The menace of the Cronulla riots lessens with the GFC. After the shopping riots in the UK in 2011, and the absence of any repeat here, our 2005 example of mob violence appears to be an isolated case of too much sun and beer. Yet the twenty-first century Australian contradiction begins with something like Cronulla: an argument over territory abetted by technology. More than 270 000 text messages were sent to mobiles phones across Sydney, calling for a show of strength at the beach. Radio personality Alan Jones read one of the offending missives on air three days before the incident. 'And the message urges Aussies . . . to take revenge against Lebs and Wogs,' Jones told his 2GB listeners on 8 December. 'Now, it's got pretty nasty when you start talking like this. It says: "This Sunday, every Aussie in the Shire get down to North Cronulla to support Leb- and Wog-bashing day."' Jones didn't endorse that sentiment, but its broadcasting lent it newsworthiness, which in the digital age can grant a hearing for race-baiting.

The logic of foul-mouth tribalism leads, inevitably, to a coarsening in the political debate. By 2011, Jones was quoting colourful listener feedback to demean Julia Gillard. 'Another one says "Please, please don't have that lying bitch on your program again, I had to move the dial to another station. I guess it was worth the once to show us all what a beep lying, beep backstabbing, beep treacherous, beep beep she is."' This is where the media is most certainly to blame in the digital age. Newspapers and radio and television stations have surrendered their online sites to anonymous commentators who type things on a computer they would never say to one another in person. The commonsense filters that were used to keep the letters-to-the-editor page civil, and to prevent the cranks from getting on air, don't apply in cyberspace because the medium rewards those who generate the most outrage.

The internet has disrupted and distracted politics, and through it the society it mirrors. The last medium to revolutionise the relationship between leader and community was television. It changed the way leaders talked and presented themselves, and altered community values, because the public could now judge by appearance without meeting their leader in the flesh, or having to read a word they typed. Gough Whitlam's 1972 election campaign is memorable because we saw it on the TV. Billy McMahon is the national reference point for failure because the camera showed he was prone to gaffe, and easy to ridicule. But television did something else: it beamed the world's insecurities into our living rooms.

Politicians had mastered television by the 1980s. The strong, and the charming, triumphed. The Anglo world had its last great leaders at the same time – Reagan, Thatcher and Hawke – in part because they commanded the small screen. The politicians who master the digital age will need brains and very thick skins. The leadership game hasn't changed. It's just the unfamiliar new playing field that is testing player and spectator alike.

The people, though, have been changed. The digital age has accelerated their sense of entitlement. Technology creates feedback loops of instant gratification and anger. We yell if the computer screen freezes for even a second. Social media offers the allure of inclusion, but it self-selects its reality. It is human nature to seek out those who think like you do. But the danger in conversing only with those you agree with is you stop learning. To take a contrary view, by seeking out those who don't share your opinions, is to invite abuse in reply. To break this cycle of segmentation, leaders need to rediscover the power of a few big ideas to reconnect our feuding tribes.

CONCLUSION:

THE AUSTRALIAN MOMENT

Are we in danger of becoming a great country? When I put the question to politicians and officials in interviews for this book, the majority response is to laugh or sigh. There is a brief flicker of recognition. Each person genuinely considers the possibility because no other nation has what we have. But then the gut takes over. The Australian insistence that we don't take ourselves too seriously will surely kick in to destroy the opportunity. We will find some way to talk ourselves back to where we came from. "It's a nice idea, but I don't see it happening," is the general tenor of the response.

The most endearing part of our character today is the new calmness in the face of real danger. A double-dip recession in the global economy might end our unbroken run of prosperity. Yet it is easy to imagine that even the worst case from here for Australia would only be half as bad as for the United States or Europe.

Australia is the West's last best role model. We are tapping the potential of the Asian ascendancy because we face the region as an open market and open society. China buys our stuff and we take some of its smartest people in return – dirt in exchange for brains. An American or a European might think it is easy for us to gloat when we are blessed with the world's biggest quarry in China's backyard, and clear blue skies that its people want to study under. But China didn't get us through the initial phase of the GFC. The communist stimulus only kicked in later in 2009, well after the first phase of ours had done its job.

The infuriating thing about reporting national affairs since the Great Escape is that both sides want to reduce an act of collective will to a petty partisan contest for credit. Each makes claims that are frankly laughable. Labor says, 'We saved you.' The Coalition says, 'No you didn't, it was China, or the Howard–Costello surpluses. Anyway, look at that waste . . .' The public, meanwhile, screams, 'What recession? That wasn't a recession, but your so-called recovery feels like one.'

At the heart of this contemporary argument is a fundamental misunderstanding between politics and the community. The origins of our Great Escape are in the fear our institutions and people addressed at around the same time. In 2006, before anyone knew about the risks of subprime lending, Australian households and the Reserve Bank began a synchronised but unconscious rebuilding of their respective monetary buffers. John Howard, the populist, misread this shift as a grand conspiracy against his government's call for Australians to keep spending. So did Kevin Rudd. He sought power on Howard's terms, with almost as many promises. The only difference between them, really, was WorkChoices, once Howard had agreed to an emissions trading scheme.

Rudd shone during the GFC because he took advice. It was out of character for him to allow someone else to tell him what he didn't know. In fact, no leader on either side since Paul Keating paid as much attention to what the Reserve Bank and Treasury had to say as Rudd did in those first few weeks of the GFC.

The price of our Great Escape appears to be steep when we recall the surpluses that existed just before the GFC. But those surpluses should have been larger to begin with. Not $10 billion or

$20 billion a year, but $50 billion. The Howard government left the nation exposed by spending the first round of the resources wind-fall. The public redeemed the situation by saving those handouts anyway.

If the Australians of the past two generations could meet face to face, our twenty-first century selves would tell our 1970s selves to stop arguing. Stagflation ended the Golden Age by exposing the limit of government's ability to secure social cohesion through price fixing. Australia has thrived over the past twenty years because it no longer kids itself that government can control the dollar, dictate what imports we can buy, or achieve wage equality by bureaucratic command. But we stopped short of a full embrace of deregulation, and here is where we really stood out. The ordeal of the 'recession we had to have' taught us that financial markets have to answer to independently minded regulators.

But the leaders of the stagflation decade also played an impor-tant role. Gough Whitlam's push for the poor to study at university and for women to re-enter work after having children combined with Malcolm Fraser's active termination of the White Australia policy to bless us with a population with the right mix of skill and temperament to survive the trials of globalisation. Howard saw this social reform to completion, against the urgings of his former self, who wanted to slow the rate of Asian immigration.

The Australian model can pick global trends better than the American and British models because it doesn't carry the bag-gage of past glories. There is no preconceived notion of Australian stature that felt threatened when first a Japan and then a China changed the global pecking order.

The Australian Moment can lead to national greatness if we are prepared to keep growing. This might seem a simple thing to say, but growth in this decade will not come as easily as it did in the last. Money needs to be put aside to invest on behalf of our children and to create a surplus large enough to handle the next shock as well as we did the last. Our cities need to be retooled, our boom–bust ecology defied with a plan to secure the water supply, and our Indigenous people welcomed to the national heart. All this requires a level of restraint we are not normally used to. We have to stop being bludgers in prosperity.

We also need to take our own backyard more seriously. A little less time in Bali and a lot more in Beijing and Mumbai is required if we are to truly unlock the possibilities of the Asian century, and to be aware of its risks. Sitting back and allowing the mining sector to dictate the relationship will deny the other 90 per cent of the economy a productive engagement with the region, and condemn Australia to a new form of insularity. The alternative to national greatness is to become the rich white trash of Asia.

We will never be big enough in our own right to ignore global trends. So we need to be mindful that the competition between the US and China offers both opportunity and danger. The Chinese may well continue to prosper, to our advantage. But the Americans retain their ability to reset international prices in their own favour, and against the interests of our quarry, as they did in the 1980s. If we are to avoid another banana republic scenario, we must remain one step ahead of everyone else. We have already proven, in politics and the community, that we can anticipate crisis and think our way through it. Now we must learn to respect what the other already knows. The public saw the GFC coming before its leaders, but its leaders saw the best way out of it.

The present day only feels uncertain because both sides of politics have been coasting intellectually for at least ten years. The social reforms of the 1970s and the economic reforms of the 1980s and 1990s were sufficient to get us through the GFC. But without a new generation of leadership that can tap Australia's willingness to continue to change, the Great Escape will be a comment on a successful past, not the confirmation of Australian greatness.

AFTERWORD

TO THE 2015 EDITION:

BACKLASH AND BURNOUT

Julia Gillard appeared to have demography on her side. Her personal story echoed Australia's over the previous four decades, placing her in a rare category of prime minister: one who approximately resembled the people she served. She was the young immigrant of the 1960s; the beneficiary of Gough Whitlam's free university education at the end of the '70s; and a member of the first wave of professional women to enter the workforce in the '80s.

On Gillard's first day at university in 1979, men working full-time held 61 per cent of all jobs. On her final day as the nation's leader in 2013, they held just 45 per cent of a more diverse workforce. That 16-percentage-point shift from a blue-collar to a pink-collar economy was a fault line.

'I think we underestimate the amount of time it takes for social change to settle,' Gillard says in an interview after leaving office. 'When society undergoes that kind of transformation its reverberations and echoes are felt for generations.'

Gillard thinks it was inevitable that some men saw a woman in the Lodge as an affront. 'For many women who in their lives had felt soft or hard discrimination, it was a bit of a "go girl" moment,' she says. 'But for many men who figured to themselves, perhaps not even consciously, "I am missing out on some things because my world has had to make space for women in the workplace – it's not perhaps the life I was expecting, it's certainly not the life my father had" – for those men it was a sort of flashpoint. "We're getting pushed and pulled around here, and now it's even happening at the highest level and we've got a woman as prime minister."'

Women claimed 3.1 million of the 5.4 million jobs created between 1979 and 2013, but that did not translate to more power. More than half the new female positions were part-time. The majority of new jobs for men were still full-time, but the share working part-time was now at an all-time high. These two changes account for the 16-point shift away from men working full-time. Women working part-time lifted their stake in the economy from 12 per cent of all jobs in 1979 to 21 per cent by 2013. Men working part-time rose from 3 to 9 per cent. By contrast, women working full-time improved their share by a single point in thirty-four years, to 25 per cent.

Gillard does not blame the men who were uncomfortable with her ascension. The political system was struggling to cope with their diminished expectations and elevated resentments long before she took charge. What did surprise her was how the backlash intensified with time.

'I thought the gender stuff would be visible at the start and then fall away,' Gillard says. 'Actually the reverse was true. The longer I was prime minister, the more I think gender influenced political reactions to me and political reporting. Partly that was because we were in a fight about political honesty around carbon pricing. I think it's easy to weave negative cultural stereotypes about women around that kind of agenda. But it's a troubling sign [and] I hope for the next woman it very quickly washes out of the system.'

Gillard received a level of scrutiny that no male in the same position would have faced. However, she didn't necessarily receive the worst media treatment in Australian political history. The press gallery ridicule of Billy McMahon in the early 1970s was analogous to the shock jock and tabloid assaults on Gillard. McMahon's appearance and his speech patterns were ridiculed as a matter of house style. Whitlamites may protest that the public endorsed this character assessment of McMahon by voting him out. Voters didn't like Gillard either, but that did not excuse the pack for its vitriol.

Australians have a perverse relationship with power. Our anti-authoritarian side is more likely to reveal itself when a leader is down. You could say we are an equal opportunity abuser, because every condemned prime minister is jeered on the way to the ballot box. Our sympathy for the human being appears restored only when they deliver their concession speech.

Tony Abbott rallied the mob by chanting that Gillard was an illegitimate prime minister. He argued that Gillard had no right to lead the nation, even though she had effective control of both houses of parliament.

'If the prime minister wants to make, politically speaking, an honest woman of herself, she needs to seek a mandate for a carbon tax and she should do that at the next election,' the opposition leader said in February 2011. No parsing of that quote can diminish the calculated sexism in the words 'honest woman'.

Coincidentally, that morning Gillard appeared on the Alan Jones radio program in Sydney. 'Do you understand, Julia, that you are the issue today, because there are people now saying your name is not Julia but Ju-liar, and they are saying that we've got a liar running the country,' Jones barked at the prime minister.

When Jones told a Young Liberal fundraiser eighteen months later that Gillard's father had died of shame, his partisan audience chortled. Tacky asides of this nature were an inevitable consequence of the tone Abbott had set. His aggression had released his media supporters from the constraint of civility.

I suspect Abbott never understood the fire with which he was playing. You could see the shock in his eyes when Gillard delivered her so-called misogyny speech in October 2012, just days after the fundraiser comment. Every man would recognise the flicker of panic as Abbott switched from blokey guffaw to 'hang on, she might have a point'. This was the son being told off by the mother, the partner receiving the ultimatum. There was another look on Abbott's face that day – exhaustion. He seemed to shrink as Gillard approached her finale. Then, as he glanced at his watch, she mocked him with a gesture that could never be scripted. Abbott threw his hands up, the child protesting that he wasn't guilty of that either.

The speech resonated in the digital age because it was an old-school debate, about a matter beyond politics. To a public conditioned to leaders who eyeball the camera and recite slogans, it was a revelation. Gillard addressed her opponent directly, and Abbott's reaction made the speech more gripping. You winced for him.

But the two-million-plus views on YouTube could not save Gillard's leadership; gender did not explain the initial collapse in her electoral support, nor her policy errors as prime minister. No Australian leader had lost favour as quickly without an economic crisis. At her first election in 2010 Gillard saved Labor from an impeding defeat, but ceded its majority. In 2013 her colleagues removed her before she could contest a second, fearing electoral wipeout. Even Gough Whitlam won a second term, and he carried the burden of the first oil shock. In the United States, Barack Obama was re-elected as president in 2012 despite the handicaps of much higher unemployment than Australia's and opponents who were prepared to play the race card against him.

It is possible that Australians would have warmed to Gillard if she led a majority government with a coherent program and without the personality clashes with Kevin Rudd. Possible but not certain, because Gillard had taken power the wrong way. The mistake she readily concedes now is that she gave voters an unsatisfactory account of why she seized the Labor leadership in 2010.

'Do you tell a story about government chaos and dysfunction, when on anyone's analysis you are only a matter of months at best from the next election, or do you try and use a proxy explanation – a good government lost its way – and move on? I chose to move on. Even if I had chosen to tell the backstory, in the highly charged media environment we were in, I don't think it would have dominated reporting because the media had already convinced themselves they knew everything about the story.'

The reticence made her seem shifty. The public had no prior warning of her ambition, which reinforced the perception that she had stabbed Rudd in the back. When she protested that she had been drafted, her critics replied that she was beholden to the faceless men of the Labor machine. This was the catch 22 of the challenge: Gillard could not correct the contradictory first impressions of being both schemer and puppet.

'As deputy prime minister I had been loyal to Kevin; I had not been out in the media or anywhere shaping a political personality around me as a leader,' she says. 'If Peter Costello in the run-up to the 2007 election had challenged John Howard for the prime ministership, I think the reaction of the Australian people would have been, "Well, you know we kind of saw that coming,"' she says. 'Certainly with Paul Keating and Bob Hawke everybody saw that coming, so there was no degree of shock. I hadn't done any of those things that Paul had done to position himself or Peter had done to position himself.'

Hawke and Keating had fallen out at approximately the same time in the life of their government as Rudd and Gillard: at the two-year mark, after the prime minister rolled the treasurer at the 1985 tax summit. But they stayed together for six more years. The consumption tax was also the issue that tested Howard and

Costello in their first and second terms in office. But they too maintained a long working relationship. Rudd and Gillard, and their respective backers, did not have the maturity to resolve their first serious argument. Gillard moved against Rudd on the very day their working relationship broke down.

'The one thing that had been holding the government together was [my] ability to work with and for Kevin, and in many circumstances to effectively substitute for him in internal decision-making,' she says. With Rudd's consent, she organised his diary, wrote his speeches, and even spoke for him at meetings he didn't attend. That, Gillard believed, gave her effective authority over Rudd's office as well. So when she read in the *Sydney Morning Herald* on 23 June 2010 that Rudd's chief of staff had canvassed almost half the Labor caucus to gauge whether the prime minister still had their support, Gillard felt betrayed. 'It was clear on that day, from that newspaper piece and the circumstances that surrounded it, that degree of trust between us had dissolved and that he no longer had that trust in me.' For Gillard, the key paragraph in the article said Rudd 'does not necessarily fully trust the public assurances of his deputy that she is not interested in the leadership'. She had been loyal. If he did not believe this, she felt, then all was lost.

'I had done everything I could to support Kevin in his leadership. We had huge, piling political problems. I thought we were on our way to losing the next election.'

The Rudd camp believed that Gillard had been plotting beforehand, but whether this is true is immaterial. Whatever the case, the leadership challenge does not reflect well on either of them. No previous government had indulged a feud so close to an election.

Five serving prime ministers have been removed by their parties, three conservative and two Labor: Billy Hughes in 1923, Robert Menzies in 1941, John Gorton in 1971, Hawke in 1991 and Rudd in 2010. Only Hawke left parliament to grant his successor a clear run to the next election. The Gillard camp believed that

Rudd should have resigned from politics after surrendering the prime ministership without a caucus ballot. But there was no precedent that decreed a deposed leader was prohibited from asking for their old job back.

As Gillard acknowledges, the community was conditioned to rivalries within governments. Taking this observation to its logical political conclusion, voters would not have been shocked to learn that Rudd was plotting a counter-coup.

The Rudd camp was convinced from the day Gillard formed her minority government that she could not win the next election. But the caucus was reluctant to make the change. Most hadn't forgiven Rudd for his conduct in his first term, and at a formal challenge in February 2012 they voted decisively for Gillard, 71 to 31. His second tilt in March 2013 was called off because he still did not have the numbers. But as the election approached and Gillard looked set to lead Labor to its heaviest defeat since James Scullin in 1931, the inevitability of his restoration was apparent.

The demography that created the most distress for Julia Gillard was the parliament itself. There has never been a parliament, or a Labor government, that looked less like the people it served. Of the 226 members and senators, 92 had been previously employed in the system as party or trade union officials, political staffers, lobbyists or in state or local government. The next largest bloc comprised the 57 who had worked in business. Another 30 had been lawyers like Gillard. At the other end of the gene pool, farmers, teachers, nurses and doctors numbered just 17 in total. This monoculture, many decades in the making, had neither the policy nous nor the political deftness of touch to satisfy an increasingly fragmented electorate.

There was a plodding uniformity to the character of Labor ministers. Pragmatic in their views and robotic in their delivery, they seemed determined to be incomprehensible. A certain under-stated greyness might have been excusable in one or two ministers, but not in Treasury, where voters had been conditioned to expect a forceful personality. Treasurers on both sides live, to some extent, in the shadows of Paul Keating and Peter Costello. They have to be the policy purist, the persuader within government and a tutor to the electorate. They must also be willing to take on a populist prime minister on a matter of principle. Wayne Swan only ticked the first of those four boxes. He was across his brief, but painfully unable to sell it. A former Queensland state Labor party secretary, Swan was the highest ranking of the machine men in the Rudd and Gillard governments and it showed. Even his closest friends in government admit privately that he struggled as an orator. Swan compounded the government's problems by reinforcing the worst political traits of its leaders: Kevin Rudd's risk-aversion and Julia Gillard's retreat to jargon.

Labor was most credible when Rudd and Swan were united by the global financial crisis, and the advice of public servants was taken seriously. Labor was its most politically nimble when Rudd and Gillard faced a common enemy in John Howard, and the party organisation didn't meddle in the affairs of the caucus. But crisis management and campaign skills do not translate to government if there is no unity of purpose.

Initially, Gillard thought it was Rudd's personality that was the problem. But she repeated his mistakes, with policies too big for the public to comprehend, and too compromised to inspire. This is where the parliament's lack of diversity counted against Labor. Raised in the winner-takes-all world of backroom politics, most ministers lacked the experience to prioritise reform, and to patiently argue for it when public opinion was against it.

Both Rudd and Gillard yielded to the same authority-sapping urges as Howard in his final term, and money was wasted on vote-buying exercises that failed to shift a single vote. When it became clear that handouts merely increased electoral cynicism, the government tried to pick symbolic fights on behalf of the mainstream. They took a swing at mining barons, then media moguls, then asylum seekers, and finally single mothers. When the shouting aroused more opposition than support, they reverted to pleading by handout.

Nevertheless, Gillard had more policies to her name than Rudd. He had introduced the national broadband network and changes to hospital funding. She revived carbon pricing and a watered-down version of the mining tax, moved to reform schools funding and piloted a national disability insurance scheme. But only the NDIS survived the change of government in the form that Labor had envisaged. The mining tax and carbon price were both repealed, while the fate of the other policies remains to be seen.

Gillard was prime minister for three years and three days; three months longer than Rudd. They governed for the equivalent of two Whitlam terms – Gough, in fact, was toppled one month earlier than Gillard.

Rudd and Gillard succumbed, together and apart, to the workaholic's curse. They logged the most hours per day in the office without the legacy to show for it. Their respective work methods damned the issue of climate change, which took a reform that had bipartisan support at the 2007 election and turned it to political poison within a term. It was also the primary source of resentment between them. Rudd felt that Gillard had let him down in 2010 on the ETS. He needed her to keep him on track, to avoid the calamity of April that year when he walked away from the scheme. But her focus wasn't on the next tricky step in the reform journey. She just wanted to clear his in-tray in preparation for an election. Climate change wasn't her issue.

'I wasn't, when we came to government, engaged in carbon-pricing policy,' she says. 'I had elected to put together as portfolios employment and workplace relations, and education. I wanted to get rid of WorkChoices, build Fair Work. I wanted to do the skills work that lay around employment, [and] all of the human capital work – early childhood education, childcare, primary schools, high schools, vocational education, universities – a huge workload. As deputy prime minister I was necessarily on every cabinet sub-committee and I thought to myself, particularly in that WorkChoices eradication period, I've got to make some decisions here about how I'm going to use my time. So I looked at the climate change sub-committee and said: "I'm just not going to do that one."'

With hindsight, she says she should have been involved. But that would have required a sacrifice elsewhere.

'In any event, carbon policy moved relatively quickly from being in the province of the cabinet sub-committee to the troika of Kevin and Wayne and Penny [Wong] in her portfolio responsibility for climate change. I would have had to make a decision to become the fourth wheel in that process, and I just think physically it would have been very difficult for me to do it and acquit all of my other functions.'

The cost of her lack of engagement multiplied after she became leader. In the 2010 election campaign she promised there would be no carbon tax under a government she led, although she did say she supported a market-based mechanism to reduce carbon population. The two statements are incompatible. An ETS begins with a fixed price – in other words, a temporary carbon tax. In both Howard's proposed scheme and in Rudd's there was a carbon tax. She would have seen the trap if she was across the issue.

Gillard was damned either way. If she had sought a fresh mandate for a carbon price – that is, waited three years – it is difficult to see how she would have avoided a scare campaign in the meantime.

In fact, Gillard hadn't ruled out a price on carbon at the 2010 election, so the question of mandate is neither here nor there. She had the numbers on the floor of the parliament to pass legislation.

But she made two further mistakes that doomed her reform. She allowed her opponent to label her proposed fixed price a 'carbon tax' with no qualification, and she agreed to the Greens' demand for a three-year period before moving to a flexible-price ETS. That made the carbon price a sitting duck for the next parliament. Labor's final error came when it switched back to Rudd in 2013. He disowned Gillard's carbon price, saying he would move to an ETS a year earlier if re-elected. Then he ignored the issue during the campaign. For a second election in a row, Labor felt it best not mention the policy that occupied most of its time.

The Rudd–Gillard rivalry was never really about policy, but policy was its ultimate victim. The election-eve leadership coups, from Rudd to Gillard and from Gillard to Rudd, discouraged the new leader from talking up their predecessor's record. In 2010, Gillard could not mention the great escape from the GFC without prompting a question on Rudd's removal. In 2013, Rudd avoided the NDIS. Bob Hawke contrasts this with the sense of a shared mission he had with Paul Keating. They fought, but not to the detriment of their program.

'Despite some arguments and disputations that Paul and I had, we were united in a commitment to reforming the country and we basically agreed on fundamentals,' he says. 'We really were about changing the country, and we did, so that provides a buoyancy that was not there in this period.'

Kevin Rudd won back the Labor leadership on 27 June 2013, three years and three days after his overthrow. He had almost doubled his support from the previous year's ballot, a sweet vindication of 57 votes to 45. The last man to have two lives as prime minister was Robert Menzies. But they were interrupted by more than eight years in opposition. Rudd was our first prime minister to come back in the same governing cycle.

On his return, Rudd found the prime minister's chair did not command the authority he had expected. The first change he noticed was in the media. It had shielded him when he bad-mouthed Julia Gillard. Now it turned on him, with the same vindictive force that it had applied to her. Sydney's *Daily Telegraph* did not even pretend to be objective. It opened the 2013 election campaign with a front-page editorial under the headline 'Kick This Mob Out'. More entertaining, but no less slanted was Brisbane's *Courier-Mail*, which greeted the announcement that former Queensland premier Peter Beattie would stand as a Labor candidate in a marginal Liberal seat with the headline 'Send in the Clown'.

I doubt whether these News Limited tabloids shifted a single vote. It's more likely their obsession with politics accelerated circulation falls in their respective markets. The *Daily Telegraph* suffered the biggest loss in Rupert Murdoch's stable, with circulation 15 per cent lower in the September quarter 2013 compared to the same quarter in 2012. Similar falls were recorded by the Fairfax metropolitan papers. The concern is not the side they selected, but that they did so at all. In Melbourne, *The Age* published the equivalent insult to their readers before the election with a front-page editorial on the Labor leadership. The once-revered Fairfax broadsheet urged Gillard to give up the prime ministership: 'We are not saying Ms Gillard should stand aside because of Labor's policies,' the editorial explained. The newspaper just wanted to make Labor more competitive, in the interests of democracy. Media organisations have barracked in the past, but were careful to avoid the appearance of political devotion. Now they just yelled for their team, pleading with the board to sack the coach.

Labor went to Rudd in desperation, and without a realistic expectation of victory. There might have been a small chance if Rudd had called an immediate election, but he waited, and by the time he set the date for 7 September, voters had made up their minds to be rid of the government.

It was a heavy defeat but not a landslide, the life-support switch flicked off instead of a brutal execution. Labor ceded 17 seats to the Coalition in total. Eight were in Tony Abbott's home state of New South Wales, three each in Victoria and Tasmania, two in Queensland and one in South Australia.

On its two preceding exits from government, Labor had surrendered almost twice as many seats – 31 in 1996 and 30 in 1975. Labor's final seat count of 55 in a parliament of 150 compared with 49 out of 148 in 1996 and 36 out of 127 in 1975.

The difference this time was the primary vote on exit. Paul Keating's in 1996 had been 38.8 per cent. Gough Whitlam's in 1975 was 42.8 per cent. Rudd's was 33.4 per cent, which raises the existential challenge for Labor of whether it can aspire to a strong majority government again. In their six soap-operatic years in office, Rudd and Gillard had reduced Labor's primary support by exactly 10 percentage points – one million voters. The only thing that gave them a second term in 2010 and prevented a wipeout on the floor of the parliament in 2013 was the alternative.

Since 2007 the Coalition has claimed just one third of Labor's primary vote loss (3.5 points), which underlines the ambivalence the electorate has felt about an Abbott-led government. The majority of Labor's lost vote went to the Palmer United Party (5.5 per cent). The Greens picked up just 0.9 points.

As one Coalition strategist noted the day after the election: 'Well, that was interesting. The 4–5 per cent who left Labor and parked in "other", poll after poll from 2010, never did move to the Coalition. Luckily Clive's preferences came our way. And the Greens fell badly too. If the Greens had gotten the same vote as in 2010, Rudd would have held on.'

The Coalition's primary vote of 45.5 per cent was its lowest entry into government since the formation of the modern Liberal Party. Menzies had won in 1949 with a primary vote of 50.3 per cent;

Malcolm Fraser set the record of 53.1 per cent in 1975; while John Howard had 47.3 per cent in 1996.

The 2013 election was not a vote for stability, but another deliberate shot at the two-party system from a politics-weary community. Minor parties claimed 21.1 per cent of the primary vote. In the previous two change-of-government elections of 2007 and 1996, that figure was less than 15 per cent. Minor parties did even better in the senate, where the balance of power was seized by a clutch of anti-politicians.

Liberal Party pollster and strategist Mark Textor says voters are less attached to the major parties today because the old relationship between government and voter has broken down.

'Before the great reforms of the '80s, governments guaranteed a lot of things. They guaranteed a job in the public service, a pension for life, certain Australian industries,' he says. 'People understood that that was changing. But if you're offering me less loyalty as a government, I can offer you less loyalty as a voter. If I'm being disempowered in terms of my relationship with government, I'll re-empower myself by being more activist as a voter. I'll demand more as a voter so I'll be more needy, and I'll want a performance bonus from you.'

Protest parties such as Clive Palmer's, and Pauline Hanson's before it, are bottom feeders, Textor explains: democracy's corporate raiders. 'What these candidates do is feed off the distressed assets.'

This perspective from the winner's lectern is revealing because it highlights the vulnerability of the incumbent, regardless of political leaning. First-term Coalition state governments in Victoria and New South Wales had caught the Labor disease, disposing of the two premiers who took them into office.

Textor says the biggest change he has seen over the past two decades is the separation of the political conversation from the public conversation. The community continues to process information at the same speed, he says, but the machinery of politics and media has sped up, making itself incomprehensible.

'Rather than what papers used to do with budgets – which is here's who wins, here's who loses, here's the tax rates for families, here's the new benefits for pensioners – we now have an entire class of people who will not make a living unless they can go on the ABC's *Drum* program or Sky News or some other channel and literally just talk about the politics of an announcement. They're usually not too skilled on the detail because they're not economists, [nor] professional journalists who are paid to provide detail, they're commentators.

'So they take a very simple issue – road funding, or Tony Abbott's paid parental leave scheme – and immediately start taking it to the next level, accelerating it into politics. What it will mean for certain cohorts, what it will mean in terms of the dynamics of parliament, what it will mean for the next marketing campaign, what it will mean between the tensions of different leaders in different parties. That's the fast lane, accelerating the issue into the rocketship of politics.

'Stuck in the slow lane are a bunch of punters, and they just want to know what does this mean for me? What is the tax rate? What is the funding model? What are the upsides and the downsides before you start telling me about the politics? And as one lady in a focus group said: "It's like being in a taxi where the taxi driver is constantly changing between stations looking for the perfect answer, looking for the perfect bit of music. Suddenly you hear something for a while and think, Geez I want to know more about that, but then the taxi driver switches again. And off you run at a million miles an hour." So what we now have is an entire political industry incentivised financially and career-wise to artificially derive a simple issue into pure politics. And what the people want is basic information.'

Gillard makes the same point. People don't obsess about politics.

'They lift their eyes periodically,' she says. '"I need to vote in an election, or something big has happened," but they don't follow it every day, every minute. But there's a class of people who do, and they furiously talk to each other. I think [the public] actually do want some of the underlying story, but no one gives it to them. And in election campaigns now you put out a policy, often [reporters] don't bother to analyse the policy so much as the politics of the policy. So there's a mum who's trying to work out "Does that new childcare policy mean I'm going to end up with more money at the end of the week?" No one's actually bothered to tell her that. They're too busy saying, "Well, you know this is all about whether Tony Abbott thinks he's got an issue with women and the contrast with Labor and blah, blah, blah." So the basic questions about policy change don't get answered any more.'

Australia has now experienced two changes of government that involved an explicit mandate to reverse poorly framed and atrociously marketed reforms. Rudd and Gillard abolished Howard's WorkChoices legislation. Abbott abolished Gillard's carbon price. The two policies are not quite analogous: WorkChoices does not qualify as genuine reform because it forced trade unions to accept a sacrifice without asking anything of the employer. But it shared with carbon pricing an overzealous repeal in which tribal fetishes trumped national policy needs.

Labor replaced WorkChoices with a pro-union policy that turned the clock back to the early 1990s. Carbon pricing was abolished as an act of political revenge, and at the time of writing there is no credible scheme in prospect to reduce Australia's greenhouse gas emissions. The irony is that Gillard's scheme actually worked. Emissions fell in its first eighteen months of operation. The economy did not crash. To give up a reform that did what it claimed is unusual. The Abbott government had the option of scrapping the fixed carbon price and moving to an ETS instead, with the perfect political cover: the Chinese are planning to establish the world's largest ETS in our neighbourhood. But the Coalition has assumed away the problem of climate change and bet the future of the economy on coal. The last act of Australian policy isolationism on this scale was the tariff, and the lesson of that error is that it can take many decades to recognise the damage caused by these decisions.

In the meantime, governments will continue to suffer early burnout until a new contract can be written between the main parties, the media and the community that takes policy seriously enough to explain and to implement it in the crowded lane of real life.

The former prime ministers are polite but terse in their appraisal of Kevin Rudd.

Malcolm Fraser did not know Rudd very well, but says 'his apology to Aboriginals was well received'.

Bob Hawke offers no direct comment: 'I'd rather not talk about Kevin Rudd. I don't think it'd be useful to anyone.' He praises the government's handling of the GFC in the plural, by referring to the Rudd–Gillard government. '[They] made the right decisions. They spent money. And that's what was needed.'

John Howard cannot find a stand-alone compliment for Rudd, and like Hawke resorts to the collective. 'Both Kevin Rudd and Julia Gillard put an emphasis on the importance of education,' Howard says. 'Now whilst I might disagree with some of the methods, the elevation of education to such an important issue is itself something to be complimented.'

Of Rudd's predecessors, only Paul Keating was generous. 'Kevin Rudd brought the Labor Party back to office and he did everything right in terms of the financial crisis. He saved us the heartache that North America and Europe went through in terms of bank failures and the stress on the financial system and the rise of unemployment. He avoided all of those things and if he did nothing else, that he did well enough.'

Gillard was the only other leader to offer an extensive tribute. She says Rudd was the 'right person in the right chair' during the GFC. 'This was an environment in which Kevin excelled,' she says. 'Cometh the hour, cometh the man. Never has that saying been more true than in the global financial crisis. Everything about his work capacity, his leadership style came to the fore in a good way during those very difficult days. And for he and Wayne [Swan], whose political relationship had been characterised by at best mutual wariness and at worst something a lot harsher than that, all of that got left to the wayside, just pushed aside. They just worked together incredibly during that period of time.'

She also hails 'the absolutely golden moment of the apology to the Stolen Generations – it will be remembered for all of time and it should be'.

Gillard herself evokes more sympathy than applause from the older guard.

Fraser says, 'Julia Gillard will always be remembered as our first female prime minister. It ended unhappily for her, and who knows what might have happened if she had had full loyalty from her own party.'

Hawke says, 'Julia's an interesting character. You have her in a group of people and she's a great communicator. Nothing forced about it. Get her on a television box and she's a different person. I said to her from the beginning, I said, "Julia, the secret of television is not to think about the hundreds of thousands or millions of people out there, you're talking to one person." And she said, "Yes, that's right." But she never seemed to get that. And communication is an enormously important part of leadership.'

Keating notes the 'controversy of her becoming prime minister' but says that doesn't detract from her policy initiatives. 'In education and the National Disability Insurance Scheme [Gillard added] to the Labor standard in these important areas of social policy.'

Rudd talks up the symbolism. 'As for Julia,' he says, she gave 'extraordinary hope and opportunity to Australian women when she became our first deputy prime minister, when she became our first woman prime minister.'

'There'll always be debate about the circumstances,' he says. 'But I think as a strong voice for women, despite all the rancour and I think a very unhealthy degree of misogyny she was able to name and shame, I think that's a strong contribution.'

The sense of unfinished business is palpable in these assessments. Labor did not fulfil its traditional role in national politics as policy innovator.

The narcissism of the Rudd–Gillard government era, and the media's own flight down the low roads of trivia and vendetta, are signs of a systemic weakness, if not failure. This was apparent when the first edition of this book was published in 2012, and while I remain an optimist, I suspect politics has a few years of mediocrity up its sleeve before we can make something our Moment. It may be that both sides need a cycle of disappointment in government before the system corrects. The economic reforms of the Hawke–Keating government, and their consolidation under the Howard–Costello government, were shaped by the economic crisis of the Whitlam–Fraser era. The next generation of Labor and Coalition governments will hopefully look at the poll-driven pettiness of the Rudd–Gillard–Abbott era with the same motivated distaste. It would be a shame for Australia to pass up its Moment because it was afraid of success.

APPENDIX

This book became the basis for a three-part documentary for the ABC, *Making Australia Great*, which was filmed over the course of 2014.

I re-interviewed, among others, every prime minister from Malcolm Fraser to Julia Gillard, treasurer Peter Costello, former Treasury department secretary Ken Henry and Reserve Bank governors Bernier Fraser, Ian Macfarlane and Glenn Stevens. Some views have evolved with time, while others are on the record for the first time. Notably, the officials are now freer to talk about the GFC than they were when the first edition of this book was being researched and written.

I also asked our leaders and policy-makers to look to the future, to see if we can make something of this Moment. Their answers add to the argument in the body of this book. What follows are the highlights of those interviews.

Why we avoided the GFC, or, as the rest of the world still calls it, the Great Recession:

Former Treasury department secretary Ken Henry: We expected to have a recession. You don't know for a long, long time afterwards whether you've managed to avoid a recession or not. You don't expect to get any thanks for it. Why? Because who was aware that they had been saved by a government from recession? After all, there are so many other vested interests out there that wanted to say that it wasn't the government that saved the Australian economy from recession, it was them. Or it was China that saved the Australian economy from recession.

There's no doubt in the minds of people [who were] in the Treasury at the time, and a lot of work has been done on this, that without those fiscal stimulus packages the Australian economy would have gone into a very deep recession. But think about some of the other possible reasons for Australia avoiding recession. These are not things that we hadn't thought about. In fact they're all the things that I said to Prime Minister Rudd on 11 October 2008. But I [also] said it's not enough, it's not going to be enough. Things like the Reserve Bank cutting interest rates and continuing to cut interest rates – yes, I said to Prime Minister Rudd, that will happen, but it's not enough. Things like the currency depreciating – I said, yep, that will happen, but that is not going to be enough.

There are those who say that it was China, [but the] Chinese economy actually suffered a bigger slowdown that any of the industrialised countries. Of course, the support provided by China and Korea – but by China in particular, coming back strongly through the second half of 2009 – was very important in providing support to the Australian economy through 2009, through 2010 and so on. And some of those who say, 'But it was China who saved the Australian economy from recession' will even admit that it was Chinese fiscal stimulus that did the work. Curiously, the Chinese fiscal stimulus saves the Australian economy from recession, not the Australian fiscal stimulus. Well, I don't believe a word of it.

Former Reserve Bank governor Ian Macfarlane: The first and immediate thing is the banking system didn't fail. So we didn't have bank runs and panics. You could probably sum up the more fundamental reason in three words – China, commodity prices, resource investment. Our economy was plugged into the strong Asian part, producing products that went up in price, and we had much less connection with the extremely weak North Atlantic part. I think our policies were right. I think our monetary policy and our fiscal policy, or certainly the initial phase of fiscal policy, were right. We didn't have this problem of fragmented regulators who didn't know what was going on because they thought the other regulator was doing it.

Macfarlane supports the first stimulus package of cash handouts, interest rate cuts and bank guarantees but questions the second, in which the government invested in school buildings and home insulation.

When you try and attach a counter-cyclical or fiscal stimulus onto some good word like 'education' or 'environment', you get into trouble. The first phase was just giving people money to spend, and the government didn't tell you how to spend it. And I think the first phase was the one that worked; it was quite effective and it hit at exactly the right time – in the fourth quarter of 2008 and the first quarter of 2009.

On how long our winning streak can continue:

Ken Henry: The thing must end at some point. I think everybody would agree on that. This is the big question: how concerned should we be about that? And of course the answer is it depends how deep it is. Doesn't matter if the Australian economy has a couple of quarters of negative growth, where instead of the economy growing

by three quarters of a percentage point it goes backward by 0.1 or
something. Does that really matter? Politically, that matters a lot.
But does it really matter? Well, it probably doesn't matter a hell of a
lot to Australia. But if it's a recession that gives us 10 per cent unemployment then we really should be worried. We should do whatever
we can to avoid that. I forget what the figures are, and I really should
have these in my head – perhaps they should be tattooed somewhere
on the anatomy of every macro-policy advisor – but a very large
proportion of people aged over forty-five who lost their jobs in the
early-1990s recession never worked a day again in their lives. A very
large proportion – more than 50 per cent. That is a consequence that
should be avoided – not at any cost, but at any reasonable cost.

On future opportunities and risks:

Reserve Bank governor Glenn Stevens: I try to be the glass-half-
full guy. Most central banks' governors through most of my career
were more often giving lectures: 'Be careful, don't borrow too
much, and governments, you know, get those deficits down,' and
so on. People should be calmer. I seem to have spent much of my
almost eight years in this role saying to people, 'It's not quite that
bad, come on, let's buck up a little, we can manage.' I wouldn't
have expected to have to do that, but I think we almost enjoy tend-
ing to wallow in this 'we'll all be ruined' kind of attitude.

Ken Henry: One of the things that kept me awake at night [as
secretary of the Treasury] was whether Australia was positioned to
deal properly [and] effectively with the strong growth in population that is in prospect. Whether we understood the implications
for urban amenity, for the environment. The sort of population
increase that we're looking at over the next several decades could
be overwhelmingly positive for Australia. It could make Australia
a much more vibrant country. A country that has all the good

things that large cities in other parts of the world demonstrate in terms of dynamism, cultural diversity and access to cultural activity. It could and if done properly, it will. But as we've discovered in the past decade, if we don't do it well it could be truly bad, with increasing urban congestion, increasing environmental problems. Another thing that worried me was whether we were going to prove, as a country, capable of dealing effectively with quite significant social issues, like entrenched Indigenous disadvantage. This is one of the wealthiest countries in the world [and] there should be no excuse for the poor quality of lives and the gaps in life expectancy that we see between non-Indigenous and Indigenous Australians. There is no excuse for that. Another thing that concerns me is the way we deal with our natural resources. When I think about the attitude that we take to the exploitation of Australia's natural resources, mineral resources and energy resources, we have a finders-keepers mentality. That's it. We encourage the private sector to make off with the resources. Now, of course there are wider economic benefits associated with private interests making off with the resources. But that mindset is actually quite unusual for a resource-rich country.

There's a lot of things that can keep you awake at night, but there's also reason to be optimistic. Other times in our history, very difficult times, we've demonstrated an ability to analyse challenges appropriately, with clarity [and] clear thinking, and to set up policy and institutional frameworks to deal effectively with those challenges. And provided we recognise that these things are challenges, then we should prove capable of doing so again.

Former Reserve Bank governor Bernie Fraser: I've got clearer views about climate change now because of some work that I've been doing, and things have to change there. I'm also a bit more concerned about population than I would have been twenty years ago. I would have thought that strong population growth, supported by immigration, was good for the workforce and growth in the workforce, and that [along] with productivity [it] was really what determined the growth rates. But now, maybe it's maturity or advancing years or something, over the last couple of decades I've come to the view that it's much better to have a competent society. You have to be competent, but one has to have regard also to fairness and opportunities and standards of education and health. Then you get these issues of age and how you're going to pay for an ageing population, how you're going to maintain some growth in the workforce and so on. So sustainability to me is quite a big issue but it's not, unfortunately, for politicians because they're focused on at most three years, where we're talking about 40–50 years. What's determined for population today is the same [as] for climate change – it is going to have consequences way out, as far as you want to think about.

On the Australian character:

Former treasurer Peter Costello: I think what drove us in the '80s and the late '90s was this feeling that somehow we were falling behind. When we got in front, we got a bit complacent. If we come back through the pack [again], I hope that will be a spur to recover our reforming zeal. I think Australia ought to take itself a little more seriously. We don't have to be a follower. We can be a leader. We have been a leader, we can do it again. People can feel that Australia has something to offer the region and the world. There's no reason why we shouldn't be talking to others about what's worked here, because we have a story to tell – and it's a good story.

John Howard: Australia will grow, it will prosper, it will remain very cohesive. And one of the reasons why is that it does have a great sense of balance. Australians don't like lunatic fringes, they don't like extremists, they don't like bigots.

Peter Costello: I think one of the endearing things also about Australians is there's this reluctance to give their leaders credit. And that's endearing, in a way, because I think it means they'll never be swept away by extremism, and they'll never be swept away by ideologues, and they'll never be swept away by ideology. That's part of the strength of the Australian character, but I do think if they were able to look at the achievements and compare them with other countries, they would feel justifiably proud.

On leadership:

Paul Keating: I think the public are so smart, they know nonsense when they hear it. Policy remarks made without integrity are noticed immediately, so I think leaders of integrity who propose better propositions to the public, important ideas, will always be gratefully received, and I think those big ideas have a magnetism about them that does draw even the disparate commentary we get now in social media. Let's regard the social media as iron filings and the ideas as magnets. You switch the magnet on and the iron filings start to come to it. But if there's no magnetism, if there's no political energy, there's no integrity. You can't get the response. So I think the response will be there with leadership. Leadership is the key to getting the response.

Bob Hawke: I think there's a great deal of legitimate concern about the way democracy's operating here and in other countries. Now, let me make the point that this is not something unique to Australia. I would make the assertion that we are at a unique point in history. This is the first time since the end of the Second World War that there hasn't been at least one outstanding political leader anywhere in the world, in the democratic world. Name me one. Now why is this? I can't pretend to say that I know all the answers, but I think one factor has been, in this country and in others, the increasing intrusiveness of the media into the private lives of politicians and their families.

Bernie Fraser: Being sort of on the fringe of policymaking and governments for fifty years now, I can't recall ever in the past getting to the point we're at now, where everything is so combative. Whether it's Labor or Coalition, what do they stand for? They can't agree on anything, but in earlier times even the oppositions would regularly concede that a government idea had some merit and it would contribute to the progress and prosperity of the community. But these days everything, wherever it comes from, whatever the colour of the government, is opposed. One wonders what these oppositions and governments stand for, because they're both doing the same thing when they're in opposition.

On the media:

Paul Keating: Well, I think the political system visited this on themselves. John Howard would do radio and press conferences virtually most days. I never did this. The prime minister's there to think about the whole system and where it's going, not be a media tart. You can have the sugar hit of being a media tart, but in the end what happens? Everything you say is devalued by the frequency and velocity of you saying it. So therefore if you think, What am I here to do? You are here to think about the future and guide it. I think that [fewer] media appearances and more thinking and more guidance will be rewarded in a more respectable coverage of the things the government says and does. But if the government wishes itself to be part of the silly spin, then it can hardly blame the media for the whole notion that you're in the washing machine being thrown around. Can you change it from where we are? That's a different point. But I still think no country's ever going to prosper without deep thinking and public policy presentation. If you think deeply and you have the presentation, the reward will be there. I'm not on Twitter now, so the chances are I wouldn't be on Twitter [as prime minister]. I'd give it a good go – staying away, I mean.

Julia Gillard: I think the combination of new technology, new media and politics right around the western world hasn't settled yet. It's like our democratic rhythms [are] disrupted by all of this new information and instant information. No one's found the new rhythm yet. We didn't as a government. Even masters of the online media age like President Obama, I think, have struggled with this sort of disruptive impact in our democracy. There's no one right answer. If you chase the media cycle, then it's more, more, more, more, more, clutter, clutter, clutter. A lot of the quality [of media coverage] is too low, and you get political problems. If you retreat and say, 'I'm not engaging in the media scrum all of the time,' then it will be a very short period of time before the analysis is [that] you're not doing anything.

Bob Hawke: The media has become more confrontational, and this is another reason why a lot of people [interested in politics] would say, 'Why the hell am I going to get into that?' So I would certainly like to see the media generally take a more constructive role. That doesn't mean they have to be supportive, but to give an opportunity for the development of discussion about ideas. [However] I've never been one within my party that's embraced the idea that all our problems are bloody media. At times they have been a pain in the arse, that's for sure. But in politics basically the worst wounds are the self-inflicted ones.

On what a great Australia would look like:

Malcolm Fraser: We'd have political leaders before us who'd give us a real option about the future. We'd have genuine debates about policy, and perhaps about values. We would be even more of a multi-cultural society than we are today. We'd be respected in our own region. We would have overcome our differences with Indonesia. We would have worked through the United Nations, especially at a time when we were on the Security Council, to try and reinvigorate the world's approach to refugees worldwide. There should be a global commitment to try and get rid of UNHCR refugee camps and long-term people in those camps.

Bob Hawke: Well, if you're asking about what we need to do now to fulfil our potential, there's one thing which stands out so obviously that it's amazing. We should take the world's nuclear waste and we should go in for uranium enrichment. If we did that we'd totally transform the fiscal situation. We'd create a very large amount of employment in this country. But more important than anything else, we would make the world a safer place. It's what my Chinese friends call a win-win situation. Win for us, win for the world. We have got the world's safest geological formations in remote areas, and don't talk about 'not in my backyard'. We've got the biggest bloody backyard in the world.

Paul Keating: I'd like it to be what I always hoped it would be. That is, an open, competitive, cosmopolitan country, a tolerant country, a republic, not just focusing on the Asian region but integrated with it to a greater degree. And I think that public policy should be about basically guiding that kind of transition. This is an immigrant country, the most successful settler of immigrant people, people from abroad. It has a natural capacity to be cosmopolitan; it is at its heart cosmopolitan. I think those sort of values should be uppermost. There should be a kindliness rather than hardness attaching to the way public policy views its responsibilities to the community at large, and I think it's completely necessary that we become a republic. The republic will lift the body energy. It'll lift the blood flow, it'll put some sprightliness into us. It'll say a lot of important things to us about ourselves, rather than simply being a country that needs to borrow the monarch of another country. I mean, how sad in the end is that? So we go to Asia as an Australian republic with our heads high, we come to reasonable terms with the Aborigines – we've admitted to the dispossession, we tried to make good their losses and improve their lives and their health and their participation – and we do what we can with some of the skills we've developed in foreign policy and the rest to try and ease Asia down, to keep it peaceful and safe and to use this energy to lift our living standards.

John Howard: When I talk about a bigger Australia, a 'big Australia', I don't have a particular population figure in mind – I think that's foolish. You take the number of migrants each year that you feel the nation can absorb. As far as the pressure it places on the economy, well, there are benefits and pressure. Migration's always been seen as good for the housing industry because the [migrants] want houses to live in. As far as infrastructure is concerned, one of the unarguable responsibilities of government is to provide a decent education system, and another is to provide a decent infrastructure. And through whatever combination of public or private investment you choose, it's got to be provided. And it is an ongoing issue. There have been cases in the past, and probably are now, where there's been a lag in the infrastructure, there's no doubt about that. There have been failures in the past, and the answer, though, is not to say, 'Put up the shutters, keep people out. The city's overcrowded.' The answer is to make the city operate more efficiently.

Julia Gillard: I'd like to see an Australia where we've got strong economic growth, [where] we have got all of our settings right so that we are ultimate winners of this century of change, that we are at home in our place in the world, deeply economically integrated into Asia and experiencing all the prosperity that can come with that. We've ensured that this is inclusive growth, that there is space in this economy and opportunities in this economy for kids from all sorts of circumstances, and enabling them to get a great education is the key to that. I would hope that we would have settled the intersections between economic growth and our impact on our environment, including the difficult questions about carbon emissions trading, climate change.

Kevin Rudd: Building the great Australia of the future is why I hope most of us get into public life. Certainly ain't for the salary, let me tell you. So what does it look like? For me it has been and remains a secure Australia, a competitive Australia, a compassionate Australia and a sustainable Australia, an Australia that does not regard all those as mutual contradictions. We're a country that's smart enough to actually walk in these directions at the same time, and that is half the vision. The other half is an Australia that has a view of its place in the world whereby we are part of the global problem-solvers, the regional problem-solvers. We're a creative middle power with universal values, with regional interests and with global interests, and we're in the business of helping solve problems beyond our borders as well. So if that's a big Australia, that's the one I believe in, and I think we're capable of doing that.

ACKNOWLEDGEMENTS

Thank you to family and friends who have tolerated my absences and/or even longer monologues while I researched and wrote this thing. In alphabetical order you are: Allison Sloan, Annabel Crabb, Barrie Cassidy, Bronwen Colman, Diane Colman, Elisabeth Wynhausen, Erasmia Melvin, Esther Anatolitis, Fiona Hando, Foong Ling Kong, Gabrielle Chan, Gavin Randles, Geoff Ginn, Jo Setright, Joe Fulco, Joel Deane, Julia Balderstone, Kate Legge, Kellie Mayo, Lynne Gallagher, Margaret Easterbrook, Michael Williams, Natasha Cica, Nick Harford, Nina Field, Patricia Karvelas, Patrick Lawnham, Peta Stevenson, Rebecca Huntley, Susan Hornbeck, Stephen Lunn and Tom Dusevic.

Special appreciation to those who lent me their out-of-print books: Toby Colman, Marie Claire Gateaux, Jeff Jenkins and Brian McKeown.

Also, to Michael Bowers and Andrew Meares for their help on the pics, and to the former prime ministers, their staff and the dozens of officials who gave their valuable time to this project.

Finally, thank you to Chris Mitchell at *The Australian* for giving me generous leave to write, and to Ben Ball and Michael Nolan at Penguin for being such good fun to work with and for turning my rough manuscript into a real book.

NOTES

CHAPTER 1

9   **barely one in ten Australians thought it was 'all right'** *Age* Poll No. 5,
    February 1972. Unless noted otherwise, all opinion polls quoted for
    the 1960s, '70s, and '80s were accessed from the Australian Data
    Archive. www.ada.edu.au/social-science/home

11 **His predecessor, the seventy-year-old Arthur Calwell** Graham
    Freudenberg, *A Certain Grandeur*, Viking, revised edition 2009, p.15.

13 **a self-described 'democratic socialist'** 'Labor and the Future', *The
    Australian*, 18 February, 1967.
    Lyndon Johnson's 'Great Society' speech is cited in Randall B. Wood,
    LBJ: Architect of American Ambition, Free Press 2006, p.466.

14 **Labor picked up 17 seats** Election results are taken from The
    University of Western Australia's Australian Politics and Elections
    Database. elections.uwa.edu.au/electionsearch.lasso?ID=2
    See also: www.aph.gov.au/library/pubs/rb/2004-05/05rb11.htm
    From 1993 onward, I also use the Australian Electoral Commission's
    website and CD-ROMs. www.aec.gov.au
    I've left out the by-elections that occurred between terms. Labor had
    picked up an extra seat before the 1969 election, which it held at the
    general election. In 1975, the Coalition famously won the seat of Bass
    from Labor, which it retained at that year's general election. Labor
    also had an extra seat before the 1983 election, which it kept.
    Conversely, before the 1990, 1996 and 2001 elections the government
    of the day lost a seat each that was subsequently recovered at the

general election. To maintain consistency, I haven't counted these cases in the final tallies either.

17 **They talked about the Vietnam War** Whitlam's meeting with Zhou is detailed in *A Certain Grandeur,* pp. 210–14; McMahon's reply is from Laurie Oakes, *Whitlam PM,* Angus and Robertson, 1973, p.225. The Chinese regarded Whitlam as a hero. On the thirtieth anniversary of the normalisation of relations, in 2002, Whitlam and Freudenberg were invited to China for a celebration. 'All toasts always ended with Chinese officials quoting the Chinese proverb, "When you go to draw the water at the well, remember who dug the well".'

18 **Bill Snedden, put his name to a prescient cabinet submission** National Archives, Cabinet minute, Series No. A5908, submission No. 195. All subsequent documents used from the National Archives will be referred to by their relevant numbers.
    Cabinet record can be found at: www.naa.gov.au/collection/explore/cabinet/index.aspx

19 **'stagflation' . . . had been coined in 1965** British Conservative politician Iain Macleod used the phrase in a parliamentary debate in 1965: 'We now have the worst of both worlds – not just inflation on the one side or stagnation on the other, but both of them together. We have a sort of "stagflation" situation.' hansard.millbanksystems.com/commons/1965/nov/17/economic-affairs#S5CV0720P0_19651117_HOC_286|publisher=hansard|title=|date=17

22 **The popular imagination was grabbed by Poseidon** The summary of the Poseidon bubble is from John Simon, 'Three Australian Asset-price Bubbles', *RBA Annual Conference Volume* for 2003. www.rba.gov.au/publications/confs/2003/simon.pdf

CHAPTER 2

27 **'rare feeling of national self-respect'** The Robert Drewe passage was cited by Gough Whitlam in a speech in Old Parliament House to mark the thirtieth anniversary of his election, 2 December 2002.

28 **There is a scene in the first Barry McKenzie movie** aso.gov.au/titles/features/adventures-barry-mckenzie/clip3/
    The mother country had abandoned us www.margaretthatcher.org/document/102136

30 **As Blanche d'Alpuget wrote in her biography** Blanche d'Alpuget, *Hawke: The Early Years,* Melbourne University Press 2010, p.303.

Plot any chart from the early 1970s The average wage data cited is
taken from table 4.17 in the RBA's *Australian Economic Statistics*.
For a comparison with the Korean War wool boom of the early
1950s, the more revealing figure is male average weekly earnings.
The figures for the two booms are similar. Between 1949–50 and
1951–2, the male average wage rose by 9.6 per cent, then 19 per cent,
then 22.6 per cent. Between 1972–3 and 1974–5, it was 9 per cent, 16.2
per cent and 25.4 per cent. Whitlam ruled during a terms of trade
boom and some of the wage rises can be attributed to the tightness
in the labour market. For a comparative study of the disruptive terms
of trade boom of the early '70s and the China-led boom since 2003,
see Treasury official David Gruen's speech to the Australian Business
Economists, 24 November 2011: www.treasury.gov.au/contentitem.
asp?NavId=008&ContentID=2237

34 **Not all margarine was bad** As cited in the *Industry Assistance
    Commission Annual Report 1973–74*, p.7.
    Whitlam seemed an unlikely convert The detail of the cabinet
    debate on tariffs is contained in Alan Reid, *The Whitlam Venture*,
    Hill of Content, 1976, pp.115–18.
    For a longer policy summary see Andrew Leigh, 'Trade Liberalisation
    and the Australian Labor Party', *Australian Journal of Politics and
    History*, Volume 48, Number 4, 2002. Leigh wrote: 'Since the late
    1960s, Whitlam had been the main champion of lower protection
    among his ALP colleagues. He pointed out that protectionism raised
    prices for consumers, and caused industries to become reliant on
    tariffs. Moreover it was economically inefficient since the real cost of
    protection was hidden from taxpayer. Finally, Whitlam argued, high
    levels of industry protection hurt workers in developing nations.' p.493.

37 **Whitlam's next attempt to wrestle with inflation** Bill Hayden's
    submission on inflation: cabinet minute, 8 October 1973. Series
    No.A5915; submission No. 697.

39 **The minutes of the 12 October discussion** Series No. A5931; Control
    symbol CL740.

40 **Sir Frederick believed that economic management and equity should
    not be confused** The exchange is cited in Bill Guy, *A Life on the Left:
    A Biography of Clyde Cameron*, Wakefield Press, 1999, p.292.

43 For a timeline on Watergate, plus the original *Washington Post*
    reports, see: www.washingtonpost.com/wp-srv/onpolitics/watergate/
    chronology.htm

CHAPTER 3

46   **The Whitlam era was only four months old** Reg Withers issued his threat in the Senate on 8 March 1973.

55   **Frank Crean, the treasurer who had been ignored** The 20 July 1974 submission was titled 'The Inflationary Crisis', Series No. A5915; submission No. 1133. The follow-up submissions mentioned in this passage are No. 1243, the August Economic Situation and Prospects report to cabinet, No. 1245 and No. 1325.

57   **Treasury made it harder for the government** The extraordinary thing about Crean's aggressive submissions is they insisted that unemployment would rise only marginally. It fell to Crean's successor Jim Cairns to deliver Treasury's mea culpa in January 1975: 'Persons registered for employment at the end of December (1974) totaled 267 000 – 4.5 per cent of the labour force. A year earlier those figures had been 102 700 and 1.8 per cent. The trend in unemployment has been strongly upwards in the past six months and is likely to continue upwards for a few more months at least.' Submission No. 1534.

'A pervasive sense of gloom' had taken hold The declassified US cables were sourced from: aad.archives.gov/aad/index.jsp. The dates, and titles, of the cables that are quoted in sequence are:

16 July 1973, Whitlam visit – political overview of Australia since visit prime minister Mamahon [sic]

5 April 1974, President of Labor Party and trade union council uneasy about election chances

15 May 1974, Robert J. Hawke: Profile

19 July 1974, Views of Opposition leader Snedden July 18

30 July 1974, Discussion with ALP president Robert J. Hawke

29 August 1974, Australia's troubles and Whitlam's troubles – a gathering crisis

16 November 1974, Australian economic and political situation: Views of Rupert Murdock [sic], managing director of News Ltd and associated companies

62   **Australia had caught up** The National Bureau of Economic Research, which plots the US business cycle, says this US recession began in December 1973 and ran until March 1975, and that the sixteen-months duration was the longest to that date since the 1930s. Note, the dates for recession were not formally announced until 1979. www.nber.org/cycles/cyclesmain.html

CHAPTER 4

64 The Treasury documents on the loans affair are sourced partly from
    Ian Hancock's summary for the National Archives, and from my own
    search of the files:
    'Proposed Loan from Arab Source'. Series No. A571
    'Scotland Yard and other reports on Mr T. Khemlani'
    'Proposal for borrowing $US4 billion from Middle East sources.
    Record of conversation with Mr R H. Dean (London) 13 December 1974'
    'Record of conversation with Mr R H Dean, 10.10 pm 13 December 1974'
    'Proposal to borrow $US4 billion from Middle East sources from Sir
    Frederick Wheeler to Treasurer, 13 December 1974'
    'Points that might be made' 13 December 1974
    'Unsolicited loan offers – treatment by the government'
    See also: www.naa.gov.au/about-us/publications/fact-sheets/fs239.aspx

65 **Connor fancied himself** The opening sequence is taken from Laurie
    Oakes, *Crash Through or Crash: The Unmaking of a Prime Minister*,
    Drummond, 1976, pp.53–56. Cameron's version is in Bill Guy, *A Life
    on the Left*, pp.296–99.

69 **'Why did Connor change his mind?'** Graham Freudenberg,
    A Certain Grandeur, pp.358–59.

71 **US president George W. Bush** georgewbush-whitehouse.archives.
    gov/news/releases/2002/10/20021015-7.html
    See also: georgewbush-whitehouse.archives.gov/news/
    releases/2002/06/20020617-2.html

76 **'[Field] was certainly no supporter of Whitlam'** Alan Reid,
    The Whitlam Venture, pp.348–49.

77 **Hayden's budget was designed to be Labor's correction** Cabinet
    warnings taken from Series No. A5915; submission No.1778 and Series
    No. A5915; submission No. 1928.

78 **'The Hayden budget surprised the Liberals** Laurie Oakes, *Crash
    Through or Crash*, p.126. Fraser's reply is cited on p.148.

79 **Fraser announced the decision to delay** The war of words between
    Fraser and Whitlam is cited by Laurie Oakes, *Crash Through or Crash*,
    pp.176–78.

80 **the Americans were ready to write Fraser's political obituary**
    7 November 1975, 'Australian Political Crisis'

CHAPTER 5

85   Paul Kelly yielded a revealing quote from Sir Garfield Barwick
     in an interview for his book *November 1975*, Allen &Unwin, 1995,
     p.228: 'Barwick: No, I didn't dislike Whitlam . . . the trouble with
     [Whitlam] was he'd have taken the rest of us down with him. You
     don't realise what the situation would have been in Gough had not
     been displaced. We'd have had chaos, public servants unpaid, bills
     unpaid, absolutely terrifying.'

86   **In one famous ad** As reproduced in Sally Young, *The Persuaders: Inside
     the Hidden Machine of Political Advertising*, Pluto Press, 2004, p.121.
     Technically speaking Once Fraser became caretaker prime minister,
     his approval numbers turned positive. The first Gallup Poll of December
     1975 had only 44.3 per cent approving of the way he handled the job
     of opposition leader, and 49.5 per cent disapproving. But 58.9 per cent
     approved of how he was handling the caretaker prime ministership, while
     only 30.3 per cent disapproved. Whitlam's numbers as prime minister
     were worse (40.3 per cent approved and 54.6 per cent disapproved).

CHAPTER 6

92   **We will not succeed in bringing down unemployment** Series No.
     A12909; submission No. 38.

94   The Callaghan government's cabinet papers on the 1976 IMF
     loan to Great Britain can found at: www.nationalarchives.gov.uk/
     cabinetpapers/themes/imf-crisis.htm.
     The issue was too sensitive Series No. A13075; submission No. 1931.

96   **An earnest cabinet submission** Series No. 12909; submission No. 2763.

97   **Masters preached the hypocrisy** Roy Masters was interviewed for
     the ABC documentary *The Fibros and the Silvertails*, 2008. The quote
     was taken from: www.abc.net.au/rn/sportsfactor/stories/2008/2377853.
     htm#transcript.

99   **In *The Lucky Country*** Donald Horne, *The Luck Country: Australia in
     the Sixties*, Penguin, 1964, p.209.

102 **The value of dubious deductions escalated** The figures cited are from
     Trevor Boucher, *Blatant, Artificial and Contrived: Tax Schemes of the
     70s and 80s*, ATO, 2010, p.176.

103 **Howard picked up the Treasury tune** Series No. A12909; submission
     No. 2342.

104 **'My dear Treasurer . . .'** Series No. A13075; submission No. 6491.

TRANSITIONS I

107 **Donald Horne observed** Donald Horne, *The Lucky Country*, p.78.

111 **including John and Moira Gillard** The prime minister's migration record is available on the National Archives database, Series No. A1877. Here is the extract, with date of embarkation, the name of the ship: 07/02/1966 FAIRSKY; GILLARD John Oliver born 15 August 1929; Moira (nee Mackenzie) born 9 February 1928; Alison Mary born 19 November 1958; Julia Eileen born 29 September 1961; travelled per FAIRSKY departing Southampton on 7 February 1966 under the Assisted Passage Migration Scheme.
And my mum's details, Series No. A2478:
GIORI Thomai born 1942 – Greek – travelled per MIQAN flight departing in 1962 under Intergovernmental Committee for European Migration.

112 **John Howard told me something similar** Joint interview with *The Australian's* Brad Norington, December 2006.

114 **'two Wongs do not make a White'** *Hansard*, 2 December 1947. The John Curtin comment is sourced from:www.immi.gov.au/media/fact-sheets/08abolition.htm.
The cabinet discussions on the Vietnamese refugee issue are, in order of quotation: Series No: A12909, submission 2771; Series No: A12390, submission 380.
The US cables cited, in order:
1 May 1975, Background to visit to Washington of Prime Minister Whitlam 7–8 May
8 May 1975, Policy towards admitting Vietnamese refugees
17 May 1975, Australian position on Vietnamese refugees
21 May 1975, Australian position on Vietnamese refugee

CHAPTER 7

125 **John Howard recorded these two related thoughts** Series No: A12909, submission 3340.

126 **Even Howard had caught the fever** Series No: A12909, submission 3869.

128 **Every leader overcorrects** Paul Kelly, *The Hawke Ascendancy*, Allen & Unwin, 2008, p.35.

CHAPTER 8

139 **The Hawke camp had targeted** The summary of Bob Hawke's second challenge is taken from Paul Kelly, *The Hawke Ascendancy*. John Button's letter to Bill Hayden is extracted in the book's prologue.

146 **The final word belongs** The international comparisons for employment by industry are taken from: www.bls.gov/fls/#laborforce. See tables under 'Annual labour force statistics, 1970–2010.'

CHAPTER 9

158 **Keating took his own notes at the meeting** Here is the full note, quoting Stone: 'The problem for the government if we move to some kind of float is what it does for other things. A 5 per cent depreciation is looking like a 20 per cent tariff cut – a major shock injected into the system. A shock needs to be put into your calculations. Our exchange rate should not be strengthening against the rest of the world. The present market sentiment, is just that: sentiment and irrational sentiment at that. In six months' time, people will say our exchange rate is over-valued but it could do a lot of damage in the meantime . . . If we are going to give the economy a shock, I would rather give it the financial sector than the productive sector.'

CHAPTER 10

166 **In 1984, the treasurer began urging** As cited in Edna Carew, *Keating: A Biography*, Allen & Unwin, 1988, p.106.

168 **Kelty told Paul Kelly** Paul Kelly, *The End of Certainty: Power, Politics & Business in Australia*, Allen & Unwin, 1994, p.68.

169 Hugh Mackay's characterisation of the baby boomers was as cited in his reply to my *Quarterly Essay* No. 40: *Trivial Pursuit*, in *QE* 41, Black Inc, 2011. The Mind & Mood research cited was from the March 1984 report, 'Money'.

CHAPTER 11

179 **Hawke was flying to Tokyo** Paul Kelly, *The End of Certainty*, p.216.

182 **Finance minister Peter Walsh wrote** Peter Walsh, *Confessions of a Failed Finance Minister*, Random House, 1995, p.151.

CHAPTER 12

191   **Peter Walsh said Keating told cabinet** Peter Walsh, *Confessions of a Failed Finance Minister*, p.183.

192   **Even the average size of our dwellings is unremarkable** The figures were cited in the June 2008 report of Senate select committee on housing affordability in Australia, p.17.

194   **Behind closed doors, however, Keating was having doubts** The Keating note is cited in John Edwards, *Keating: The Inside Story, Penguin Books*, 1996, p.375.

195   **increased their risk-taking after the October 1987 stock-market crash** The stories of Bond and Skase, and the estimates of the money lost by the banks, are sourced from Trevor Sykes, *The Bold Riders*, Allen & Unwin, 1996.

CHAPTER 13

209   **But history was playing with Keating that day** The September quarter national accounts, released on 29 November 1990, can be seen here: www.abs.gov.au/AUSSTATS/abs@.nsf/ DetailsPage/5206.0Sep%201990?OpenDocument. They showed the economy contracted in the December quarter 1989, grew in the March quarter 1990, then shrunk again in the June and September quarters – the two that Keating was talking to. The ABS prefers a different measure of GDP now, and its revisions based on that standard – the so-called chain volume method – turned the minus sign for the June quarter 1990 into a plus. If this had been the result at the time, Keating would no doubt have waited until 1991 before entertaining the idea of calling it the recession we had to have.

CHAPTER 14

214   Keating's National Press Club address is taken from *Men and Women of Australia*, Random House, 2005, edited by Michael Fullilove, pp.123–8, and from Michael Gordon, *A Question of Leadership*, University of Queensland Press, 1993, pp.4–6.

217   **Undoubtedly John Curtin would have drawn a higher approval rating** The only Australian Gallup Poll to test 'feelings about Mr Curtin as prime minister' was on 31 July 1943. The results: 26.9 per cent said he was doing an 'excellent job', another 39.7 per cent said

he was doing a 'fairly good job' and 23.7 per cent said he was doing 'some good things'. Only 9.6 per cent said he was 'not a success'.

227 **once known by his published approval rating as 'Mr 75 per cent'**
As mentioned in Chapter 10, one poll had his rating at 80 per cent. Here is the extract, from the Australian Social Science Data Archive: Australian Gallup Polls, March 1984
MR HAWKE AS PRIME MINISTER
Approve: 80.4%
Disapprove: 18.4%
50/50: 1.2%

CHAPTER 15

238 **a deficit that widens even when growth returns to the economy**
Interestingly, the total cost of the government's stimulus for 1992–93 was just $2.7 billion, counting every new item of spending since the final weeks of Bob Hawke's prime ministership. The forecast deficit for that year was $13.4 billion, so the larger explanation was the collapse in revenue and the higher-than-expected unemployment rate.

240 **Keating used this statement** Don Watson, *Recollections of a Bleeding Heart*, Random House, 2002, p.248.

CHAPTER 16

250 The 'L-A-W law' quote came in answer to a question on 10 February 1993: 'They've been legislated. They are not a promise, they are law: L-A-W law. And the difference between a legislated tax cut and some opposition speaker's manifesto is all the world of difference. They were signed into law at the end of the last parliamentary system.'

256 **Howard had disowned his former self on Asian immigration** 'I was wrong on Asians, says Howard', *The Australian*, 7 January 1995, p.1.

TRANSITIONS II

263 **The generational shift between old and new Australia** The figures for age of youngest child at which mothers return to work are my calculations from customised census tables from 1976 to 2006, supplied to me at *The Australian* newspaper by the Australian Bureau of Statistics. For the figures of tertiary education for the baby

boomers and Generation X, see:www.abs.gov.au/AUSSTATS/abs@.
nsf/DetailsPage/3101.0Jun%202010?OpenDocument.

268 **The Saints hailed from Brisbane's south-west** The best account of
Brisbane's role in punk rock is in Andrew Stafford, *Pig City: From
The Saints to Savage Garden*, University of Queensland Press, 2004.

CHAPTER 17

274 **Howard conducted a ring-around** The John Anderson quotes are
from the ABC-TV series, *The Howard Years*, narrated and interviewed
by Fran Kelly.
There had been twelve mass murders See table 1, Simon Chapman;
P Alpers; K Agho; M Jones, 'Australia's 1996 gun law reforms: faster
falls in firearm deaths, firearm suicides and a decade without mass
shootings', BMJ Publishing Group, 2006.

278 **The insistence on surplus budgeting** Until this point in the book,
the budget numbers reflect those published at the time. Each new
government makes a change to the budget accounting methodology
which, perhaps not coincidentally, makes their predecessor appear
less virtuous. The spending-to-GDP figures are based on the
coalition's new estimates of the Labor years. Paul Keating's record was
diminished by the exercise, taking away one of his published surpluses.

284 **'We are no longer seen as some kind of anxious outsider'** 'My great
sorrow: Howard gives a glimpse of his private side', Kate Hannon,
Daily Telegraph, 5 December 1997.

285 **the real 'miracle economy'** Paul Krugman's comment was reported in
'White favoured colour of money', Michael Stutchbury, *The Weekend
Australian*, 14 November 1998.

CHAPTER 18

290 **'I spent a lot of time thinking in hospital'** Howard's earlier interview
with me was recorded for *The Longest Decade*, Scribe, 2006.
The GST was no more popular in 1998 For a summary of the public
attitudes to the GST, see News Poll. The GST polls were not a
reliable guide to either the 1988 or 2001 election results.

297 David Hale interviewed for the ABC's *7.30 Report*, 11 September
2000: www.abc.net.au/7.30/stories/s174698.htm

CHAPTER 19

305 **China was still competing with Italy for sixth place** www.chinadaily.
com.cn/english/doc/2005-12/20/content_504977.htm

319 It is worth recording, at length, Howard's ETS promise on 3 June 2007:
'This will be a world-class emissions trading system, more
comprehensive, more rigorously grounded in economics and
with better governance than anything in Europe. Implementing an
emissions trading scheme and setting a long-term goal for reducing
emissions will be the most momentous economic decisions Australia
will take in the next decade. This emissions trading system must
be built to last. It needs to last not five or ten years, it needs to last
the whole of the twenty-first century if Australia is to meet our
global responsibilities and further build our economic prosperity.
This is a great economic challenge for Australia as well as a great
environmental challenge. Significantly reducing emissions will mean
higher costs for businesses and households, there is no escaping that
and anyone who pretends to do otherwise is not a serious participant
in this hugely important public policy debate. It will change the
entire cost structure of our economy. We must get this right; if we
get this wrong it will do enormous damage to our economy, to jobs
and to the economic wellbeing of ordinary Australians, especially
low-income households.'

320 **voters said they preferred less tax over an increase in social spending**
The attitudes to tax cuts and social spending are sourced from Ian
McAllister and Juliet Clark, 'Trends in Public Opinion: Results from
the Australian Election Study, 1987–2004', Australian Social Science
Data Archive.

CHAPTER 20

331 **US investment bank Lehman Brothers collapsed** The details of the
Lehman Brothers collapse, as they were reported on the day: www.
marketwatch.com/story/lehman-folds-with-record-613-billion-
debt?siteid=rss. I've relied on David Wessel, *In Fed We Trust: Ben
Bernanke's War on the Great Panic*, Scribe, 2009, for an outline of the
US end of the story. I chaired a session at the 2010 Sydney Writers'
Festival with Wessel and Paul Keating that covered the GFC: www.
abc.net.au/tv/bigideas/stories/2010/06/28/2938830.htm.

337 **And even after it acknowledged that recession was underway**
Ken Henry quoted in Lenore Taylor and David Uren, *Shitstorm*,
Melbourne University Press, pp.74–75.

341 **Tom Albanese, the American-born chief executive of Rio Tinto**
Tom Albanese was interviewed by 2GB's Alan Jones on 3 June 2010.
The focus group I sat in on was conducted by Rebecca Huntley, a
director of Ipsos Mackay research.

TRANSITIONS III

362 **Cronulla the 'race riots in paradise'** The article from *The Economist* is
here: www.economist.com/node/5310512
More than 270 000 text messages See The Australian
Communications and Media Authority investigation of Alan Jones'
broadcast: www.acma.gov.au/WEB/STANDARD/pc=PC_310133

363 **Jones was quoting colourful listener feedback to demean Julia
Gillard** Alan Jones' thoughts on Julia Gillard: www.abc.net.au/
mediawatch/transcripts/s3272172.htm

AFTERWORD

369 **Gillard says in an interview** Conducted in Adelaide, 4 July 2014

371 **'If the prime minister wants to make, politically speaking, an honest
women of herself'**
'… there are people now saying your name is not Julia but Ju-liar'
The respective comments of Tony Abbott and Alan Jones were made
on 25 January 2011. www.news.com.au/national/tony-abbott-tells-
julia-gillard-to-make-an-honest-womanof-herself-on-carbon-tax/
story-e6frfkvr-1226012034629

371 **'died of shame'** For a summary of the Jones speech, and his apology, see:
www.dailytelegraph.com.au/jones-says-gillards-dad-died-of-shame/
story-e6freuy9-1226484128451?nk=3f9fc8116e47a692e950c13bf00afcc9

372 **The speech resonated in the digital age** www.youtube.com/
watch?v=ihd7ofrwQXo

374 **she read in the *Sydney Morning Herald*** Article by Peter Hartcher and
Phillip Coorey www.smh.com.au/national/rudds-secret-polling-on-
his-leadership-20100622-yvrc.html

375 **The demography that created the most distress** The 'traits and
trends' of the hung parliament were revealed in research by Martin

Lumb, Parliamentary Library: www.aph.gov.au/About_Parliament/
Parliamentary_Departments/Parliamentary_Library/pubs/rp/
rp1314/43rdParl

380 **Now it turned on him** www.dailytelegraph.com.au/
news/opinion/consign-rudd-to-the-bin-of-history/
story-fni0cwl5-1226691046953?nk=22f121780f70fe848cb019d1ccabb887
www.couriermail.com.au/news/queensland/prime-minister-
kevin-rudd-begs-spinner-peter-beattie-to-help-rescue-labor/
story-fnihsrf2-1226693889409

The election circulation figures were taken from Matthew Knott,
Crikey: www.crikey.com.au/2013/11/08/circulation-results-teles-anti-
rudd-campaign-falls-flat/?wpmp_switcher=mobile

The Age's front-page editorial was published on 22 June 2013, five days
before Kevin Rudd reclaimed the Labor leadership: www.theage.com.
au/federal-politics/editorial/for-the-sake-of-the-nation-ms-gillard-
should-stand-aside-20130621-2006e.html

382 **Liberal Party pollster and strategist Mark Textor** Interviewed 17 June
2014

384 **Gillard's scheme actually worked** www.environment.gov.au/
climate-change/greenhouse-gas-measurement/publications/quarterly-
update-australias-national-greenhouse-gas-inventory-december-2013

A NOTE ON THE DATA

I've relied on the Australian Bureau of Statistics and the Reserve Bank of
Australia websites for jobs, inflation and GDP figures, both domestic and
international: www.abs.gov.au and www.rba.gov.au/statistics/

The latest fiscal data used in the book was taken from the mid-year review
for the 2010–11 budget. The most recent national accounts used were for
the June quarter 2011.

For Australian house prices before 1990, and for trade union coverage, I've
relied on the ABS Year Books.

For house prices between 1990 and 2003, I've relied on the Reserve Bank,
RP Data-Rismark Index, and from 2003 the ABS.

More detailed US material used in the book is also officially sourced at:
www.bls.gov/data/ and www.whitehouse.gov/omb/budget/Historicals/

INDEX